W9-BLN-309

Global
Prospects
for
Education

Errata—*Global Prospects for Education: Development, Culture, and Schooling*

The following line from p. 325 is repeated on the top of p. 326:

body principle, few used their school knowledge to solve the problems.

The following line is missing from the top of p. 327:

The probability that the child's competence is in place is symbolized

The following line from p. 327 is repeated on the top of p. 328:

lished. Rarely were their authors motivated by a desire to improve the

The following line is missing fom the top of p. 329:

standing of any concept. It requires a high level of understanding to

Global Prospects for Education

for

Development, Culture, and Schooling

EDITED BY

Scott G. Paris
Henry M. Wellman

American Psychological Association
Washington, DC

Published by
American Psychological Association
750 First Street, NE
Washington, DC 20002

Copies may be ordered from
APA Order Department
P.O. Box 92984
Washington, DC 20090-2984

In the UK and Europe, copies may be ordered from
American Psychological Association
3 Henrietta Street
Covent Garden, London
WC2E 8LU England

Typeset in Minion by EPS Group Inc., Easton, MD
Printer: Edwards Brothers, Inc., Ann Arbor, MI
Cover Designer: Minker Design, Bethesda, MD
Technical/Production Editor: Catherine R. W. Hudson

Library of Congress Cataloging-in-Publication Data
Global prospects for education : development, culture, and schooling / edited by
  Scott G. Paris and Henry M. Wellman.— 1st ed.
      p.   cm.
      Festschrift for Harold Stevenson.
      Includes bibliographical references and index.
      ISBN 1-55798-492-1
      1. Academic achievement—Psychological aspects—Cross-cultural
  studies.   2. Child development—Cross-cultural studies.   3. Cognition in children
  —Cross-cultural studies.   4. Mathematical ability—Cross-cultural
  studies.   5. Educational anthropology—Cross-cultural studies.   6. Education—
  Social aspects—Cross-cultural studies.   7. Stevenson, Harold W. (Harold
  William), 1924– .   I. Paris, Scott G., 1946– .   II. Wellman, Henry M.
  LB1062.6.G57   1998
  370.1'52—dc21   97-49911
                                                                       CIP

British Library Cataloguing-in-Publication Data
A CIP record is available from the British Library.

Printed in the United States of America
First Edition

Contents

Part Two: Developmental Aspects of Literacy

Part Three: Developmental Psychology, Social Policy, and Education

Contributors

Hiroshi Azuma, Professor, Department of Child Development and Juvenile Culture, Shirayuri College, Tokyo, Japan

Peter Bryant, Professor, Department of Experimental Psychology, Oxford University, Oxford, England

Guo-Peng Chen, Associate Professor, East China Normal University, Peoples Republic of China

Anne E. Cunningham, University of California, Berkeley, United States

David C. Geary, Professor, Department of Psychology, University of Missouri, Columbia, United States

Jacqueline J. Goodnow, Professor, Behavioural Sciences, Macquarie University, Sydney, Australia

Carmen O. Hamson, Postdoctoral Fellow, Department of Psychology, University of Missouri, Columbia, United States

Giyoo Hatano, Professor, Department of Human Relations, Keio University, Japan

Mary K. Hoard, Doctoral student, Department of Psychology, University of Missouri, Columbia, United States

Kayoko Inagaki, Professor of Psychology, Chiba University, Japan

Shin-Ying Lee, Research Scientist, Center for Human Growth and Development, University of Michigan, Ann Arbor, United States

Fan Liu, Research Scientist, China Central Institute for Educational Sciences, Beijing, China, and Visiting Scholar, Department of Psychology, University of Missouri, Columbia, United States

Frank B. Murray, Department of Psychology, University of Delaware, Wilmington, United States

Terezinha Nunes, Professor, Department of Child Development and Learning, Institute of Education, University College, London, England

Scott G. Paris, Professor of Psychology and Education, University of Michigan, Ann Arbor, United States

Keith E. Stanovich, Professor, Department of Instruction and Special Education, University of Toronto, Canada

James W. Stigler, Professor, Department of Psychology, University of California, Los Angeles, United States

Sally J. Styfco, Head Start Research Associate, Yale University, New Haven, CT, United States

Christina E. van Kraayenoord, Senior Lecturer, Department of Education, University of Queensland, Brisbane, Australia

Daniel A. Wagner, Professor, Department of Education, Director, National Center on Adult Literacy, and Director, International Literacy Institute, University of Pennsylvania, Philadelphia, United States

Henry M. Wellman, Professor of Psychology and Research Scientist, Center for Human Growth and Development, University of Michigan, Ann Arbor, United States

Richard F. West, James Madison University, Harrisonburg, Virginia, United States

Edward Zigler, Sterling Professor of Psychology, Yale University, New Haven, CT, United States

Preface

Children's learning is a central concern of parents, educators, and policymakers around the world and an enduring focus of research by Harold Stevenson. The authors in this volume examine themes of children's development, culture, and schooling that represent a convergence of factors in Dr. Stevenson's research throughout his career. From his earliest studies of children's learning to his most recent cross-national examinations of educational achievement and practices, Harold Stevenson has studied child development and schooling with an ever-widening global perspective.

The authors who contributed to this Festschrift are a distinguished group of individuals. They are not only internationally recognized scholars, they are also colleagues and friends, and many are former students of Harold Stevenson who have benefited from his collaboration, inspiration, and mentoring. This legacy of scholars is one of Dr. Stevenson's outstanding contributions to psychology and education. An individual can make a contribution to a profession through research, collaborative projects, teaching, leadership, and policy making. What distinguishes Harold Stevenson is that he has contributed extensively to the field of psychology, generally, and to child developmental research, specifically, in all of these roles. Moreover, his contributions have been amazingly sustained and cumulative, beginning in the 1950s and 1960s when Dr. Stevenson and a handful of other researchers extended psychological studies of children's learning, and continue today. It is fair to say that his current research with his many collaborators is yielding the most intriguing, informative, and influential research of his career.

It has been an honor and a pleasure for us to organize this tribute to our respected colleague and friend. We offer the volume as thanks to him for his many contributions to the field and to chilren's lives. Dr. Stevenson's legacy lies in his research, the studies that he has inspired in others, the students that he has trained, and the professional organizations that he has led and nurtured. Our understanding of children's education and learning would be significantly impoverished without Harold Stevenson's example, research, teaching, and leadership. Lest readers infer that Dr. Stevenson's efforts are now at an end, we wish to clarify that he has *not* retired. Our celebration is in lieu of his retirement—which given his youth and energy is a long way off. Thus, our tribute is to his continuing professional and personal contributions to psychology. We also honor his warmth, his zest for life, and his dedication to friends and family that are so clear to everyone who knows him.

This volume was made possible by a Festschrift Conference grant from the American Psychological Association as well as through funding from the Center for Human Growth and Development and the Department of Psychology at the University of Michigan. The conference and volume were supported by many individuals, including Mary Jo Beck, Sheba Shakir, Deborah Apsley, and Kate Restrick. We want to thank them and all the participants for helping us to honor Harold Stevenson's contributions to the field of child development.

About Harold

Harold Stevenson is Professor of Psychology and Fellow, Center for Human Growth and Development, at the University of Michigan. He also holds several concurrent appointments, including the following: Adjunct Professor of Psychology, Peking University; Visiting Professor, Tohoku Fukushi University; and Adjunct Professor, Institute of Psychology, Chinese Academy of Sciences. Harold has received many honors, including the following: the G. Stanley Hall Award, APA, Division of Developmental Psychology, 1988; the SRCD Award for Distinguished Scientific Contributions to Child Development, 1993; the James Mc-Keen Cattell Fellow Award in Applied Psychology, 1994; the American Federation of Teachers, Quest Award, 1995; the Urie Bronfenbrenner Award, APA, Division of Developmental Psychology, 1996; and an Honorary ScD degree, University of Minnesota, 1996. The list of organizations he has headed, editorial boards on which he has served, and national committee memberships that he has held is truly impressive. Moreover, he has maintained his leadership in these endeavors throughout the past 40 years. Colleagues around the world know his deep commitment to psychological and educational organizations that have supported research and policies to improve the lives of children and families.

Among the many books he has authored and edited are *The Learning Gap* (1992) with J. Stigler, *Child Development and Education in Japan* (1996) with H. Azuma and K. Hakuta, *Research in Child Development and Social Policy* (1984) with A. Siegel, *Learning and Motivation in the Classroom* (1983) with S. Paris and G. Olson, and *Cross-Cultural Studies of Child Development* (1981) with D. Wagner. Additional books and articles are listed at the back of this volume. What is missing from this list of achievements are the personal glimpses of his dedication to his family, his constant availability to students, his legendary sit-ups and bike riding, his impatience with administrative obstacles, and his graciousness as a host to visitors, colleagues, and students in his home.

A review of Harold's career reveals his pioneering work on many topics. Harold was responsible for initiating much of the basic and applied research on the effects of tangible and social rewards on children's learning, children's learning of central versus incidental content, the influence of anxiety and failure on children's learning, and their learning from filmed or televised displays. His recent investigations analyze academic learning, instruction, and achievement in several cultures, especially the United States, China, and Japan. During the past 15 years, Harold's research on children's academic achievement in different countries has been widely cited by educators and politicians who aspire to improve American schools. Harold's current research continues his abiding interest in children's learning, parental variables, and educational instruction, yet it includes a wide range of international studies and comparisons. It has long been realized that comparing learning and achievement across contrasting cultures, instructional practices, and educational arrangements can stimulate educational reforms, but the obstacles to collecting the required, culturally comparable but representative data are monumental. Harold's research has yielded a treasure trove of exemplary methods, rigorous data, and persuasive findings.

Harold's approach is typically direct, ingenious, and rigorous. To devise a test of children's mathematics achievement in three very different cultures, he began by extensively analyzing the mathematics textbooks and curricula used in the three countries. Only concepts taught at the same grades in all three cultures were included on the test. This test was then given to statistically representative samples of children in the various countries. Beyond testing mathematics skills, his research program encompasses tests of reading, information acquisition, and basic cognition as well as observation and analyses of curricula, in-class teaching behavior, and at-home informal teaching. His research now includes projects in Hungary, Canada, Britain, and Germany (as well as the United States, Japan, China, Taiwan, and Hong Kong) and also includes surveys and interviews of teachers, students, and parents. The total research program is a comprehensive and complicated endeavor with multiple controls and safeguards for interpreting the data. Thus, the findings stand as a model of empirical clarity in an extremely difficult research area.

Harold has greatly magnified his distinguished research contributions to the field by training and inspiring a continuous stream of influential students. It would be hard to exaggerate his impact in this fashion. The list of his academic apprentices is replete with impressive scholars: Ed Zigler, Mort Weir, Rachel Clifton, Alex Siegel, Richard Odom, Kennedy Hill, and Hayne Reese, to name some of his early students at Texas and Minnesota. More recently his students include Vonnie McLoyd, Dan Wagner, Jeff Bisanz, James Stigler, Shin-Ying Lee, Chun Chen, David Crystal, Andrew Fuligni, Xiaotong Mu, Heidi Schweingruber, and others from the University of Michigan. To have fostered a fraction of the expertise and influence obvious in this list of students would be a dream of many great teachers.

Furthermore, Harold has been extremely influential in establishing and invigorating a number of important organizations that guide and initiate applied psychological research. Harold was instrumental in helping expand the Society for Research in Child Development into its present national and international status. He was one of the youngest presidents ever of the society, serving in 1969–1971. He was also the president of APA Division 7 (1964–65) and of the International Society for the Study of Behavioral Development (1988–1992). In the 1980s, Harold was a key figure in the formation of the Bush Programs in Child Development and Social Policy, a national network of university centers at Yale, Michigan, North Carolina, and UCLA that focused on the use of child development research to inform and shape social policies that affected children and families. These centers greatly accelerated the impact of developmental science on policy and, ultimately, children's lives. Similarly, through several programs housed at the University of Michigan, Harold has been responsible for the establishment of relations and cooperative programs between psychologists in the United States and the People's Republic of China. At one point in the late 1980s, more than half the official visitors to China in the area of psychology and more than half the postdoctoral Chinese scholars in psychology studying in the United States had been sponsored by the programs under his direction.

The recipients of Harold's leadership activities, research, and acumen are clearly his colleagues and the field at large.

Global
for Prospects
Education

Introduction

Children's learning and instruction are fundamental topics of concern for psychologists, educators, and parents. Learning fuels and shapes developing expertise, instruction guides and motivates learning of valued competencies, and formal and informal educational settings provide support and application of new knowledge. The study of children in diverse contexts is necessary in order to understand the forces that shape development and the roles played by parents, teachers, peers, and culture. The study of children bridges disciplines and is at the crossroads of psychology, education, and anthropology. Many of the chapters in this volume reflect the interdisciplinary perspectives of the authors and are intended to stimulate thinking about children's learning from multiple perspectives.

Beyond a celebration of Harold Stevenson's distinguished contributions, this volume was designed to advance an important scientific agenda: sharing and integrating expert knowledge about children's development and schooling around the world. The focus is on exemplary research in children's academic learning and educational achievement; research that informs us about basic mechanisms of learning and development and that provides strategies for effective instruction and education. The festschrift provides a timely and fitting vehicle for addressing these important issues that are also at the heart of Harold's research.

Enhancing educational achievement, optimizing the development of each student, and adjusting educational opportunities in response to changes in families and social conditions are pressing issues around the world as each country seeks to maximize the development of human capital through education. The critical task of educating children for the challenges of the next century must be built on a foundation of research, knowledge, and successful practices. Sustained, intensive, multicultural, and cognitively oriented investigations of reading, mathematics, science, technology, second language learning, and the like are necessary to assess and improve educational opportunities for students. Cognitive developmental psychologists, in collaboration with teachers and educational researchers, have a great deal to offer the educational enterprise—a focus on learners and their developing understanding of mathematics, literacy, and science; empirical methods to assess and evaluate children's knowledge; and capacities to conduct large-scale systematic research programs. Moreover, educational and instructional settings provide crucial contexts for studying basic cognitive processes. Schools are laboratories par excellence for understanding children's developing skills, learning strategies, and conceptual knowledge, some of the most fundamental topics of psychological research.

This volume brings together psychological and educational researchers who exemplify syntheses between developmental theories and educational practices. The authors have been selected to represent diverse international and cultural perspectives. The chapters are diverse, yet coherent, reflecting Harold's diverse yet programmatic contributions. The volume is organized into three broad themes; cross-cultural studies of academic achievement, developmental aspects of literacy, and connections among developmental psychology, social policy, and education. We provide capsule summaries of each chapter in these sections as an overview of the volume.

Geary, Hamson, Chen, Liu, and Hoard begin the volume with a description of their biocultural model of academic development. They argue that primary abilities are shaped by evolutionary forces whereas secondary abilities are shaped by cultural forces. Secondary abilities, such as success in school subjects, depend on cultural valuation of the abilities and motivational supports and, thus, reflect the effects of cultural contexts on educational achievement. The authors point out that East Asian and American students do not differ much on primary abilities and therefore, conclude that cross-national differences in academic achievement are due to differences in secondary abilities that might be traced to cultural practices.

Lee's chapter examines the reasons for differences in academic achievement among students in China, Japan, and the United States. She reports detailed observational and qualitative analyses of classroom interactions in each country. For example, the research team found that students in East Asian classrooms were cognitively engaged in mathematics learning activities more than 80% of the time whereas students in the United States were only engaged about 60% of the time. In addition, East Asian teachers more than American teachers explained concepts and allowed students to evaluate the accuracy of their own as well as their peers' answers to problems. The frequency of four different kinds of instruction was noted in each country; using different examples of a problem, extending students' answers, relating answers to abstract concepts, and facilitating deeper understanding. Teachers in first and fifth grade classes in Chicago used each of these tactics less often than teachers in China and Japan. Thus, Lee argues that students in American classes had fewer opportunities to construct meaning and to understand the mathematical concepts presented in the curriculum. Lee examines differences in preservice and inservice professional activities of teachers and notes that East Asian teachers have more opportunities to work together, prepare lessons, grade student work, and meet students individually than American teachers. She concludes that many of the achievement differences observed in students may be derived from different cultural expectations about teaching and learning and different instructional practices of teachers.

Hatano and Inagaki address Stevenson's own research program directly. They aptly describe the merits and uniqueness of this cross-national research on mathematics achievement—its careful methods, its striking and informative findings, and the interest in Asian teaching practices that the research has naturally fostered. Hatano and Inagaki also provide a larger, culturally based analysis of the Stevenson research, specially focused on the implications of the research for changing educational practices in the United States. They do this by articulating several less-obvious cultural values and practices that shape Japanese students' mathematics instruction and achievement—the different beliefs held by Japanese and U.S. teachers with regard to the significance and role of children's errors or mistakes, the socialization of children as listeners and observers versus active participants, and efforts to form classroom communities where children care about others' ideas rather than just their own ideas and performances. Hatano and Inagaki argue that performance and instruction are shaped by myriad interlocking cultural beliefs and practices that provide an important context and infrastructure for specific practices and results. Thus, cross-national differences in math performance and math instruction do not translate easily into prescriptions for improving instruction and outcomes in the United States.

Goodnow uses the monograph by Stevenson and Lee (1990) as a vehicle to examine different features of cultural contexts. She argues against simplified explanations of cultural differences and notes that complex interactions must be identified. For example, in Stevenson's research, variables that predict differences between cultures may not predict differences within cultures, and vice versa. Goodnow analyzes how cultural valuation of academic achievement, a key difference between East Asian and American parents in Stevenson's research, might be elaborated into more complex explanations. She considers how achievement may be important for different groups of people and for different cultural goals. Indeed, relative importance of achievement means that the value of education must be compared to other culturally available opportunities and expectations and Goodnow illustrates how these can vary widely across and within cultures. She argues that each culture offers different expectations about leeways, trade-offs, and negotiations about acceptable academic performance of children. Furthermore, these expectations depend on children's perceptions of the value of achievement and the self-images they construct. Her provocative chapter offers several directions for future research on cultural differences in academic achievement.

Stigler's focus is on methods for improving educational instruction. We need to systematically improve classroom instruction, he argues, and to do this we need careful, informative observational data about actual classroom practices. Yet those data are surprisingly difficult to collect in dynamic classrooms and have often been unavailable. Stigler analyzes the difficulties in classroom observational research, but more importantly, he advances a solution—a new system of computerized video observation. He outlines the requirements of an observational system and describes the system that he and his colleagues developed in a cross-national study of educational practices in three countries—the United States, Japan, and Germany. Stigler provides some revealing initial analyses of that study to demonstrate the value of video analyses of classroom instruction and the richness of the data.

The second section of the volume is focused on literacy development and the various authors consider how reading and literacy are influenced across the life span. Bryant and Nunes discuss the difficulties of learning to read across cultures in many different languages. They note that Stevenson and colleagues showed convincingly that Japanese orthography does not prevent Japanese children from having problems learning to read. They raise the provocative issue of the pervasive link between grammar and spelling, a connection that has often been ignored in favor of analyses of phonological correspondence between written and oral language. Bryant and Nunes trace the development of children's spelling and show that early attempts are guided by phonetic cues in their invented spellings but incorporate increasing grammatical knowledge. They describe a large study of English children and how they cope with non-phonetic verb endings like -ed which is the basis for a 5-stage model of orthographic development. This developmental sequence captures children's changing ideas about the nature of orthography from phonetic to grammatically based conventions. This developmental sequence raises compelling questions for instruction in early literacy.

Paris and van Kraayenoord note that assessment of early reading development is difficult and often relies on assessments of vocabulary and decoding rather than comprehension of text. The rationale for their study was the need to create new assessments of reading that measure a wider variety of cognitive skills and the need to create practical assessment activities for teachers that are compatible with their usual instruction. They describe a longitudinal research project in Australia where they gave 5- to 10-year-old children a variety of reading tasks designed to measure comprehension, metacognition, and strategies among young readers. The tasks assessed the strategies that children use to select appropriate books, the strategies that children use to make and monitor reading, and the understanding that children create as they examine a wordless picture book. These skills were correlated with measures of reading comprehension and metacognition and examined again two years later. Paris and van Kraayenoord found that some tasks were sensitive to developmental differences among young children and some were reasonably good predictors two years later of reading comprehension and strategy use. The tasks are compatible with American and Australian instructional practices that emphasize meaning-making and strategy use while reading and may be adapted by teachers for diagnostic use in classrooms.

Wagner analyzes a neglected topic in psychology and education, retention of skills. He reviews cognitive aspects of forgetting and transfer related to skill retention and then considers several important educational examples of skill loss including students' loss of skills during summer vacation and foreign language loss over time. Wagner then considers literacy retention and describes the problems endemic with this research. His research and other studies of adult literacy in the United States show that loss of skills is minimal if post-educational experiences reinforce the use of literacy skills. Wagner concludes his chapter by focusing on the policy issues surrounding literacy retention and the unanswered questions in the field that need to be addressed.

Stanovich, Cunningham, and West examine how literacy proficiency varies as a function of the amount of reading that people do. Many studies have investigated the antecedents of literacy, for example, instructional approaches and family variables, that lead to differences among people in reading achievement. Few have investigated the consequences of differences in the volume of reading among individuals. Stanovich and colleagues describe their intriguing research program focused on how the amount of reading that people do influences their cognition and knowledge. Their main finding is that the more a person reads, controlling for many other factors, the more he or she knows about a great many things. For example, in one intriguing analysis they show that "exposure to print" rather than just "exposure to information" is important, by comparing the everyday knowledge of world events evident in subjects with heavy exposure to print (e.g., spending lots of time reading newspaper) versus heavy exposure to other information sources (e.g., watching lots of TV news). Stanovich and colleagues use these data to advance arguments about the importance of reading, the goals of reading instruction, the influence of reading on information processing, and the nature of cognition itself.

The third section of the volume addresses policy issues that connect developmental and educational psychology with larger issues such as cross-cultural research, teacher training, and early educational programs for children at risk. Azuma reviews research by Stevenson and his colleagues that has revealed superior mathematical performance in Asian, particularly Japanese, students. He takes a holistic-cultural view of these findings and suggests that Japanese students' performance is supported by a variety of factors that stem from the influence of "Japanese collectivism." Japanese collectivism supports communal, societal, and specifically educational, practices such as deep-seated family support for the school system and for educational achievement, the use of classroom group management practices that foster communities of learners rather than individuals, and an emphasis on interpersonal relations rather than individual expression. Azuma then argues that these same values lead to negative as well as positive outcomes when seen in a context larger than just mathematics achievement. Here he provides analyses of two seemingly different but related phenomena: first, the role and influence of nationwide college entrance examinations in the Japanese system, and second, the occurrence of bullying in Japanese schools. His analyses of the Japanese cultural ethos embed both positive and negative features of Japanese education in a set of beliefs and practices that transcend education.

Murray examines the connections between current reforms in teacher education and tenets of developmental psychology. He analyzes educational slogans such as "developmentally appropriate" instruction and "all children can learn" and the "spiral curriculum" from an historical perspective that identifies the roots of these terms in developmental psychology. Murray argues that many of these developmental concepts failed to have enduring effects because they became only slogans and not part of teachers' fundamental pedagogical understanding. He then illustrates how a focus on "teaching for understanding" can be predicated on a developmental and constructivist view of learning and development, such as Piaget's, and how developmental research has identified important factors in the teaching–learning process. He contends that a deeper understanding of developmental theories, as well as enriched understanding of the complexities of subject matter, can help teachers use the concepts to make substantive changes in classroom practices.

Zigler and Styfco conclude the volume with an historical review of Head Start, the rationale, philosophy, problems, and promises of this landmark educational program to help families at educational risk. They embed their analysis of Head Start in the social and educational philosophies of the 1960s and connect it to longitudinal studies that have shown the value of early educational intervention. Zigler and Styfco then outline four lessons that the field has learned about successful preschool programs and use these lessons as the foundation for policy recommendations for educational interventions for children. Written by the founder of Head Start, this chapter shows how social policies can be based on sound empirical research and benefit millions of children directly.

In summary, these chapters examine a wide variety of issues that influence children's learning, development, and education. The international perspectives reveal the universal concerns with these topics in psychology and education as well as the specific influences of culture and context. The chapters include empirical analyses of children's learning and educational instruction, conceptual frameworks for understanding cultural influences on development, and policy implications of basic research for teacher training and educational reform. We believe these chapters reflect enduring themes of Harold Stevenson's research and represent a stimulating tribute to his career.

PART ONE

Cross-Cultural Studies of Academic Achievement

1

A Biocultural Model of Academic Development

David C. Geary, Carmen O. Hamson, Guo-Peng Chen,
Fan Liu, and Mary K. Hoard

Individual and group differences in educational outcomes have far-reaching social and economic implications because the ever increasing demands of technologically complex societies require larger and larger segments of the population to be educated at historically unprecedented levels. In addition, educational outcomes are strongly related to the well-being of individuals within these societies and to society in general, through their relation to employability, wages, and on-the-job productivity (e.g., Boissiere, Knight, & Sabot, 1985; Rivera-Batiz, 1992). A complete understanding of individual and group differences in educational outcomes will require the analysis of children's academic development at multiple levels, ranging from the influence of evolved biases in children's cognitive and motivational patterns to cultural influences on the organization of children's schooling.

The research of Harold Stevenson and his colleagues represents groundbreaking contributions to the understanding of how cultural, cognitive, and developmental processes influence children's academic

The preparation of this chapter was supported, in part, by Grant 1R01-HD27931 from the National Institute of Child Health and Human Development.

development and, as such, has made seminal contributions to the understanding of individual and group differences in educational outcomes. These contributions include, among others, the identification of substantial cross-cultural differences in children's mathematical development (e.g., Stevenson, Lee, & Stigler, 1986) and the documentation of cultural (e.g., the relative valuation of mathematics), educational, and cognitive factors that contribute to these differences (e.g., Stevenson, Lee, Chen, Stigler, Hsu, & Kitamura, 1990; Stevenson, Parker, Wilkinson, Hegion, & Fish, 1976; Stevenson & Stigler, 1992).

The goal of this chapter is to add another layer of analysis to the work of Stevenson and his colleagues. In particular we consider the ways that evolved biases in children's cognitive, developmental, and motivational patterns interact with broader cultural factors to influence academic development. First we provide the basic framework for considering the interaction between evolutionary and cultural processes during children's schooling. We then provide an illustration of how this approach to academic development can be used to understand differences in arithmetic competence of individuals from China and the United States.

THEORETICAL FOUNDATION

Evolved cognitive modules are systems of interrelated cognitive, motivational, emotional, and behavioral processes that have been designed by evolutionary pressures to address specific and recurring problems of adaptation in ancestral environments (Cosmides & Tooby, 1994; Fodor, 1983; Geary, 1998). The functioning of modules results in biases in the ways in which people process and respond to social (e.g., facial expressions) and ecological (e.g., classification of flora and fauna; Atran, 1994; Keil, 1992) information. A complete understanding of how these modules might be adapted by educational practices for nonevolutionary functions requires a distinction between evolved cognitive abilities and those abilities that arise from cultural practices, termed *primary* and *secondary* abilities, respectively (Geary, 1995a). The distinction between primary and secondary abilities and a brief discussion of how secondary abilities can emerge from primary modules is presented next. We then focus on developmental and motivational processes that appear to influence the acquisition of these cognitive competencies.

Primary and Secondary Abilities

Primary abilities are forms of cognition that have been shaped by evolutionary processes, appear to be universal, and might be conceptualized as constellations of socially based and ecologically based modules (Fodor, 1983; Geary, 1998). Secondary cognitive abilities, in contrast, are not universal and are shaped by cultural rather than evolutionary processes (Geary, 1995a; Rozin, 1976). Because different motivational and experiential processes appear to be necessary for the acquisition of primary and secondary abilities, a distinction between the two has important implications for understanding children's cognitive and academic development (Geary, 1995a, 1996a; Rozin, 1976).

Primary Abilities

There is little question that human beings are social animals (Baumeister & Leary, 1995) and that a host of neurobiological, cognitive, emotional, and behavioral systems have evolved to deal with the pressures associated with the development and regulation of social relationships (Alexander, 1979; Dunbar, 1993; Karmiloff-Smith, Klima, Bellugi, Grant, & Baron-Cohen, 1995). For instance, socioemotional reactions, such as anger and guilt, appear to have enabled the evolution of reciprocal social relationships (Trivers, 1971) and allow for the development of long-term friendships (Youniss, 1986). This is because long-term friendships are based on reciprocal exchange or roughly an equal amount of give and take in the relationship. Anger (more give than take) and guilt (more take than give) motivate behaviors that maintain this reciprocity. The socially based primary abilities that enable the emergence of such individual friendships as well as more complex social systems are likely encompassed within several social modules, including language (Pinker & Bloom, 1990), facial processing, and *theory of mind*, which represents the cognitive competencies that allow

15

individuals to make inferences about the intentions, beliefs, emotional states, and so on of other people (Cosmides, 1989; Karmiloff-Smith et al., 1995; Leslie, 1987).

Ecologically based primary abilities appear to be organized into physical and biological modules. These modules encompass the perceptual and cognitive systems that enable living in the physical, as contrasted with the social, world and make possible the exploitation of the biological environments within which we live and develop (Geary, 1998; Shepard, 1994). Examples of the associated cognitive competencies include the ability to generate mental representations or maps of familiar ecologies (Landau, Gleitman, & Spelke, 1981), the tendency to develop incidental memories for the location and organization of objects in these ecologies (Silverman & Eals, 1992), and, in preindustrial societies, the development of taxonomies of flora and fauna in the ecology that support survival (Atran, 1994; Geary, 1998; Gelman, 1990). In addition to the competencies associated with social, biological, and physical modules, there appear to be other primary competencies, such as primary numerical abilities (Geary, 1995a).

Secondary Abilities

The emergence of secondary abilities appears to arise from cultural practices that enable the use of primary cognitive modules in ways that are unrelated to their original evolutionary function. There appear to be at least two ways in which primary cognitive competencies can be used for the development of secondary abilities: the redescription and elaboration of innate implicit knowledge (typically recasting the knowledge in verbal form) and *cognitive co-optation* (Geary, 1996a; Karmiloff-Smith, 1992; Rozin, 1976).

With respect to the former, the initial development of primary abilities appears to be guided by innate, implicit knowledge of the domain (Gelman, 1990); a domain can be represented by the class of information processed by a given module (e.g., social modules are sensitive to human social behaviors, such as facial expressions). This knowledge automatically directs the attentional systems of an infant to specific features of the environment (e.g., human faces), structures the processing of this information, and guides the infant's behaviors toward engaging the environment. In contrast, implicit knowledge associated with secondary abilities (e.g., typing, reading, carpentry), and the automatic execution of the component processes associated with these abilities, develop only *after* exposure to the content of the domain (see, e.g., Schacter, 1994). Thus, while both primary and secondary abilities include implicit knowledge and the automatic processing of content-specific information, implicit knowledge provides the foundation for the development of primary abilities but is simply one outcome of the development of secondary abilities. In fact, the initial development of secondary abilities appears to be heavily dependent on an explicit understanding of the associated principles; the way in which the mastery of many secondary abilities, especially those taught in school, is tested (e.g., essay exams) is based on the assumption that conceptual and factual knowledge can be articulated.

The development of secondary abilities often involves an explicit redescription of the implicit skeletal knowledge associated with primary domains (Geary, 1995a; Gelman, 1990; Karmiloff-Smith, 1992; Rozin, 1976). As an example, consider that the primary systems that support movement in the physical world include skeletal knowledge of many features of Euclidean geometry (Gallistel, 1990). This is because Euclidean geometry is an approximate mathematical representation of the organization of the physical world, at least those features of the world that our sensory and perceptual systems process (Shepard, 1994), and navigation is based on an implicit understanding of this organization. For instance, it has been shown that many species of animal implicitly understand that the most efficient way to move from one location to another is to go "as the crow flies," or in a straight line (Gould, 1986). Euclid's redescription of this implicit knowledge is reflected in his first postulate, 'a line can be drawn from any point to any point, that is, a line is a straight line.' Euclid's explicit formalization of this innate and implicit skeletal principle allowed for the cultural transmission of this knowledge, which, in turn, contributed to the development of mathematics and architecture, among other fields.

As another example, consider that children are able to form and maintain friendships based on reciprocity without having read Trivers'

17

(1971) seminal article on the evolution of reciprocal altruism. Stated otherwise, an explicit understanding of the reciprocal basis of long-term friendships is not needed to develop friendships. However, the social behavior of children indicates an *implicit* understanding of the importance of reciprocity in long-term social relationships—children who do not reciprocate are socially rejected (Newcomb, Bukowski, & Pattee, 1993). Social behaviors are more or less automatically constrained by an implicit understanding of the costs and benefits of reciprocal relationships, but the explicit understanding of these same principles was only achieved through considerable scientific effort (e.g., Cosmides, 1989; Trivers, 1971).

In short, the initial conceptual knowledge needed to achieve primary goals (e.g., developing social relationships) is built into the cognitive and biological systems that were designed, by evolution, to function in the social, biological, and physical world. Much, though not necessarily all, of this knowledge is unconscious or implicit. In contrast, the knowledge needed to achieve secondary goals (e.g., learning formal geometric theorems) is not built into these systems but secondary abilities can emerge as primary implicit knowledge is formalized and described by means of language or mathematics. One result of any such redescription is that the implicit becomes explicit. Once explicit, this knowledge can be transmitted culturally (e.g., taught in school).

Cognitive co-optation involves the use of primary cognitive systems in ways that are unrelated to the original evolutionary function of these systems. For instance, the cognitive systems that support the generation of mental maps of familiar locations can be used in ways unrelated to navigation, such as for the representation of quantitative information presented in mathematical word problems (Geary, 1996a). Lewis (1989) demonstrated that the frequency of errors associated with solving word problems can be greatly reduced if the quantitative relationships in the word problem are diagrammed, or represented spatially. It is very unlikely that the evolution of the visuospatial system was in any way related to the solving of mathematical word problems, but nevertheless this system can be co-opted to aid in the solution of such problems.

There is, however, a critical difference between generating mental maps associated with navigation and generating spatial diagrams of mathematical relationships. This difference is reflected in the ease with which these cognitive skills are acquired. Mental maps of familiar ecologies develop more or less automatically and effortlessly (Landau et al., 1981), but most people need to be taught explicitly how to diagram mathematical relationships (Lewis, 1989). Even with formal instruction, learning how to diagram mathematical relationships is typically a tedious and difficult task. Nevertheless, the end result is often a new, secondary, cognitive skill; in this example, a formal step-by-step system of rules for diagramming the mathematical relationships that are presented in word problems (Lewis, 1989).

Developmental and Motivational Processes

There are a number of developmental and motivational factors, outlined below, that appear to differentially affect the acquisition of primary and secondary abilities. An understanding of these differences has important implications for conceptualizing the source of individual and group differences in educational outcomes.

Developmental Processes

The first critical difference associated with the development of primary and secondary abilities concerns the initial organization of the associated competencies, and the second concerns the contexts within which these competencies develop.

As noted earlier, the skeletal structure of the competencies associated with primary abilities appears to be built into the architecture of the underlying neurobiological systems (Gelman, 1990; Shepard, 1994). Skeletal structure means that primary competencies are biologically prepared to emerge with appropriate developmental experiences, not that these competencies are fully developed in children. It appears that the natural play and exploratory behaviors of children result in the experiences necessary for the development of primary abilities (Eibl-Eibesfeldt, 1989; Geary, 1995a). This is not to say that play is the only activity associated with the emergence of primary abilities. Parent–child interactions or even formal schooling might influence the emergence of primary competencies. Schooling, for example, might accelerate the expression of these competencies. Nevertheless, the position here is that play is likely to be necessary for the fleshing out of many of the cognitive competencies that have emerged through evolutionary selection (see Geary, 1995a).

As one example of the potential relation between play and the development of primary abilities, consider the early social behavior and activities of infants and preschool children. Initially, infants have a number of skeletal competencies that support social interactions, including an implicit conceptual understanding of the difference between people and nonpeople. In addition, infants have a rudimentary understanding of the emotions signaled by facial expressions, as well as those behaviors that enable social interactions (Bower, 1982). These behaviors would include visual tracking of human movement and smiling at familiar people, among others. The net result of these competencies is that infants orient themselves to the social environment, such as human faces, and respond to social stimulation with positive emotions (Bower, 1982; McGuinness & Pribram, 1979). The positive emotions associated with social stimulation motivate continued engagement with people (Campos, Campos, & Barrett, 1989), which, in turn, produces experiences that are needed for the continued development of the infants' social competencies.

All of these behaviors reflect the basic skeletal competencies of the primary social modules (e.g., language, facial processing) and appear to be further elaborated as children engage in social play (Baumeister & Leary, 1995). Sociodramatic play, for instance, appears to be an important vehicle for elaborating children's social competencies, such as learning the implicit scripts that choreograph many social interactions. Beginning at around 3 years old, children practice social scripts in the context of their play (Rubin, Fein, & Vandenberg, 1983). Initially, this type of play involves using dolls or other toys to act out everyday social experiences (e.g., dinner). The use of toys allows the child to practice coordinating social interactions at a point where the child does not yet have the competencies to do so effectively with other children. Later, particularly between the ages of 4 to 6 years, children rehearse and then expand on these scripts with groups of other children (Rubin et al., 1983). Thus, from 3 to 6 years old, children's play activities involve increasingly complex patterns of social interaction, patterns that very likely build on and elaborate the initial skeletal structures associated with the social modules.

The architecture for secondary abilities (e.g., typing, reading, and carpentry), in contrast, is not biologically prepared and, as a result, the acquisition of these abilities is slow and effortful and occurs, for the most part, only with formal or informal instruction (Geary, 1995a; Siegler & Crowley, 1994). Formal and informal instruction can, of course, occur in many settings, including at home, in peer groups, and through apprenticeship programs (e.g., to learn auto mechanics), but the primary setting within which most children in technologically complex societies learn most secondary competencies is school. School-taught secondary abilities are thus the focus of all later discussion in this chapter of secondary learning, but this should not be taken to mean that there are not other forms of secondary learning (e.g., driving a car) or other contexts within which such learning can occur.

In this view, schools essentially involve the society-level organization of children's activities such that children acquire social and cognitive skills that otherwise would not emerge. It is not a coincidence that many secondary abilities (e.g., reading) emerge largely in technologically complex societies (Whiting & Whiting, 1975). Neither is it a coincidence that the need for near universal schooling arises in such societies only after technological changes make it necessary for individuals to universally develop school-taught competencies to enter the workforce. One implication of this perspective, which we address below, is that a complete understanding of individual and group differences in the development of school-taught abilities requires consideration of the factors that influence the motivation to learn in school. Nature has not provided a *universal* interest in secondary learning (e.g., reading) nor has nature provided inherent positive emotional responses to engaging in the activities that will facilitate the acquisition of secondary competencies (see Geary, 1995a).

Motivational Processes

Heckhausen and Schulz (1995; see also Schulz & Heckhausen, 1996) have recently argued that a fundamental—and arguably the most general—human motivation is the desire to control or exert some level of influence on the environments within which we live and develop; control is defined as "bringing the environment into line with one's wishes" (Heckhausen & Schulz, 1995, p. 285). When this control motivation is viewed from an evolutionary perspective, human beings are predicted to be fundamentally motivated to attempt to organize and control social, biological, and physical environments in ways that enhance their reproduction and survival and the reproduction and survival of their kin (e.g., Betzig, 1993). The near universal goal of attempting to control these environments likely created selection pressures for the evolution of an ensemble of modules designed for interfacing the social, biological, and physical environments (Geary, 1998), as described earlier.

For humans, the general activities associated with the control of these environments would be focused on the acquisition of resources and social status, the development and maintenance of reciprocal social relationships, the finding of a mate, and the healthy development of one's children (Alexander, 1979; Buss & Schmitt, 1993; MacDonald, 1988). Reproduction and survival are directly dependent on the acquisition of physical (e.g., water) and biological (e.g., food) resources and on the development of social relationships. Social status is important because it influences an individual's level of control over other people and thus enables greater success in bringing the environment into line with one's wishes. Social status, in turn, is typically achieved by political means, through control of the biological and physical environments that support survival, or through both.

From this perspective, children's play and exploratory behavior provide a natural means of rehearsing the primary competencies needed to effectively achieve some level of control over these environments in adulthood (children, of course, seek some level of control as well). The associated motivational (and emotional; see Geary, 1998) systems direct the behavior of children toward engaging the social, biological, and physical environments in ways that flesh out primary cognitive abilities. The earlier described patterns for sociodramatic play provide one example for social modules; games such as hide and seek and baseball (e.g., through tracking the trajectory of moving objects in three-dimensional space) potentially influence the fleshing out of the competencies associated with physical modules (Geary, 1995b).

Motivational systems are complex, however, because attempts to achieve some level of control often result in failure. *Motivational mechanisms* "help the individual to cope with failure and [foster] primary control by channeling motivational resources toward selected action goals" (Heckhausen & Schulz, 1995, p. 284). Motivational mechanisms involve expectancy of goal attainment, value of goal attainment, and causal attributions of behavioral outcomes (e.g., lack of ability). For instance, nearly all individuals naturally seek out some social affiliations, and motivational mechanisms are likely to be more or less automatically and universally triggered with social failures. Even with such failures, most individuals will continue to seek social affiliations (Baumeister & Leary, 1995). Therefore, the goal of developing social affiliations is likely inherent. Furthermore, motivational processes automatically enable individuals to continue attempts to seek out or maintain social relationships even after conflicts arise or there is a failure to achieve this primary goal.

In contrast to the inherent motivation to attempt to control the social, biological, and physical environments within which people live (Heckhausen & Schulz, 1995), as well as in contrast to the resulting inherent motivation to develop the cognitive competencies needed to achieve some level of control in these environments, the motivation to develop secondary abilities comes from the demands of the wider society and not the inherent interests of children. Many children are, of course, motivated to learn in school (Ames & Archer, 1988; Nicholls, 1984). The point is, if the goal is universal education, then school and supporting environments (e.g., home) need to be structured so that the motivation to acquire secondary abilities is a feature of instructional activities; we cannot rely on children's "natural curiosity" or "natural enthusiasm for learning."

Without such social supports, it is predicted that when individuals fail to achieve secondary goals it is more likely to result in the long-term devaluation of the associated competencies than is the case when individuals fail to achieve the primary goals. In this view, the sociocultural value of secondary abilities and attributions that affect motivational processes is potentially very important sources of individual and group differences in educational outcomes. In other words, cultural differences in the value of secondary cognitive abilities might result in differences in the degree to which motivational systems are engaged when acquiring school-taught competencies becomes difficult and prone to failure. Moreover, wider economic changes might result in changes in the relative value of secondary abilities even within cultures—many individuals attend college because a college degree affects later earnings (resource control is a primary goal) and not because of an inherent enjoyment of learning (Coleman, 1993).

As an example from secondary mathematics (Geary, 1995a), experimental manipulations that change adolescents' perceptions of the use and economic value of mathematics have resulted in adolescents taking additional mathematics courses (Fennema, Wolleat, Pedro, & Becker, 1981). Moreover, there is some evidence that the difference in the mathematical achievement of individuals from the United States and East Asian nations is related, in part, to differences in the cultural value of mathematics and the perceived attributes of mathematics learning (i.e., the relative importance of effort and ability for learning mathematics; Stevenson et al., 1990). These differences in the value of secondary mathematics would presumably operate by maintaining goal-directed behavior when learning mathematics becomes difficult and prone to failure (e.g., see Ames & Archer, 1988).

This perspective does not mean that no one will be motivated to pursue secondary learning (Geary, 1995a). Rather, from this perspective, the motivation to pursue primary goals will be more or less universal but the motivation to pursue secondary goals will not. Two important implications follow from this view: (a) universal education will be dependent on the cultural valuation of secondary abilities (Stevenson & Stigler, 1992), and (b) given free choice, most individuals will prefer to pursue primary instead of secondary goals. Stated otherwise, the near universal development of secondary abilities will require, to some extent, the cultural suppression of primary activities (e.g., socializing) and the redirection of behavior toward secondary learning.

Implications

A general overview of the differences between primary and secondary abilities that seem most relevant to children's academic development is presented in Table 1, although these differences are probably somewhat exaggerated.

Overall, the demarcation of cognitive competencies into primary and secondary abilities provides a potentially useful organizing frame-

Table 1
Important Differences Between Primary and Secondary Abilities

Dimension	Primary	Secondary
Organization of Abilities	Implicit knowledge	Explicit knowledge
	Biologically prepared architecture	Socially prepared architecture
Learning and Development	More or less automatic	Slow and effortful
	Emerges with natural activities	Emerges with formal schooling
Motivational Processes	Valuation of primary goals is biologically prepared	Valuation of secondary goals is culturally dependent
	With a failure to achieve primary goals, motivational processes are automatically triggered.	With a failure to achieve secondary goals, the triggering of motivational processes is more strongly influenced by social than biological factors.

work for approaching the issue of individual and group differences in academic development (Geary, 1995a, 1996a). For primary domains, congenital or early environmental factors are implicated as the primary source of any such differences. For secondary domains, (a) cultural factors that influence motivational processes, (b) schooling, (c) the supporting primary cognitive systems (e.g., working memory), and (d) differences in general intelligence (IQ) are implicated as the source of individual or group differences in secondary learning.

With respect to the latter, IQ might reflect individual differences in the ability to use primary systems for secondary learning, which would be reflected, to some extent, in individual differences in school achievement (Geary, 1996a). This argument is based on the finding that IQ is a good predictor of learning in school (Stevenson et al., 1976) and that most school-based learning involves acquiring secondary abilities. This view has, in fact, been implied in the claim that the advantage of East Asian children over children in the United States in educational outcomes is largely due to a group difference, favoring East Asians, in intelligence (Rushton, 1995).

CULTURAL VARIATION IN ACADEMIC ACHIEVEMENT

The perspective presented in the first part of this chapter indicates that a thorough assessment of group and individual differences in educational outcomes will require a determination of whether any such differences emerge for primary or secondary abilities (Geary, 1996a, 1996b) and whether any differences in secondary abilities can be attributed to differences in intelligence, schooling (broadly defined, including, e.g., parental support of schooling), motivational factors, or differences in the primary systems that support secondary abilities.

On the basis of this perspective, a brief overview of differences, or a lack thereof, in the primary and secondary mathematical competencies of East Asian and American children is presented below. We then present a study that addresses the issue of whether differences in the intelligence of individuals from East Asia and the United States is the source of the East Asian advantage in secondary mathematical domains. The relation between schooling and the development of secondary arithmetical abilities is then examined through comparisons of the pattern of arithmetical competencies across several generations of individuals from China and the United States. The discussion closes with a few comments on motivational factors and the primary systems that support secondary arithmetical competencies.

Primary and Secondary Competencies

Primary numerical and arithmetical abilities are evident in human infants and preschool children throughout the world. These abilities include quickly apprehending the quantities of small sets, as well as rudimentary counting and arithmetical competencies (Geary, 1995a). There appear to be no differences in the primary numerical and arithmetical abilities of American and East Asian children, but consistent and substantive differences in nearly all secondary mathematical areas (Fuson & Kwon, 1992; Geary, 1996b; Geary, Bow-Thomas, Liu, & Siegler, 1996; Geary, Fan, & Bow-Thomas, 1992). The implications of this pattern are important, as the pattern suggests that the East Asian advantage in mathematics does not have biological origins (Geary, 1996b). Furthermore, educational interventions directed at closing the mathematical achievement gap between the United States and the East Asian nations should focus on fostering U.S. children's acquisition of secondary mathematical competencies and should also focus on factors that promote (e.g., schooling) the acquisition of these competencies.

Some of the early differences in the secondary numerical and arithmetical competencies of East Asian and American children appear to be due to differences in the structure of number words past 10, and, when comparisons are made between China and the United States, the speed with which number words can be articulated. In East Asian languages, counting past 10 is translated as "ten one," "ten two," "ten three," and so on. These number words mirror the underlying base-10 structure of the Arabic number system. As such, these number words appear to facilitate East Asian children's counting past 10 and their conceptual understanding of certain arithmetical concepts, such as trading in complex arithmetic (e.g., 47 + 39; Fuson & Kwon, 1992; Miller, Smith, Zhu, & Zhang, 1995).

In addition, Chinese number words can be pronounced more quickly than English number words, which affords Chinese individuals about a 2-digit span advantage over their American peers (Stigler, Lee, & Stevenson, 1986). Chen and Stevenson (1988) found no differences between Chinese and American preschool children in the ability to keep information active in phonological memory, indicating that the Chinese advantage in digit span is not due to group differences in the primary systems (e.g., phonological memory; Geary, Bow-Thomas, Fan, & Siegler, 1993) that support memory span (see also Stevenson, Stigler, Lee, Lucker, Kitamura, & Hsu, 1985). Rather, the Chinese advantage in digit span is simply due to differences in the surface structure of number words. Nevertheless, this span advantage appears to enable Chinese children to abandon the developmentally immature finger counting strategy for solving simple arithmetic problems, in favor of verbal counting, at a younger age than American children (Geary, Bow-Thomas, et al., 1993; Geary, Bow-Thomas, et al., 1996).

However, these differences in number words result only in very *selective* East Asian advantages in early numerical and arithmetical competencies and, given this, are not likely to be the principal source of the mathematical achievement gap when comparing the United States and East Asian nations (Geary, Bow-Thomas, et al., 1996). For competencies that do not appear to be related to the structure of number words, cross-national differences in secondary mathematical achievement might then be related to differences in the schooling, broadly defined, of East Asian and American children. In addition, differences may be related to factors that might influence the acquisition of school-taught secondary competencies, including intelligence and motivational processes (e.g., valuation).

Intelligence

As noted earlier, individual differences in intelligence are strong predictors of individual differences in educational outcomes (Stevenson et al., 1976), and group differences in intelligence have been implicated as the source of the academic achievement gap comparing children from East Asia and the United States. Preliminary results for a study conducted in our laboratory, however, suggest that a group difference in IQ is not the source of the mathematical achievement advantage of East Asians over Americans. These results are in keeping with the earlier findings of Stevenson and his colleagues (Stevenson et al., 1985).

In our study, relatively select groups of high school seniors were administered the Raven's Progressive Matrices Test, a nonverbal measure of general intelligence (Raven, Court, & Raven, 1993), and sets of arithmetical computational and reasoning tests (see Geary, Hamson, Chen, Liu, Hoard, & Salthouse, 1997). The computational tests were timed paper-and-pencil tests of skill at solving simple subtraction (e.g., $9 - 3, 5 - 2$), complex subtraction (e.g., $43 - 5, 29 - 2$), and complex addition (e.g., $34 + 97 + 12, 9 + 62 + 61$) problems. The reasoning tests were Necessary Arithmetic Operations (NAO) and Arithmetic Aptitude (AA; Ekstrom, French, & Harman, 1976). Both tests require the solving of multi-step arithmetic word problems, but NAO only requires participants to indicate the order in which arithmetic operations (e.g., multiplication then division) need to be used in order to solve the problem—no computations are needed. Items for AA require the participants to solve multi-step word problems.

For the most part, all of the arithmetic tests appear to assess school-taught secondary mathematical abilities, and are comparable to tests used in large-scale economic studies. The results of these studies indicate that performance on these types of tests is predictive of employability, wages, and productivity (Boissiere et al., 1985; Rivera-Batiz, 1992), above and beyond the influence of intelligence, reading ability, race, sex, and years of schooling.

The groups were relatively select because only about 30% of urban Chinese adolescents attend academic high schools. A comparable population in the United States, after factoring in the dropout rate, appears to be high-school seniors enrolled in calculus, precalculus, and college algebra classes. Thus, to ensure that comparable samples were assessed, we compared U.S. seniors enrolled in these classes ($n = 55$) to Chinese seniors in academic high schools ($n = 80$). The mean IQ of 120 ($SD =$

11) and 118 ($SD = 10$) of the Chinese and American samples, respectively, did not differ significantly ($p > .10$).

However, the Chinese adolescents outscored ($ps < .01$) their American peers on all of the arithmetic tests, as shown in Table 2. The column labeled d (effect size) represents the difference between the mean performance of the Chinese 12th graders and the mean of the American 12th graders in terms of standard deviation (SD) units derived from the Chinese sample (Cohen, 1988); the percentile column in Table 2 indicates the level at which the average American 12th grader performed relative to the Chinese sample. For simple subtraction, the performance of the average American 12th grader, from this relatively

Table 2

Test Performance for the Chinese and American 12th Graders

| Test | China | | United States | | | |
	M	SD	M	SD	d	%tile
Computational tests	138.3	10.8	116.2	23.3	2.05	2
Simple subtraction						
Complex subtraction	68.1	16.9	37.4	9.3	1.82	3
Complex addition	47.2	8.6	36.0	8.3	1.30	10
Reasoning tests						
Necessary arithmetic	19.4	4.1	17.3	4.6	0.51	31
operations						
Arithmetic aptitude	22.4	4.7	15.2	5.5	1.53	6

Note. Effect size, d, provides an estimate of the magnitude of the group differences and was calculated as follows:

$$d = \frac{M\ (\text{China}) - M\ (\text{U.S.})}{SD\ (\text{China})},$$

where M (China) and M (U.S.) are the mean scores of the Chinese and U.S. samples, respectively, and SD (China) is the standard deviation of M (China). Positive scores indicate a Chinese advantage.

Percentile is derived from d (Cohen, 1988) and represents the percentile ranking of the mean U.S. score in relation to the Chinese sample. For instance, for simple subtraction, the average U.S. student scored at the second percentile of the Chinese sample; 98% of the Chinese students outscored the average U.S. student.

elite group of American high school students, was 2.05 *SD*s below the Chinese mean. The adjacent percentile column indicates that in simple subtraction the average American 12th grader would perform at the 2nd percentile in an academic Chinese high school (i.e., 98% of Chinese 12th graders scored above the average American student). Overall, the American 12th graders are at or below the 10th percentile on all arithmetic measures, except NAO, where they are at the 31st percentile.

The overall pattern indicates (a) a substantial Chinese advantage in computational arithmetic, (b) a moderate advantage in arithmetical reasoning (as indexed by performance on the NAO test), and (c) a substantial advantage in the ability to solve complex multi-step word problems (as indexed by performance on the AA test). The finding of substantive differences in the secondary arithmetical competencies of Chinese and U.S. adolescents with comparable IQ scores suggests that differences in the schooling or the secondary motivational processes—or both—of East Asian and American children, not differences in intelligence, are the source of the achievement gap in mathematics.

Schooling

One approach that can be used to study the effects of schooling on the development of secondary academic competencies is to compare the pattern of academic development across generations as well as across cultures (Geary, Salthouse, Chen, & Fan, 1996). This approach is particularly useful for examining the influence of schooling on arithmetical development because there is evidence that the level of competency in secondary arithmetic has declined across generations in the United States (e.g., Schaie, 1993, 1996). Any decline in academic competencies in the United States is unlikely to be related to population-wide changes in IQ, given that performance on IQ tests tends to increase from one generation to the next (Flynn, 1987), but rather strongly implicates changes in schooling and perhaps cultural factors that influence the motivation to learn in school.

Of course, changes in the numbers of individuals who attend school from one generation to the next complicate such comparisons. Given this, it is important that cross-generational and cross-cultural comparisons are for groups that have comparable educational levels, as well as comparable performance on IQ tests, as described above. In one recent study, comparably and relatively well educated groups (14.0 to 14.7 mean years of education across groups) of younger (college students) and older (*M* age = 73, United States; *M* age = 66, China) adults from the United States and China were administered sets of psychometric tests of arithmetical abilities (e.g., 36 + 86 + 14, 37 − 9), perceptual speed (e.g., speed of reading numbers), and spatial abilities (e.g., skill at rotating images in three dimensions; Geary, Salthouse, et al., 1996).

For the older groups, there were no substantive cross-national differences in any of the three ability domains. Similarly, there were no substantive differences for the younger adults on the perceptual speed or spatial measures. In contrast, the Chinese college students outperformed their U.S. peers on all of the arithmetic tests, and the magnitude of the Chinese advantage was comparable to the advantage of Chinese high school students over American high school students noted in Table 2. Thus, the often found advantage of contemporary East Asians over Americans in secondary mathematics (e.g., Stevenson, Chen, & Lee, 1993) is not evident, at least in complex arithmetic, for Chinese and American adults who were educated earlier in this century.

Comparisons of the performance of younger and older groups within nations was also very informative. Consistent with general findings in cognitive aging research (e.g., Salthouse, 1991), the younger Chinese adults outperformed their older same-nation peers in all three ability domains (i.e., computational arithmetic, perceptual speed, and spatial). Moreover, the magnitude of the advantage of the younger Chinese adults over the older Chinese adults was highly similar across domains, suggesting that normal aging affects computational abilities in arithmetic along with the other types of cognitive abilities. For the Americans, the same pattern emerged for the perceptual speed and spatial measures, but not for performance on the arithmetic tests. In fact, there was no substantive difference in the arithmetical computational abilities of the younger and older Americans.

The within-nation pattern suggests that the comparable arithmetical abilities of older Chinese and older American adults is not due to

Americans eventually catching up to their Chinese peers. The pattern does not support the position that arithmetical abilities gradually increase throughout the life span. If this were the case, then the younger Chinese adults would not have outscored their older peers in arithmetic. In fact, the finding that the relative advantage of the younger Chinese adults over the older Chinese adults was essentially the same across all three ability domains indicates that the arithmetical abilities of the younger Chinese adults were not exceptional. Rather, the Chinese pattern for performance on the arithmetic tests suggests that the older Chinese adults were probably comparable to the younger Chinese adults when they were in their 20s and the current difference largely reflects standard age-related changes in cognitive performance (Salthouse, 1991). These patterns, combined with the *selective* advantage of younger Chinese adults over their same-age American peers in arithmetic, suggest that the comparable arithmetical abilities of younger and older adults reflects declining competencies, across generations, in the United States (see also Geary, Frensch, & Wiley, 1993; Schaie, 1996).

An aspect of the earlier described study replicated the finding of comparable arithmetical competencies of Chinese and American adults who were educated earlier in this century. Here, Chinese ($n = 56$) and American ($n = 47$) adults between the ages of 60 and 80 years and with between 9 and 16 years of formal schooling were administered the same IQ and arithmetical tests administered to the 12th graders. The mean IQs of the Chinese and American samples were 105 ($SD = 10$) and 113 ($SD = 14$), respectively, and differed significantly ($p < .01$). The American sample was also somewhat better educated than the Chinese sample; the mean years of schooling for the Chinese and American samples were 11.0 ($SD = 2.2$) and 13.8 ($SD = 2.0$; $p < .01$), respectively. The mean arithmetic test performance of the Chinese sample was therefore adjusted to control for the American IQ and schooling advantage.

The relative performance of the American and Chinese adults on the arithmetic tests, after controlling for IQ and schooling differences, is presented in Table 3. There were no significant differences for four of the five tests ($ps > .05$). The one test, complex addition, that did show a difference favored the Americans ($p < .01$). A comparison of

Table 3

Test Performance for the Chinese and American Elderly Adults

Test	China		United States		d	%tile
	M	SD	M	SD		
Computational tests	92.8	30.8	94.7	20.4	−.06	52
Simple subtraction						
Complex subtraction	30.1	17.4	35.4	10.8	−.30	62
Complex addition	26.9	12.2	39.0	11.4	−.99	84
Reasoning tests						
Necessary arithmetic operations	12.3	3.9	12.4	5.8	−.03	51
Arithmetic aptitude	10.5	4.6	10.2	7.2	.07	47

Note. Effect size, *d*, provides an estimate of the magnitude of the group differences and was calculated as follows:

$$d = \frac{M\ (\text{China}) - M\ (\text{U.S.})}{SD\ (\text{China})},$$

where M (China) and M (U.S.) are the mean scores of the Chinese and U.S. samples, respectively, and SD (China) is the standard deviation of M (China). Positive scores indicate a Chinese advantage, negative scores a U.S. advantage.

Percentile is derived from d (Cohen, 1988) and represents the percentile ranking of the mean U.S. score in relation to the Chinese sample. For instance, for simple subtraction, the average U.S. participant scored at the 52nd percentile of the Chinese sample.

the percentile column of Table 3 with the same column of Table 2 underscores the magnitude of the cross-generational decline in the arithmetical competencies of Americans relative to their Chinese peers. For the four tests on which the American high school students are at or below the Chinese 10th percentile, the older Americans score between the 47th and 84th Chinese percentile.

Another, more direct, method of estimating the extent to which schooling influences the magnitude of the mathematics achievement gap comparing the United States and East Asian nations is to compare changes in the mathematical competencies of American and East Asian children across the academic year. Geary, Bow-Thomas, et al. (1996)

conducted such a study. In this study, groups of kindergarten through third-grade children were administered a paper-and-pencil addition test (e.g., 5 + 3 =), a digit span measure, and an addition strategy assessment toward the beginning and toward the end of the U.S. school year. The addition strategy assessment provided information on the types of strategies the children used to solve simple addition problems (e.g., 3 + 2, 8 + 6) as well as information on the speed and accuracy of their strategy use. The results indicated that the Chinese children had about a 2-digit span advantage over the American children, presumably reflecting differences in the speed of articulating Chinese and English number words (Stigler et al., 1986), but the magnitude of this advantage did not change from one grade to the next. This finding suggests that differences in the schooling of Chinese and American children do not greatly affect digit span.

However, there were large differences, favoring the Chinese children, in performance on the paper-and-pencil addition test and on the addition strategy assessment that appeared to be related, in part, to differences in the schooling of Chinese and American children. For instance, for the Chinese kindergarten and first-grade children, there was a clear shift in the use of counting strategies to the use of direct retrieval to solve simple addition problems from the beginning to the end of the academic year; the Chinese children retrieved nearly all basic addition facts by the end of first grade (Geary et al., 1992). For the American children, in contrast, there was little change in the distribution of strategy choices from the beginning to the end of the academic year at any grade level, although there was a shift toward more direct retrieval across grade levels. Still, by the end of third grade the American children were only correctly retrieving about 1/2 of the basic addition facts.

Performance differences on the paper-and-pencil test were also dramatic. For instance, at the beginning of the academic year the American third graders correctly solved, on average, 36 simple addition problems in 2 minutes. At the end of the year, these third graders correctly solved 39 problems, a gain of 3 problems. The Chinese third graders, in contrast, correctly solved 84 problems in 2 minutes at the beginning of the year and 118 problems at the end of the year, a gain of 34 problems.

Because the Chinese academic year extends almost 2 months beyond the U.S. academic year, the comparison of U.S. and Chinese students at the end of the U.S. school year actually underestimates the gap between the competencies of Chinese and American students at the end of each grade level. Nevertheless, within the confines of the U.S. school year, American students begin each grade level behind their Chinese peers in basic arithmetical competencies and the gap grows over the course of the school year.

Motivational Processes and Supporting Primary Systems

Although we did not measure motivational processes in these studies, the research of Stevenson and his colleagues (Stevenson et al., 1990; Stevenson & Stigler, 1992) suggests that differences between East Asian and American cultures in the relative valuation of mathematics and in the relative emphasis on effort rather than ability for school learning are very likely to be important proximate mechanisms contributing to the mathematics achievement gap of contemporary East Asian and American children. An important issue is whether these school-related motivational processes have changed from one generation to the next in the United States—an issue we hope is addressed with future studies.

As noted earlier, the research of Stevenson and his colleagues suggests that the advantage of East Asian children over American children in secondary arithmetic does not appear to be due to a group difference in the primary systems that support the emergence of these secondary abilities (Chen & Stevenson, 1988; Stevenson et al., 1985). The one exception might be the well-developed spatial abilities of Japanese children relative to their American peers. Well-developed spatial abilities might result in a selective advantage in learning how to diagram spatially the mathematical relationships depicted in mathematical word problems and in acquiring certain aspects of geometry (Geary, 1996a, 1996b). However, this difference in spatial ability cannot be related to broad racial categories, because Japanese children also outperform Chinese children on spatial tests and because there are no spatial ability differences comparing individuals from China and the United States (Geary, Salthouse et al., 1996; Stevenson et al., 1985).

CONCLUSION

A complete understanding of individual and group differences in educational outcomes will require the consideration of these differences from many levels as well as a consideration of how processes at these different levels interact. At the broadest level are cultural influences on the organization of children's activities. Within technologically complex societies, the organization of children's activities is centered on schooling. Across technologically complex societies, general cultural beliefs about children's learning will influence instructional activities, motivational processes that affect school learning, and the relative emphasis on one type of secondary learning or another (e.g., reading vs. mathematics; Stevenson & Stigler, 1992).

These broad cultural influences are layered on top of the more primary cognitive abilities and motivational patterns of children (Geary, 1995a). In this view, the primary motivation of children is to learn about and attempt to control the social, biological, and physical ecologies within which they live. The cognitive competencies that enable learning about the social, biological, and physical world comprise natural social and ecological cognitive modules, among others (e.g., primary numerical abilities). The initial skeletal structure of these cognitive modules is built into the organization of the underlying neurobiological substrate (Gelman, 1990), and this substrate and skeletal knowledge are fleshed out as children engage in natural play or social activities.

The interactions between these primary cognitive abilities and cultural influences on learning occur, for the most part, in the context of school (broadly defined to include parental influences on secondary learning). From this perspective, schooling involves organizing children's activities so that unnatural, or secondary, cognitive competencies emerge from more primary evolved competencies. This perspective explains differences in the ease with which primary (e.g., language) and secondary (e.g., reading) abilities are acquired by children, the importance of instruction for the emergence of secondary but not primary competencies, as well as the mechanisms through which broad cultural factors, such as valuation of secondary mathematics, can lead to substantive cross-national differences in secondary but not primary abilities

(Geary, 1996b). These interactions are more complex than suggested in this chapter, no doubt. Nevertheless, the general framework presented here should prove useful in further theoretical and empirical studies of children's academic development.

REFERENCES

Alexander, R. (1979). *Darwinism and human affairs*. Seattle, WA: University of Washington Press.

Ames, C., & Archer, J. (1988). Achievement goals in the classroom: Students' learning strategies and motivational processes. *Journal of Educational Psychology, 80,* 260–267.

Atran, S. (1994). Core domains versus scientific theories: Evidence from systematics and Itza-Maya folkbiology. In L. A. Hirschfeld & S. A. Gelman (Eds.), *Mapping the mind: Domain specificity in cognition and culture* (pp. 316–340). New York: Cambridge University Press.

Baumeister, R. F., & Leary, M. R. (1995). The need to belong: Desire for interpersonal attachment as a fundamental human motivation. *Psychological Bulletin, 117,* 497–529.

Betzig, L. (1993). Sex, succession, and stratification in the first six civilizations: How powerful men reproduced, passed power on to their sons, and used power to defend their wealth, women, and children. In L. Ellis (Ed.), *Social stratification and socioeconomic inequality: Volume 1: A comparative biosocial analysis* (pp. 37–74). Westport, CT: Praeger.

Boissiere, M., Knight, J. B., & Sabot, R. H. (1985). Earnings, schooling, ability, and cognitive skills. *American Economic Review, 75,* 1016–1030.

Bower, T. G. R. (1982). *Development in infancy* (2nd ed.). San Francisco: Freeman.

Buss, D. M., & Schmitt, D. P. (1993). Sexual strategies theory: An evolutionary perspective on human mating. *Psychological Review, 100,* 204–233.

Campos, J. J., Campos, R. G., & Barrett, K. C. (1989). Emergent themes in the study of emotional development and emotion regulation. *Developmental Psychology, 25,* 394–402.

Chen, C., & Stevenson, H. W. (1988). Cross-linguistic differences in digit span of preschool children. *Journal of Experimental Child Psychology, 46,* 150–158.

Cohen, J. (1988). *Statistical power analysis for the behavioral sciences* (2nd ed.). Hillsdale, NJ: Erlbaum.

Coleman, M. T. (1993). Movements in the earnings-schooling relationship, 1940–88. *Journal of Human Resources, 28,* 660–680.

Cosmides, L. (1989). The logic of social exchange: Has natural selection shaped how human beings reason? Studies with the Wason selection task. *Cognition, 31,* 187–276.

Cosmides, L., & Tooby, J. (1994). Origins of domain specificity: The evolution of functional organization. In L. A. Hirschfeld & S. A. Gelman (Eds.), *Mapping the mind: Domain specificity in cognition and culture* (pp. 85–116). New York: Cambridge University Press.

Dunbar, R. I. M. (1993). Coevolution of neocortical size, group size and language in humans. *Behavioral and Brain Sciences, 16,* 681–735.

Eibl-Eibesfeldt, I. (1989). *Human ethology.* New York: Aldine de Gruyter.

Ekstrom, R. B., French, J. W., & Harman, H. H. (1976). *Manual for kit of factor-referenced cognitive tests 1976.* Princeton, NJ: Educational Testing Service.

Fennema, E., Wolleat, P. L., Pedro, J. D., & Becker, A. D. (1981). Increasing women's participation in mathematics: An intervention study. *Journal for Research in Mathematics Education, 12,* 3–14.

Flynn, J. R. (1987). Massive IQ gains in 14 nations: What IQ tests really measure. *Psychological Bulletin, 101,* 171–191.

Fodor, J. A. (1983). *The modularity of mind: An essay on faculty psychology.* Cambridge, MA: MIT Press.

Fuson, K. C., & Kwon, Y. (1992). Korean children's understanding of multidigit addition and subtraction. *Child Development, 63,* 491–506.

Gallistel, C. R. (1990). *The organization of learning.* Cambridge, MA: MIT Press and Bradford Books.

Geary, D. C. (1995a). Reflections of evolution and culture in children's cognition: Implications for mathematical development and instruction. *American Psychologist, 50,* 24–37.

Geary, D. C. (1995b). Sexual selection and sex differences in spatial cognition. *Learning and Individual Differences, 7,* 289–301.

Geary, D. C. (1996a). Sexual selection and sex differences in mathematical abilities. *Behavioral and Brain Sciences, 19,* 229–284.

Geary, D. C. (1996b). Biology, culture, and cross-national differences in mathematical ability. In R. J. Sternberg & T. Ben-Zeev (Eds.), *The nature of mathematical thinking* (pp. 145–171). Hillsdale, NJ: Erlbaum.

Geary, D. C. (1998). The functional architecture of evolved cognitive modules: Implications for behavioral genetic research. *Human Biology, 70,* 183–196.

Geary, D. C., Bow-Thomas, C. C., Fan, L., & Siegler, R. S. (1993). Even before formal instruction, Chinese children outperform American children in mental addition. *Cognitive Development, 8,* 517–529.

Geary, D. C., Bow-Thomas, C. C., Liu, F., & Siegler, R. S. (1996). Development of arithmetical competencies in Chinese and American children: Influence of age, language, and schooling. *Child Development, 67,* 2022–2044.

Geary, D. C., Fan, L., & Bow-Thomas, C. C. (1992). Numerical cognition: Loci of ability differences comparing children from China and the United States. *Psychological Science, 3,* 180–185.

Geary, D. C., Frensch, P. A., & Wiley, J. G. (1993). Simple and complex mental subtraction: Strategy choice and speed-of-processing differences in younger and older adults. *Psychology and Aging, 8,* 242–256.

Geary, D. C., Hamson, C. O., Chen, G.-P., Liu, F., Hoard, M. K., & Salthouse, T. A. (1997). Computational and reasoning abilities in arithmetic: Cross-generational change in China and the United States. *Psychonomic Bulletin and Review, 4,* 425–430.

Geary, D. C., Salthouse, T. A., Chen, G. P., & Fan, L. (1996). Are East Asian versus American differences in arithmetical ability a recent phenomenon? *Developmental Psychology, 32,* 254–262.

Gelman, R. (1990). First principles organize attention to and learning about relevant data: Number and animate-inanimate distinction as examples. *Cognitive Science, 14,* 79–106.

Gould, J. L. (1986). The locale map of honey bees: Do insects have cognitive maps? *Science, 232,* 861–863.

Heckhausen, J., & Schulz, R. (1995). A life-span theory of control. *Psychological Review, 102,* 284–304.

Karmiloff-Smith, A. (1992). *Beyond modularity: A developmental perspective on cognitive science.* Cambridge, MA: MIT Press and Bradford Books.

Karmiloff-Smith, A., Klima, E., Bellugi, U., Grant, J., & Baron-Cohen, S. (1995). Is there a social module? Language, face processing, and theory of mind in individuals with Williams Syndrome. *Journal of Cognitive Neuroscience, 7,* 196–208.

Keil, F. C. (1992). The origins of an autonomous biology. In M. R. Gunnar &

M. Maratsos (Eds.), *Modularity and constraints in language and cognition: The Minnesota symposia on child psychology* (Vol. 25, pp. 103–137). Hillsdale, NJ: Erlbaum.

Landau, B., Gleitman, H., & Spelke, E. (1981). Spatial knowledge and geometric representation in a child blind from birth. *Science, 213,* 1275–1278.

Lewis, A. B. (1989). Training students to represent arithmetic word problems. *Journal of Educational Psychology, 81,* 521–531.

Leslie, A. M. (1987). Pretense and representation: The origins of "theory of mind." *Psychological Review, 94,* 412–426.

Luria, A. R. (1980). *Higher cortical functions in man* (2nd ed.). New York: Basic Books.

MacDonald, K. B. (1988). *Social and personality development: An evolutionary synthesis.* New York: Plenum.

McGuinness, D., & Pribram, K. H. (1979). The origins of sensory bias in the development of gender differences in perception and cognition. In M. Bortner (Ed.), *Cognitive growth and development: Essays in memory of Herbert G. Birch* (pp. 3–56). New York: Brunner/Mazel.

Miller, K. F., Smith, C. M., Zhu, J., & Zhang, H. (1995). Preschool origins of cross-national differences in mathematical competence: The role of number-naming systems. *Psychological Science, 6,* 56–60.

Newcomb, A. F., Bukowski, W. M., & Pattee, L. (1993). Children's peer relations: A meta-analytic review of popular, rejected, neglected, controversial, and average sociometric status. *Psychological Bulletin, 113,* 99–128.

Nicholls, J. G. (1984). Achievement motivation: Conceptions of ability, subjective experience, task choice, and performance. *Psychological Review, 91,* 328–346.

Pinker, S., & Bloom, P. (1990). Natural language and natural selection. *Behavioral and Brain Sciences, 13,* 707–784.

Raven, J. C., Court, J. H., & Raven, J. (1993). *Manual for Raven's Progressive Matrices and Vocabulary Scales.* London: H. K. Lewis.

Rivera-Batiz, F. L. (1992). Quantitative literacy and the likelihood of employment among young adults in the United States. *Journal of Human Resources, 27,* 313–328.

Rozin, P. (1976). The evolution of intelligence and access to the cognitive unconscious. In J. M. Sprague & A. N. Epstein (Eds.), *Progress in psycho-*

biology and physiological psychology (Vol. 6, pp. 245–280). New York: Academic Press.

Rubin, K. H., Fein, G. G., & Vandenberg, B. (1983). Play. In P. Mussen & E. M. Hetherington (Eds.), *Handbook of child psychology: Socialization, personality, and social development* (Vol. 4, pp. 693–774). New York: Wiley.

Rushton, J. P. (1995). *Race, evolution, and behavior: A life history perspective.* New Brunswick, NJ: Transaction Publishers.

Salthouse, T. A. (1991). Mediation of adult age differences in cognition by reductions in working memory and speed of processing. *Psychological Science, 2,* 179–183.

Schacter, D. L. (1994). Priming and multiple memory systems: Perceptual mechanisms of implicit memory. In D. L. Schacter & E. Tulving (Eds.), *Memory systems 1994* (pp. 233–268). Cambridge, MA: The MIT Press.

Schaie, W. K. (1993). The Seattle longitudinal study of adult intelligence. *Current Directions in Psychological Science, 2,* 134–137.

Schaie, K. W. (1996). *Intellectual development in adulthood: The Seattle longitudinal study.* New York: Cambridge University Press.

Schulz, R., & Heckhausen, J. (1996). A life span model of successful aging. *American Psychologist, 51,* 702–714.

Shepard, R. N. (1994). Perceptual-cognitive universals as reflections of the world. *Psychonomic Bulletin and Review, 1,* 2–28.

Siegler, R. S., & Crowley, K. (1994). Constraints on learning in nonprivileged domains. *Cognitive Psychology, 27,* 194–226.

Silverman, I., & Eals, M. (1992). Sex differences in spatial abilities: Evolutionary theory and data. In J. H. Barkow, L. Cosmides, & J. Tooby (Eds.), *The adapted mind: Evolutionary psychology and the generation of culture* (pp. 533–549). New York: Oxford University Press.

Stevenson, H. W., Chen, C., & Lee, S. Y. (1993). Mathematics achievement of Chinese, Japanese, and American children: Ten years later. *Science, 259,* 53–58.

Stevenson, H. W., Lee, S. Y., Chen, C., Stigler, J. W., Hsu, C. C., & Kitamura, S. (1990). Contexts of achievement: A study of American, Chinese, and Japanese children. *Monographs of the Society for Research in Child Development, 55* (1-2, Serial Mo. 221).

Stevenson, H. W., Lee, S. Y., & Stigler, J. W. (1986). Mathematics achievement of Chinese, Japanese, and American children. *Science, 231,* 693–699.

Stevenson, H. W., Parker, T., Wilkinson, A., Hegion, A., & Fish, E. (1976). Longitudinal study of individual differences in cognitive development and scholastic achievement. *Journal of Educational Psychology, 68,* 377–400.

Stevenson, H. W., & Stigler, J. W. (1992). *The learning gap: Why our schools are failing and what we can learn from Japanese and Chinese education.* New York: Summit Books.

Stevenson, H. W., Stigler, J. W., Lee, S. Y., Lucker, G. W., Kitamura, S., & Hsu, C. C. (1985). Cognitive performance and academic achievement of Japanese, Chinese, and American children. *Child Development, 56,* 718–734.

Stigler, J. W., Lee, S. Y., & Stevenson, H. W. (1986). Digit memory in Chinese and English: Evidence for a temporally limited store. *Cognition, 23,* 1–20.

Trivers, R. L. (1971). The evolution of reciprocal altruism. *Quarterly Review of Biology, 46,* 35–57.

Whiting, B. B., & Whiting, J. W. M. (1975). *Children of six cultures: A psychocultural analysis.* Cambridge, MA: Harvard University Press.

Youniss, J. (1986). Development in reciprocity through friendship. In C. Zahn-Waxler, E. M. Cummings, & R. Iannotti (Eds.), *Altruism and aggression: Biological and social origins* (pp. 88–106). New York: Cambridge University Press.

2

Mathematics Learning and Teaching in the School Context: Reflections From Cross-Cultural Comparisons

Shin-Ying Lee

Since the 1980s, numerous reports have described the crisis that exists in American mathematics education. American students have lagged behind their peers in many other industrial nations (e.g., Garden, 1987; Husen, 1967; Lapointe, Mead, & Phillips, 1989; Lapointe, Mead, & Askew, 1992; McKnight et al., 1987; Stevenson, Lee, & Stigler, 1986; Stevenson, Chen, & Lee, 1993). The concerns about the poor performance in mathematics have aroused national attention, as was reflected in the publication *A Nation at Risk* (National Commission on Excellence in Education, 1983). Since then there have been strong calls for recommendations concerning educational reforms. Instigated by the Governors Conference in 1989, President Bush announced "Education Goals 2000." One of the goals stated that "By the year 2000, U.S. stu-

This chapter was prepared for the Festschrift Conference to honor Harold Stevenson who has been a great mentor and colleague to me. Data reported in this chapter were based on several projects funded to Harold Stevenson by the National Science Foundation (Grant MDR 89564683), W. T. Grant Foundation and the U.S. Department of Education (subcontract from Westat, Inc. RN 93005001). I wish to thank the many people who have worked on the various projects over the years, in particular, Chuansheng Chen, David Crystal, Terresa Graham, Carol Kinney, Salley Lubeck, and Roberta Nevison-Law who have contributed significantly to the data reported in this chapter.

dents will be first in the world in mathematics and science achievement." Decisions are being made at national, state, and local levels that seek to establish standards for curricula and to change teaching practices in American classrooms.

Although the need to improve American students' mathematics achievement is clear, the reform efforts do not seem to be yielding significant effects. Evidence has shown that American students have made little improvement in mathematics performance over the past decade (National Assessment of Educational Progress, 1990; Ravitch, 1995; Stevenson et al., 1993). Reports from the National Assessment of Educational Progress, the "Nation's Report Card," also pointed out that math proficiency is lower today than it was in the early 1970s. Results are equally discouraging for elementary, middle, and high school students, and for students enrolled in advantaged urban and suburban schools as well as in poor inner-city schools (U.S. Department of Education, 1994a).

Our research group, directed by Harold Stevenson, has conducted a series of cross-cultural studies during the past 2 decades to compare the mathematics achievement of Chinese, Japanese, and American students. The main purposes were to investigate and identify the correlates of children's mathematics achievement in these three cultures. What are the factors embedded in the different cultures that would enhance or inhibit the mathematics competency of their students? We found that students from Japan, Taiwan, and China achieved significantly higher levels of mathematics competency than did the American students. The advantage of the East Asian students began in elementary school and persisted through high school (Stevenson et al., 1993). Differences in both family and school contexts were found to relate significantly to the level of academic achievement among students in the different locations (Stevenson et al., 1990b; Stevenson & Stigler, 1992). Within each country, factors such as level of parental education, children's cognitive abilities, and children's attitudes toward achievement all relate significantly with children's levels of achievement. Those factors suggest explanations for individual differences in mathematics performance within each country. However, it is the beliefs and education practices that differ between the countries that may offer explanation for the achievement gap between the countries.

RESEARCH METHODS

In the studies, we have used quantitative as well as qualitative approaches to understand the contexts of mathematics achievement. The major effort used quantitative methods to make the cross-cultural comparisons. We have tested more than 24,000 students from representative samples of 1st, 5th, and 11th grade students from metropolitan areas of Beijing, China; Sendai, Japan; Taipei, Taiwan; and Minneapolis and Chicago, Cook County, Illinois in the United States. Structured interviews were conducted with more than 5,000 parents, 6,500 students, and 400 teachers. We also made systematic time sampling and narrative observations in 800 math classes in the elementary schools in the four locations (see Stevenson et al., 1990a; Stevenson, 1996 for more details of the sampling and the methods used in these studies).

Recently, as a project affiliated with the Third International Mathematics and Science Study (TIMSS), we conducted a case study adopting a qualitative approach to interviews, discussions, and observations of smaller numbers of students, parents, and teachers. The researchers also shadowed and observed the teachers for a day in school, interviewed the administrators, and spent time in the teachers' lounge and school hallways. Extensive field notes were taken and analyzed by experienced researchers. The goal of the case studies was to extend our information beyond what could be revealed from the quantitative data and to provide a richer context of the family, school, and cultural practices that may relate to mathematics and science achievement in the different countries. The study was conducted in three representative cities in Japan, Germany, and the United States with students in grades 4, 8, and 12 from high, average, and low achieving schools (see Stevenson, 1996 for detailed description of the study).

As our research projects continue to investigate the factors that relate to the academic achievement of students in the different countries, the present chapter focuses on one specific aspect of the findings that may offer suggestion for the improvement of the mathematics performance of American students. Constructive thinking experiences in math classes are compared between American elementary school children and children who go to school in Japan, Taiwan, and China. The teacher's working conditions that contribute to their overall effectiveness are also examined.

DIFFERENCES IN ACHIEVEMENT

We developed the mathematics tests on the basis of careful analyses of the mathematics textbooks used in each of the locations. The items included in the test were concepts introduced in the textbooks in all of the locations and at the same or adjacent grade levels. The results of the tests thus allowed us to examine students' level of achievement

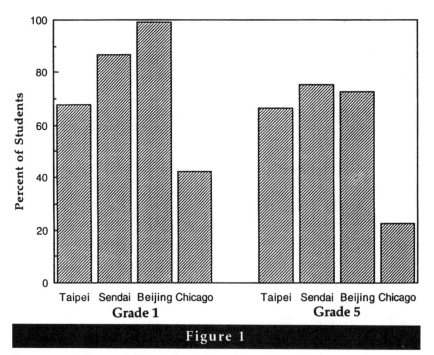

Figure 1

Percentage of first- and fifth-grade students from Taipei, Sendai, Beijing, and Chicago who achieved at or above the grade level in mathematics.

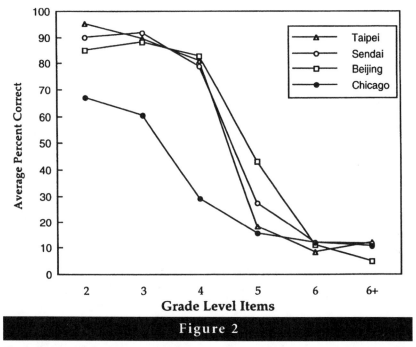

Figure 2

The average percent correct on different grade level math concepts by fifth graders in Taipei, Sendai, Beijing, and Chicago.

according to the grade level expected in the curriculum. The comparisons revealed that the majority of the East Asian students, but only a small percentage of the American students, were achieving at their grade level. Between 70% and 99% of the first-grade students in the three East Asian locations, compared with only about 40% of the American students, were achieving at or above first-grade level in math (Figure 1). By 5th grade, about 70% of the Chinese, Japanese, and Taiwanese students were achieving at or above the 5th-grade level whereas less than 25% of the American students reached the grade level.

Another way to understand the students' level of math achievement is to examine how well they have mastered the concepts they should have learned during earlier years. Figure 2 shows that the 5th graders in the three East Asian locations correctly answered over 80% of the math questions assessing concepts introduced in earlier grades. Amer-

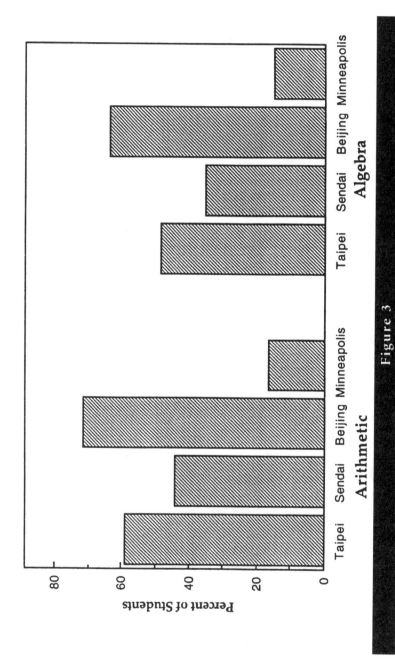

Figure 3

Percentage of 11th-grade students from Taipei, Sendai, Beijing, and Minneapolis who achieved 70% correctness for tests of arithmetic and algebra.

ican 5th graders, on the other hand, responded correctly to 60% of the questions tapping 2nd and 3rd grade concepts and only 30% of the 4th grade concepts. Similar trends were found among the high school students. Whereas the East Asian 11th grade students were competent in arithmetic and algebra, significantly fewer American 11th graders reached the same level of competency (Figure 3).

The results of the mathematics achievement of American students are consistent with the report from the National Education Goals Panel (1996). This report showed that between 7% and 28% of the fourth-grade students and between 8% and 37% of the eighth-grade students in the United States attained the "proficient" or "advanced" levels in math according to the data from National Assessment of Educational Progress.

"Mathematics for all" is one of the major reform ideas popular in the United States. The comparative achievement data from our findings showed that it is the education in the East Asian countries that develop mathematics knowledge for the majority of East Asian children. Students in Japan, China, and Taiwan learn the grade level materials and therefore are meeting the education standard set by the curriculum, whereas only a small percentage of the American students are able to do so. The results clearly suggested that the poor mathematics achievement of American students in the international comparative studies was due to the fact that so few of the American students are keeping up with the curriculum requirements. What goes on in the mathematics classes in the different locations should reveal significant information. How do American students' classroom experiences differ from their peers in other, high-achieving countries?

EXPERIENCE IN THE MATH CLASSROOMS

Classroom setting is believed to provide the most influential environment for students to construct mathematical knowledge, and teachers have the most important role in structuring the learning activities (Cobb, 1994). Many suggestions have been made to improve mathematics instruction in the United States. The Curriculum and Evaluation Standards for School Mathematics published by the National Council of Teachers of Mathematics (NCTM) in 1989 recommended a more integrated curriculum that emphasizes mathematical problem-solving and reasoning abilities. Several other curriculum reform efforts also proposed that all students need to develop higher order thinking skills and students should learn by actively constructing their own knowledge rather than by passively receiving information or instruction (U.S. Department of Education, 1994b).

Can we relate the mathematics competency of the East Asian students to the frequency with which their teachers engage in constructive thinking activities that promote mathematics learning? It is impossible here to describe fully the mathematics instruction that we observed in the different countries (see Lee, Graham, & Stevenson, 1996; Stevenson & Lee, 1995; Stevenson & Stigler, 1992; Stigler & Perry, 1988). In this chapter, we chose to compare two specific aspects of classroom experience among the students in different countries: the role of students as active learners and the teaching practices that facilitate students' thinking skills. Both aspects are the essential components of constructivism.

In our observational study of mathematics classrooms, we selected 10 elementary schools in Beijing, China; Sendai, Japan; and Taipei, Taiwan, and 20 elementary schools in the Chicago metropolitan area (Cook County) in the United States. The schools were chosen to represent the wide range of schools in each metropolitan area. The larger number of schools in Chicago was necessary to represent the diverse ethnic, racial, and socioeconomic groups residing in the metropolitan area. In each school we randomly selected two first- and two fifth-grade classrooms for study. Both time-sampling and narrative observations were conducted in the math lessons to capture the instructional and learning processes in the classrooms. Trained observers visited each classroom four times over a 2-week period. We sought through these observations to gain a better understanding of the teaching and learning experiences afforded by teachers in the classrooms of each culture.

Students As Active Learners

A fundamental assumption about constructive learning is that students must actively participate in the learning situation to maximize the learning outcome. Students must be psychologically "connected" to what is going on during the lessons. The connection can be reflected in how much they are concentrating on the task at hand, paying attention to the teacher, engaging in the learning task, and participating in the class activities and discussions.

Engaging Behavior

In our observation, the class was considered to be engaged when the majority of the class members were either attending to the teacher or were actively involved in the task that had been defined by the teacher. It is evident in Figure 4 that the percentage of time children were engaged in mathematics learning activities was remarkably high in East

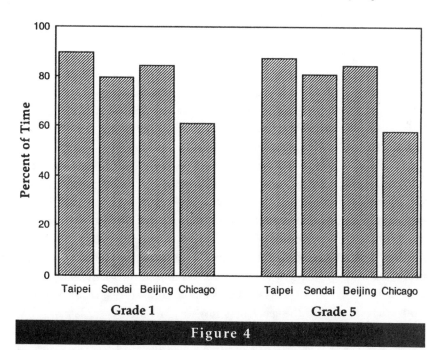

Figure 4

Percentage of time first- and fifth-grade students from Taipei, Sendai, Beijing, and Chicago are attending to teacher or task in the mathematics class.

Asian classrooms—over 80% of the time in all three locations. American students, on the other hand, were less frequently engaged in the learning processes. They were attentive for about 60% of the time.

Verbal Explanation and Evaluation by Students

Verbal explanations of mathematical concepts and procedures are one of the most common forms of knowledge transmission that occur during mathematics instruction. These explanations can be provided by the teacher or by the students in the class. When the teacher explains, the students can listen actively or passively. When the teacher elicits explanations from students, the students have to be actively engaged in thinking. Results from Table 1 show that except for first-grade classes in Beijing, more than 90% of East Asian classroom teachers explained mathematical knowledge in their lessons, compared with about 65% of the American first-grade teachers and 80% of the American fifth-grade teachers. If the strategy of the American teachers was to engage the active thinking processes of the students rather than to act as the provider of information, then a high frequency of explanation by students in the American classrooms would be expected. This was not the case. The frequency of students engaged in verbal explanation of mathematics was also the lowest in the American classes. Although this practice occurred in 70% of the American first-grade classes and 80% of the fifth-grade classes, the frequency of students offering their ideas was significantly higher in the East Asian classes.

In addition to involving students in the processes of discussing the mathematical problems, East Asian teachers also more frequently involved students in the evaluation of the relevance or correctness of their own or their fellow classmates' responses than did the American teachers. Having students evaluate each others' work provides a good opportunity for all the students to think about how they would solve the problems and encourages students to pay attention to the alternative approaches used by others. Under these circumstances, students learn from each other and the teacher is not the sole arbiter in determining what is correct. East Asian teachers also commonly involved students in self-evaluation processes. They often asked the students to raise their hands if their answers were correct or incorrect, and to raise their hands

Table 1

Percentage of Classes With Teachers' and Students' Explanation and Evaluation

	First Grade				Fifth Grade			
	Taipei, Taiwan	Sendai, Japan	Beijing, China	Chicago, United States	Taipei, Taiwan	Sendai, Japan	Beijing, China	Chicago, United States
Explanation								
By teacher	92.1	91.2	77.5	64.2	93.7	98.7	93.4	79.5
By student(s)	89.6	89.6	98.7	69.7	93.7	98.7	100.0	80.4
Evaluation								
By teacher	57.9	72.5	65.0	51.9	84.6	82.5	64.5	58.8
By student(s)	69.6	70.4	61.3	31.4	65.0	62.5	63.2	52.7

if they understood or did not understand the problem. The practice provided students with the experience of monitoring their own progress as well as reflecting on their own level of understanding. In more than 60% of the East Asian first- and fifth-grade classes, students were involved in the evaluation processes. American teachers adopted the practice less frequently. Evaluation processes were observed in about 30% of the first-grade classes and 50% of the fifth-grade classes (see Table 1).

Moreover, when American teachers invited students to offer their explanations or answers, they usually called on the students who volunteered. Other students may or may not have been actively involved, but as long as they were not disturbing the class, the teacher seldom invited them to offer their answers or ideas. In East Asian classrooms, the educational philosophy is to have all students in the class involved in the learning processes. The teachers therefore call on all students to participate in the discussion, explanation, and evaluation processes. Not knowing who the teacher will call on next, all students must pay attention to the lesson and be actively engaged in the thinking processes.

Thus, while "students as active learners" is an important aspect in the American education reform, it is in more of the East Asian classes, not American classes, that we observed students engaging in the active learning role. East Asian students have more opportunities to produce, explain, and evaluate solutions to mathematical problems. The experiences not only help to maintain the students' active engagement in the class, but also create a critical element of successful learning outcome.

Promoting Students' Thinking and Understanding

Another essential component of constructive thinking is that students should discover, construct, use, and generate their own meanings of math, and they should understand the concepts by building relationships and connections with their prior knowledge. The teacher's role in the class should therefore be to stimulate students by introducing activities that would lead to problem solving behavior. We identified four different ways teachers in the different locations accomplished this goal.

Table 2
Percentage of Classes With Different Instructional Processes

	First Grade				Fifth Grade			
	Taipei, Taiwan	Sendai, Japan	Beijing, China	Chicago, United States	Taipei, Taiwan	Sendai, Japan	Beijing, China	Chicago, United States
Using different examples	74.2	46.3	76.3	28.9	47.1	47.5	55.3	30.4
Extending students' answers	41.3	33.8	37.5	7.9	22.5	57.5	71.1	22.7
Relating to abstract concepts	31.3	49.6	53.8	18.0	37.9	52.5	73.7	24.6
Facilitating deeper understanding	52.9	26.3	43.8	2.8	20.0	22.5	68.4	13.3

Table 2 presents the frequency of the four instructional strategies used by teachers.

Using Different Examples

One strategy teachers used to induce constructive thinking was to use different types of problems to illustrate the same mathematical principle. For example, within the same lesson teachers might use word problems, numerical computation, diagrams, and concrete manipulatives to approach the same concept. These different experiences can offer more opportunities for students to understand the concept. The students also experience how different procedures may reflect and be applicable to the same concept. These kinds of practices reduce the number of drills in which students must do the same thing over and over again. Different students also have the opportunity to understand the concept from different approaches. Those students who have only an intuitive idea about how to solve the problem may gain a more solid conceptual understanding. The practice of presenting one mathematical concept in a number of different ways occurred in significantly more of the East Asian classrooms than in the American classrooms. Fewer than 30% of the American teachers supplied multiple examples in their lessons (see Table 2).

Extending Students' Answers

A second technique used by teachers to facilitate children's understanding of mathematical concepts and reasoning ability was elaborating on the students' responses. If students in the class offered a simple or incorrect answer, the teacher would ask them how they solved the problem. When students responded with a correct answer, the teacher would ask them to think of other ways to solve the problem. East Asian teachers also believe incorrect answers and incomplete or confused responses provide good opportunities to guide all students for further discussion. Thus, they often purposefully select students with different answers to share their responses as a means of enriching or enlivening the discussion. As a result, there is a more detailed discussion of why some approaches to solving the problem work and some do not, and why some procedures for solving the problem are more efficient than others. In all cases, teachers probe questions on the basis of students' responses and lead the discussions to promote students' understanding of mathematics.

Teachers elaborated on students' answers in more than 33% of the East Asian first-grade classrooms and only in 8% of the American first-grade classrooms. At fifth grade, elaboration occurred in more than 70% of the classes in Beijing and more than 55% of the classes in Sendai but occurred in less than 25% of the Chicago and Taipei classrooms.

Usui (1996), in his observation of American math classes from the perspective of a Japanese educator, described the teaching style in the American classrooms as the *Question-Answer Cycle*. The teacher behaved like the host on a quiz show. The teacher asked a question, a student answered. The teacher then announced whether each answer was correct. Students were not asked to explain how they came up with their answer, and the teacher did not explain why the answer was correct or incorrect. The sequence was repeated several times. In each case, there was very little discussion among students. This is very different from Chinese and Japanese classrooms, where the teacher's role is more like a coordinator than a judge. Teachers provide questions to constantly stimulate students to engage in active thinking about the different perspectives of the problem.

Relating Concrete Operations to Abstract Concepts

Competence in mathematics requires procedural skills and conceptual knowledge. Procedural skills focus on learning the steps necessary to solve particular types of math problems correctly. When students learn to solve a mathematical problem by acquiring the mechanical steps involved without a real understanding of the concept, they have not really acquired the mathematical thinking that is necessary for problem-solving. As a consequence, they are more likely to make mistakes, forget how to apply the procedure, or have difficulties applying the procedure when the situation is changed.

To characterize the lessons we observed in the four locations, we identified lessons that contained only procedural information and those that included both conceptual and procedural information. Figure 5 shows that in almost all classes in all the locations, students were ex-

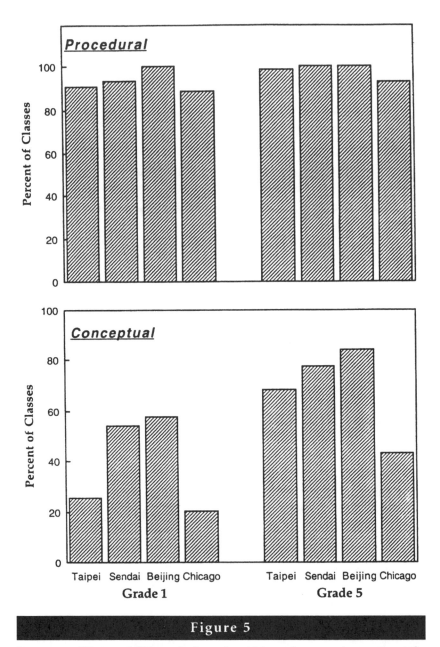

Figure 5

Percentage of first- and fifth-grade classes in which teachers were instructing at the procedural and conceptual level.

posed to procedural knowledge. American students, however, were found to have many fewer opportunities to engage in a conceptual level of learning than had their East Asian peers.

Teachers have to create special experiences to help students explicitly connect the learning of concrete procedural operations to more general rules or principles. Teachers may use manipulatives to demonstrate the operation being discussed and then come back to the more general and abstract concept, or they may present a concrete problem for students to solve and then follow with a discussion of the conceptual explanation or definition of the problem. Teachers in more than 50% of the Japanese and Chinese classes provided learning experiences relating concrete operations to abstract concepts while less than 25% of the American teachers did this (see Table 2).

Facilitating Deeper Understanding

The quality of the mathematical thinking in which the students are engaged depends both on how the student responds to the question as well as how the teacher asks the question. When teachers present questions to elicit more sophisticated responses from students, they are providing an opportunity to facilitate students' deeper understanding of mathematics. We assessed students' level of mathematical thinking by examining the characteristics of verbal responses students offered in the lessons. The responses could be of five types. Students usually responded with a simple numerical response when teachers asked computational questions. When they were asked to identify certain mathematical properties, identification responses were presented. Procedural responses referred to the situation in which students explained the computational steps they used to solve the mathematics problem. Students gave conceptual responses when they explained the fundamental concepts that were involved in solving the problem. When students had to explain both why and how they solved the mathematical problem, they were responding at both the procedural and conceptual levels. Finally, students could describe the logical steps to solve the problem in the form of an equation.

Table 3 shows that in all locations more teachers elicited simpler levels of students' responses than more abstract conceptual levels of

Table 3

Percentages of Classes With Different Levels of Student Responses

	First Grade				Fifth Grade			
	Sendai, Japan	Beijing, China	Taipei, Taiwan	Chicago, United States	Sendai, Japan	Beijing, China	Taipei, Taiwan	Chicago, United States
Numerical answer	65.0	86.3	69.2	69.2	81.3	97.4	83.8	73.0
Identification	67.9	88.8	72.1	49.8	75.0	80.3	62.1	52.3
Procedural explanation	57.1	57.5	61.7	30.6	70.0	94.7	77.5	60.1
Conceptual explanation	9.2	45.0	12.5	6.0	17.5	46.1	23.3	14.0
Procedural/conceptual explanation	21.3	25.0	8.8	2.6	17.5	48.7	17.9	5.4
Equational explanation	25.0	65.0	15.0	10.5	63.8	71.1	40.0	7.4

responses and that these occurred more frequently in fifth-grade classes than in first-grade classes. American teachers, however, elicited significantly fewer responses requiring students to identify certain mathematical characteristics or to describe the procedures they used to solve the mathematics problems than did the East Asian teachers. The frequency of conceptual responses and the use of equations was extremely low in the American classes. They were observed in only 6% and 11% of the first-grade classes. East Asian teachers, especially Chinese teachers in Beijing, created many more opportunities for their students to think conceptually and abstractly.

In the fifth-grade classes, similar cross-cultural differences were found. American classes, compared to the East Asian classes, had the lowest frequency of any type of responses. Conceptual responses occurred very infrequently. Teachers from China elicited the most responses of a conceptual nature from their students when compared with teachers in the other countries. The gap between the teachers' practices in American and East Asian classes was most marked in the frequency with which students were asked to respond by providing a mathematical equation. In more than 60% of the Japanese and Chinese classes, and in more than 40% of the Taiwanese classes, students expressed their thinking with a mathematical equation, but this occurred in only 8% of the American fifth-grade classes. We observed significantly more East Asian classes, especially in China, than American classes where the students were expected to think in a way that required an in-depth understanding of the mathematics concepts in the lessons.

We found American teachers were less likely to use any of the techniques that we identified as facilitating students' constructive thinking and conceptual understanding of mathematics than were teachers in the East Asian countries. Regardless of the emphasis on "teaching for understanding" in the recent trend of math education in the United States, the theory has not had a strong influence on common practices in American classrooms.

Comparing the teaching approach of Chinese, Japanese, and Taiwanese teachers we found differences in the frequency of applying the particular teaching techniques among Chinese teachers, in general, provided the most opportunities for their students to learn mathematics in a constructive fashion. Students in Taiwan had the least experience of the Asian students to think of mathematics constructively, although they were as actively involved in the lessons as their Chinese and Japanese peers.

In summary, more East Asian than American students are having the kinds of experience American educators and cognitive psychologists are advocating. In the East Asian math classes, students are actively involved with the learning tasks, they have opportunities to think mathematically, and teachers are also applying teaching strategies to lead the students to engage in constructive thinking processes. The findings are not the results that most Americans would have predicted. In the minds of American educators, as well as many of the Asian educators, it is American education that emphasizes problem solving and conceptual approaches to learning. Our data clearly show that regardless of the strong emphasis on the reform of mathematics teaching in the United States, we infrequently observed these constructive teaching practices in the American classrooms. Although the stereotypical Asian education includes a strong emphasis on drilling of procedural skills, the data illustrated that East Asian students also have frequent classroom experience that facilitates their conceptual understanding of mathematics.

Most American teachers have been exposed to the idea of creating constructive thinking experiences for their students. They often respond that the techniques just described are ones that they themselves practice. One must ask why East Asian teachers have more success applying the constructive approaches in their classrooms while fewer American teachers do. What are the characteristics of the teachers in different countries and what are their working conditions that may or may not facilitate the effective mathematics instruction for the students?

TEACHERS

The teachers we observed in the structured observational study we have just described were all experienced professionals. The teachers in Taipei, Sendai, Beijing, and Chicago had taught in elementary schools for an average of 14, 16, 21, and 16 years, respectively. However, their educational histories differed greatly. Only 78% of the Sendai teachers, 23% of the Taipei teachers, and none of the Beijing teachers had received a bachelor's degree. The remainder of Japanese and Taiwanese teachers had received a teacher's certificate from a 2-year junior college. All of the teachers in Beijing had only regular high school or 2-year junior college teacher training education. In contrast, American teachers had much higher levels of formal education. All of the Chicago teachers who participated in our study had received their bachelor's degree and 41% had also received a master's degree. It is, therefore, not the formal level of education the East Asian teachers had received that determined the ways they taught in the classrooms.

Teachers develop their teaching skills through the experience they accumulate during their teaching years. There are inevitably individual differences in the effectiveness of teachers within any country. But the systematic differences we observed between American teachers and the East Asian teachers had to be related to certain structural differences in the teachers' teaching experience. To examine these differences, I compared data collected in our TIMSS case study in which semi-structured interviews and observations of small numbers of teachers and principals from representative samples of schools across different regions in Japan and the United States were conducted (see Kinney, in press; Lubeck, in press, for details of the study). China and Taiwan did not participate in the TIMSS study. The comparisons in this chapter focus on the ways teachers in each country are trained on the job and on the ways their everyday working conditions create both differential constraints and opportunities for teaching. The qualitative data provides a rich base of information for us to gain an in-depth understanding of the working environment for teachers.

Inservice Training

Professional development of teachers is a central topic in discussions of education reform in the United States (Carnegie Forum on Education and the Economy, 1986; National Commission on Teaching and America's Future, 1996). At the present time, there is the common awareness that better trained teachers are needed to improve the achievement level of American students. The professional development of teachers involves teachers' coursework and training prior to receiving certification (preservice training), and any subsequent education, training, coaching, or learning opportunities from which certified teachers can benefit (inservice training). In both Japan and the United States, there are clear guidelines and requirements for pre- and inservice training. The fact that many Japanese teachers received fewer years of formal education but demonstrated more effective teaching skills in the mathematics classrooms than the American teachers suggests that the experience of inservice training is a significant factor.

Japanese teacher inservice training not only happens outside of school as provided by the city or prefecture board of education, but more importantly, it also takes place regularly and frequently within each school. Schools provide supportive environments where training, nurturing, and sharing are all part of a teacher's daily experience. There are extensive training opportunities, close working relationships with other teachers, and established mechanisms for continual sharing of information from the first days of a teacher's career. For American teachers, inservice training differs by school districts, but it generally means meeting the requirement that is necessary for maintaining one's teaching certificate.

In Japan, there are 90 hours of teacher training time for the first-year elementary school teacher, 60 of which are spent within their school. The new teachers are paired with experienced teachers who teach the same grade students or are paired with a skilled teacher who is on leave for the year and is assigned to help several new teachers. The training emphasizes the sharing of information among teachers and encourages the transmission of knowledge and experience in teaching.

Many American teachers had a very different beginning experience in their career. Though some new teachers had a wonderful and caring teacher as their mentor, many more did not. In most of the cases, the teachers described their beginning teaching experience as the "tough love" and "trial by fire" approach. Many teachers interviewed in the case study started their teaching careers as substitute teachers in the school districts. They got moved around the building, grade level, and subject level depending on the need of the school district or school building. When a permanent position opened, it was frequently assigned right before school started. The teacher had to pick up the class and teach the full load with very little help from the other teachers and with little support from school administrators.

American teachers are obligated to participate in professional development activities by certification and recertification requirements. The majority of teachers' professional development time is spent on district-run activities. According to Little (1989), more than one fourth of staff development participant hours were targeted toward "generic pedagogy," which is independent of any subject matter or curriculum content. Therefore, teachers are called upon to enact new ideas but they may not understand them and may not know how to bring the ideas to their everyday teaching. As for the training in mathematics, the topics do not necessarily address teachers' concern about their everyday teaching. These kind of ideas often require sophisticated knowledge of subject matter and well-developed pedagogical abilities that most teachers have not had the opportunity to develop.

Japanese teachers' inservice and ongoing training occur at the city, school, and grade levels. At the city level teachers are required to participate in training outside school during their 6th, 10th, and 20th years of teaching. In addition to attending lectures, they have to submit lengthy lesson plans, and engage in discussion and self-reflection with other teachers. Teachers perceive this as an opportunity to interact with teachers at other schools who are in the same career stage. Within each school building, twice a year, some teachers in the school are asked to give a demonstration lesson with a real class of students, and all other teachers observe and discuss the instructional methods. In addition, most importantly, there are teacher-run subject study groups that meet every week. The meetings usually address issues that relate to day-to-day teaching. Some of the examples are how to plan a lesson for a specific math topic, how to use the blackboard effectively, how to start the lesson to motivate students' interests in the topic, how to facilitate group discussion, and how to maintain students' attention during the lesson. Those topics are related to "hands-on" experiences that teachers can apply in their daily instructions. Through the weekly meetings teachers in the same school rely on each other to generate ideas for teaching. During the school year, they also observe each other's classes and share reflection on each other's teaching. The weekly meeting is very time-consuming for teachers. It is usually held after school but the majority of teachers find the meetings as well as the observation of other teachers' teaching very helpful. The meetings provide opportunities for teachers to collaborate with each other and to generate ideas for more effective teaching.

Similar to the ways Japanese teachers encourage students to share their mathematical thinking with classmates and to evaluate each other's approach to solve the problems, Japanese schools provide experiences for teachers to learn to teach. The teachers actively participate in the meetings and engage themselves in the constructive thinking about teaching in the group. Japanese inservice training, therefore, is an ongoing effort of formal observations of model classes and informal discussions with colleagues so that all the teachers gradually polish their instructional skills to become more effective teachers. This format of inservice training seeks to enhance teachers' prevailing competence through their existing repertoire.

Almost no teacher interviewed in the United States had similar kinds of inservice training experience. The elements of active participation and reflection on teaching are usually missing in the professional development programs. Teachers worked in isolation from one another with little time to plan together or share their knowledge. Most teachers had not seen other teachers teach. Many teachers continued to teach the way they began teaching regardless of the efforts of inservice training.

THE WORKING CONDITION OF THE TEACHERS

Teachers in East Asian countries and the United States all work very hard. However, the general working condition differs in several ways.

East Asian elementary school teachers spend more time in school than the American elementary school teachers. The teachers who participated in our observation study in Taipei, Sendai, and Beijing reported spending on the average 9.1, 9.5, and 9.7 hours a day in school, respectively. Chicago teachers reported that they remained at school for an average of 7.3 hours. Chicago teachers, however, had to spend a higher proportion of their time on instruction per day than the East Asian teachers did. They had to teach an average of 5.1 classes per day, whereas teachers in Taipei taught 4.7 classes; Sendai, 4.9 classes; and Beijing, only 2.7 classes per day.

Because the teachers remained at school longer and had fewer teaching hours, teachers in the East Asian locations had several more hours a day to interact with other teachers, prepare lessons, work with individual students, and correct students' work. In all East Asian schools, every teacher also had a desk at which to work in a shared teachers' room, a setting that promotes sharing of ideas among the teachers. American teachers, on the other hand, are in front of the class most of the time they are in school. When they have time to work, it is usually in the classrooms by themselves. Other reports have also stated that American primary teachers spend a higher proportion of their time on instruction per week than primary teachers in any other economically advanced nation (Nelson & O'Brien, 1993). According to a survey conducted in 1991, American public elementary school teachers averaged 3 hours per week for preparation during the school day. That is equivalent to 35 minutes per day or 8 minutes of preparation time for every hour in the classroom (Choy, Henke, Alt, Medrich, & Bobbitt, 1993). With inadequate time to prepare lessons, it seems unlikely that anyone can offer effective instruction.

Data from the case study showed that although Japanese teachers do not have to spend as much time in class teaching, their working days are very busy. They have to meet with other teachers, work with individual students, eat lunch with the students, supervise extracurricular activities, and plan the school events. The majority of teachers have to work several hours at home each day and on the weekends. The difference between the Japanese and American teachers is how they feel about their working condition. Most Japanese teachers feel they are responsible for and in control of what occurs in their school. They feel effective at the basic tasks of teaching and do not express a sense of powerlessness in the face of students' problematic behaviors. Many American teachers, however, report that they are overworked, highly stressed, and not rewarded for their effort. The feeling was captured by one teacher interviewed in the case study:

> [A] teacher is the implementor of all district, state, and federal policies; a whole array of expectations, objectives, goals, outcomes, standards, and skills that policy makers and the public have decided are the responsibility of the schools and therefore, the teachers. Educators are constantly mandated to add more courses, that is, AIDS education, sex education, safety, drugs, recycling, all need to be included in the curriculum.

Although Japanese students are known to attain a high level of academic achievement, Japanese schools are set up as supportive environments to help students and teachers engage in learning and teaching activities in a sociable manner. During the day, schools allow time for social interactions among the students and teachers. Efforts are made to invest in the development of the teachers and to provide an environment that would make teaching an enjoyable experience. Extracurricular activities are formed not only for the students but also for the teachers, such as team sports, flower arrangement, choir, and so forth. As one elementary school principal put it, "If you don't look at teachers with a long term view and raise them that way, you can't get good teachers. We think of raising children, and also raising teachers, all as a part of education." The efforts Japanese schools put forth to create an environment where teachers are supportive of each other is reflected in the following quote from a Japanese principal:

> The most important thing is the teamwork among the teachers. They all work together to raise the children. If you just try to get your own class to improve, it won't happen, but if you do

it as a grade, or even with the whole school, it will work. For example, if there is a problem with a particular child, it isn't only the home room teacher but this teacher, and this teacher, and this teacher, too, everyone tries to help. In that way we get a unified understanding. So I guess that no matter what we try to do we do it all together, cooperating. If there is a problem, we all investigate in various ways and provide guidance to each other. And in the end, the important thing is that that child is in one teacher's home room, so we talk about how to give responsibility for that child back to that teacher. In that way the connections between the teachers and children are built and strengthened.

The emphasis in the Japanese school is obviously on the importance of team work and cooperation. The bottom line is how all teachers can help a home room teacher deal with their classroom.

In the United States, although cooperative learning is frequently emphasized as an effective way to promote students' learning, it is not the common experience of the teachers we interviewed. Most teachers have little time or opportunity to work collaboratively with others. An elementary school teacher from a low-achieving school expressed her frustration:

I am overwhelmed at having yet another new set of books and a different grade level of children to teach. I hate the curriculum but I have to use it. I have no one to talk to about what I am doing. I don't know if this is what I should be teaching. Is it too hard for the students? Is it too easy? I have never taught children this age before. All I got from the principal was reprimands and threats rather than any assistance. No one is there to help me to do a better job.

American policy makers, school administrators, and math educators are eager to improve the mathematics learning experience and outcome of the students. However, the emphasis on "outcome-based" and "accountability" without setting up a supportive working condition for the

71

teachers may simply put more pressure on teachers and that may not be conducive to better teaching in class.

THE IMPLEMENTATION OF EDUCATION REFORM

There have been many efforts in the United States in the last decade to introduce teaching practices that aim at improving the achievement level of the students within the community, for example, the ideas of teaching for understanding, cooperative learning, interdisciplinary curricula, portfolio, and other alternative assessments. There is usually little coordination, however, between school, district, state, and federal levels, which results in the "transitory" nature of many curricular innovations. The programs would be implemented for several years and then discontinued because of lack of funding or change of personnel. American teachers, therefore, have seen many innovations come and go and have become cynical about any approach that promises to be "the answer." Many of those reforms also ignored the constraints under which teachers work. There is little consideration of what teachers and schools need to know to put the reform idea into effect. Teachers are expected to implement the program with or without the appropriate understanding of the concepts and supporting materials for implementing the program. Many teachers are tired and resistant; many choose to change professions rather than change the way they teach.

Reform in Japan, in contrast, is usually orchestrated by the long-term planning of Monbusuo (Ministry of Education, Science, and Culture) at the national level. Academic experts and experienced teachers are usually involved in the planning process to design change, and they aim to implement the programs in all schools. The programs are coordinated with curriculum changes and the availability of supplemental teaching materials and suggestions for instructional approaches. Program development is followed by frequent meetings within each school, and teachers work together to gradually develop instructional techniques to help implement the new ideas.

CONCLUSION

American students are not achieving in mathematics at a level comparable to students from East Asian countries. They are also not improving to the degree that educators and policy makers would like to see. The widespread attention on education reform holds pressure and promise for change, but the confusing array of ideas on how classrooms should look leave teachers with the difficult task of sorting out what is really essential to how they teach in the classrooms. Many of the reforms turned out to be visions or trends of education, not programs for practice. As Hiebert et al. (1996) pointed out, the reforms are images and ideals of what teaching and learning could be, but the processes of implementation are not clear. Even with the high expectation of the establishment of NCTM standards as a new framework for school mathematics, educators have come to realize that the standards are difficult to be translated into action and hard to sustain.

Data from our cross-cultural comparative studies of mathematics achievement in Japan, Taiwan, China, and the United States showed that the American education reform ideas about mathematics teaching are actualized in the East Asian classrooms. Teachers there were effective in providing the constructive instructional discourse in the lessons. Students there were exposed to classroom activities in ways that enhance their mathematical competency whereas fewer American students were.

Teachers everywhere teach from what they know, what they believe about learning, and what their working environments allow them to accomplish. East Asian teachers work in school environments that provide the structure and opportunities for them to improve their teaching skills. Meanwhile, the development of new approaches to teaching is facilitated by processes that encourage teacher collaboration and collegiality. The working conditions for most American teachers, except in the most affluent schools, are not as supportive. American teachers are lacking in time and support from the schools to learn to teach effectively.

Many of the differences we found between the working experience of American and East Asian teachers parallel the cross-cultural differences of students' experiences in their math classes. In East Asian schools, both teachers and students actively participate in the learning activities, they learn from each other and they have to reflect their own thoughts frequently in the group. When teachers have personally experienced the conditions conducive to learning, they can apply those elements in their teaching more readily. In American schools, although reform efforts place strong emphasis on the improvement of the learning experience of the students, much less emphasis is placed on the improvement of teachers' teaching skills. As Darling-Hammond (1996) pointed out, most American teachers cannot produce the kind of learning demanded by the new reforms, not because they do not want to, but because they do not know how. Teaching for understanding cannot be packaged for teacher-proof implementation. This kind of teaching is more complex because it requires deeper knowledge of subjects and more flexible forms of pedagogy, which was never included in the professional training of teachers in the United States.

The cross-cultural differences we found in the educational practices reflect some fundamental difference in cultural beliefs. In the East Asian philosophy, there is the high expectation that everyone can learn. It is believed that all students, except in the extreme case, can learn the defined content materials if they are given the opportunity to learn and if they work hard to practice (Stevenson & Stigler, 1992). Similarly, it is also believed that all teachers can teach if they are properly trained and guided to be teachers. Schools should provide supportive environments and lots of opportunities for teachers to engage in the conversation about teaching. It is an optimistic view of education. In the United States, there is the strong belief that people are born with individual differences and therefore are expected to perform and behave differently. It is often believed that a good teacher is born rather than made and a good teacher should find his or her own way of teaching. The belief not only makes it difficult to develop common standards for students but also makes it challenging to instill changes in teaching techniques. It is this view that may undermine the improvement of the teaching and learning of American students and teachers.

REFERENCES

Carnegie Forum on Education and the Economy, Task Force on Teaching as a Profession. (1986). *A nation prepared: Teachers for the 21st century.* New York: Author.

Choy, S. P., Henke, R. R., Alt, M. N., Medrich, E. A., & Bobbitt, S. A. (1993). *Schools and staffing in the United States: A statistical profile, 1990–91.* Washington, DC: U.S. Government Printing Office.

Cobb, P. (1994). Where is the mind? Constructivist and sociocultural perspectives on mathematical development. *Educational Researcher, 23,* 13–20.

Darling-Hammond, L. (1996). The right to learn and the advancement of teaching: Research, policy, and practice for democratic education. *Educational Researcher, 25,* 5–17.

Garden, R. A. (1987). The second IEA mathematics study. *Comparative Education Review, 31,* 47–68.

Hiebert, J., Carpenter, T. P., Fennema, E., Fuson, K., Human, P., Murray, H., Olivier, A., & Wearne, D. (1996). Problem solving as a basis for reform in curriculum and instruction: The case of mathematics. *Educational Researcher, 25,* 12–21.

Husen, T. (Ed.). (1967). *International study of achievement in mathematics, Vols. I and II.* Stockholm: Almqvist & Wiksell.

Kinney, C. (in press). Teachers and the teaching profession in Japan. In J. LeTendre, H. W. Stevenson, & R. Nerison-Low (Eds.), *The Education in Japan: Case study findings.* Report for the TIMSS Case Studies project.

Lapointe, A. E., Mead, N. A., & Askew, J. M. (1992). *Learning mathematics.* Princeton, NJ: Educational Testing Service.

Lapointe, A. E., Mead, N. A., & Phillips, G. (1989). *A world of differences.* Princeton, NJ: Educational Testing Service.

Lee, S. Y., Graham, T., & Stevenson, H. W. (1996). Teachers and teaching: Elementary schools in Japan and the United States. In T. Rohlen & G. LeTendre (Eds.), *Teaching and learning in Japan* (pp. 157–189). New York: Cambridge University Press.

Little, J. W. (1989). District policy choices and teachers' professional development opportunities. *Education Evaluation and Policy Analysis, 11,* 165–179.

Lubeck, S. (in press). Teachers and the teaching profession in the U.S. In R.

Nevison-Law, H. W. Stevenson, & B. Hofer (Eds.), *The Education in the United States: Case study findings.* Report for the TIMSS Case Studies project.

McKnight, C. C., Crosswhite, F. J., Dossey, J. A., Kifer, E., Swafford, J. O., Travers, K. J., & Cooney, T. J. (1987). *The underachieving curriculum: Assessing U.S. school mathematics from an international perspective.* Champaign, IL: Stipes.

National Commission on Excellence in Education. (1983). *A nation at risk: The imperative for educational reform.* Washington, DC: U.S. Government Printing Office.

National Commission on Teaching and America's Future. (1996). *What matters most: Teaching for America's future.* Washington, DC: U.S. Government Printing Office.

National Council of Teachers of Mathematics. (1989). *Curriculum and evaluation standards for school mathematics.* Reston, VA: Author.

National Education Goals Panel. (1996). *Profile of 1994–95 state assessment systems and reported results.* Washington, DC: Author.

Nelson, F. H., & O'Brien, T. (1993). *How U.S. teachers measure up internationally: A comparative study of teacher pay, training, and conditions of service.* Washington, DC: American Federation of Teachers, AFL-CIO.

Ravitch, D. (1995). *National standards in American education: A citizen's guide.* Washington, DC: Brookings Institution.

Stevenson, H. W. (In press). The case study project of TIMSS. In G. Kaiser (Ed.), *Comparative studies of mathematics achievement.*

Stevenson, H. W., Chen, C., & Lee, S. Y. (1993). Mathematics achievement of Chinese, Japanese & American children: Ten years later. *Science, 259,* 53–58.

Stevenson, H. W., & Lee, S. Y. (1995). The East Asian version of whole-class teaching. *Educational Policy, 9,* 152–168.

Stevenson, H. W., Lee, S., Chen, C., Lummis, M., Stigler, J., Fan, L., & Ge, F. (1990a). Mathematics achievement of children in China and the United States. *Child Development, 61,* 1053–1066.

Stevenson, H. W., Lee, S., Chen, C., Stigler, J. W., Hsu, C., & Kitamura, S. (1990b). Contexts of achievement: A study of American, Chinese, and Japanese children. *Monographs of the Society for Research in Child Development,* Vol. 55, Serial No. 221.

Stevenson, H. W., Lee, S., & Stigler, J. W. (1986). Mathematics achievement of Chinese, Japanese, and American children. *Science, 231,* 693–699.

Stevenson, H. W., & Stigler, J. W. (1992). *The learning gap.* New York: Summit Books.

Stigler, J. W., & Perry, M. (1988). Mathematics learning in Japanese, Chinese, and American classrooms. In G. G. Saxe & M. Gearhart (Eds.), *Children's mathematics* (pp. 27–54). San Francisco: Jossey-Bass.

U.S. Department of Education, Office of Research. (1994a). *Issues of curriculum reform in science, mathematics and higher order thinking across the disciplines.* Washington, DC: Author.

U.S. Department of Education (1994b). *NAEP 1992 trends in academic progress.* Washington, DC: U.S. Government Printing Office.

Usui, H. (1996). Differences in teacher classroom behaviors in USA and Japan: A field note. *Annual Report 1994–1995, Research and Clinical Center for Child Development, Faculty of Education, Hokkaido University,* 18, 63–85.

3

Cultural Contexts of Schooling Revisited: A Review of *The Learning Gap* From a Cultural Psychology Perspective

Giyoo Hatano and Kayoko Inagaki

A series of cross-national studies on mathematics achievement conducted by Harold Stevenson and his associates has had a tremendous impact on both psychology and education. Stevenson is still active and the research program is ongoing, but we believe what he and his associates have already achieved deserves careful examination. In this chapter, we consider Stevenson and Stigler's (1992) summary and discussion of policy issues from *The Learning Gap*. We also examine the first two large studies that are reported in detail in academic journals and some book chapters that are major empirical sources for this book. These studies are the Minneapolis-Sendai-Taipei study (Study 1)[1] and the Beijing-Chicago-Sendai-Taipei study (Study 2).[2] This series of studies is undoubtedly one of the best in quality and the best known of those that are concerned with the cultural contexts of schooling and its cognitive products. More specifically, these studies have at least four distinctive merits. We describe them below.

---

[1]Reported by Stevenson and Lee (1990a), Stevenson, Stigler, Lee, Lucker, Kitamura, and Hsu (1985), and Stigler, Lee, and Stevenson (1986, 1987).
[2]In Perry, VanderStoep, and Yu (1993), Stigler and Perry (1988), Stigler and Fernandez (1995), and Stigler, Lee, and Stevenson (1990).

MERITS OF THE STEVENSON–STIGLER STUDIES

Appropriate Selection of Cognitive and Contextual Variables

Informative target cognitive and contextual variables for cross-national comparison were chosen for both the studies we are discussing. Mathematics achievement constitutes an especially important criterion for judging academic success in a variety of cultures including American, Chinese, and Japanese. Moreover, what is considered essential or important in mathematics achievement at the elementary school level is highly similar across these cultures. In this sense, mathematics is probably the most appropriate target for cross-national comparison among school subjects.

Because mathematics achievement is expected to be a direct product of the educational (teaching–learning) practice of mathematics, cross-cultural similarities and differences in mathematics achievement can be interpreted in terms of different characteristics of the educational practices in these cultures. Many other variables can then be treated as constituting the cultural background of this educational practice, for example, providing the pressure for students to participate in mathematics learning actively and successfully. The research program led by Stevenson adopted this strategy. It is quite consistent with the recent emphasis on the notion of "practice" as a link between culture and cognitive development and the larger cultural contexts as an influence on the pattern of practices (e.g., Goodnow, Miller, & Kessel, 1995; Saljo, 1991). In other words, unlike many earlier cross-cultural studies of cognitive development, this series of studies by Stevenson and colleagues is not vulnerable to the criticism of methodological behaviorism (Lucariello, 1995), that is, applying a fixed set of measurements to different cultures without sensitivity or without a theoretical framework.

Careful Methodological Considerations

The series of studies by Stevenson and colleagues was conducted with impressive methodological rigor. A reasonably large representative sample was used. About 1,500 children from 20 classrooms at each of the two grade levels in Taipei (Taiwan), Sendai (Japan), and Minneapolis (United States) participated in Study 1, and more than 5,000 children from 20 classrooms at each of the two grade levels in Taipei and Sendai, and 40 classrooms at each grade level in Chicago, participated in Study 2. (Beijing was included for some measures.) Almost 1,000 kindergartners also participated in Study 1. They constituted a representative sample of children from these cities; for example, in Study 1, two 1st-grade and two 5th-grade classrooms were randomly chosen in each school, and from each classroom six boys and six girls were randomly chosen.

The test Stevenson and his colleagues used was constructed with the greatest care to be a tool that made possible culturally fair comparison; it was based on a detailed analysis of the mathematics curricula in the three countries, representing important shared topics. Although the test used in Study 1 tended to overemphasize computational skills, the test in Study 2 was designed to evaluate not only computational skills but also conceptual understanding in many aspects of elementary school mathematics (i.e., word problems, number concepts and equations, mathematical operations, graphing, estimation, visualization, transformation of spatial relations, and mental calculation). Whereas the test of computational skills in Study 2 was carried out as a group test for a large sample, the other tests were individually administered.

The classroom experiences of the three countries were assessed by extensive observations using rigorous time-sampling methods in Study 1 and narrative analyses in Study 2; observers visited each classroom 40 times over a period of 2 to 4 weeks, and thus, 800 mathematics instructional sessions were observed at each grade level in each city. Trained observers traced either the children's behaviors or teacher's behaviors in math classes (Stigler, Lee, & Stevenson, 1987).

The interviews, which contained both objective and open-ended questions, were administered to students' parents and teachers to obtain background information. The interviews included questions about the children's everyday lives, the parents' interest in their child's academic achievement, the parents' and child's beliefs about the relative influence of effort and ability on academic achievement, and so on.

Large Cross-National Differences

These studies yielded striking differences in mathematics achievements among the three cultures, particularly between the American children and the Asian children. This is a merit of the research because it leads to clear interpretations of the findings as opposed to disputes about the statistical or everyday significance of the results. In Study 1 the first-grade Chinese children as well as the Japanese children clearly outperformed the American children. At the fifth-grade level the difference in performance between the American and the Asian children was even greater. For example, even the highest score for an American fifth-grade classroom was below the lowest score of an Asian fifth-grade classroom. At the first-grade level, only 15 American children were among the 100 top scorers on the mathematics test, and at the fifth-grade level, only 1 American child was included (Stevenson & Stigler, 1992; Stigler, Lee, & Stevenson, 1986). This gap between the performance of the American children and the Asian children was reconfirmed in Study 2. In addition, Study 2 revealed that the Asian children on the average outperformed the American children not only in computational skills but also in mathematical understanding; the average scores of the American children were remarkably low in comparison with the other countries on all the tests including number concepts, geometry, word problems, and so forth (Stigler, Lee, & Stevenson, 1990).

From the results of these studies, it is clear that the United States is not first in mathematics achievement, at least in the last part of the 20th century. American children's inferiority in the mathematics achievement cannot be attributed to their general cognitive functioning, because Stevenson et al. (1985) found no difference in cognitive functioning among Chinese, Japanese, and American children. The fact that the gap in mathematics achievement between the American and the Asian children is widened with ascending grade levels strongly suggests that schooling, more specifically, the educational practices of teaching–learning mathematics at school, is primarily responsible for these results.

Studies 1 and 2 revealed corresponding differences in the educational practice among the three cultures, and Study 1 found some cross-cultural differences in background factors. We will describe in detail the former in the section "Interactions in the Mathematics Classroom," and the latter in the section "Sociocultural Contextual Factors Outside School."

Enhancing Interest in Asia

Last but not least, the Stevenson research program directed the attention of Americans to education in Asian countries. Their cross-national comparisons have yielded a unique set of policy implications. Stevenson and his associates recommended that the United States learn from East Asian countries, not vice versa. This recommendation, coupled with the strength of the empirical results mentioned above, has interested a number of American (mainstream) educational researchers in Asian education. As Hatano (1990) has noted, this may open truly bidirectional conversation between American and Asian investigators, and thus may have a democratizing effect within the community of educational researchers.

The significance of the argument by Stevenson and Stigler (1992) that the pedagogical methods of East Asian public schooling deserve special consideration as sources of inspiration for the reform of American education needs to be emphasized, because it has rarely been proposed that the politically strongest and technologically most advanced country has something to learn about education and schooling from less strong and less advanced countries. In the present century, few societies are fully insulated against external cultural influence. However, a historically recurrent type of encounter between different cultural traditions is one in which the more politically powerful group seeks to impose its cultural tools and ideas on another less powerful group. Whereas this phenomenon used to take the form of hegemonic imposition, in recent years it has been replaced by the modernization theory (Serpell & Hatano, 1997). This theory supposes that less advanced countries can develop, both economically and socially, by importing the technologies and systems of more advanced countries. This idea is proposed as a universalistic principle to justify the transplantation of many Western cultural inventions into other societies. Even when it takes a milder form of recommending that less powerful groups import advanced tools deliberately and with some adaptations, the direction of the influence is almost always from the western to nonwestern countries. For example, it is often assumed, even among cross-cultural psychologists, either explicitly or implicitly, that by adopting the western system of schooling and incorporating western ideas Third World countries can develop economically (Serpell, 1993). Stevenson and his associates may be the first American scholars who suggest that western countries can profitably learn about schooling from nonwestern countries.

Beyond Merits: Defining Some Problems

Even the best research program inevitably has some soft points. As also pointed out by Hatano (1990), we are concerned that Stevenson and his associates may have sometimes failed to identify critical components in the cultural configuration of school and community practices that produce high mathematics achievement, that the interpretations they offer of their findings may sometimes ignore the culturally embedded nature of pedagogical methods, and thus, that in their recommendations that are based on these interpretations they may have overestimated the feasibility of transplanting these methods from one culture to another. Among other things, we are concerned that Stevenson and his associates are too universalistic at times, though they have reversed the rationale of the modernization theory. We will take up these issues in this chapter as well.

INTERACTIONS IN THE
MATHEMATICS CLASSROOM

The teaching–learning practice in mathematics is a part of institutionalized, public basic schooling, which is more or less similar all over the world. Institutionalized public basic schooling is usually expected, unlike apprenticeship, to provide children with the opportunities to acquire basic literacy and other foundational skills that may not have any immediate practical value. It is conducted by teachers who are regarded as specialists and are in charge of choosing the contents and methods of teaching. The teachers usually rely on didactic methods that require students to manipulate symbols instead of handling real objects in meaningful contexts (Serpell & Hatano, 1997). In addition, at the elementary school level, the contents of mathematics teaching–learning are more or less similar across nations. In this sense, the educational practice of mathematics teaching–learning might be expected to be essentially the same kind of practice in China, Japan, and the United States. However, this is not the case.

Cross-Cultural Differences in the Mathematics Teaching–Learning Practice

There are remarkable differences in a number of features, both quantitative and qualitative, of the mathematics teaching–learning practices in China, Japan, and the United States. Several of these are documented by Stevenson and his associates. Study 1, for example, revealed some impressive quantitative differences among the three cultures.

First, according to the estimate by Stigler and Perry (1988), the average number of hours spent each week in mathematics differed greatly among the three cultures. At the first grade level, American teachers spent an average of 2.9 hours in mathematics instruction, whereas Japanese teachers spent 6.0 hours in mathematics instruction. Chinese teachers fell in between, spending 3.9 hours in mathematics instruction. At the fifth-grade level, 3.4, 11.4, and 7.6 hours were spent on average in mathematics instruction by American, Chinese, and Japanese teachers, respectively.

Second, their extensive observations revealed that the percentage of the total time in mathematics classes when students were led by teachers also differed cross-culturally. Whereas no one was leading the students' activity 9% of the time in China and 26% of the time in Japan, American students were not supervised as much as 51% of the time. This lack of supervision was partly because American teachers spent more time working with individuals and less time with the whole class than Asian teachers did. Therefore, children in the three cultures differed not only in the frequency of participation in the educational practice of mathematics but also in the extent of active involvement in it.

Qualitative differences in the teaching–learning practice in mathematics were also found in Study 2. Two of these differences seem particularly important. One concerns the types of questions that were asked and how often they were asked. Perry, VanderStoep, and Yu (1993) found that at the first-grade level teachers in the three cultures asked computational and rote recall questions equally often but that Japanese and Chinese teachers asked computing-in-context questions (word problems) and also questions about problem-solving strategies much more often than did American teachers. Stigler and Perry (1988) also noted that Japanese and Chinese teachers often spent an entire lesson discussing one or two problems, offering a marked contrast with American teachers who seemed to try to ask as many questions as they could.

The other striking cross-cultural difference in the educational practice in mathematics concerned how student's answers, especially erroneous answers, were treated by the teacher. American teachers often gave positive feedback to students' correct answers by offering praise. They had a high tolerance for errors; at least they seldom discussed students' errors in public. In contrast, Chinese and Japanese teachers were more likely to ask students "to explain their answers" and to then call upon other students "to evaluate their correctness" (Stevenson & Stigler, 1992, p. 191). In response to other students' negative feedback and criticisms, a student may have struggled to remedy his or her original answer continuously in public.

In spite of these and other differences, Stevenson and Stigler (1992) conclude:

> The techniques used by Chinese and Japanese teachers are not new to the teaching profession—nor are they foreign or exotic. In fact, they are ones often recommended by American educators. What the Chinese and Japanese examples demonstrate so compellingly is that when widely and consistently implemented, such practices can produce extraordinary outcomes. (p. 198)

Some differences are merely matters of degree, "breadth and consistency," to use their words. Others, which may appear to be of a more qualitative nature, are actually differences in the use of the same component techniques. The various instructional methods in the three cultures are almost all seen as legitimate ones for teaching elementary school arithmetic within institutionalized public basic schooling.

However, this does not mean that American and Asian educational practices in mathematics are qualitatively the same. We do not believe this is what Stevenson and Stigler intend to claim. The term *practice* means that a sequence of activities is not only recurrent but also is followed by most of the members of a group and taken for granted (Miller and Goodnow, 1995). Thus, if some features of a Chinese or Japanese mathematics lesson surprise, puzzle, or confuse American teachers, this implies that their practice is qualitatively different from Americans', even though these features are in line with the recommendations of leading American educators.

Stevenson and Stigler expect American teachers to find some features in the Japanese or Chinese lessons strange, such as the prolonged display of pupil's errors, concentration on one or two problems for an entire lesson, use of a very slow instructional pace, and so on. Likewise, we believe, many Japanese teachers find some features of the American lesson "unnatural." For example, successively asking the same question to many students, as in the following example, often puzzles them.

Example 1
T: Emily, what did you end up with?
S1: 3 tens and 4.
T: Sounds good. Omar?
S2: 3 tens and 4.
T: OK, Scott?
S3: 3 tens and 4.
T: Dan?
S4: 3 tens and 4.

We expect many Japanese teachers to ask "Do you agree (with S1)?" instead of repeating the same question with feedback, so that S2, S3, and others will be able to connect their answer to S1's. This is, from the Japanese teachers' viewpoint, an important first step, a step of requiring students to examine other students' ideas. In the upper elementary grades, Japanese teachers often attempt to induce collective examination activities by offering a student's answer as an object of thinking. Using terminology by Wertsch and Bivens (1992), students' utterances are treated as "thinking devices or objects to which one can respond." We have found many instances of such attempts in the lessons collected in a joint project with Jim Stigler and in collaboration with S. Amaiwa and H. Yoshida that consisted of 17 videotaped lessons of fifth-graders learning fractions. The attempts were made first by the teacher, as in Example 2, but later by the children themselves, as in Example 3.

> Example 2
> C1: We can make 40/60 into 4/6 by deleting 0s.
> T: (To all other students) What do you all think? Do you follow what C1 says? Can we remove 0s from 40/60? Why does he think so?
> C2: But . . . 40/60 means 40 out of those divided into 60, whereas 4/6 means 4 out of 6 . . .
> T: A little different, you mean. What do you think?

> Example 3
> C: My idea is similar to Takashi's—dividing (a circle) here at even numbers results in 4/6. (to all other students) What do you all think?

Students in the Japanese mathematics classroom are not only encouraged to offer their own ideas but also to evaluate and incorporate ideas proposed by others. Such an attempt of coordinating ideas may be critically important for the construction of mathematical knowledge.

How to Interpret the Cross-Cultural Differences in Practice

What caused such differences? Were the cross-cultural differences due to simple ignorance of or lack of commitment to some learning principles of teachers in either culture? If so, it could be rather straightforward to reduce the difference. However, we do not believe this to be the case.

We assume that there are underlying processes that produce cross-cultural differences such as those observed by Stevenson and Stigler. Let us offer three interpretations for the differences between the United States and Japan. We exclude China from the following discussion, because we are not sure whether Chinese and Japanese practices show similar tendencies for the same underlying reasons. This point will be discussed at the end of this section. The three interpretations are as follows: (a) teachers hold different folk-pedagogies, (b) they hold basically the same folk pedagogy, but it is adjusted to different learners, and (c) teachers differ in confidence and motivation. Needless to say, these are not mutually exclusive, but we might assess how far each of them can go to explain the observed differences. We will thus examine each of them in detail below.

Different Folk Pedagogies

It is possible that American and Japanese teachers are committed to different folk-pedagogies as regards the best way for students to learn mathematics. Stevenson and Stigler (1992) sometimes suggested the interpretation, more specifically, that American teachers are more behavioristic and Japanese teachers are more constructivistic. For example, they wrote: ". . . Asian teachers subscribe to what would be considered in the West a constructivist view of learning. According to this view, knowledge is regarded as something that must be constructed by the child rather than as a set of facts and skills that can be imparted by the teacher" (p. 197). They specifically contrast this with the folk-pedagogy held by American teachers, as evident in the following response to students' errors, "People should strive to avoid errors and to give only the correct response—a routine that fits our culture and has been strengthened by the writings of behavioral psychologists . . ." (p. 17). Stigler and Fernandez (1995) elaborated this point, "American teachers try hard to keep errors out of the mathematics classroom, and especially out of the public discourse. This may be because they are afraid that students will remember the wrong answers, a notion that probably can be traced to behaviorist theories of learning" (p. 117).

It is somewhat puzzling that American teachers are less constructivistic than their Japanese counterparts, in spite of the fact that many leading mathematics educators in the United States tend to be constructivists, sometimes even radically so (von Glasersfeld, 1991). We believe that teachers become more constructivistic, not by persuasion, but by being presented concrete examples of children's mathematical construction. It is also critical whether teachers themselves are encouraged to construct knowledge, for example, to find their own way of teaching, rather than to be instructed 'the best way' and required to follow it. This latter point will be discussed later. In any case, the success of some constructivistic programs in the United States, for example, Cognitively Guided Instruction (Carpenter, Fennema, Peterson, Chiang, & Loef, 1989), strongly suggests that it is possible to change American teachers' folk-pedagogy toward constructivism, though it may take time.

Another important dimension of teachers' folk-pedagogy concerns individualism. Stated more specifically, we mean teachers' beliefs about whether diverse children learn more from each other or whether they benefit most from individualized lessons. American teachers' inclination toward individualism, as pointed out by Stevenson and Stigler, is closely related to teachers' spending a considerable amount of time working with individuals.

Whereas American teachers have willingly accepted large individual differences even in a single classroom and have tried to optimize instruction by individualizing it, Japanese teachers have tended to emphasize the significance of students sharing experiences and ideas. Recently, teachers in both countries seem to pay attention to advantages of the other approach. However, just as it is hard for Japanese teachers to adapt their lesson to individual students, American teachers may not be accustomed to organizing whole class activities.

Differential Adjustment to Learners

The second interpretation supposes that, although both American and Japanese teachers have basically the same folk-pedagogy, they have adjusted it to different learners. The practice of teaching–learning mathematics is co-constructed by the teacher and the students. Although the teacher has the primary responsibility and often takes the initiative, the students' contributions cannot be ignored. Which students' characteristics may produce cross-culturally different educational practices in mathematics? We think two tendencies of students, which are not explicitly discussed by Stevenson and Stigler, are particularly important.

The first characteristic might be called socialization for speakership and listenership. We believe that American students have been trained to be good speakers, for example, to express their ideas clearly and persuasively. In contrast, Japanese children are good listeners, trained to listen to significant others eagerly and carefully. They are not frustrated nor do they become inattentive even when they have little opportunity for verbally expressing their own ideas, as long as they have some sense of participation. We believe this to be an important prerequisite for an extended whole-class discussion in Japan.

Let us refer to our findings supporting this notion. In our study of the effects of the whole-class discussion on science learning (Hatano & Inagaki, 1991), students were divided according to whether they belonged to the majority or the minority at the beginning of the discussion and whether they spoke at least once or not at all during the discussion. Students' learning was assessed in terms of the elaborateness of their explanations. We found that the explanations given by the silent participants were only slightly less elaborate than those of the vocal ones, and the minority participants' explanations were as elaborate as those of the majority participants.

Some of the silent participants actively tried to find "agent(s)" who "spoke for" them in the discussion, and if they could, they tended to give elaborate explanations afterward. Even when silent participants could not find such an agent because they belonged to a minority, some of them seemed to have responded with their opponents' arguments in mind and elaborated their explanations by incorporating challenging ideas into their initial thought. We believe these silent-participants enjoyed the lesson, though in this study we did not ask questions to see if this was so.

The second students' tendency that we believe is critical concerns their involvement in the class. In other words, what is critical is whether a mathematics classroom constitutes a community of learners (Brown, 1994) or, more precisely, a caring community "where all students know and care about one another as people, know how to talk and listen to one another respectfully, and have the safety provided by strong, shared class norms of kindness, helpfulness, and putting our strength together" (Lewis, 1995, p. 177). We expected to find a mathematics class to be such a caring community much more often in Japan than in the United States.

Relatedly, Lewis (1995) points out that Japanese classrooms are not just cognitive environments; "wholehearted involvement, persistence, and thoughtful problem solving are regarded as important goals for children's learning" (p. 176). She draws our attention to the fact that Japanese "teachers work hard to create a community of learners who respond supportively to one another's thoughts and feelings" (p. 176). Moreover, she strongly suggests that, without appreciating the critical efforts by Japanese teachers, it would be impossible for children to learn from their mistakes through listening and responding to one another's ideas. In other words, if American teachers, without paying due attention to "the infrastructure for exploring mistakes" (Lewis, 1995, p. 177), borrow the common Japanese practice of using individual students' mathematics mistakes as the basis for class discussion, the results may be tragic. Certainly Japanese teachers' effortful attempts to establish a caring community have to be appreciated. It also must be emphasized that Japanese children have a definite tendency to form such a community for mathematics lessons. As Lewis aptly puts it, making an error in public would damage American as well as Japanese children's self-esteem unless they are assured and convinced that their classroom constitutes a caring community.

On the basis of this social foundation of the caring community, Japanese teachers often convey, either explicitly or implicitly, their belief that students' mistakes really facilitate learning in the community. They often succeed; consider, for example, this impressive episode of first-graders' internalization of this belief from Itoi and Nishio (1977). The pupils were presented a comparison problem, "There are 12 boys and

8 girls. How many more boys than girls are there?" A majority of the pupils answered correctly "four more boys," but five incorrectly added the numbers (12 + 8), which produced an answer of 20. One of them insisted that subtraction could not be used, because it was impossible to take 8 girls away from 12 boys. None of the pupils who had answered correctly could offer a persuasive argument against this assertion. After a little while, some pupils proposed to try it out—12 boys and 8 girls of the class made two lines in front of the blackboard. As a result, a new idea emerged and convinced every pupil, that is, both 12 and 8 in the subtraction are boys, but those 8 are boys who hold hands with girls (thus we can take 8 away from 12). When they were asked who contributed to their lesson most, they almost unanimously nominated the child who had insisted on the wrong idea, because their understanding before the discussion was not deep enough for generating a persuasive argument against that idea. An important point here is that Japanese students are willing to disclose their possibly or even probably erroneous answers within the context of and for the benefit of their caring community.

If the above interpretations are correct, we must conclude that the observed differences in the mathematics teaching–learning practice were not due to simple ignorance of or the lack of commitment to some learning principles. A target practice is supported and compensated by many other practices. Extended whole-class discussion is possible only when most students are willing to be good listeners. Requiring students to display their solutions can be productive only when students form a caring community for mathematics lessons. In contrast, teachers must ask as many questions as possible if this is the only way to maintain the interest of the students. Teachers' fear of damaging a child's self-esteem by public failure is real unless the class is a caring community. All of these considerations make us skeptical of the feasibility of transplanting Japanese teaching strategies to the United States. Although it is possible to import teaching procedures from Japanese classrooms, they may not prove to be effective in the United States or they may not be fully accepted by American teachers.

Differences in Teachers' Confidence and Motivation

This third possibility is a sensitive one, and we are not willing to undertake criticisms of American teachers. We do want to refer to Stevenson and Stigler's comment that American teachers may "feel insecure about the depth of their own mathematical training" (1992, p. 191). We would like to emphasize that teachers can encourage students' construction of mathematical knowledge only when they are encouraged to construct their own knowledge, either about mathematics or about teaching. It should be noted that in Japan elementary school teachers are expected, and often supported, to be experts on how to teach specific subject-matter contents. Moreover, a variety of their voluntary organizations have proposed innovative instructional methods largely on the basis of their experience. Their status in the Japanese society is very close to that of professionals. However, compared with changing interrelated practices and values, it is relatively easy to modify the variables of confidence and motivation through teacher education and community support for teachers. Thus, if these teacher variables are some of the main causes of cross-cultural differences in the educational practice, we can be optimistic about the use of the Japanese model in the United States.

Do Japanese and Chinese Educational Practices Have Much in Common?

As alluded to at the beginning of this section, we are a bit skeptical whether Chinese and Japanese mathematics classrooms can be grouped as "Asian," at least not without losing much information. We are not simply claiming that Japan is unique. In fact, Chinese philosophical and social thoughts constitute a very important component of the Japanese intellectual tradition, although this fact is sometimes concealed by more recent European and American influences. Among others, direct and indirect influences of Confucianism cannot be ignored even in the recent and current educational practices. Furthermore, it is often asserted, especially by Westerners (e.g., Tobin, Wu, & Davidson, 1989), that the emphasis on modeling and being modeled is still prevalent in Japanese education.

However, Stigler and Perry (1988) indicate that, though very few differences emerged between Chinese and Japanese classrooms in their quantitative analyses, Chinese and Japanese were contrastive in terms of style: The Chinese classrooms were more performance oriented, the Japanese classrooms more reflective, and the American classrooms neither consistently. Moreover, economic and political contexts surrounding schools are fairly different between Sendai and Taipei, even more so between Sendai and Beijing. Grouping the two Asian countries together and contrasting them with the United States, a strategy taken by Stevenson and Stigler, can be justified only to simplify the story for the sake of the American lay audience.

SOCIOCULTURAL CONTEXTUAL FACTORS OUTSIDE SCHOOL

Practices do not exist in isolation (Miller & Goodnow, 1995). The practice of teaching–learning mathematics in school is not only embedded in a larger culture but is also part of the practice of socializing children, requesting and enabling children to acquire skills needed for their future life and the economy of the society. Such a school practice is also supported by the educational practice at home. Among other things, how much pressure children receive from their families to participate in the educational practice and to perform well in school can be expected to influence mathematics achievement.

Out-of-School Causal Factors for Mathematics Achievement

Stevenson and Lee (1990a), as part of Study 1, attempted to identify out-of-school causal factors for the cross-national differences in mathematics achievement that they had reported earlier. Through interviews with children and their mothers, the authors examined five clusters of variables as candidates for sociocultural conditions facilitating achievement: emphasis on academic achievement, involvement of parents and other members of the society, realism in evaluation, moderately high standards of performance, and emphasis on effort. Stevenson and Lee

(1990a) were particularly interested in identifying "the most salient reasons for poor performance" of the American children (p. 103).

Stevenson and Lee's conclusion provides a simple, convincing story explaining why the Asian countries produce high mathematics achievement in their children. Asian culture emphasizes and gives priority to mathematical learning. In China and Japan, high achievement in mathematics is seen by mature members of the culture to be an important goal for its less mature members. Asian adults assess their children's accomplishments carefully and, whenever help is needed, are willing to give it so that the children will accomplish more. It is assumed by almost all Asians that effort makes a difference in the level of one's accomplishments.

This story suggests that a culture may impose selected values on its less mature members through the process that does not take a dictatorial form. As noted by Stevenson and Lee, Japanese mothers, known as *kyoiku mama*, attempt "to provide a nurturant and protective atmosphere for learning" (p. 99). Mediating individuals and groups provide warmth, kindness, and respect for the individual efforts. They socialize less mature members in a subtle way; making the best use of their closeness, they lead them to internalize the cultural values. Once these values are internalized, the motivation to pursue them comes from within the individual.

Cultural imposition through close relationships between more mature and less mature members can be seen in many other areas. Consider the example of national sports. When a country has a national sport as part of its culture—that is, contests that almost all members find interesting to participate in or watch—the team representing that country tends to be strong, even if its population is small. This means that, if we were somehow to measure children's skill for playing the given sport, their average score would be very high in that country. Since the culture values being good at it, considerable time is allocated for participating in the sport, and peers, if not parents, pay close attention to less mature members' mastery, and are willing to help as well as encourage mastery of the sport.

In this type of cultural imposition children have almost no other choice than to seek the mastery of culturally prescribed skills. In contrast, there are also many skills that are viewed as culturally provided alternatives, and for which freedom of choice is allowed. We think that school mathematics is a national (in the sense used above) intellectual pursuit in Asian countries, but not in the United States. Whereas students cannot escape from it in the former, in the latter they are told (at least implicitly) that if they are poor at or dislike mathematics, they are free to seek achievement in some other area.

This difference in whether the acquisition of skill in school mathematics is compulsory or optional seems related to the emphasis placed on effort. It has often been claimed, even prior to Stevenson and Lee (1990a), that the Japanese people might be characterized by their belief in effort. For example, Hatano (1982b, p. 58) indicated that "while Japanese people think that effort makes a difference everywhere (i.e., even when one lacks ability), Americans tend to regard effort meaningful only insofar as one is smart (bright) or talented enough in the field." He even hinted that this belief in effort facilitates students' calculation skills (Hatano, 1982a). However, such claims may have overemphasized the cultural difference. We would like to propose here a more "domain-specific" assumption, namely that, whereas people generally tend to place much more importance on effort, with regards to competencies that every member of the society is expected to acquire, ability may be considered more important in the case of optional competencies. It is likely that the American culture allows its members to decline gaining competence in more domains than its Japanese or other Asian counterparts (Geary, 1994), permitting Americans to preserve their belief in ability without being fatalists. Our working hypothesis is that as a society becomes richer and comes to offer a wider variety of options to children, people in that society tend to lose their belief in effort. In other words, the emphasis on effort irrespective of ability, which leads to devoting more time to an area in which one performs poorly, is incongruent with the idea of choosing an area that best suits one's talent from available options. Japan's economic success may thus lead to the erosion of Japanese belief in effort in coming decades.

Can Asian Countries Be Taken as a Model for the United States?

The central issue we would like to discuss here is whether it is possible to improve education in a culture such as the United States, by incorporating ideas and techniques of socialization developed in another culture. Stevenson has long been interested in seeing developmental research make a contribution in setting social policy. Accordingly, Stevenson and Lee (1990a) aimed, not only at understanding the causes of cross-national differences in mathematics achievement, but also at reducing the differences, more specifically, in assisting the United States to catch up with the Asian countries. In fact, their findings provided important bases for Stevenson and Stigler's (1992) claims and proposals.

As Hatano (1990) suggests, a high incidence of low achievement in mathematics can be likened to a high incidence of a certain disease. If so, is it a disease of deficiency, like beriberi? In other words, is its cause singular, and is it prevented or cured by a specific procedure? As beriberi is caused by the lack of vitamin B1 and is prevented by ingesting vitamin B1, is low mathematics achievement caused by one sociocultural factor, and can it be greatly reduced by manipulating that factor? Alternatively, is this "disease" more like stomach cancer, with many causes and mediating variables? Although epidemiology has suggested a number of foods as candidates for its "major causes," the removal of any single food cannot have a dramatic effect.

Culture-conscious, policy-oriented research of the kind exemplified by Stevenson and Stigler (1992) should try to identify variables that when changed are likely to solve or alleviate the target problem and that people within a culture will not mind changing. If a rice-based society or group suffers from a high incidence of beriberi, the introduction of rice boiled with barley into the diet, for example, would be suggested as a solution to its high incidence. The reduction of beriberi becomes possible with minimal sacrifice, and most people might be willing to accept that level of sacrifice because the benefit more than compensates. Thus, if low mathematics achievement in the United States is like a high incidence of beriberi, then doing good policy-

98

oriented research is easy, and the recommendations that are based on such work can be straightforward.

However, if low mathematics achievement is like a high incidence of stomach cancer, then policy-oriented researchers must be much more cautious in designing studies, deriving conclusions, and making recommendations. Although a high incidence of such cancer is always a problem, it does not necessarily mean that a group that is characterized by low incidence is the healthier one; the low incidence of this form of disease may be accompanied by the high incidence of a different but equally serious illness. Moreover, attempts to decrease its incidence by manipulation of selected variables are likely to be difficult and, even if successful, may have negative side effects. Likewise, hasty attempts to reduce the incidence of low mathematics achievement may induce new weaknesses that are often raised about, if not empirically confirmed for, Asian education, for example, the lack of spontaneity and creativity of students.

Suppose for the current discussion that the Asian countries really are more successful in facilitating children's mathematical learning. Many Japanese educational researchers and teachers are not satisfied with the current mathematics education in Japan, especially because many Japanese children feel that mathematics is too hard and thus learning it cannot be fun, as revealed in Stevenson and Lee (1990a), but take this as a reasonable price for their high mathematics achievement. Can the comparative "underachievement" in mathematics in the United States then be reduced, without undue sacrifice, by changing the relevant sociocultural conditions of the United States to approximate those of the Asian countries?

We believe that the answer to this question cannot be simply affirmative. Let us put aside again the issue of possible negative emotional reactions accompanying high mathematics achievement. However, if our previous arguments are correct, then attempting to change American sociocultural conditions to the Asian sociocultural conditions, so as to improve children's mathematics achievement, would be nearly impossible without posing a threat to important American cultural values. If American children's low mathematics achievement is generally a consequence of their cultural milieu—such as the availability of a broader range of possibilities and the encouragement to pursue whatever is individually more challenging—then attempting to reduce low mathematics achievement could disturb the core of the American culture. Because every culture has a more or less coherent matrix of values, policy-oriented researchers such as Stevenson and Stigler (1992) must consider carefully whether an intended change can be induced in the given matrix at all and whether doing so will do harm to the matrix's coherence.

We are confident that Stevenson disagrees with this assessment. In fact, Stevenson and Lee (1990b) rebutted Hatano's (1990) commentary. Leaving aside the question of whether Asian students reveal mathematical understanding and intuition, they argued first, that cultural improvements by observing other cultures are often possible; as an example, they offer the revision of a Japanese textbook series that took many of the ideas from the "New Math" curriculum developed in the United States in the 1960s. Second, more specifically, American children's lower achievement in mathematics can be reduced without great cultural confusion because the essential recommendations, that is, good teaching, interested parents, and hard work, should enhance important elements in any culture, unless these go too far. Finally, Stevenson and Lee (1990b) assert that American students, though they may enjoy the wide variety of options open to them, seldom achieve excellence in any of them, and often suffer from illiteracy, school dropout, and unemployment.

It is true, as Stevenson and his associates (Stevenson & Lee, 1990b; Stevenson & Stigler, 1992) assert, that such Asian characteristics as the emphasis on scholastic achievement and the belief in effort per se may not be alien to the American culture. However, we do not think that is the real issue. More critical is whether mathematics achievement is regarded as one of the few markers of maturity and whether it is considered rational to devote considerable time and effort to study and practice in an area which does not seem suitable to one's aptitudes. In this sense, we believe that American culture is considerably different from Japanese or Chinese culture, and that the possibility of transplanting advantageous Asian features for mathematics achievement is limited.

CONCLUSIONS

Let us conclude this chapter by summarizing our arguments. As cultural psychologists, we believe that pedagogical methods are culturally embedded, and that transplanting them from one culture to another is not always feasible (Serpell & Hatano, 1997). Needless to say, we are not claiming that nothing can be learned about education from other cultures. We assume that when a practice is prevailing in a culture, more effective tools for this practice can be imported from other cultures with some adaptations. For example, updating textbooks is often done by reference to textbooks in other countries. Alternatively, observing another culture enables people to make extensive use of resources (tools, activities, or systems) that are already available but are not widespread in their own culture. Japan's adoption of the Western system of schooling had been prepared by a variety of indigenous forms of schooling (Dore, 1965). In this sense, some "Asian" instructional procedures may be applied to the American classroom in a way that is adapted to American children's prior tendencies and concurrent activities. Even some Asian socialization practices may be incorporated in this way. However, we want to emphasize that such transplantation requires great care and inventiveness.

We predict that universal approaches that are based on the modernization theory, which assumes the context-free effectiveness of tools and procedures even when their rationale is reversed, will bring about limited success at best. Cross-cultural studies, especially good studies like those by Stevenson and his associates, allow us to reassess the strengths as well as the weaknesses of our own educational system, and such reassessment is a prelude to an attempt to improve the system (Stevenson & Lee, 1990b). However, we believe it impossible to improve the system simply by importing the educational technologies and their supporting beliefs developed in another culture. It is necessary to "translate" these educational technologies and beliefs so that they can be harmonious with indigenous practices. For example, it could be recommended for American educators to place an expertise in mathematics, or even a collective pursuit of it, among the variety of options open to children. We hope this emphasis on the necessity of "translation" is not incompatible with the stated goal of Stevenson and Stigler (1992), that is, using the Asian pedagogical methods as sources of inspiration for the reform of American education.

REFERENCES

Brown, A. L. (1994). The advancement of learning. *Educational Researcher, 23,* 4–12.

Carpenter, T. P., Fennema, E., Peterson, P. L., Chiang, C. P., & Loef, M. (1989). Using knowledge of children's mathematics thinking in classroom teaching: An experimental study. *American Educational Research Journal, 26,* 499–531.

Dore, R. P. (1965). *Education in Tokugawa Japan.* Routledge & Kegan Paul.

Geary, D. C. (1994). *Children's mathematical development: Research and practical applications.* Washington, DC: American Psychological Association.

Goodnow, J. J., Miller, J. P., & Kessel, F. (Eds.) (1995). *Cultural practices as contexts for development.* San Francisco: Jossey-Bass.

Hatano, G. (1982a). Learning to add and subtract: A Japanese perspective. In T. P. Carpenter, J. M. Moser, & T. A. Romberg (Eds.), *Addition and subtraction: A cognitive perspective* (pp. 211–223). Hillsdale, NJ: Erlbaum.

Hatano, G. (1982b). Should parents be teachers too? A Japanese view. *Dokkyo University Bulletin of Liberal Arts, 17,* 54–72.

Hatano, G. (1990). Commentary: Toward the cultural psychology of mathematical cognition. *Monographs of the Society for Research in Child Development, 221* (55, 108–115).

Hatano, G., & Inagaki, K. (1991). Sharing cognition through collective comprehension activity. In L. B. Resnick, J. M. Levine, & S. D. Teasley (Eds.), *Perspectives on socially shared cognition* (pp. 331–348). Washington, DC: American Psychological Association.

Itoi, H., & Nishio, T. (1977). *Even a deviant child is entertained.* Tokyo: Ayumishuppan. [in Japanese]

Lewis, C. C. (1995). *Educating hearts and minds: Reflections on Japanese pre-*

school and elementary education. Cambridge, England: Cambridge University Press.

Lucariello, J. (1995). Mind, culture, and person: Elements in a cultural psychology. *Human Development, 38,* 2–18.

Miller, P. J., & Goodnow, J. J. (1995). Cultural practices: Toward an integration of culture and development. In J. J. Goodnow, P. J. Miller, & F. Kessel (Eds.), *Cultural practices as contexts for development* (pp. 5–16). San Francisco: Jossey-Bass.

Perry, M., VanderStoep, S. M., & Yu, S. L. (1993). Asking questions in first-grade mathematics classes: Potential influences on mathematical thought. *Journal of Educational Psychology, 85,* 31–40.

Saljo, R. (1991). Introduction: Culture and learning. *Learning and Instruction, 1,* 179–185.

Serpell, R. (1993). *The significance of schooling: Life-journeys in an African society.* Cambridge, England: Cambridge University Press.

Serpell, R., & Hatano, G. (1997). Education, schooling and literacy in a cross-cultural perspective. In J. W. Berry, P. R. Dasen, & T. S. Saraswathi (Eds.), *Handbook of cross-cultural psychology* (Vol. 2). Boston: Allyn & Bacon.

Stevenson, H. W., & Lee, S. (1990a). Contexts of achievement: A study of American, Chinese, and Japanese children. *Monographs of the Society for Research in Child Development, 221*(55), 1–107.

Stevenson, H. W., & Lee, S. (1990b). Reply: To achieve. *Monographs of the Society for Research in Child Development, 221*(55), 116–119.

Stevenson, H. W., & Stigler, J. W. (1992). *The learning gap.* New York: Summit Books.

Stevenson, H. W., Stigler, J. W., Lee, S., Lucker, G. W., Kitamura, S., & Hsu, C. (1985). Cognitive performance and achievement of Japanese, Chinese, and American children. *Child Development, 56,* 718–734.

Stigler, J. W., & Fernandez, C. (1995). Learning mathematics from classroom instruction: Cross-cultural and experimental perspectives. In C. A. Nelson (Ed.), *Basic and applied perspectives on learning, cognition, and development.* The Minnesota symposia on child psychology (Vol. 28), 103–130.

Stigler, J. W., Lee, S., & Stevenson, H. W. (1986). Mathematical achievement of Chinese, Japanese, and American children. *Science, 231,* 693–699.

Stigler, J. W., Lee, S., & Stevenson, H. W. (1987). Mathematics classrooms in Japan, Taiwan, and the United States. *Child Development, 58,* 1272–1285.

Stigler, J. W., Lee, S., & Stevenson, H. W. (1990). *Mathematical knowledge of Japanese, Chinese, and American elementary school children.* Reston, VA: National Council of Teachers of Mathematics.

Stigler, J. W., & Perry, M. (1988). Mathematics learning in Japanese, Chinese, and American classrooms. In G. B. Saxe & M. Gearhart (Eds.), *Children's mathematics* (pp. 27–54). San Francisco: Jossey-Bass.

Tobin, J. J., Wu, D. Y. H., & Davidson, D. H. (1989). *Preschool in three cultures.* New Haven, CT: Yale University Press.

von Glasersfeld, E. (Ed.). (1991). *Radical constructivism in mathematics education.* Dordrecht, The Netherlands: Kluwer.

Wertsch, J., & Bivens, J. A. (1992). The social origins of individual mental functioning: Alternatives and perspectives. *The Quarterly Newsletter of the Laboratory of Comparative Human Cognition, 14,* 35–44.

4

Contexts of Achievement

Jacqueline J. Goodnow

Festschrifts provide an excellent opportunity to look back and to note how much has been accomplished by a specific person or in a particular field. Harold Stevenson's successes to date certainly warrant such reflection. Festschrifts also, however, present occasions to look toward the future. That is the direction I take in this chapter. I do so partly because one of the signs of a successful research program is that it continues to raise questions and possibilities even after it has been in place for some time. I do so also because one of Harold Stevenson's best qualities is his tendency to look forward rather than to rest on past laurels.

My focus in this chapter then is on some questions and possibilities that Stevenson's research might well explore in a further round of studies. In this respect, one may note the considerable overlap between this chapter and the one by Hatano (chapter 3, this volume). There is still work to be done—work sparked by what has already been completed.

To anchor my proposals, I use as a base the monograph by Stevenson and Lee (1990) titled "Contexts of Achievement." That 1990 monograph is by no means the last comment by Stevenson and his colleagues on contexts of achievement. Within a single source, however, it provides starting points for the research directions I wish to highlight.

I have divided those directions into two main forms. The first consists of asking what inferences about contexts can one draw from the several result patterns that emerge from comparisons across cultural contexts. The second has to do with ways of extending the analysis of a feature of contexts emphasized by Stevenson and Lee (1990): the nature of expectations.

This second direction is given the most attention and is itself divided into two parts, both of which have some degree of foreshadowing in Stevenson and Lee (1990). The first deals with expectations related to the importance of various forms of achievement. The second has to do with expectations related to leeway when it comes to performance. Importance by itself, I propose, is an incomplete account of what gives rise to performance. It needs to be balanced by attention to leeway— to the presence of flexibility, tradeoffs, or negotiations with regard to what is acceptable.

Within this second direction, both importance and leeway are discussed as features of contexts, that is, as expectations held by teachers or parents or built into a school structure. The final section, necessarily brief, asks how these expectations come to be translated into the expectations and the performance of children.

Before beginning, a brief note is in order with regard to the term *contexts*, or *social contexts*, which is currently used in two main senses. These are interrelated but nonetheless lead in different directions.

The first refers to conditions influencing performance at any one time. Whereas once the emphasis fell on the logical demands of the task and the individual's mental capacity or knowledge base, contextual arguments add that every encounter with a task is also a social interaction. Tasks are often undertaken in conjunction with others, or in the company of others. Even when a person officially works "alone," the task is "socially structured": Others assign it, set the scene, influence the availability of resources, or limit the forms that performance may take. It is this sense of the term *context*, equivalent in many ways to the term *situation*, that then leads easily to comparisons of performance under various interaction conditions (i.e., working alone compared with working with others, working with people who accept one's lead compared with working with people who challenge one's position).

The second main sense of context has a more developmental connotation. It refers to conditions influencing the course of changes in performance or the level of achievement reached over time. Whereas once the emphasis fell on internally driven, age-related shifts in mental capacity, contextual arguments call for attention to conditions that give rise to different degrees of familiarity with particular task strategies, to varying investments of effort, to different readinesses to interpret any current situation in particular ways. This second sense of the term, often encapsulated in the phrase "cultural context," leads easily to comparisons of performance across groups with a history, known or inferred, of particular kinds of experience. This second sense of the term is the sense in which Stevenson and Lee (1990) used the phrase "contexts of achievement." It is also the sense in which I use the term throughout this chapter.

RESULT PATTERNS AND INFERENCES
ABOUT CONTEXTS

By and large, research on contexts and performance proceeds in two ways. In one, we observe differences in performance and then work back to differences in context. We note, for instance, differences in achievement on tests of mathematical skill and ask why. In the other, we observe differences in context and ask what differences in performance might follow. We note, for instance, that two cultures differ in the way reading is taught or in the kind of alphabet or orthography used, and we ask what consequences these differences might have. With either strategy, we are now at a point where we can anticipate some particular result patterns.

Stevenson and his colleagues have worked with both strategies. I limit my comments, however, to the strategy of working from group differences, largely because that strategy has predominated within this research program. I shall also concentrate on three anticipatable result patterns: (a) differences in means and distributions, (b) differences both between groups and within groups, and (c) no differences between groups.

The first of those result patterns is illustrated in part of the report by Stevenson and Lee (1990). The mean reading scores for their U.S. sample were not significantly different from those obtained with the Chinese and Japanese samples. The U.S. sample, however, contained the largest proportion of both bottom scorers and top scorers for the three samples combined.

What kind of contextual picture might account for such a pattern of results? One possibility is that in the U.S. school system individual differences have more free rein, either because the meanings of words can be discovered by children (characters need to be taught, character by character) or because less classroom effort is expended on seeing that every student reaches a certain level. There may be more tolerance both for exceeding and for dropping below a class average. At the least, the contextual factors at work are unlikely to be the same as those that apply when differences occur in the means but not in the distributions.

For the second anticipatable pattern, I turn again to the Stevenson and Lee (1990) report:

> Paradoxically, variables such as years of parents' education— that offer likely explanations of differences in performance among children within a culture—do not necessarily prove to be useful in discussing cross-cultural differences in perfor- mance. Conversely, variables reflecting motivational differences (e.g., emphases on effort) varied directly with levels of achieve- ment between cultures but do not vary with levels of achieve- ment within cultures.... In sum, variables that predict differ- ences in performance between cultures may not be the same variables as those that predict differences among individuals within a culture. (p. 116)

That particular pattern is not unique to a single study. It comes up again, for instance, in current reports by Shin-Ying Lee and by Jim Stigler (this volume). We need to ask the following: What does it mean when a set of variables predicts differences across national groups but not differences within a group, or differences across cultural groups taken as a whole but not differences among subgroups—groups varying, for instance, in gender, ethnicity, or socioeconomic status? It would be wonderfully parsimonious if the same factors accounted for diversity across and diversity within groups. The evidence, however, is against that neat pattern being the one we may happily expect and any theory of contextual effects will need to come to terms with the possibility of predictors that are differentially related to particular kinds of diversity.

The third and last pattern consists of finding no differences in performance scores across groups, inviting the inference that these groups share similar contexts. The same end point, however, may be reached by different routes, and the route may reflect the nature of the context more than the end point does. A report by Steinberg, Darling, and Fletcher (1996) provides an example. African-American and European-American students, they noted, may both be doing well in U.S. high schools. For the former group, however, a strong school performance may be correlated with what is often termed *authoritarian* parenting. The same strength of school performance among Euro-American children may not be correlated with that style of parenting but may be correlated instead with a more relaxed style. Authoritarian parenting may in fact now give rise to negative correlations with school achievement.

With results such as these, it is difficult to argue that a single variable such as style of parenting is the basis of strong school performance. Perhaps what also matters is the extent to which a parent's style is in keeping with that used by most other parents in the same ethnic or social group, encouraging children to regard that style as reasonable, as a sign of responsible parenting, or as a mark of group identity. Perhaps what matters is some kind of interaction between what parents do and the circumstances that a child encounters. If one is to cope with a hostile or undermining school environment, for instance, one may well need the kind of unquestioning belief in the need to achieve that authoritarian parenting may encourage. The possibilities are several. What is clear is that similarities in achievement do not allow the conclusion that the background contexts and the routes to achievement are similar.

Clear also is the implication, from all three result patterns, that we need to think in terms of the interplay of multiple contextual variables. We may well do best to think of various features of contexts as softening each other's effects, as canceling each other out, as supporting one another, as having cumulative effects, as creating opportunities for impact, or for sustaining each other's impact.

Thinking in terms of multiple interactions, however, does not tell us what the variables are that we might put into any design. We still have to locate and specify features of contexts that we expect to be significant influences on performance in their own right and also to have interacting effects. It is in relation to this challenge that interest arises in the nature of expectations (in particular, expectations dealing with the importance of various kinds of performance and with the acceptability of various kinds of leeway in a performance).

EXPECTATIONS OF IMPORTANCE

One of Stevenson and Lee's (1990) major proposals is that differences exist across the three cultures considered—China, Japan, and the United States—in the relative importance attached to achievement in particular areas. There are, for instance, differences in the importance attached to achievement in reading as compared with mathematics. There are also differences in the importance attached to being a well-rounded, well-adjusted, happy individual as compared with being a good student.

This proposal helps account for the achievement differences that Stevenson and Lee (1990) observed. It also has the advantage of fitting nicely with other proposals to the effect that in any educational setting some particular ways of thinking and speaking are highly valued, whereas others are barely tolerated and still others are actively discouraged (e.g., Goodnow, 1990; Wertsch, 1991). Part of cognitive development in itself may then consist of the acquisition of these "cognitive values" (Goodnow, 1990).

The simple specification of degrees of importance, however, is not likely to offer a sufficient account of how differences in performance come about. To take Stevenson and Lee's (1990) proposal further, what might be added? Below is a set of possible expansions.

EXPANDING THE CONCEPT OF IMPORTANCE

Important for Whom?

One way in which the notion of importance has already been expanded consists of noting that the same expectations are not held out for all members of a group: a possibility that may help account for variations in performance within cultural groups. The expansion is most apparent in studies asking about the extent to which mathematics is regarded as more important for males than for females (e.g., Eccles & Jacobs, 1986; Parsons, Adler, & Kaczala, 1982). The same kind of expansion could also be made with regard to children from different socioeconomic backgrounds or to children seen as falling into various categories of ability (e.g., what is regarded as important for "the gifted" is not likely to be the same as what is regarded as important for those who are "slow"). What needs to be considered then in any analysis of context is not only the specification of what is regarded as important for most people but also the specification of the distinctions drawn between the people for whom a particular area of achievement is regarded as more versus less important.

Important for What Purpose?

Variations in importance can easily prompt speculation about how they arise. Why, for instance, is mathematics so highly prized in Chinese and Japanese schools? Why are Islamic studies at the top of the list in most schools in Malaysia? Answering those questions can lead in the direction of seeking conditions within a culture's history and structure. Islamic studies, for example, derives part of its importance in Malaysia from a social structure in which state and church are not firmly separated and advancement in many fields is influenced by the extent of demonstrated commitment to a particular religion. That direction, however, does not easily lead to predictions about children's performance. An alternate direction holds more promise for that purpose. This consists of attention to the kinds of justification that are offered in face-to-face interactions, for example, by teachers to parents, by parents and teachers to children, and—in time—by children to others or to themselves.

Some justifications, for instance, are highly specific. For example, an individual is told that he or she needs to reach a certain level of achievement to attend a particular school, enter a particular program, or progress from a particular grade to the next. Others are extremely general. This area of knowledge, for example, will help one cope with modern life (a frequent argument for the importance of acquiring computer skills). This area will develop one's capacity to reason (as in the argument that Latin helps develop logical thought). Still others have the appeal of conferring on the achiever a particular kind of identity —an identity, for instance, as one of the "bright" students or, as Hatano (1990) and Nunes (1995) emphasized, an identity as an educated or "schooled" person.

Does the kind of justification offered make a difference to performance? One line of impact lies in the extent to which a justification is open to challenge or question. It is feasible to determine whether a particular level of achievement will lead to a specific next step. In contrast, it is difficult to disprove the argument that achievement of this or that kind will be "good for you," or the argument—already within the repertoire of primary school children in Australia—that "if you don't go to school, you'll grow up 'dumb'" (Goodnow & Burns, 1985).

A further line of impact lies in the extent to which a justification helps sustain effort over a long and difficult period. Justifications in terms of identity, Hatano (1990) proposed, are particularly relevant when there are no obvious instrumental reasons for a long-term commitment. Learning to read in Japanese offers a specific example (Hatano, 1995). Japanese orthography contains two sets of syllabaries, made up, respectively, of kana characters and a combination of kana and kanji characters. The former is learned first, and most foreigners stop with this highly functional system (the second is considerably more difficult). What then persuades Japanese school children to make the major effort needed to learn the second system? The answer, Hatano (1995) proposed, lies in the linking made between this reading skill and identity. To be regarded as an educated Japanese, skill with the second system is essential.

Justifications in terms of identity, however, are not always facilitators of school performance or of school-like performance. One reminder on that score comes from Nunes (1995). In everyday life, adults may avoid the use of school-taught heuristics for solving arithmetic problems on the grounds that these are inappropriate for a "practical" person (Nunes, 1995). Within school, links to identity may also lead to avoidance of the forms of achievement that adults promote. Being one of "the lads" was part of a pattern of reluctant effort, both in school and on the shop floor, within the group of English boys that Willis (1977) studied. Avoiding the label of *burnout* (in the sense of being no longer resistant to adult pressure) was part of avoiding the science subjects promoted by teachers and parents in a U.S. high school (Eckert, 1989). In effect, we need to know both the kinds of justification that are offered for achievement by adults and the degree of appeal that they have for particular audiences.

Important Relative to What?

Importance is always relative. What we need to know for the analysis of contexts is the nature of the contrast cases. In Stevenson and Lee's (1990) analysis, for example, the importance of mathematics is contrasted with reading. Outside school, the contrast is between homework and a variety of other after-school activities (e.g., time with friends, household jobs, lessons in "nonschool" subjects).

Are there ways of taking further a contrast between what is "more" versus "less" important? One way to do so, I suggest, is to regard activities as being placed in four groups, each associated with degrees or occasions of effort.

In the first group are activities regarded as *top priority*. Every effort will be made to secure achievement in these areas. There is likely also to be no choice offered in this area: Competence must be achieved. In China and Japan, mathematics and being "a good student" emerge from Stevenson and Lee's (1990) report as being placed in this category.

113

The second group consists of activities regarded as *important but not top priority*. Effort toward achievement is expected in these areas but the degree expected is less than for the activities in the first set and may be cut back if achievement in the first set falls below expectations. Reading appears to be in this category in China and Japan, but not in the United States.

For examples of the third and fourth groups, I need to step outside the Stevenson and Lee (1990) report. The third consists of *lost opportunities:* activities foregone with a sense of regret and with the intention of picking them up again if circumstances permit. Not being able to take on a part-time paid job is in this category for many Australian students in the last year of high school (a year for concentrating on the final exam) and often during the first year of college (a time of uncertainty as to what is possible; J. Bowes, personal communication, May 1995). The same activity, I suspect, would not be in this category in China or Japan.

The final category covers areas of *acceptable ignorance* or *acceptable incompetence* (Goodnow, 1996). These are areas in which no effort is expected. Aiming at achievement in these areas may even be regarded with amusement or as wasted time. For an example, I draw from a comparison of Lebanese-Australian with Anglo-Australian mothers of children in the first year of school (Goodnow, Cashmore, Cotton, & Knight, 1984). (The term *Lebanese-Australian* refers to mothers born in Lebanon but who emigrated to Australia as adults or after their own schooling had been completed. The term *Anglo-Australian* refers to mothers with a monolingual English-speaking background.) The teachers wished to know why children from Lebanese-Australian families were often so "poorly prepared" for the first year of school and why so few of the mothers seemed interested in or enthusiastic about what the children did in kindergarten. A large part of the problem turned out to be that the Lebanese-Australian mothers regarded many of the children's activities (e.g., marching to music, singing, acting out stories, learning to tie one's shoelaces or button one's coat) in kindergarten and even first grade as a "waste of time": not simply low priority but useless. What, one mother asked, did these activities have to do with her son's becoming a doctor?

This set of four groups, it may be noted, includes no reference to *penalty activities:* the activities people will be assigned if they fail to achieve or to make an effort toward achievement in the valued areas. In Taiwan, I am told, "household jobs" are in this category. They would not usually be placed in this group by Australian parents. Penalty activities clearly have a place in any full analysis of ratings of importance, if only because they are important to avoid. The four divisions considered, however, will take us a considerable distance toward specifying differences among contexts in expectations of importance. (We might well, for example, ask people in various social groups to divide school activities into the several groups outlined.) The same divisions will also take us some distance toward making finer links between these expectations and levels of achievement or of effort toward achievement.

LEEWAY IN PERFORMANCE

Even when importance is more finely specified, importance by itself is not likely to offer a sufficient account of how differences in performance come about. What other conditions might be added?

One addition from Stevenson and Lee (1990) has to do with the steps that parents take to increase the likelihood that children can achieve in valued areas: steps such as expecting few household jobs or buying a desk to be used for the specific purpose of doing homework. That kind of addition, in the general form of implementation steps being added to the setting of goals, historically has been regarded as an important variable in analyses of achievement (e.g., Bourdieu, 1979; Jackson & Marsden, 1966). In effect, Stevenson and Lee's (1990) proposal helps strengthen a general concern with contexts as varying in the provision of implementation procedures for the goals that are set.

A second suggestion has less of a history and is the one to which I give attention. The variable in question is the nature of leeway. Any expectation about achievement comes not only with a tag indicating its importance but also with a tag indicating how much flexibility there is with regard to meeting a set goal. Flexibility with regard to time is the form of leeway suggested within the Michigan program and I shall begin with that. Added, however, are proposals related to the need to consider more widely the possibilities of flexibility, negotiations, and tradeoffs. The route to performance, I propose, reflects the combination of expectations about importance and about leeway, and both need specification.

INTRODUCING THE CONCEPT OF LEEWAY IN TIME TABLES

How much time can elapse before the decision is made that an expectation is not being met? Within the Michigan program, this kind of question appears in the form of asking the question, At what point do mothers become concerned about a child's falling below the mean of the class? When this kind of performance appears in Year 5, there is little difference among mothers from several cultural groups. In contrast, when this kind of performance appears in Year 1, mothers in the United States are the least likely of the groups considered to express concern (Chen & Uttal, 1988; Stevenson & Lee, 1990). When children are young, the results suggest, mothers in the United States are more prepared to wait for "good" performances to appear.

The reasons for this kind of difference are not yet clear. It may be that, in the U.S. school system, fewer decisions are made at the end of Year 1 about where a child will be placed in Year 2. It may also be that the culture as a whole contains a stronger belief in the possibilities of "catching up," of children being "late bloomers." Regardless of the base, however, here is an aspect of context that must affect performance and is underappreciated. How might this kind of possibility be taken further?

One possible research direction consists of turning to the structure of a society or a school system, asking where and when timelines contain various degrees or forms of leeway. This is the direction taken, for the analysis of societies, by Erikson (1968) and by Neugarten (1979). Erikson has pointed out that most societies contain "moratoria": periods in a person's life when there is greater tolerance than at other times for delay and time out. In Erikson's analysis, adolescence or youth is one such period. In Neugarten's analysis, periods after a war or after individual trauma have a similar quality. These are times when there is a certain level of forgiveness if the usual timetables are not met, provided that the reasons for doing so are acceptable.

This kind of analysis might well be extended to school systems. One might well ask, for instance, at what points or under what circumstances a school system has the greatest or the least tolerance for variable rates of progress toward an expected goal. The Australian school system, for example, contains a segment known as "infants' schools" or "infants' classes," covering a period from kindergarten (age 5) to Year 2 or Year 3. These schools are less common than they once were. In them, however, the tradition is one of considerable tolerance for individual differences in the rate at which children move toward the level of competence needed later in primary school.

Being "young," however, may not be the only circumstance that allows a flexible timeline. Universities also often exhibit flexible timelines toward the completion of a degree. In Australia, that flexibility is less than it once was. Nonetheless, the general level of flexibility with regard to time still remains more marked than it is for most of the Australian high school period. For any part of the education system then, one may well ask what circumstances or justifications accompany the presence of flexible timelines.

The exploration of leeway in time, however, does not need to proceed only at the structural level. At the level of face-to-face interactions, Nucci (1995) has drawn attention to the willingness of American parents, as compared with Brazilian parents, to allow children to make certain decisions for themselves (e.g., decisions about what to wear). Nucci also added that after a certain period of time has elapsed American parents begin to structure a child's choices. They begin, for example, to suggest what might be worn or to narrow the choices down to a few alternatives. We know very little about the nature of these grace periods, about their length or about the nature of the signals used to indicate that a grace period has elapsed or is about to end. Data of that kind, however, would clearly add to our understanding of the steps between a goal being set and the translation of that goal into performance.

EXPANDING THE CONCEPT OF LEEWAY

The General Possibility of Leeway, Negotiations, and Tradeoffs

Flexibility with regard to time is one aspect of a more general property, namely, the extent to which any expectation comes with some degree of flexibility or tolerance for how it will be met. The full exploration of leeway calls for attention to these other forms.

Leeway With Regard to Correct Answers

Mathematics provides an example of leeway with correct answers. At least in Australia and the United States, mathematics is often taught with an insistence on a precisely correct answer. If the correct answer is 4, then 3 is as wrong an answer as 33. Being close to the correct answer is as wrong as being out toward the edge of the target board in a game of darts: Only a "bull's eye" matters. I have seen only one classroom wherein children were explicitly taught to estimate the range within which an answer might fall. Is the answer likely to be, for example, less than 100? Less than 50? Less than 10? Apart from its relevance to everyday life, estimating the range of an answer—in particular, being able to recognize an improbable answer—is an important part of monitoring one's performance on any number problem. In addition, a lack of leeway on this score, especially if combined with the lack of leeway on procedures that Stodolsky (1988) has documented for U.S. classes in mathematics, may contribute to a lack of enthusiasm for the subject and to students' turning, if they can, to subjects that allow greater flexibility with regard to what will be treated as a correct or interesting answer.

Leeway With Regard to Acceptable
Alternatives or Tradeoffs

If we are to understand achievement, it is clearly useful to know how far others will accept a performance that to varying degrees falls short of an original expectation. It is also useful to know what will be accepted as an alternative to doing well in a particular area. To return to mathematics as an example, are there alternative routes—even in China or Japan—to being regarded as "a good student" or as "bright?" Would excellence in any other subject be accepted as a possible substitution? If there are no acceptable substitutes for doing well in mathematics, then we clearly have another contributing factor to efforts at achievement in this area.

Tradeoffs, I suggest, offer a particularly useful way of analyzing contexts of achievement and of helping to fill in the set of variables that give rise to specific levels of performance or effort. Each culture, for instance, may be thought of as offering particular kinds of tradeoffs, amazing or incomprehensible to others. Australians, for example, are regularly amused and amazed that U.S. universities allow football scholarships. Although sport is important in a country, there is no way of trading excellence in athletic skills for academic points.

Australians are also amazed by what seems to them to be a narrow base when it comes to considering academic excellence: an aggregate score for verbal skills and an aggregate score for number skills. Australians are accustomed to a system in which aggregate scores matter. In fact, the aggregate score on a state exam at the end of Year 12 determines entry not only into college but also into particular faculties, from medicine to veterinary science, dentistry, law, engineering, general science, or general arts. (With two exceptions, Australian universities are all supported by state or federal funds.) Again, with a few exceptions (one medical school, and some programs preparing teachers for preschools), there are none of the interviews with prospective students that usually occur in the United States. Students taking the Year-12 exams are assigned a number, eliminating attention to gender or ethnicity and making the aggregate score still more the determining criterion.

The bases to that all-important score, however, are many and varied, allowing for multiple tradeoffs in areas of skill. At the moment, for example, there are within the state of New South Wales around 50 subjects that are counted as "examinable subjects," that is, as subjects for which the state board will set an exam, mark it, and count it toward an aggregate on the basis of a student's chosen combination of 10 units (units represent the school subjects for which an examination is taken, either at a baseline 2-unit level or at a more advanced 3- or 4-unit level). For one student, for instance, the aggregate might be based on a combination of 4-unit mathematics, 2-unit physics, 2-unit chemistry, and 2-unit English. For another, the aggregate might be based on five subjects, all studied at 2-unit level: English, history, geography, Japanese, and Indonesian. The exams for which one sits need not be taught at the school one attends. Mandarin and Modern Greek, for instance, are examinable subjects but they are taught in a limited number of schools. The system might strike observers from outside the culture as very strange. Without a knowledge of the tradeoffs that are possible, however, national patterns of achievement would be difficult to interpret.

A knowledge of tradeoff patterns might in fact help account for some particular attributions for achievement. Where there are many options, Hatano (1990) suggests, and students have the opportunity to decline having to achieve in areas where they do not expect to shine, success may more often be attributed to talent than to effort. In contrast, attributions to effort as the basis for success—often commented on as the pattern for Chinese and Japanese students—may well be more likely when students operate within a system where the number of options is smaller and the possibility of "doing something else" is more limited.

The General Acceptability of Negotiations

How acceptable is it to negotiate with others about what one will do, especially if those others have a status generally regarded as higher than one's own? Within analyses of life in the English-speaking world, for example, there is a strong tendency toward regarding negotiations between parents and children as a given. In fact, socialization may even be described as directed not so much toward achieving compliance as it is directed toward teaching children the difference between acceptable and unacceptable ways to negotiate what may or may not be done (Kuczynski & Kochanska, 1990; Leonard, 1993).

The same kind of point has been made with regard to classrooms and to parent–teacher interactions. Teachers and students, it has been argued, negotiate an "agenda" that is acceptable to both (Mehan, 1979), or a degree and kind of order in the classroom that will be tolerable for both (e.g., Davies, 1982). Parents negotiate with teachers and school administrators, seeking alternative arrangements for their children and developing a sense of which person is likely to be the most approachable or the most able to make a hoped-for change (Alexander & Entwisle, 1988). Would it be best, for instance, to go to the child's classroom teacher or to the school principal?

It is tempting at this point to think that whole school systems or whole cultures might be described as varying in the degree to which they regard negotiation as possible or reasonable. More probable, I suggest, are differences in what is regarded as negotiable, in the people seen as having the right to negotiate (e.g., children may be seen as having little right to do so) and in the approval given to various ways of negotiating). This is not to argue that people approach all situations with an interest in determining what is negotiable. On the contrary, many situations are so taken for granted that alternatives are looked for only when challenges or difficulties arise (Bourdieu, 1990). What is normative, what is routine, carries us along without asking questions (Miller & Goodnow, 1995). The general point remains, however, that ideas and practices related to negotiations have considerable promise as one more way by which we may begin to specify the presence of leeway and the steps between the setting of a goal and its translation into performance.

TRANSLATING OTHERS' EXPECTATIONS INTO ONE'S OWN

To move from features of contexts to the actual performance of children, I have proposed that several steps need to be taken. We need to ask about the possible implications of particular differences in patterns of achievement. We also need to specify as clearly as possible the features of contexts that we consider to be influential: features such as the extent to which particular forms of achievement are regarded as important and as allowing various degrees and kinds of leeway.

One additional step needs also to be considered. For their performance to be influenced, children themselves need to make assessments of importance and leeway. These assessments may come to be similar to those of the adults in their social world. Chinese and Japanese children, for example, may come to regard mathematics as possessing the same degree of importance that their parents and teachers do (Stevenson & Lee, 1990). Similarity in assessments, however, cannot be taken for granted. In addition, regardless of the extent of similarity across generations, we need to ask, What are the processes by which children's own assessments come about?

That question has received considerable attention within analyses of socialization. These analyses have not been made with the phenomenon of school achievement in mind. The proposals offered within them, however, are useful additions to the examination of school performance.

Useful at the start is the insistence that the direction of influences is never one way. Particularly in school situations, it is tempting to think of influence as flowing from adults' expectations to children's expectations or assessments. That direction of influence undoubtedly occurs. Children's performances, however, also influence adults' assessments. Children's assessments of importance—the importance of school achievement, for instance, or of going to school at all—can also prompt a reassessment by adults. It is the recognition of mutual influence and mutual interdependence that underlies a variety of proposals to the effect that individuals and contexts "create one another" (Briggs, 1992), "shape each other" (Cole, 1985), "make each other up" (Shweder, 1990), or "co-construct" each other (Valsiner, 1988). The specific proposals may vary. The point agreed on, however, is that any account of differences in behaviors across contexts needs to consider the interwoven contributions of the context and of the individual.

A further useful addition consists of the proposal that the process of translation or influence—in any direction—is best thought of as involving several steps, with different conditions influencing each of these (Cashmore & Goodnow, 1985; Goodnow, 1992, 1995, 1996; Grusec & Goodnow, 1994). At the least, two steps are involved. One of these has to do with the perception of the other's message or position, a perception that may be accurate or inaccurate. The other has to do with the acceptance or rejection of the perceived position. The first step may be particularly influenced by conditions such as the clarity of the first person's position, diminishing the likelihood of error in assessing where the other stands. The second step may be more strongly influenced by the extent to which there is a sense of similarity or identity between oneself and the other, or a sense that the other's position would be a rewarding position to adopt.

Stepwise analyses of influence have predominantly arisen within analyses concerned with cross-generation agreement or with the meaning and bases of internalization. When applied to the occurrence of particular patterns of achievement, what do such analyses highlight?

Suppose we simplify matters by considering one part of the chain of influences: children's perception and possible acceptance of the degree of importance that parents and teachers assign to subjects such as mathematics and to school achievement in general.

Highlighted at the start are conditions influencing the likelihood that children will be aware of the adults' positions and perceive them accurately. We need to know, for example, about the extent to which, and the ways in which, parents and teachers make their position clear. The relative importance of mathematics, for instance, may be made clear not only verbally but also by such nonverbal means as the place it is given in the timetable: never the last subject of the day and never omitted in favor of some "lesser" event. In contrast, it may be far less easy for children to decipher advice to the effect that they should "do well" or "could do better."

Highlighted also are conditions that influence the likelihood that an adult's message will be accepted or rejected. One of those conditions is the extent to which children assess the adult's position as realistic.

The children of immigrant parents, for instance, are less sanguine about the kinds of jobs they will ultimately attain, or should aim for, than they describe their parents as being (Cashmore & Goodnow, 1985). A further condition relevant to school performance is the extent to which an adult's message is reinforced by the messages that others provide. The emphasis within developmental psychology tends to fall easily on the individual and on the family. Within analyses of cultural contexts, however, attention is given also to the extent to which there is consensus within the group. The greater the consensus in the group, it is argued, the more likely it is that a viewpoint will remain unexamined or unquestioned (e.g., Watson-Gegeo, 1992) and that individuals will assume that others think as they themselves do (Frijda & Mesquita, 1994).

Consensus within the group is not usually taken into account as a factor influencing school achievement. Its relevance to school achievement, however, is nicely brought out by results demonstrating that the presence of "like-minded" people both within the school and within the neighborhood helps students sustain the interest in achievement that they bring to high school (Steinberg et al., 1996). We have become accustomed to thinking of socialization as best sustained by an individual's coming to incorporate a particular value into the image of self or to feel that interest in a topic has been self-generated rather than being a response to external pressure or inducement. In the process, however, we may have come to shortchange the significance of being in the company of similar others. School achievement would appear to be an area where that imbalance might be usefully corrected.

In sum, there is a large agenda of research questions and possibilities still to be tackled within research on contexts of achievement. I have concentrated on questions and possibilities arising from specific parts of the Michigan program. That is in part because these are central to the analysis of achievement. It is also because I hope that this particular concentration will serve a specific purpose. My hope is that Harold Stevenson and his colleagues, far from seeing their work as over, will build still further on the challenging body of theory and research that they have already developed.

REFERENCES

Alexander, K. L., & Entwisle, D. R. (1988). Achievement in the first two years of school: Patterns and processes. *Monographs of the Society for Research in Child Development, 53* (2, Serial No. 218).

Bourdieu, P. (1979). *Distinction: A social critique of the judgment of taste*. London: Routledge & Kegan Paul.

Bourdieu, P. (1990). *A logic of practice*. Stanford, CA: Stanford University Press.

Briggs, J. (1992). Mazes of meaning: How a child and a culture create each other. In W. A. Corsaro & P. J. Miller (Eds.), *Interpretive approaches to children's socialization* (pp. 25–50). San Francisco: Jossey-Bass.

Cashmore, J., & Goodnow, J. J. (1985). Agreement between generations: A two-process model. *Child Development, 56,* 493–501.

Chen, C., & Uttal, D. H. (1988). Cultural values, parents' beliefs, and children's achievement in the United States and China. *Human Development, 31,* 351–358.

Cole, M. (1985). The zone of proximal development: Where culture and cognition create each other. In J. V. Wertsch (Ed.), *Culture, communication, and cognition* (pp. 146–161). Cambridge, England: Cambridge University Press.

Davies, B. (1982). *Life in the classroom and playground: The accounts of primary school children*. London: Routledge & Kegan Paul.

Eccles, J., & Jacobs, J. E. (1986). Social forces shape math attitudes and performance. *Signs: Journal of Women in Culture and Society, 11,* 367–380.

Eckert, P. (1989). *Jocks and burnouts*. New York: Teachers' College Press.

Erikson, E. (1968). *Identity: Youth and crisis*. New York: W. W. Norton.

Frijda, N. H., & Mesquita, B. (1994). The social roles and functions of emotions. In S. Kitayama & H. R. Markus (Eds.), *Emotion and culture* (pp. 51–88). Washington, DC: American Psychological Association.

Goodnow, J. J. (1990). The socialization of cognition: What's involved? In J. Stigler, R. A. Shweder, & G. Herdt (Eds.), *Cultural psychology: Essays on comparative human development* (pp. 259–286). Cambridge, England: Cambridge University Press.

Goodnow, J. J. (1992). Parents' ideas, children's ideas: The bases of congruence and divergence. In I. Sigel, A.V. McGillicuddy-DeLisi, & J. J. Goodnow (Eds.), *Parental belief systems* (2nd ed., pp. 293–318). Hillsdale, NJ: Erlbaum.

Goodnow, J. J. (1995). Acceptable disagreement across generations. In J. G. Smetana (Ed.), *Beliefs about parenting: Origins and developmental implications* (pp. 51–64). San Francisco: Jossey-Bass.

Goodnow, J. J. (1996). Acceptable ignorance, negotiable disagreement: An alternative view of learning. In D. R. Olson & N. Torrance (Eds.), *Handbook of education and human development* (pp. 345–368). Oxford, England: Blackwell.

Goodnow, J. J., & Burns, A. (1985). *Home and school: Child's eye view.* Sydney, Australia: Allen & Unwin.

Goodnow, J. J., Cashmore, J., Cotton, S., & Knight, R. (1984). Mothers' developmental timetables in two cultural groups. *International Journal of Psychology, 19,* 193–205.

Grusec, J. E., & Goodnow, J. J. (1994). The impact of parental methods on the child's internalization of values: A reconceptualization of current points of view. *Developmental Psychology, 30,* 4–19.

Hatano, G. (1990). Toward the cultural psychology of mathematical cognition: Commentary. *Monographs of the Society for Research in Child Development, 55* (Serial No. 221).

Hatano, G. (1995). The psychology of Japanese literacy: Expanding "the practice account." In L. Martin, K. Nelson, & E. Tobach (Eds.), *Sociocultural psychology: Theory and practice of doing and knowing* (pp. 250–275). Cambridge, England: Cambridge University Press.

Jackson, B., & Marsden, D. (1966). *Education and the working class.* Harmondsworth, England: Penguin.

Kuczynski, L., & Kochanska, G. (1990). Development of children's noncompliance strategies from toddlerhood to age 5. *Developmental Psychology, 26,* 398–408.

Leonard, R. (1993). Mother–child disputes as arenas for fostering negotiation skills. *Early Development and Parenting, 2,* 157–167.

Mehan, H. (1979). *Learning lessons: Social organization in the classroom.* Cambridge, MA: Harvard University Press.

Miller, P. J., & Goodnow, J. J. (1995). Cultural practices: Towards an integration of culture and development. In J. J. Goodnow, P. J. Miller, & F. Kessel (Eds.), *Cultural practices as contexts for development* (pp. 5–16). San Francisco: Jossey-Bass.

Neugarten, B. L. (1979). Time, age, and the life cycle. *American Journal of Psychiatry, 136*, 887–894.

Nucci, L. (1995). Mothers' beliefs regarding the personal domain of children. In J. G. Smetana (Ed.), *Beliefs about parenting: Origins and developmental implications* (pp. 81–98). San Francisco: Jossey-Bass.

Nunes, T. (1995). Cultural practices and the conception of individual differences: Theoretical and empirical considerations. In J. J. Goodnow, P. J. Miller, & F. Kessel (Eds.), *Cultural practices as contexts for development* (pp. 91–104). San Francisco: Jossey-Bass.

Parsons, J. G., Adler, T. F., & Kaczala, C. M. (1982). Socialization of achievement attitudes and beliefs. *Child Development, 53*, 310–321.

Shweder, R. A. (1990). Cultural psychology: What is it? In J. Stigler, R. A. Shweder, & G. Herdt (Eds.), *Cultural psychology: Essays on comparative human development* (pp. 1–43). Cambridge, England: Cambridge University Press.

Steinberg, L., Darling, N. E., & Fletcher, A. C. (1996). Authoritative parenting and adolescent adjustment: An ecological journey. In P. Moen, G. H. Elder, Jr., & K. Luescher (Eds.), *Examining lives in context* (pp. 423–466). New York: Guilford Press.

Stevenson, H., & Lee, S.-Y. (1990). Contexts of achievement. *Monographs of the Society for Research in Child Development, 55* (1–2, Serial No. 221).

Stodolsky, S. (1988). *The subject matters: Classroom activity in mathematics and social studies.* Chicago: University of Chicago Press.

Valsiner, J. (1988). Ontogeny of co-construction of culture within socially organized environmental settings. In J. Valsiner (Ed.), *Child development within culturally structured environments* (Vol. 2, pp. 283–297). Norwood, NJ: Erlbaum.

Watson-Gegeo, K. A. (1992). Thick explanation in the ethnographic study of child socialization: A longitudinal study of the problem of schooling for Kwara'ae (Solomon Islands) children. In W. A. Corsaro & P. J. Miller (Eds.), *Interpretive approaches to children's socialization* (pp. 51–66). San Francisco: Jossey-Bass.

Wertsch, J. V. (1991). *Voices of the mind.* Cambridge, MA: Harvard University Press.

Willis, P. (1977). *Learning to labour.* Aldershot, England: Gower.

5

Video Surveys: New Data for the Improvement of Classroom Instruction

James W. Stigler

This chapter explores the use of large-scale video surveys for the study and improvement of classroom instruction. I begin by discussing the current lack of information about classroom instruction, and argue that both understanding and improvement of classroom learning will require the collection of classroom process data. I next discuss video as data, pointing out its potentials and pitfalls. Finally, these points are illustrated by briefly describing the first large-scale video survey of classroom instruction, the video component of the Third International Mathematics and Science Study.

IMPROVING SCHOOLS

There has been a great deal of activity over the past decade focused on the improvement of schools. The motivation for these efforts is clear:

This chapter was prepared for the Festschrift in honor of Harold W. Stevenson. Portions of this chapter have been adapted from Stigler, J. W., Gonzales, P., Kawanaka, T., Knoll, S., & Serrano, A. (1997). *Methods and Findings of the TIMSS Videotape Classroom Study.* Washington, DC: U.S. Government Printing Office.

American students, compared with students in other industrialized countries, show poor levels of achievement, especially in mathematics and science. Yet despite efforts to improve schools, we still have not seen marked gains in achievement. Why is this?

A detailed analysis of current reform efforts is outside the scope of this chapter. However, I do wish to make the point that most of these efforts have placed relatively little emphasis on classroom instruction as a locus of change. Some reform efforts pursue what might be called political solutions to the problem. Voucher plans, and the movement for school choice, for example, assume that education will be improved much like species evolve; if customers—that is parents and children—are allowed to choose the school they wish to attend, good schools will thrive and bad ones will die, thus leading to an overall improvement in education. According to these views, the problem with schools is that they have not been subject to proper systems of control, systems that could be provided by market forces.

Other approaches to improving schools use what might be termed a "sandwich model." If clear content standards are specified (i.e., outcome goals) and then clear performance standards are defined so that we can measure whether or not we have achieved the content standards, then we can simply hold schools accountable for student outcomes. Left unspecified in this approach is what should come between the goals and the outcomes; this is left up to individual teachers and schools. If schools are held accountable for clearly specified outcomes, they will find a way to achieve the outcomes, or so the assumption goes.

Missing from each of these plans is any clear idea of why students are not learning in the first place, and what processes need to change in order to improve student performance. Classrooms, which must surely be the place in which students learn most of what they know about mathematics, are rarely alluded to in such plans. Some reformers say, "Who cares what teachers do to achieve results? Results are all that matter. Just reward the teachers who are successful, and the rest will take care of itself." Further, some even imply that to "tell" teachers how to teach, or even to intimate that they need to be told, is to deprofessionalize teachers. Teachers, these reformers say, can figure out for themselves, as professionals, how best to produce high-achieving students.

This line of thinking appears flawed to me, for several reasons. First, it assumes that teachers are failing to produce high levels of achievement because they have not been rewarded for doing so, or held accountable for not doing so. It further suggests that if the proper rewards were in place, achievement would follow. However, the vast majority of teachers work hard to teach to the best of their abilities. If their students do not learn, we can assume that most of these teachers would not know how to change their instruction in order to succeed. Further, I would argue that the lack of focus on classroom instruction as a process that can be studied and improved actually contributes to the deprofessionalization of teachers. Professions are distinguished as such, in part, by a shared body of knowledge about practice. No one would argue that a surgeon should not be told how to cut, that she should figure it out for herself. Deemphasizing the importance of teaching as a learnable craft serves to deemphasize the professionalism of teachers.

Emphasizing outcomes at the expense of processes also contradicts much of what we have learned over the past decade in efforts to improve quality in industry. The legendary W. Edwards Deming made the point that quality will not be improved by mass inspections of the product, but rather by careful examination of the processes that produce the product. Without examining the process and understanding what needs to be done to improve quality, it is not even possible to train workers effectively; the relevant information would be unavailable. Inspection can boost average quality somewhat, but not shift the whole distribution of outcomes upward.

The point is this: Efforts to improve schools need to include a focus on the processes of classroom instruction. This may not sound revolutionary; in fact, it may even sound obvious. As we will see in the next section, however, it is a point strangely absent from the debate over school improvement.

A DETOUR TO CALIFORNIA

As many states have struggled in recent years to improve teaching and learning in their schools, California has stood at the forefront. In the 1980s, the State of California published curriculum frameworks that laid out in some detail a set of standards for what should happen in the state's classrooms. The California Frameworks, as they are known, have been regarded by some as model blueprints for the reform of classroom teaching and learning in both reading and language arts and mathematics.

Over this same period, however, the achievement of California's students has declined. In the last National Assessment of Educational Progress (NAEP) California's students ranked last of the fifty states in both reading and mathematics, scoring significantly higher only than the territory of Guam. The paradox here was not lost on California's new Superintendent of Public Instruction. If the Frameworks are so good, why is achievement so low? In 1995, the superintendent formed two task forces—one for reading and language arts and one for mathematics—to assess the situation and to make recommendations that could be implemented immediately to turn the situation around. I served on the mathematics task force.

At the first meeting of the mathematics task force, discussion turned to the Framework. Did it overemphasize problem solving and concep-tual understanding at the expense of computational skills? Of course, there were many points of view expressed, but as the discussion progressed, one point became clear. Although the Framework had been the official State policy for some 8 years, there was no information regarding the extent to which the Framework was being implemented in California's schools. There were some case studies showing the dif-ficulties encountered by some teachers who struggled to implement the Framework, but no state-wide data relevant to the question. In fact, although the California Department of Education does collect data on student outcomes, it collects no data on any aspect of classroom in-struction.

This lack of data did not deter the Superintendent from immedi-ately adopting an addendum to the Framework stressing the importance of calculation skills in a balanced mathematics curriculum. At the same time, a decision was made to revise the Framework, a process that is currently underway. Still, the State has no plans to begin collecting data regarding what happens in classrooms. Is it any wonder that swings of the pendulum, rather than progress on the road to improvement, characterize the history of educational change in the United States?

We adopt a policy, but outcomes do not improve. Instead of studying how the policy was implemented, we decide that the policy must be mistaken, then adopt a different policy. Again, we take no steps to study whether the policy is implemented inside classrooms, or if implemented, how effectively the policy works. In this context, debate on the future of education necessarily stays at the level of ideology and opinion. Experts in a room debate and decide, but never gather the kind of data that could inform their decisions. It is hard to see how instruction could systematically improve under such circumstances.

WANTED: DATA ON THE PROCESS OF INSTRUCTION

Data on the process of classroom instruction are necessary for at least two reasons. First, data are necessary as a foundation on which to construct a theory of classroom instruction. Second, they are necessary as a means of evaluating the implementation and effectiveness of educational policy. In this section I will reflect on what such data should look like, or, which kinds of data would be most useful for the improvement of instruction.

To be most useful, data on classroom process should meet at least the following three criteria:

1. Data should be sampled and analyzed in meaningful units, the smallest of which, for instruction, would be the lesson. Instruction is a system, consisting of many parts functioning together. These parts include actions of the teacher and students as well as the goals,

materials, and classroom environments in which the instruction takes place. Because instruction is a complex system, it is important to study units in which the basic functioning of the constituent parts is maintained in a valid way. Of course, a full understanding of instruction requires attention to units other than the lesson: Teachers plan lessons in sequences, for example, that may span several weeks of classroom time. The point is simply that the lesson is the smallest unit that has validity for both researchers and practitioners, and that can be aggregated meaningfully in larger studies.

2. Data should be concrete, maintaining the full richness and complexity of classroom lessons, yet at the same time, be amenable to quantitative analyses. Quantifying dimensions of classroom instruction is important: How else can we study the relative effectiveness of different instructional styles, or monitor the implementation of educational policies over time. On the other hand, research on teaching will be limited if it cannot connect theories of teaching with concrete examples from real classrooms. The debate over teaching practices—for example, the debate over the California frameworks—is greatly hindered by the fact that researchers, teachers, and the public lack a common understanding, in concrete terms, of what words such as *hands-on* or *problem solving* actually mean. Not only does this lack of concrete referents impede research on teaching, but it also greatly impoverishes attempts to communicate the results of research.

3. Data should be relevant to multiple theories of instruction. Much of the classroom process data collected in the 1960s and 1970s was based on what was then the predominant theory of how children learn, that is, reinforcement theory. Researchers coded, for example, the frequency with which reinforcers were dispensed by teachers, in the form of praise or other kinds of rewards. This was logical at the time, but renders the data largely irrelevant to the interests of present-day researchers. If data are to maintain their relevance across changes in theoretical orientations they must be analyzable from multiple perspectives.

What kind of data might meet these criteria? Questionnaire assessments fall short on various grounds. By their very nature, they presuppose what is important about classroom instruction. If views of what to ask change over time, older data are rendered irrelevant. Additionally, questionnaires do not allow for qualitative analysis of instructional processes. We cannot study responses to a questionnaire and discover some new fact about classroom instruction—although we can learn how teachers believe they are teaching. Finally, the validity of questionnaires seems particularly problematic in the current environment, which lacks a vocabulary of shared meanings for describing instruction. A questionnaire that asks, for example, whether a teacher uses problem solving in the classroom assumes that a shared meaning for the term *problem solving* exists, both among teachers and among researchers. Unfortunately, such a shared meaning generally does not exist.

Observational checklists and objective coding schemes suffer from many of the same problems, especially when collected by live observers in the field. Although the meanings of the categories may be more comparable across observers than across questionnaire respondents— assuming that observers are carefully trained—they still provide a view of the classroom that is narrowly relevant to the investigator's specific purpose. For this reason, most data resulting from coding schemes applied by live observers are not of interest to other researchers working from other theoretical perspectives, or to anyone who wants a full description of teaching in the classroom context.

Because of concerns such as these I have been exploring the use of video records as data on which to build a science both for understanding and for improving classroom instruction.

VIDEO AS DATA

Observational studies have a long history in the social sciences. Video, as a type of observational data, is more recent. In this section I briefly explore some of the unique advantages, and unique challenges, of using video as data. I start with the advantages.

Advantages of Video Data

Video Data Are Concrete and Prequantitative

Whereas other forms of observational data presuppose particular theories of instruction and learning, video is generally open to interpretation from multiple perspectives. Because of this, it is possible to interest researchers from a diversity of disciplines and theoretical orientations in the analysis of a single set of video data.

This fact holds exciting prospects for the study of classroom instruction. Classroom instruction has been studied by researchers from a number of disciplines: psychology, anthropology, and sociology, to name a few. But rarely has it been possible for these researchers to analyze, interpret, and come to some common understandings of a set of data. This is because data collected by psychologists have not contained enough detail to satisfy the kind of interpretive activity favored by anthropologists. Similarly, data collected by anthropologists have sometimes appeared impressionistic and of questionable representativeness to psychologists. A carefully sampled set of video observations would be of interest to both groups, thus providing a basis for multidisciplinary collaboration.

In the same vein, video will have a longer shelf-life than other kinds of data. Researchers in the future, armed with different theories and different analytic techniques, will still be able to make sense of video records collected today. They will be able to study, for example, changes in instruction over time, an endeavor not possible today due to our lack of valid historical data on instructional practices.

A Source of New Ideas

Another advantage follows from the concrete nature of video data, but is important enough to warrant separate mention. Video data, unlike questionnaires or live observational coding schemes, allow for discovery of new ideas about teaching. Because these new ideas are concrete and grounded in practice, they have immediate practical significance for teachers. Questionnaires and coding schemes can help us to spot trends and relationships, but they cannot uncover a new way to teach the Pythagorean Theorem.

Video Allows Merging of Qualitative and Quantitative Analysis

Video makes it possible to merge qualitative and quantitative analyses in a way not possible with other kinds of data. With live-observer coding schemes the qualitative and quantitative analyses are done sequentially: First, initial qualitative analyses lead to the construction of the coding scheme; then, implementation of the coding scheme leads to a reevaluation of the qualitative analysis.

When video is available it is possible to move much more quickly between the two modes of analysis. Once a code is applied, the researcher can go back and look more closely at the video segments that have been categorized as similar. This kind of focused observation makes it possible to see, for example, that the segments differ from each other in some significant way, and this difference may form the basis for a new code.

This integration of qualitative and quantitative analysis has important implications for the development of theories of instruction. Theories developed in the context of video examples will have a set of such examples that can be linked to each construct in the theory. This solves a major problem with theories of instruction developed to this point: The constructs on which such theories rest often lack concrete referents, making them difficult to understand and communicate, and difficult to apply in real-life classroom settings.

Video Enables Study of Complex Processes

Classrooms are complex environments, and instruction is a complex process. Live observers are necessarily limited in what they can observe, and this places constraints on the kinds of assessments they can do. Video provides a way to overcome this problem: Observers can code video in multiple passes, coding different dimensions of classroom process on each pass. On one pass, for example, they might code the ways materials are used, on another the behavior of students.

Not only can coding be done in passes but it also can be done in slow motion. With video, for example, it is possible to transcribe the language of the classroom, enabling far more sophisticated analysis of complex discourse processes. Detailed coding of classroom discourse

137

would be unthinkable without the capacity to slow down and listen again.

Video also resolves problems of inter-rater reliability that are difficult to resolve in the context of live observations. The standard way to establish the reliability of observational measures is to send two observers to observe the same behavior, then compare the results of their coding. This is at minimum inconvenient, and is often infeasible for studies that are performed cross-culturally or in geographically distant locations. Using video to establish reliability means that the behavior can be brought to the observers instead of vice versa. Thus, in the context of a cross-cultural study, observers from different cultural and linguistic backgrounds can work collaboratively, in a controlled laboratory setting, to develop codes and establish their reliability using a common set of video data.

Using video also makes it far easier to train observers. With video, inter-rater reliability can be assessed not only between pairs of observers but between all observers and an expert "standard" observer. Disagreements can be resolved based on reviewing the video, making such disagreements into a valuable training opportunity. Also, the same segments of video can be used for training all observers, increasing the chances that coders will use categories in comparable ways.

Challenges in the Use of Video

There are also disadvantages, or significant issues that need to be addressed if video is to be used successfully.

Video Is Concrete and Vivid

The fact that video is concrete and vivid was discussed above as an advantage of video, but it also can be a disadvantage. Concrete images and anecdotes are vivid and powerful tools for representing and communicating information. One picture, it is said, is worth a thousand words. On the other hand, anecdotes can be misleading, and even completely unrepresentative of reality. Furthermore, research in cognitive psychology has shown that the human information processing system is easily misled by anecdotes, even in the face of contradictory and far more valid information. Video can be a treasure chest of insights. But it also can be deceiving unless it is collected on a large scale. Too small a library of images of teaching could mislead, and could allow researchers to mistake the superficial for the essential. A large-scale video survey, like the one described in this chapter, provides one possible way to resolve this tension between concrete images and statistical generalizations.

The Problem of Scaling Up

Most researchers who have used video to study classroom instruction have also studied very small samples: perhaps one, and usually not more than five or six, lessons. One reason for this must surely be the logistical challenges involved in implementing a video study on a large scale. In contrast with traditional surveys, which require intensive and thorough preparation up front, the most daunting part of video surveys is in the data management and analysis phase. Whereas information entered on questionnaires can easily be transformed into computer readable format, this is not so for video images. Thus, it is necessary to find a means to index the contents of the hundreds of hours of tape that can be collected in a video survey. Once data are indexed there is still the problem of coding. Coding of videotapes is renowned as highly labor intensive.

There are strategies available, however, for bringing the task under control. In the study I discuss in this chapter, we have developed specialized computer software to help us in this task. Emerging multimedia computing technologies will, over the next several years, revolutionize the conduct of video surveys, making them far more feasible than they have ever been in the past. In fact, video surveys already are a cost-effective means of studying classroom processes, generally costing less than a comparable study that uses live observers. The fact that video data can be reanalyzed for different purposes over time lowers the cost even further.

Standardization of Camera Procedures

Another issue in video research involves the effect that camera habits can have on the data. Left to their own devices, different videographers will photograph the same classroom lesson in different ways. One may focus in on individual students, another may shoot wide shots in order to give the broadest possible picture of what is happening in the classroom. Yet another might focus on the teacher or on the blackboard. Because the goal of the research is to study classroom instruction, not the videographers' camera habits, it is important to develop standardized procedures for using the camera and then to carefully train videographers to follow these procedures. This is not as simple as it might appear because deciding where to point the camera in a lesson can constrain the kinds of interpretations that will be possible using the resulting videotape. The solution requires the researcher to carefully think through the implications of different camera-use procedures, and then to decide on which standard procedures to follow in a given study.

The Problem of Observer Effects

Given that the camera is used in a consistent way, we must next consider the possible effect the camera might have on what happens in the classroom. Will students and teachers behave as usual with the camera present, or will observers get a view that is biased in some way? Might a teacher, knowing that she is to be videotaped, even prepare a special lesson just for the occasion that is unrepresentative of her normal practices?

This problem is not unique to video studies. Questionnaires have the same potential for bias: Teachers' questionnaire responses, as well as their behavior, may be biased toward cultural norms. On the other hand, it may actually be easier to gauge the degree of bias in video studies than in questionnaire studies. Teachers who try to alter their behavior for the videotaping will likely show some evidence that this is the case. Students may look puzzled or may not be able to follow routines that are clearly new for them.

It also should be noted that changing the way a teacher teaches is not accomplished easily, as much of the literature on teacher development suggests. It is highly unlikely that teaching could be improved significantly simply by placing a camera in the room. On the other hand, teachers will obviously try to do an especially good job, and may do some extra preparation, for a lesson that is to be videotaped. We may, therefore, see a somewhat idealized version of what the teacher normally does in the classroom.

In the study described in this chapter, three techniques were used for minimizing observer bias. First, instructions were standardized across teachers. Teachers generally do not want to bias the results of a study, but may inadvertently do so in an effort to help researchers. It is important, therefore, to clearly communicate the goal of the research to the teacher in carefully written, standard instructions. The teacher, when properly informed, becomes an important ally in the effort to obtain unbiased results. Teachers need to be told that the goal is to videotape a typical lesson, with typical defined as whatever they would have been doing had the videographer not shown up. Teachers can also be explicitly asked to prepare for the target lesson just as they would for a typical lesson.

Second, we attempted to assess the degree to which bias occurred. After the videotaping, teachers were asked to fill out a questionnaire in which they rated, for example, the typicality of what we would see on the videotape, and described in writing any aspect of the lesson they felt was not typical. We also asked teachers whether the lesson in the videotape was a stand-alone lesson or part of a sequence of lessons, and to describe what they did yesterday and what they plan to do in tomorrow's lesson. Lessons described as stand-alone and as having little relation to the lessons on adjoining days would be suspect for being special lessons constructed for the purpose of the videotaping. In this study, however, lessons were rarely described in this way.

Finally, researchers must use common sense in deciding the kinds of indicators that may be susceptible to bias, and taking this into account in interpreting the results of a study. It seems likely, for example, that students will try to be on their best behavior with a videographer present, and so we may not get a valid measure from video of the frequency with which teachers must discipline students. On the other hand, it seems unlikely that teachers will ask different kinds of questions while being videotaped than they would when the camera is not present. Some behaviors, such as the routines of classroom discourse, are so highly socialized as to be automatic and thus difficult to change.

Sampling and Validity

Observer effects are not the only threat to validity of video survey data. Sampling—of schools, teachers, class periods, lesson topics, and parts of the school year—is a major concern.

One key issue is the number of times any given teacher in the sample should be videotaped. This obviously will depend on the level of analysis to be used. If researchers need a valid and reliable picture of individual teachers, then they must tape the teacher multiple times as teachers vary from day to day in the kind of lesson they teach as well as in the success with which they implement the lesson. If researchers want a school level picture, or a national level picture, then they obviously can tape each teacher fewer times, provided they resist the temptation to view the resulting data as indicating anything reliable about the individual teacher.

On the other hand, taping each teacher once limits the kinds of generalizations that can be made about instruction. Teaching involves more than constructing and implementing lessons. It also involves weaving together multiple lessons into units that stretch out over days and weeks. If multiple teachers are taped once, it will be difficult to code the dynamics of teaching over the course of a unit. The important point is that one must be sensitive to the constraints that sampling decisions place on the interpretation of video data.

Another sampling issue concerns representativeness of the sample across the school year. This is especially important in cross-national surveys where centralized curricula can lead to high correlations of particular topics with particular months of the year. In Japan, for example, the eighth-grade mathematics curriculum devotes the first half of the school year to algebra, the second half to geometry. Clearly, the curriculum would not be fairly represented by taping in only one of these two parts of the year.

Finally, although initially it may seem desirable to sample particular topics in the curriculum in order to make comparisons more valid, in practice this is virtually impossible. Teachers may define topics so differently that the resulting samples become less rather than more comparable, especially across cultures. Randomization appears to be the most practical approach to ensuring the comparability of samples.

Confidentiality

The vast potential of any video dataset will still be largely untapped at the conclusion of the study. It is important, therefore, to make the data available to other researchers for further coding and analysis, especially because this potential for secondary analysis is one of the major advantages we have identified for video data. Yet, the fact that images of teachers and students appear on the tapes makes it more difficult than usual to protect the confidentiality of study participants. An important issue, therefore, concerns how procedures can be established to allow continued access to video data by researchers interested in secondary analysis.

One option is to disguise the participants by blurring their faces on the video. This can be accomplished with modern-day digital video editing tools, but it is expensive at present to do this for an entire dataset. A more practical approach is to define special access procedures that will enable us to protect the confidentiality of participants while still making the videos available as part of a restricted-use dataset. Agreement on such procedures among researchers and those with responsibility for protecting participants' confidentiality should be a high priority as more video surveys are planned.

THE VIDEO COMPONENT OF THE THIRD INTERNATIONAL MATHEMATICS AND SCIENCE STUDY

I have argued that we suffer a lack of both theory and data relevant to teaching and learning in classrooms. I have described the kind of data needed, and especially the role that video data might play in efforts to understand and improve classroom instruction. Now I turn to a specific example, the Third International Mathematics and Science Study Videotape Classroom Study. This study represents an unprecedented attempt to collect video records of classroom instruction on a large scale.

In this chapter I can only give a brief overview of the study, and present a few illustrative findings. A full description of the study can be found in Stigler, Gonzales, Kawanaka, Knoll, and Serrano (1997).

Background and Goals

The Videotape Classroom Study, a video survey of eighth-grade mathematics lessons in Germany, Japan, and the United States, was a part of the Third International Mathematics and Science Study (TIMSS), a comparative study of mathematics and science education in 41 countries (see U.S. Department of Education, 1996). Funded by the U.S. Department of Education's National Center for Education Statistics and the National Science Foundation, the video study was the first study ever to collect videotaped records of classroom instruction from nationally representative samples of teachers.

The Videotape Classroom Study had four goals:

- To provide a rich source of information regarding what goes on inside eighth-grade mathematics classes in the three countries
- To develop objective observational measures of classroom instruction to serve as quantitative indicators, at a national level, of teaching practices in the three countries
- To compare actual mathematics teaching methods in the United States and the other countries with those recommended in current reform documents and with teachers' perceptions of those recommendations
- To assess the feasibility of applying videotape methodology in future, wider-scale, national and international surveys of classroom instructional practices.

Brief Overview of Methods

The study sample included 231 eighth-grade mathematics classrooms: 100 in Germany, 50 in Japan, and 81 in the United States. Sampling was done in two stages. First, schools were sampled, then classrooms within schools. Sampling was random within strata, defined appropriately for each country. Teachers who refused to be videotaped were replaced by teachers in different schools according to the sampling plan. Principals were never allowed to substitute a different teacher or class period from the one that was randomly selected. The exact procedures used varied by country, but in each case procedures were adopted that were expected to yield a sample representative of the instruction received by eighth-grade mathematics students in each nation.

Two main types of data were collected in the video study: videotapes and questionnaire responses. We also collected supplementary materials (e.g., copies of textbook pages or worksheets) deemed helpful for understanding the lesson. Each classroom was videotaped once, on a date convenient for the teacher. One complete lesson—as defined by the teacher—was videotaped in each classroom. A primary purpose of the questionnaire was to get teachers' judgments of how typical the videotaped lesson was compared with what we would normally see in their classroom.

Teachers were initially contacted by a project coordinator in each country who explained the goals of the study and scheduled the date and time for videotaping. Because teachers knew when the taping was to take place, we knew they might attempt to prepare in some way for the event. In order to mitigate any bias that might be caused by their preparation, we gave teachers in each country a common set of instructions. We told teachers that our goal was to see what typically happens in the mathematics classrooms of their country, that is, what they would have done had we not been videotaping.

Only one camera was used to videotape each lesson, and it usually focused on the teacher. Standardized procedures for camera use were developed, and videographers were trained in the application of these procedures. (In fact, eighth-grade mathematics instruction in all three cultures is primarily whole-class and teacher directed. Studies of other subjects or at other grade levels would no doubt require different procedures for camera use, or perhaps even an additional camera, to capture the instruction.)

Tapes were encoded and stored digitally on CD-ROM, and were accessed and analyzed using multimedia database software developed

145

especially for this project. All lessons were transcribed, and then analyzed on a number of dimensions by teams of coders who were native speakers of the three languages. Analyses focused on the content and organization of the lessons, as well as on the instructional practices used by teachers during the lessons.

Constructing the Multimedia Database

Once the tapes were collected, they were sent to UCLA for transcription, coding, and analysis. The first step in this process was to digitize the video and store it in a multimedia database, together with scanned images of supplementary materials. Digital video offers several advantages over videotape for use in video studies. The resulting files are far more durable and long-lasting than videotape, and they will not wear out or degrade with repeated playing and re-playing of parts of the video, as happens during analysis. Digital video also enables random, instantaneous access to any location in the video, a feature that makes possible far more sophisticated analyses than are possible with videotape.

Once the videos were digitized, they were transcribed, and the transcripts were linked by time codes to the video in the multimedia database (see Figure 1). Transcription of videotapes is essential for coding and analysis. Without a transcript, coders have difficulty hearing, much less interpreting, the complex flow of events that stream past in a classroom lesson. It also is possible to code some aspects of instruction directly from the transcript, without viewing the video at all. We thus transcribed, as accurately as possible, the words spoken by both the teacher and the students in each lesson, and, for German and Japanese lessons, translated the transcriptions into English.

We had several reasons for translating the German and Japanese tapes into English. First, translations were used for training coders from different cultures to apply codes in a comparable way, and for establishing independent inter-rater reliability of codes across coders from different cultures. Even though a translation is never perfect, agreement between coders working with a translation can give us a rough estimate of how reliable a code is. A second purpose for the translation was to aid us in multi-language searches of the database. If we want to locate,

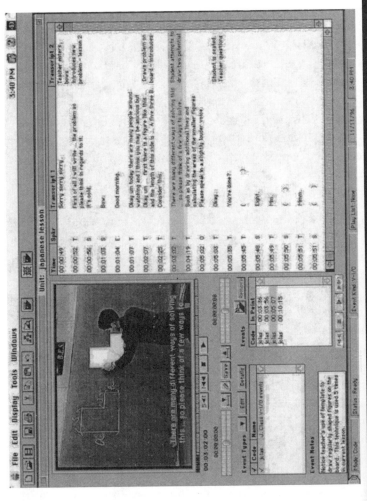

Figure 1

Multimedia database software used for transcription, coding, and analysis in the TIMSS video study. (Software is marketed as vPrism by Digital Lava, Inc., Los Angeles, CA.)

for example, times when a teacher discussed the concept of area we can search using the English word "area." Finally, having the lessons translated allows members of the research team not fluent in German or Japanese to view and understand lessons taught in those languages.

Using the multimedia database software system illustrated in Figure 1, coders had instant access to the video as they worked with the linked transcript, making it easy to retrieve the context needed for interpreting the transcript. On-screen controls allowed them to move instantly to the point in the video that corresponded to the highlighted transcript record, or to the point in the transcript closest in time to the current frame of video. Depending on the code, codes could be marked either as time codes in the video or as highlighting in the transcript. All event codes were marked, stored, and linked with a time code to the video within the same database.

Deciding What to Code

In deciding what to code we had to keep two goals in mind: First, we wanted to code aspects of instruction that related to our developing construct of instructional quality. Second, we wanted the codes we used to provide a valid picture of instruction in three different cultures.

For the first goal, we sought ideas of what to code from the research literature on the teaching and learning of mathematics, and from reform documents such as the *National Council of Teachers of Mathematics Professional Teaching Standards* that make clear recommendations about how mathematics ought to be taught. We wanted to code both the structural aspects of instruction, that is, those things that the teacher most likely planned ahead of time, and the on-line aspects of instruction, that is, the processes that unfold as the lesson progresses.

The dimensions of instruction we judged most important included the following:

- *The nature of the work environment.* How many students are in the class? Do they work in groups or individually? How are the desks arranged? Do they have access to books and other materials? Is the class interrupted frequently? Do the lessons stay on course, or do they meander into irrelevant talk?

- *The nature of the work in which the students are engaged.* How much time is devoted to skills, problem-solving, and deepening of conceptual understanding? How advanced is the curriculum? How coherent is the content across the lesson? What is the level of mathematics in which students are engaged?
- *The methods teachers use for engaging students in work.* How do teachers structure lessons? How do teachers set up for seatwork, and how do they evaluate the products of seatwork? What is the teacher's role during seatwork? What kinds of discourse do teachers engage in during classwork? What kinds of performance expectations do teachers convey to students about the nature of mathematics?

Our second goal was to accurately portray instruction in Germany, Japan, and the United States. Toward this end, we were concerned that our description of classrooms in other countries make sense from within those cultures, and not just from the American point of view. One of the major opportunities of this study, after all, was that we might discover approaches to mathematics teaching in other cultures that we would not discover looking in our culture alone. We wanted to be sure that if different cultural scripts underlie instruction in each country, we would have a way to discover these scripts.

For this reason, we also sought coding ideas from the tapes themselves. In a field test, in May, 1994, we collected nine tapes from each country. We convened a team of six code developers—two from Germany, two from Japan, and two from the United States—to spend the summer watching and discussing the contents of the tapes to develop a deep understanding of how teachers construct and implement lessons in each country.

The process was a straightforward one: we would watch a tape, discuss it, and then watch another. As we worked our way through the 27 tapes we began to generate hypotheses about what the key cross-cultural differences might be. These hypotheses formed the basis of codes, that is, objective procedures that could be used to describe the videotapes quantitatively. We also developed some hypotheses about

149

general scripts that describe the overall process of a lesson, and devised ways to validate these scripts against the video data.

First-Pass Coding: Constructing the Lesson Tables

We found it useful to have an intermediate representation of each lesson that could serve to guide coders as they tried to comprehend a lesson, and that could be coded itself. For this purpose, our first step in coding the lessons was to construct a table that maps out the lesson along several dimensions. Briefly, the table included the following information:

- *Organization of class.* Each videotape was divided into three segments: pre-lesson activities (Pre-LA), lesson, and post-lesson activities (Post-LA). The lesson needed to be defined in this way because the lesson would be the basic unit of analysis in the study.
- *Outside interruptions.* Interruptions from outside the class that take up time during the lesson (e.g., announcements over the public address system) were marked on the tables as well.
- *Organization of interaction.* The lesson was divided into periods of classwork (CW), periods of seatwork (SW), and periods of mixed organization. Seatwork segments were characterized as being Individual (students working on their own, individually), Group, or Mixed.
- *Activity segments.* Each classwork and seatwork segment was further divided, exhaustively, into activity segments according to changes in pedagogical function. We defined four major categories of activities: Setting Up, Working On, Sharing, and Teacher Talk/Demonstration. (Each of these were divided into subcategories, which will be defined more completely below.)
- *Mathematical content of the lesson.* The mathematical content of the lesson was described in detail. Content was marked, for analytical purposes, into units, which are noted on the table: Tasks, Situations, Principles/Properties/Definitions, Teacher Alternative Solution Methods (TASM), and Student Generated Solution Methods (SGSM; a more detailed description of each can be found below). In addition,

frames from the video were digitized and included in the table to help illustrate the flow and content of the lesson.

An example of what the resulting tables looked like is shown in Figure 2, which represents one of the Japanese lessons in our sample (JP-012). The table contains five columns. The first column indicates the time code at which each segment begins as well as the corresponding page number from the printed lesson transcript. The second column shows the segmentation of the lesson by organization of interaction (e.g., CW = Classwork), the third by activity (e.g., T/S = Task/Situations). The fourth and fifth columns show the symbolic description of the content and the concrete description of the content, respectively. Rows with lines between them show segment boundaries. Seatwork segments are shaded gray. The acronyms used refer to the coding categories described above.

As mentioned above, these first-pass tables served two functions. First, they were used by subsequent coders to get oriented to the contents of the videotapes. Often it takes a great deal of time for coders to figure out what is happening in a lesson. The tables ease the way, providing an overview of the structure and content of each lesson.

A second use for the tables was as objects of coding themselves. Some aspects of the lesson can be coded from the tables without even going back to the videotapes. Examples of such codes include TIMSS content category, nature of tasks and situations, and changes in mathematical complexity over the course of the lesson.

ILLUSTRATIVE RESULTS OF THE VIDEO STUDY

Because the purpose of this chapter is mainly to explore the potential of video surveys, I will present only a few, illustrative results from the video study. First, I will introduce some of the quantitative indicators used in the study. Second, I will present a more qualitative description of the instructional processes that underlie the indicators. A full description may be found in Stigler et al. (1997).

ID:
Topic: JP012
1.4.1 Transformations
Materials: Chalkboard; computer

Page # (Time)	Organi -zation	Activity	Content Symbol	Description of Content
1 (00:01)	Pre-LA			
1 (00:27)	CW	Working On: T/S/PPD	PPD1	(Computer) The triangles between two parallel lines have the same areas. 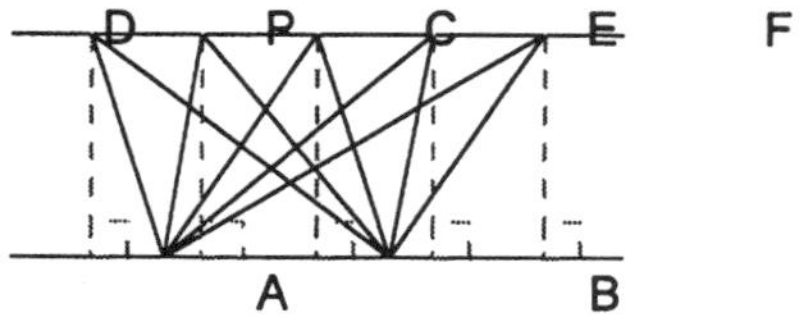
1 (01:26)		Setting Up: M	S1	(Chalkboard) There is Eda's land. There is Azusa's land. And these two peoples' border line is bent but we want to make it straight. 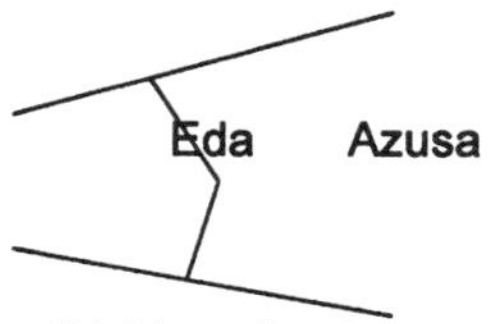
3 (03:34)			T1 [A]	Try thinking about the methods of changing this shape without changing the area.

Figure 2

Example of first-pass coding table for Japanese lesson (JP-012).

	SW: I	Working On: T/S/PPD		
3 (04:05)				
4 (07:04)	SW: SG	"People who have come up with an idea for now work with Mr. Ishikawa, and and people who want to discuss it with your friends, you can do so. And for now I have placed some hint cards up here so people who want to refer to those, please go ahead."		
16 (19:20)	CW	Sharing: T/S	SGSM1	First you make a triangle. Then you draw a line parallel to the base of triangle. Since the areas of triangles between two parallel lines are the same we can draw a line here. [See the diagram]
			SGSM2	We make a triangle and draw a line parallel to the base of the triangle by fitting it with the apex. Since the length of the base doesn't change and the height in between the parallel lines doesn't change. So wherever you draw it the area doesn't change with the triangle that we got first.

Figure continues

153

19 (22:57)		Setting Up: Phys/Dir	S2	(Chalkboard) 
19 (23:25)			T2 [A]	Without changing the area please try making it into a triangle.
19 (23:39)	SW: I	Working On: T/S/PPD		"Then people who are done please go to Mr. Ishikawa again. And people who want hints I will leave hint cards here so please look at them and try doing it. It's also fine to do it with your friends." (Hint cards unidentified.)
21 (26:47)	SW: SG		SGSM1	"We will make them ABCD." [Draw a diagonal line AC and make a triangle by drawing a parallel line going through D]
			SGSM2	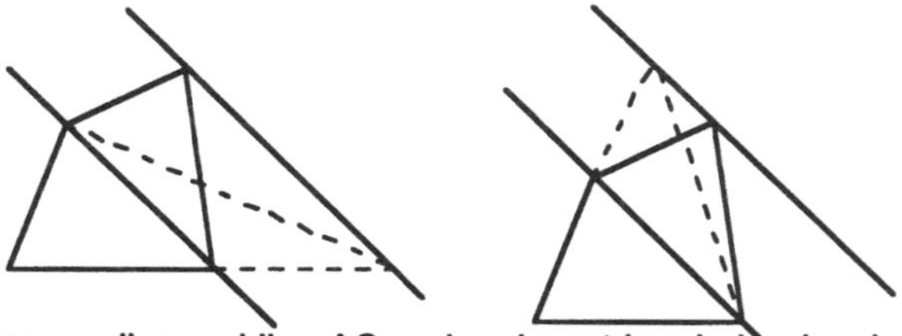
37 (46:11)	CW	Sharing: T/S	SGSM3	[Draw a diagonal line AC and make a triangle by drawing a parallel line going through B]

Figure 2 (*Continued*)

Figure continues

SGSM4

SGSM5

SGSM6

[Draw a diagonal line BD and make a triangle by drawing a parallel line going through A]

39 (48:58) 40 (49:47)		Working On: HW	SGSM7 SGSM8	[Draw a diagonal line BD and make a triangle by drawing a parallel line going through C] 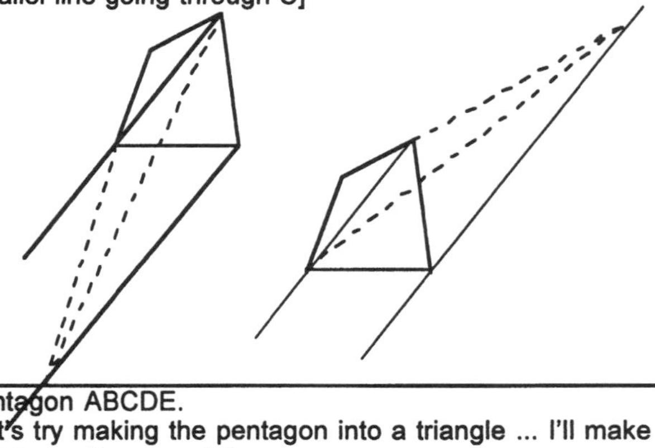
40 (50:25 ~50:45)	Post-LA		HS1 HT1	Pentagon ABCDE. "Let's try making the pentagon into a triangle … I'll make that then a homework."

Figure 2 ° (*Continued*)

Quantitative Indicators

A number of indicators were developed in the TIMSS video study that were used to compare instruction across the three countries in the study (Germany, Japan, and the United States). In this section I focus on some of the indicators used to measure (a) the kind of mathematics being taught in the three countries, and (b) the kind of thinking in which students were engaged during the lesson.

Number of Topics and Topic Segments per Lesson

Classroom instruction is inherently complex and multidimensional. For purposes of analysis, however, we must describe instruction in layers, of which mathematical content clearly is one of the most significant. It is difficult to draw the line between what is taught and how it is taught. Still, it is useful to examine content apart from the lesson in which it is embedded. The rationale for this is simple: No matter how good the teaching is, if a lesson does not include rich mathematical content it is unlikely that many students will construct a deep understanding of mathematics from the lesson.

Our first step in coding the mathematical content of the video lessons was to categorize the content of the lessons using the TIMSS content coding scheme. This coding scheme differentiates the main topics taught in the eighth-grade curricula of the 41 countries that participated in TIMSS. The complete system, which included 44 categories, is available in Robitaille, McKnight, Schmidt, Britton, Raizen, and Nicol (1993).

I will not go into detail regarding the distributions of lessons across topics in the three countries. However, some general findings are of interest. The most frequent topic in the United States sample (about 40% of the lessons) was *numbers*, which included such topics as whole number operations, fractions, decimals, and so forth. Only 13% of German lessons, and 0% of Japanese lessons, were devoted to these topics. In the German sample, the two most common topics were geometry: position, visualization, and shape, and functions, relations, and equations. In the Japanese sample, by far the most common topic was

157

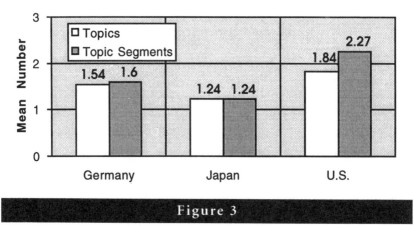

Figure 3

Average number of topics and topic segments per lesson in each country.

geometry: symmetry, congruence, and similarity, followed by validation and structure.[1]

Because a lesson could contain more than one topic, we next divided lessons into topic segments, that is, the points in the lesson at which the topic shifts from one to another. A shift in topic is a clear shift in the primary content of the lesson and is usually marked by an announcement by the teacher. For example, in one lesson the teacher says, "Okay let's still start something new today. Your school exercise book please." This is a clear signal that the topic is about to change, thus marking the beginning of a new topic segment. If a lesson had only one topic then it would, by definition, contain only one topic segment. However, many lessons had more than one topic. In this case, the number of topic segments might equal the number of topics (i.e., there could be one segment for each topic) or it might exceed the number of topics if, for example, the lesson alternated from a segment of one topic, to a segment of another, to another segment of the original topic.

As shown in Figure 3, American lessons contained significantly more topics than did Japanese lessons, and significantly more topic

---

[1]Although the German and United States lessons were sampled evenly across the entire school year, this was not the case in Japan. The preponderance of geometry in the Japanese sample is in part due to this bias. In an attempt to counteract this potential problem, we conducted some analyses on balanced subsamples of algebra and geometry lessons in each country.

Exhibit 1		
Average Grade Level of Content by International Standards		
Country	Mean	SD
Germany	8.65	1.90
Japan	9.07	1.08
United States	7.53	2.45

segments than both Japanese and German lessons. Also, German lessons contained more topic segments than did Japanese lessons.[2]

Level of Mathematical Content

It is not possible, a priori, to say that one topic is more complex than another. However, it is possible to make an empirical judgment of how advanced a topic is based on its placement in mathematics curricula around the world. We were able to make use of the TIMSS curriculum analyses, conducted by William Schmidt and his colleagues at Michigan State University, to make such a judgment. The TIMSS content codes for each lesson were assigned a number indicating the modal grade level at which the majority of the more than 40 countries studied gave the most concentrated curricular attention to the topic. Average level for each lesson was obtained by averaging the MSU index for all topics coded for the lesson.

The average grade level of topics covered in the video sample, as indicated by the MSU index, is shown in Exhibit 1. In terms of this index, the United States sample lagged significantly behind Germany and Japan.[3] By international standards, the mathematical content of

---

[2] One-way ANOVA of average number of topics across countries, $F(2,227) = 4.91, p < .01$; Bonferroni contrasts at .05 level of significance showed US > J.

[3] One-way ANOVA of average number of topic segments across countries, $F(2,227) = 7.46, p < .001$; Bonferroni contrasts at .05 level of significance showed US > G > J.

One-way ANOVA of average level of content across countries, $F(2,221) = 10.97, p < .001$; Bonferroni contrasts at .05 level of significance showed G, J > US.

U.S. lessons was at a seventh-grade level, whereas German and Japanese lessons fell at the high eighth- or even ninth-grade level.

Concepts and Applications

We next examined, for each topic covered in the lesson, whether the topic included concepts, applications, or both. We defined these terms broadly to catch all instances in which students might have constructed concepts or learned to apply them.

- *Concept* was coded when the only treatment of the topic in the lesson involved the presentation of information, through either a statement or a derivation of general mathematical principles, properties, or definitions (e.g., formulas and theorems), or statement or derivation of a method for solving a class of problems. A concept can be presented through a concrete example or abstractly. It can be introduced for the first time or simply be restated.
- *Application* was coded when the only treatment of the topic in the lesson was as an application to the solving of a specific mathematical problem. Mathematical concepts were not explicitly stated or discussed. The emphasis was on developing skills for solving specific types of problems.
- *Both* was coded when a topic included, somewhere in the lesson, both concepts and applications. (If a mathematical concept was stated that did not directly relate to the topic, it was not counted as a concept.)

As shown in Figure 4, U.S. lessons had significantly lower percentages of topics that consisted of concepts only than did either German or Japanese lessons. In addition U.S. lessons had a higher percentage of topics that consisted of applications only than did Japanese lessons.[4]

---

[4]One-way ANOVA of average percentage of topics in each lesson that include concepts across countries, $F(2,225) = 7.39$, $p < .001$; Bonferroni contrasts at .05 level of significance showed G, J > US.

One-way ANOVA of average percentage of topics in each lesson that include applications across countries, $F(2,225) = 7.83$, $p < .001$; Bonferroni contrasts at .05 level of significance showed US > J.

One-way ANOVA of average percentage of topics in each lesson that include both concepts and applications across countries, $F(2,225) = 1.3$, $p = .27$.

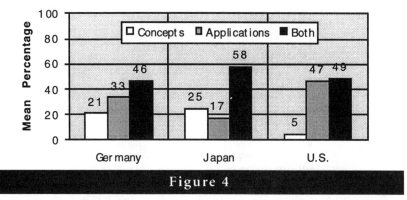

Figure 4

Average percentage of topics in each lesson that include concepts, applications, or both.

When concepts were included in the lesson, they could be stated or they could be developed. A concept was coded as *stated* if it was simply provided by the teacher or students, but not explained or derived. For example, the teacher, in the course of solving a problem at the board, might simply remind the students of the Pythagorean Theorem—for example, "The formula for finding the length of the hypotenuse of a right triangle is $a^2 + b^2 = c^2 \ldots$"—to guide the solution of the problem. The focus here is on the mathematical information itself rather than on the process of deriving it. A concept was coded as *developed* when it was derived and explained by the teacher or the teacher and students collaboratively to increase students' understanding of the concept. The form of the derivation could be through proof, experimentation, or both.

The results of coding concepts as stated versus developed are shown in Figure 5. Concepts were significantly more likely to be only stated in the American lessons than in either the German or Japanese lessons.[5]

---

[5]One-way ANOVA of average percentage of topics in each lesson that contained developed concepts across countries, $F(2,169) = 48.06$, $p < .001$; Bonferroni contrasts at .05 level of significance showed G, J > US.

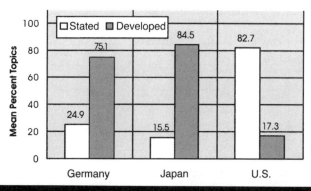

Figure 5

Average percentage of topics in each lesson that contained concepts that were developed vs. only stated.

Global Ratings of Quality

As mentioned in the introduction, one advantage of collecting video data is that they can be analyzed from multiple perspectives. We exploited this advantage in the video study by having an independent group of researchers who are experts in mathematics and mathematics teaching perform secondary analyses of the content of the lessons. There were four members of this group, which we called the Math Content Group. One had taught mathematics primarily at the high school level, one primarily at the college level but with extensive experience also teaching high school students, one primarily at the college level, and one at both college and graduate levels.[6]

The group was assigned the task of analyzing the mathematical content of each lesson based only on information contained in the lesson tables (described above). The group worked with a subsample of 90 lessons, 30 from each country. To reduce the possibility of bias, tables were disguised so that the group would not know the country of origin. This typically required only minor changes in such details as the

---

[6]This group was headed by Alfred Manaster, Professor of Mathematics at the University of California, San Diego. Other members of the group were Barbara Griggs Wells, Phillip Emig, and Wallace Etterbeek.

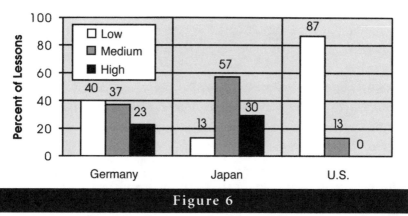

Figure 6

Percentage of lessons rated as low, medium, and high quality of mathematical content by the Math Content Group.

names of persons and currencies. The country of origin was not revealed until all coding was complete. Although the group was denied the additional information that would have been provided by looking at the videotapes, the advantage to our project of having a blind analysis of content was enormous.

The Math Content Group undertook a number of analyses. In the current chapter I will present only one: the group's overall judgment of the quality of the mathematical content of each lesson. They rated each lesson on a three point scale: low, medium, or high. Although the measure is subjective, there was high agreement among the independent raters. A summary of these ratings is presented in Figure 6. Both German and Japanese lessons received significantly higher quality ratings than U.S. lessons.[7]

Student Thinking During Seatwork

Finally, we coded the kinds of tasks students worked on during periods of seatwork. It is not possible to know what students are doing as they sit at their desks during classwork. It is possible, however, to characterize

---

[7]Comparison of lessons rated as low, medium, and high of mathematical content across countries, Pearson Chi-Square with 4 degrees of freedom = 34.03, $p < .001$; Bonferroni contrasts at .05 level of significance showed J > US, G > US.

the specific tasks they are assigned by the teacher to work on during seatwork. We coded tasks into three mutually exclusive categories:

- Practice Routine Procedures. This category was coded to describe tasks in which students were asked to apply known solution methods or procedures to the solution of routine problems.
- Invent New Solutions/Think. This was coded to describe tasks in which students had to create or invent solution methods, proofs, or procedures on their own, or in which the main task was to think or reason.
- Apply Concepts in New Situations. This was coded whenever the seatwork task did not fall into one of the other two categories. The tasks coded into this category generally involved transferring a known concept or procedure into a new situation, hence the label.

The average percentage of seatwork time spent in each of the three kinds of tasks is shown in Figure 7. Clearly, this indicator differentiates Japan from both Germany and the United States. Japanese students spent less time practicing routine procedures and more time inventing new solutions or thinking about mathematical problems.[8]

Qualitative Descriptions

I can not go into detail here on the qualitative findings of the study. However, I do want to say enough to illustrate the importance of qualitative analyses, especially in the context of quantitative indicators such as those presented above. These indicators show that the content in American classrooms lags in a general way behind that of both Ger-

[8]One-way ANOVA by country for average percentage of seatwork time spent in practice procedure $F(2,200) = 60.21$, $p < .001$; Bonferroni contrasts at .05 level of significance showed G, US > J.

One-way ANOVA by country for average percentage of seatwork time spent in application of concepts $F(2,200) = 2.63$, $p = .07$; Bonferroni contrasts at .05 level of significance revealed no significant effects.

One-way ANOVA by country for average percentage of seatwork time spent in inventing new solutions and thinking about mathematical problems $F(2,200) = 66.32$, $p < .001$; Bonferroni contrasts at .05 level of significance showed J > G, US.

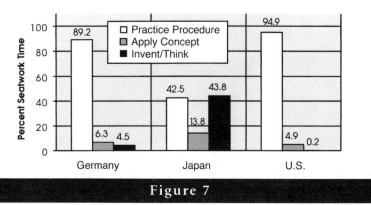

Figure 7

Average percentage of seatwork time spent in three kinds of tasks.

many and Japan. They showed that American lessons cover more topics, focus less on concepts, and, where they do include concepts, tend only to state the concepts rather than develop them. They also showed that Japanese students engage in more thinking during seatwork than either German or American students.

Although these differences are interesting, it is critical to note that nothing from these quantitative comparisons answers the key question of how teachers in Japan teach a lesson. Lessons, after all, are more than the sums of their parts. They are systems, with parts that interact in complex ways. Quantitative indicators result from the system of instruction, but they do not allow us to see the system itself. For this we need to look in a qualitative way at the videos; to describe how teaching works in different cultures. Indeed, this is another form of the same problem teachers confront when faced with recommended features of "reform" instruction: How can such features be implemented in a lesson with real students, real content, and real materials?

Qualitative analyses can allow us to identify, for example, different cultural scripts that generate the lessons in the study. To illustrate, Japanese teachers appeared to pursue a different goal than American teachers. Whereas American teachers designed their lessons to produce procedural competence, Japanese teachers appeared to stress understanding and conceptual growth as the goal of their lessons. The sequence of

165

activities in typical lessons from the two countries followed this difference in goals.

American lessons tended to start with the teacher demonstrating, step-by-step, how to solve a particular kind of problem. The demonstration usually was accomplished interactively, with students being called on to produce each new step. After the class completed several examples this way, the teacher typically assigned students to practice a few more examples on their own. As students practiced, the teacher would move from student to student, tutoring those students who experienced difficulty.

Japanese lessons proceeded in much the opposite way. Rather than give students examples to work after they had been shown how to solve them, Japanese teachers typically started the lesson with a problem and had students struggle on their own to generate a solution. The expectation was that multiple solutions would be generated. Once the students had worked for some time on the problem, the class would reconvene, and students would present their various solution methods to the class. Through skillful guidance, the Japanese teacher would lead a discussion of the alternative solutions, leading students to the conceptual understanding that was the goal of the lesson. It becomes clear from this qualitative description why Japanese lessons were found to develop concepts, and why Japanese students engaged in more thinking during the lesson.

CONCLUSION

I have attempted in this chapter to explore the potential of large-scale video surveys for the study and improvement of classroom instruction. I have presented some of the benefits of such surveys, as I see them, as well as some of the problems and issues that need to be resolved to make such surveys useful. And, I have outlined the methods used in the TIMSS Videotape Classroom Study in order to illustrate in broad strokes what a comprehensive video survey might look like.

In my view, the fact that this study was accomplished—the first-ever study to collect video records from nationally representative samples of classroom teachers—is far more significant than the specific results that have been found thus far. It often seems to me, especially in the field of educational research, that the most subtle and complex studies are conducted before the most basic and obvious ones are. Given the importance that classroom instruction must surely play in student learning and in attempts to raise achievement, it is amazing that we have not to this point tried to study instruction on a national scale. Given the debate that goes on about how teachers should teach, and given the policies that have been adopted and then scrapped as states and school districts strive to improve education, it is hard to believe that we have not systematically studied the results of such policies in the classroom.

In this vein, I would like to end by acknowledging the debt I owe to Harold Stevenson as I choose to do studies like this one. Of all the lessons I learned from Harold, one of the most important was to keep focused on the forest, even as each tree was examined in great detail by hordes of other researchers. Harold, in his career, has often done the study that, in hindsight, appeared most obviously important, yet at the time no one thought to do. In the late 1970s, for example, while other researchers were busy explaining the alleged lack of reading disabilities in Asian children, Harold was wondering whether, in fact, there was any evidence of the phenomenon others were trying to explain. It was the obvious study, yet no one had seen that. The consequences of Harold's foray into the area have, of course, been monumental. Harold always had a working compass that pointed him in the most interesting directions.

Something Alfred Binet once wrote to sum up his philosophy of science always reminded me of Harold, and sums up the rationale for our video research as well: "Prolonged meditation on facts gathered at first hand." The study of teaching, more than almost any other topic in the field of education, has been hindered by a lack of even the most basic facts. This, to me, is the promise of video studies of classroom teaching. It took a hundred years to develop valid and reliable indicators of cognitive processes. We are only beginning the job of developing such indicators of teaching. But without such indicators, and without concrete examples of the teaching we are attempting to study and improve, it will be difficult to advance theories of instruction and learning that will be useful for the improvement of teaching.

REFERENCES

Robitaille, D. F., McKnight, C., Schmidt, W. H., Britton, E., Raizen, S., & Nicol, C. (1993). *Curriculum frameworks for mathematics and science.* TIMSS Monograph No. 1. Vancouver: Pacific Educational Press.

Stigler, J. W., Gonzales, P., Kawanaka, T., Knoll, S., & Serrano, A. (1997). *Methods and findings of the TIMSS Videotape Classroom Study.* Washington, DC: U.S. Government Printing Office.

U.S. Department of Education. (1996). *Pursuing excellence: A study of U.S. eighth-grade mathematics and science teaching, learning, curriculum, and achievement in international context* (NCES 97–198). Washington, DC: U.S. Government Printing Office.

PART TWO

Developmental Aspects of Literacy

6

Learning About the Orthography: A Cross-Linguistic Approach

Peter Bryant and Terezinha Nunes

THE INFLUENCE OF HAROLD STEVENSON

To pay tribute to the work and influence of Harold Stevenson is a pleasant, but formidable task; formidable because the extraordinary richness and the range of his research make it quite impossible to catch his achievements and what he stands for in a few paragraphs. At a very broad level, one can point to what he has done for the subject or, rather, for the subjects of developmental psychology and cross-cultural psychology for he has been a leader for a long time in both, and his achievement in getting the two subjects to work together is truly impressive. The fact that psychologists move so easily now from one subject to the other and bring them together in so many interesting ways is due in no small measure to Harold Stevenson's example and effort. For this he deserves many thanks, but, to us, his actual ideas about children's development in different environments are the significant thing. These have had a strong influence on us and we are pleased to have the chance to say something about this influence.

Two of the main themes of Harold Stevenson's work have played their part in the work that we will describe in this chapter. One is his evident conviction that it is impossible to understand many developmental processes without looking at them as they happen in different cultural environments. Another has been a considerable respect on his part for the difficulty posed by the developmental hurdles that children have to cross whatever the environment. Harold Stevenson definitely does not believe in quick fixes and is suspicious of easy solutions. His argument against the position that the Japanese orthography prevents reading difficulties is surely a case in point. The data presented by Harold Stevenson and his colleagues (Stevenson, Stigler, Lee, Kitamura, & Hsu, 1985) on that topic are an instance of a phenomenon that is rather rare in psychology—a definitive statement. These data showed quite clearly that learning to read in Japanese is simply not to be taken for granted. The hurdles, to use that word again, that come with the Japanese orthography may be different from the English hurdles, but they are formidably there. Much the same could be said about Harold Stevenson's ideas about the views that parents hold on their children's progress in learning mathematics. The research that led to Harold Stevenson's warning against parental complacency (Stevenson, Stigler, Lucker, Lee, Hsu, & Kitamura, 1986) seems a marvelous example of work of great theoretical interest and of immediate practical value.

These two Stevensonian themes will provide the framework for our chapter. We will first make the point, using data from several different languages, that children who are learning to read must make connections between script and spoken language on more than one linguistic level. Not only must they make a phonological connection between alphabetic letters and sounds, they must also learn about regular connections between the morphemic structure and the spelling of the words that they read and write. We will also show that these different kinds of links afford children some difficulty, and then we will concentrate on the developmental steps to learning about the conventional spelling for morphemes, again in several different languages.

THE DIFFICULTIES OF LEARNING TO READ

Children's reading is definitely not a matter for complacency. Even in rich countries where the schools are competent and the resources quite adequate, rather more than 5% of the population never learns to read or write to a respectable standard (Rutter & Yule, 1975; Snowling, 1987). In poorer countries the problem can be a great deal worse because the educational system may not reach as many people with the same efficiency as it might in the richer nations. In Brazil, which is the country in this bracket that we know the best, around 20% of the population is functionally illiterate (Nunes, Buarque, & Bryant, 1992).

Why is reading so hard for some? The answer seems to us is that it is actually a difficult job for all children. It takes most children several years to get through the basic steps in reading and writing, and even then they continue to make mistakes right through their school years. Most adults, even, are not too certain about the spellings of some words or about some of the punctuation rules. It is a formidable obstacle and we can probably only understand the outright failures of a minority of people to read if we know what the general difficulties are.

LEARNING HOW TO SPELL INFLECTIONAL MORPHEMES

The general difficulties people have in learning to read must have something to do with the various kinds of correspondence that exist between written and spoken language. When we teach children to read and write, we are teaching them about a set of regularities. Written language corresponds to spoken language in a regular manner, and no one can be counted as a competent reader until he or she has mastered these regularities. It is important to realize that there are different kinds of correspondences between written and spoken language, different regularities. The most obvious for alphabetic orthographies are the phonologically based letter–sound correspondences. It would, however, be quite wrong to stop there, although quite a few reading experts do. There are other kinds of correspondence that involve other linguistic levels. One of these levels, on which we will concentrate in this chapter, is grammatical. In English, but not just in English, many of the conventional orthographic patterns have a grammatical basis. English has conventional spellings for morphemes that relate to the syntactic status of the words they are in. Plurals end in *s* regardless of the end of the words sounding like /s/, /z/, or /ks/. Plural words ending in /ks/ are not spelled with an *x*, so the singular noun *fox* ends in one way and the plural noun *socks* in another. As far as we know there are no exceptions to the rule that all words ending in this combination of phonemes are written with an *x* at the end when they are singular nouns and with *cks* or occasionally just *k* when they are plurals.

The endings of English past tense verbs are even more intriguing, for here there is a hierarchy of correspondence. We shall describe the spoken forms first and then we shall consider how these affect the orthography. In English there are "strong" and "weak" past tense verbs. In the strong form past tense verbs have their own stems, which are different from the present tense stems. *Did, found, felt,* and *ate* are strong past tense verbs. Weak past tense verbs share the same stem as the present tense verb. They are formed by adding the inflectional morpheme with the sound /t/ or /d/ or /id/ to the infinitive. So *helped, called,* and *waited* are examples of the weak form. A long time ago nearly all the English past tense verbs were strong ones, but as new words were added to the language, particularly from the French—new words that did not carry the past tense with them—they were simply included as weak verbs, until the weak inherited, if not the earth, at least the linguistic high ground, for they are now in the majority. In fact, some previously strong forms have now migrated to the weak form, the past tense of "help" used to be the strong "haelpt" before it became the weak "helped" (Barber, 1993).

We can consider now the printed representations of these verb endings—the conventional printed representation for inflectional morphemes. There is a regular correspondence between written and spoken English past tense verbs on which, as far as we know, no one has commented but that nevertheless is simple and obvious. The endings of strong verbs are spelled phonetically. Weak verbs on the other hand end in *ed*, which is not a phonetic spelling. We do not actually say *kiss-ed* or *burn-ed* or even *wait-ed*. These words end in the sounds /t/, /d/, and /id/ respectively, but they are all spelled as *ed*, which is, therefore, always a nonphonetic printed representation of these sounds. Weak verbs are spelled that way not because of the sound of their final morpheme, but because of their syntactic status. This nonphonetic, grammatically based spelling of the endings of weak past tense verbs means, of course, that other words with the same sound but with a different grammatical status are spelled differently. The spoken words *kissed* and *list* end in the same way, and so do *rolled* and *bold*, and so also do *drowned* and *found*. They are spelled differently because one of the words in each pair is a weak past tense verb and the other word is not.

OTHER GRAMMATICALLY BASED CONNECTIONS WITH SPELLING

There are many other examples of the connection between grammar and the English orthography, such as the *wh* opening in interrogatives (Nunes, Bryant, & Bindman, 1997) and the use of the apostrophe to denote possession (Bryant, Devine, Ledward, & Nunes, 1997), but we have probably said enough to have established the importance and the pervasiveness of the link between grammar and spelling. We can go on to make three general points about the grammatical connection. The first is that English is not alone. Nearly every other European orthography has the same phenomenon. There are many such instances in Portuguese. For example, the suffixes *ice* and *isse* are pronounced in exactly the same way, but *ice* is a derivational morpheme used in abstract nouns and *isse* is an inflectional morpheme for the subjunctive. In French, many inflectional morphemes are just not pronounced though they are spelled. The singular verb *(il) aime* and the plural *(ils) aiment* sound the same and so do the singular noun *(la) maison* and the plural *(les) maisons*. The spelling of these words then depends directly on their syntactic status.

The second point is that it is almost impossible to conceive of anyone learning all the correct ways of writing the types of words that we have been describing or of decoding correctly the printed versions of these words without also having some explicit grammatical knowledge. How else would anyone know when to put an "ed" onto the end of a word ending in a /t/ or /d/ sound and when not to? How would anyone eventually learn to put an apostrophe in genitive words but not in nominative plural words (the different between "the boy's sail" and "the boys sail")? The only possible alternative is that children learn each written word by rote. That seems implausible to us because it would take a devil of a long time to learn all that, and, as we shall show later, it is easy to demonstrate empirically that this is not how children learn the relationship between spoken and written language.

Our third point concerns the relationship between the two kinds of correspondence of spoken to written language that we have mentioned so far—phonological and grammatical correspondence. These are not amicable relations—the two are actually often in conflict. It would be pleasant to report that children simply have to learn about both kinds of correspondence and perhaps to report that they learn one before the other. However, there are obvious instances where the two kinds of correspondence tell the child contradictory things. For example, in English one learns that the last sound in words ending in /t/ should be represented by t (the phonological connection) and that it should be represented by ed in past tense verbs. It is a battlefield and we are concerned that children are often left to their own devices right in the middle of the conflict.

What happens to children in this conflict? There is evidence that before they go to school they do actually entertain hypotheses both about the link between print and phonology, and also about its connection with meaning. Emilia Ferreiro and Anna Teberosky (1983) have shown that young Spanish-speaking children discover quite early that written Spanish has something to do with sounds, but for a long time hold the hypothesis that each letter represents a syllable. Five-year-olds often believe that a word like *mariposa* (butterfly) is represented by four letters only.

It also seems that very young children—4-year-olds who have not begun to read—are quite willing to accept the idea of a direct link between meaning and written language. Brian Byrne (1996) showed 4-year-old Australian children two written words, one a singular and the other its plural. For example, he gave them the words *tree* and *trees*, with the *s* printed in a different color, and then told them which word was which so that they saw that the plural word had a red-colored *s* at the end of it. Then he gave them another singular–plural pair such as *boy* and *boys* in which the *s* was distinguished in the same way and asked which said *boy* and which *boys*. Byrne found that many, though not all, of the children managed this task quite well. In another condition the second pair of words consisted of two singular words, one of which ended with a red *s*, *bug* and *bus*. The children made no discrimination here, which shows that they did not manage the *boy/boys* discrimination by attributing to the letter *s* the function of representing the sound /s/. It begins to look as though these children understood straightaway that the letter *s* represented the plural morpheme. However, some subsequent data showed that this was not quite so. Byrne went through the same procedure, but in the second pair the two written words were *man*, and the nonexistent *mans*, and he asked the children which said *man*, and which *men*. They chose *mans* for *men* as often as they had chosen *boys* for *boys*, indicating the connection that they made was not morphemic; it was more global than that. They certainly grasped the possibility of a direct connection between a written symbol in a word and its meaning, but they probably did not realize that this is done by means of the symbol representing the inflectional morpheme. They had the wrong hypothesis—or at any rate not quite the right hypothesis–about the role of print. It seems to us that their hypothesis might have served them better if they had gone on to learn Chinese, in which many characters include a semantic radical that gives a clue to the meaning of the word.

PHONOLOGY AND LEARNING TO SPELL

If children who speak European languages need to have some understanding of the connection between grammar and orthographic principles, it is a pity that little attention has been paid to this issue in teaching schemes. For a long time the debate about teaching beginning readers has centered around phonology. People have argued about what emphasis should be given to teaching letter–sound relationships. This is a well-documented controversy that we will not enter into here, except to note that the opponents of the phonological approach to teaching reading do not offer the grammatical link as an alternative. Their alternative is to teach the child to take advantage of contextual cues offered by prose known as the *whole language* approach (Goodman, 1965, 1967). Thus the question of teaching children about the grammatical connection has not been the focus of any educational debate, as far as we know.

Whatever the rights or wrongs of teaching letter–sound relationships, it is quite clear that children's early phonological skills do play an important part in their early progress in learning to read and to spell. Again we are talking about a well-documented topic, and we need only say that measures of their ability to detect rhyme and alliteration, taken before children begin to learn to read, predict the progress that they subsequently make in learning to read and to spell extremely well (Bradley & Bryant, 1983; Ellis & Large, 1987). Successful training programs in detecting rhymes and other phonological units consistently improve children's reading levels as well (Lundberg, Frost, & Petersen, 1988; Snowling, 1996).

Although this is a well-researched topic, there are questions of the phonological unit involved in the connection between rhyme and reading that still have not been sorted out. It seems reasonable that rhyme predicts children's reading because rhyme represents a phonological unit smaller than the syllable, and therefore rhyme tasks measure children's ability to break into the syllable. But rhyme measures predict too much and too little for this idea to be completely right. In a recent study of 100 Chinese children in Hong Kong (Ho, 1994; Ho & Bryant, 1997a), it was shown that measures of rhyme detection taken before these children had learned to read predicted the progress that they had made 2 and 3 years later in the beginning stages of reading Chinese. We concluded that this must be because of the phonological component in Chinese characters. Indeed in a later study we showed that there was also a strong relationship between a rhyme detection score and the children's ability to detect Chinese pseudo-words on the basis of their phonological components (Ho & Bryant, 1997b). But these phonological components give a clue to the sound of the word that does not

necessarily require breaking into the syllable. Sometimes the phonological component may represent the syllable but with a different tone,
sometimes it may represent the rhyme, and still sometimes there may
be a vowel change when the word is pronounced. So rhyme detection
measures are not necessarily important just because they help children
start to analyze the syllables into smaller units.

Whatever the role of rhyme in early reading is, it is quite clear that
children learning an alphabetic orthography have to learn to break syllables up into phonemes fairly quickly, and they do. Their writing attests
to that. The phenomenon of young children's "invented spelling" had
been staring us in the face before Charles Read began his brilliant work
on it in the 1970s and 1980s (Read, 1971, 1986), but it was only at that
point that we realized its significance. Read showed us that children use
the letter–sound relationships that they have only just learned in a
startingly literal and original way. They sometimes even represent phonetic distinctions that we adults do not hear (e.g., *jragin* for *dragon*).
But one thing that they do not do very much is adopt the conventional
spellings for morphemes, that much is obvious from their representations of past tense verbs—*halpt, suckt, kist, watid,* and *wotid,* are words
that we have culled from Read's opus (there are many more), and one
only has to look at the writings of English children of 5, 6, and even 7
years to see that with barely an exception they blithely ignore the *ed*
ending and stick to phonetic spelling.

THE TRANSITION TO SPELLING MORPHEMES

This partiality for phonetic spelling, this early avoidance of grammatically dependent spelling sequences, is widespread. It is clearly there in
Portuguese. In this orthography, as we have seen, spelling is heavily
influenced by grammar, and the work of Terezinha Carraher Nunes
(Carraher, 1985) shows that it takes children a long time to learn. For
example the final semivowel /w/ is usually represented with an *o* but
in the third person singular of past tense verbs with that end-sound it
is written as *u.* At first, young children simply write *u* for all semivowel
/w/ sounds at the end of words because the *o* would not be a good

phonological representation; later they correct this phonetic spelling by using *o* but they do not make a distinction between grammatical classes and do not keep that *u* in past tense verbs. It is only much later that they will distinguish the grammatical categories in their writing. This overgeneralization in Portuguese, it turns out, is not at all an isolated phenomenon. Recently Totereau, Thevenin, and Fayol (1997) have looked at French children's representation of the silent inflectional morphemes in plural nouns and verbs that we mentioned earlier. Like Nunes' Brazilian children, these French children also plainly go through an invented spelling period, which means that they simply do not represent these silent inflections in writing. Later, however, they begin to bring in the *s* for plural nouns but they overgeneralize it in the most interesting way; they often spell the ends of plural verbs with an *s* as well (e.g., *ils aimes*). Later still they overgeneralize the plural morpheme the other way, giving the plural verb ending to plural nouns (e.g., *les maisonent*).

These striking overgeneralizations by Portuguese and French speaking children demonstrate that the transition from writing in a purely phonetic way to adopting the conventional grammatically determined orthographic sequences for particular morphemes is not a smooth one. There are strong signs from the evidence that we have described that for a while children begin to use the nonphonetic spelling either with no idea (Carraher, 1985) or with only a very incomplete idea (Totereau et al., 1997) of the grammatical constraints. The children realize that various sounds are not always spelled phonetically, but they do not at first recognize the grammatical basis for distinguishing between those that are spelled phonetically and those that are not.

A LONGITUDINAL STUDY WITH ENGLISH CHILDREN

Is it the same with English? We have evidence that it is. Our data come from a large scale longitudinal study of English children's understanding of the relation between spoken and written language. We looked at children's learning of a large range of grammatically and morphologically determined orthographic patterns (Nunes, Bryant, & Bindman, 1997; Bryant, Nunes, & Bindman, 1997). Here we shall focus on children's rendering of past tense verbs, the rules for which we set out in some detail earlier in this chapter, and in particular we shall concentrate on the way that they cope with the nonphonetic *ed* orthographic sequence.

When our study began the children who took part in it (368 in number) were 6, 7, and 8 years old. The study went on for 3 years, during which time we saw each child three times a year. One of the many things that we looked at in these sessions was the children's ability to spell past tense verbs that end in *ed* (the weak form) and past verbs that do not (the strong form) as well as words with similar endings that were not verbs.

First, we looked at the children's success in representing the endings of words (nonverbs and strong verbs) when these endings are spelled phonetically. Both our cross-sectional and our longitudinal data showed that children do make mistakes with these phonetic endings and that these mistakes decline with age, which suggests that some of our youngest children had not yet reached the stage of invented spelling. This developmental change, however, was overshadowed by the contrast between the children's success with these phonetic endings and their difficulties with the *ed* ending. The cross-sectional data and the longitudinal data both showed that the *ed* words were much harder, but also that there was a particularly sharp improvement in spelling these *ed* words as the children got older. In our first session hardly any of the youngest children, who were 6 years old at the time, ever produced this spelling pattern, and 2 years later the children in the oldest group, who were 10 years old by then, produced these spellings appropriately nearly all the time.

We can be sure that there are marked developmental changes in children's ability to produce the conventional grammatically determined spellings for morphemes. But an even more striking discovery was the frequency of overgeneralizations of the *ed* sequence. The youngest children, as we have remarked, hardly ever produced the *ed* spelling, but we also found that, when they began to write it, they did so in the wrong words as well. There are two ways to overgeneralize the *ed* sequence. Children might stick an *ed* on the end of strong verbs, which would mean spelling *found* as *founed* for example, but they can also put *ed* on the end of nonverbs that end in the /t/ or /d/ sound. An example of this would be writing *soft* as *sofed*. The former is a generalization to another word within the same grammatical category; the latter is a generalization to a word in a different grammatical category. We found both kinds of generalization in abundance.

In the first session (Session A), 134 out of a total of 363 children (34%) generalized the *ed* sequence to irregular past tense verbs at least once. In the next session, 9 months later, in which we tested the children's ability to write these words (Session B), the percentage of children making this mistake at least once increased to 38.3% and increased still further in another session (Session C) 1 year after that. Thus 21 months after session A the percentage of children making the mistake increased to 41.8%. Even more impressively, of the children whom we tested in Session C, 71.1% had made at least one such generalization in one of the three sessions.

We have a more remarkable fact to report about generalizations. Many children overgeneralized the *ed* spelling pattern to the wrong grammatical category: in session A, 104 of the children (28.7% of the whole sample) generalized the *ed* sequence to at least one nonverb. They wrote, for example, *soft* as *sofed* or *ground* as *grouned*. Roughly the same proportions of children made these ungrammatical generalizations in Sessions B and C as well. By Session C, over half (55.8%) of the children whom we tested in that session had made at least one such generalization to a nonverb in one or more of the three sessions. Both types of generalization increased with age, but the generalizations to nonverbs dropped off much faster with age than did the generalizations to irregular verbs, as we hypothesized.

What is the significance of these two kinds of generalization and of their developmental course? It seemed to us that our results were clearly in line with the Portuguese and French data that we have mentioned already. As first the children did not seem to handle the phonetic representations at all well, but as they grew older they took to invented spelling, which is phonetically based, with a will. Later they realized that there are exceptions to the letter–sound rules and, in this case, that some words that end in /d/ or /t/ are spelled as *ed*, but they do not at first understand the grammatical significance of the *ed* sequence and so generalize not just to other past tense verbs but also to nonverbs as well. Because these generalizations across grammatical categories decline with age more rapidly than do the generalizations to strong past tense verbs, it looks as though at a certain stage the children begin to understand that the *ed* sequence is confined to past tense verbs, though they do not grasp the difference between strong and weak past tense verbs. Finally they learn quite well which are the *ed* verbs and which are not, though whether they understand the underlying strong–weak distinction or simply learn the difference on an individual rote basis is unclear at this time.

A Developmental Model

We have, in effect, outlined a five-stage developmental hypothesis that is summarized in Table 1, and we were able to test the hypothesis in our longitudinal study. Any stage model should pass at least three tests. One is that all, or very nearly all, of the children in the appropriate age range should clearly belong to one of the stages in the model. A second requirement is that the developmental stages should be related to external criteria. Children at more advanced stages should also be the older or the educationally more successful children in the sample. The third test of a model of developmental stages is the most stringent, and unfortunately the least often applied in developmental research. Because the stages are ordered from less to more advanced, individual children over time should move in one direction but not in another. For example, if a child is at stage 2 in one session, the model predicts that he or she will be either at the same stage or at a higher stage in the next session but not at a lower stage. He or she is expected to be at stage 2, 3, or 4 in the following session but not at stage 1.

We set objective criteria for each of these stages, and, using a computer, assigned each child to either one of the five stages or to none of the stages if the child did not satisfy the criteria for any of the stages.

Table 1
The Five Developmental Stages: Their Characteristics and the Numbers of the Children Assigned to Them

Stage	Characteristics of the children's spelling at stage	Typical Spelling	Number of children in each category per session		
			A	B	C
Stage 1	Unsystematic spelling of word endings		58	53	15
Stage 2	Frequent inappropriate phonetic transcriptions of endings: failure to produce conventional spellings of morphemes	*kist, slept, soft*	78	63	29
Stage 3	Some *ed* endings, but generalizations to irregular verbs and nonverbs (i.e., failure to confine this sequence to past verbs)	*kissed, sleped, sofed*	86	67	71
Stage 4	*ed* spellings confined to past verbs, with generalizations to irregular verbs	*kissed, sleped, soft*	52	57	65
Stage 5	*ed* spellings confined to regular past verbs: *no* generalizations	*kissed, slept, soft*	63	82	112
Unclassified			26	16	6

Table 1 gives the number of children falling into the five stages in the three sessions, together with their actual ages and their reading ages in Sessions A and C. The table shows that the stage model successfully included the vast majority of children (more than 90% in each phase), which satisfies the first of our three tests.

We also found that the stages were related to external criteria in the way that we predicted. The average age and also the average reading level of the children allocated to the later stages was consistently higher than those of children at a less advanced stage according to our model (Nunes, Bryant, & Bindman, 1997). This satisfies our second test.

The crucial test for us was the third—the longitudinal test. We wanted to know whether the children would progress in one direction and not regress over time. Figure 1 presents two sets of data about the relative position of individual children in two successive sessions. One set concerns their relative position in Sessions A and B, and the other in Sessions B and C. Figure 1 shows how many children stayed at the same stage in the two sessions (these children are represented by the top left to bottom right diagonal in both tables), how many children progressed to a higher stage (children above the diagonal) and how many were at a lower stage, according to our model, in the later session (below the diagonal). Our prediction was that the vast majority of the children should either be on the diagonal or above it, and that few should be below it.

This prediction was largely successful. There were those who did slide backwards, but they were clearly in the minority, and by far most of the children, who did change stages from one session to the other, changed to a higher stage (in our model). The longitudinal data therefore support our developmental model.

THE REASONS FOR THIS
DEVELOPMENTAL SEQUENCE

The developmental sequence that we have just presented suggests that children progress first by noticing the exceptions to letter–sound rules and later by learning that these apparent exceptions have a grammatical

The stages of individual children in Sessions A and B

	Stage in Session B					
	1	2	3	4	5	Total
Stage in Session A						
1	*28*	11	8	1	1	49
2	5	*43*	10	5	6	69
3	0	3	*30*	21	19	73
4	0	1	11	*13*	17	42
5	0	1	3	11	*37*	52
Total	33	59	62	51	80	285

The stages of individual children in Sessions B and C

	Stage in Session C					
	1	2	3	4	5	Total
Stage in Session B						
1	*9*	7	9	5	0	30
2	2	*16*	15	16	8	57
3	1	1	*26*	14	19	61
4	0	0	14	*15*	23	52
5	1	0	5	7	*56*	69
Total	13	24	69	57	106	269

Note. The italics indicate the number of children who stayed in the same stage across the two sessions.

Figure 1

The stages of individual children in each session.

rationale. In other words, their progress is determined by the experiences that they have in reading and spelling. However, to understand the significance of some of those experiences they also need to be aware of the grammatical distinctions that underlie the orthographic patterns about which they are learning. Just as phonological awareness contributes to children's learning about letter–sound correspondences, so too should their awareness of syntax and morphemes be connected to their learning about grammatically determined orthographic patterns.

We tested this idea in our project by devising tests of what we can call morphosyntactic awareness. The most successful of our measures were both based on analogy. We presented either a sentence or a word and then transformed it, then we presented another rather similar word or sentence and asked the child to make the same transformation. For example, one of our word analogy problems was "teacher: taught :: writer: ?", and one of our sentence analogy problems was "Tom helps Mary: Tom helped Mary :: Tom sees Mary: ?".

These tests were strong predictors of the progress that children made in their orthographic development. We looked at the relations between grammatical awareness scores in the first session and the correct representation of the endings of *ed* verbs in subsequent sessions. The sentence and word analogy tasks predicted the amount of correct *ed* spelling in both the following sessions even after stringent controls for differences in age, IQ, and the children's reading levels. We conclude that children's learning about the printed representation of morphemes depends to a large extent on their ability to make the appropriate morphosyntactic distinctions.

CONCLUSIONS

The account that we have been giving of children's reading and spelling is really an account of their changing ideas about the nature of the orthography. Very early on children are quite ready to accept that letters represent meaning, particularly when they are asked to take a letter that distinguishes a pair of words, such as *boy–boys*, where a semantic contrast is also present (Byrne, 1996). Preschool children (perhaps a bit later) can also recognize early on that letters represent sounds (Read, 1996; Ferreiro & Teberosky, 1983). In both cases their hypotheses are correct in an approximate sense, although wrong in detail—at least in English. In the first few years at school they learn, one way or another, the correct hypothesis about the nature of letter–sound correspondences. The struggles that they have in the early stages with learning how to isolate the phoneme are time consuming, and by the time they have surmounted that hurdle they still have not mastered orthography. Children need to realize that there is a grammatical connection as well as a phonological one between oral and written language. The period of invented spelling is both an advance and, in some sense, a loss. Learning that letters represent sounds seems to persuade the child that the letters cannot mean anything else. What follows is a confused period in which the child first realizes that there are some exceptions to the letter–sound rules, but only later begins to understand the grammatical significance. This takes a very long time. Our account of this development in English was confined to one instance, the *ed* orthographic sequence, that took us to children of the age of 10 years whose representation of this segment is still not perfect. We have found, however, other examples of grammatically based orthographic sequences that take a great deal longer, for example, the use of the apostrophe to denote possession (also strongly predicted by earlier syntactic awareness tests). Even children of 11 years have very great difficulty in understanding that apostrophes are to be placed in genitive words but not in similar sounding nominative or accusative plural words (in "the boy's sail" but not in "the boys sail").

Why does it take such a long time? One simple answer may be the nature of the teaching that children receive. We could find little evidence that children in English schools are taught about the grammatical basis for *ed*. The link between this orthographic sequence and past tense verbs is not made clear, and they are certainly not taught about the significance that the distinction between strong and weak past tense verbs has for the use of this sequence. This, however, cannot be the only explanation. English children are taught about the grammatical basis for the apostrophe, and they still find it horribly difficult. French children are taught the grammatical basis for the written representation of singular and plural nouns and verbs, and yet they also have much difficulty learning the grammatical connection.

To us a more likely explanation is the conflict that we have mentioned. The phonological connection and the grammatical connection are not complementary; they actually disagree. So if a child learns only about the phonological connection, his or her progress with letter–sound correspondences may well be at a considerable cost. One form of learning may impede the other. It is not easy for the child, but it should be a lot easier if the conflict were explicitly recognized by those who teach the children. It does not seem to be so at the moment, either in English classrooms or in English reading schemes.

The grammatical connection has been neglected by teachers and to a certain extent by psychologists too because it is a lot less obvious than the phonological one, but it is an important connection because no one could possibly master orthography until he or she has understood the part that grammar plays in English spelling. It is important for another reason. It gives a vivid example of the power and interest of cross-linguistic comparisons. The actual surface forms that the grammatical connection with orthography takes are wildly different in different languages, but the underlying phenomenon is the same, and so is the development. In three different languages we have found the same change from spelling phonetically to using the grammatically based conventional sequences occasionally but with little idea of their grammatical basis, and finally to understanding the grammatical connection fully. The similarity of the developmental changes despite formidable surface differences is the most convincing evidence that we have for the developmental progression that we have suggested.

REFERENCES

Barber, C. (1993). *The English language: A historical introduction.* Cambridge, England: Cambridge University Press.

Bradley, L., & Bryant, P. E. (1983). Categorising sounds and learning to read—a causal connection. *Nature, 301,* 419–521.

Bryant, P., Devine, M., Ledward, A., & Nunes, T. (In press). Spelling with apostrophes and understanding possession. *British Journal of Educational Psychology.*

Bryant, P., Nunes, T., & Bindman, M. (In press). Backward readers' awareness of language: strengths and weaknesses. *European Journal of Psychology and Education.*

Byrne, B. (1996). The learnability of the alphabetic principle: Children's initial hypotheses about how print represents spoken language. *Applied Psycholinguistics, 17,* 401–426.

Carraher, T. N. (1985). Exploracoes sobre o desenvolvimento da competencia em ortografia em Portugues. *Psicologia: Teoria e Pesquisa, 1,* 269–285.

Ellis, N., & Large, B. (1987). The development of reading: As you seek so shall you find. *British Journal of Developmental Psychology, 78,* 1–28.

Ferreiro, E., & Teberosky, A. (1983). *Literacy before schooling.* Exeter, NH: Heinemann Educational Books.

Goodman, K. (1965). A linguistic study of cues and miscues in reading. *Elementary English, 42,* 639–643.

Goodman, K. (1967). Reading: A psycholinguistic guessing game. *Journal of the Reading Specialist,* 126–137.

Ho, C. (1994). A cross-cultural study of the precursors of reading. Unpublished doctoral thesis, University of Oxford, England.

Ho, C., & Bryant, P. (1997a). Development of phonological awareness of Chinese children in Hong Kong. *Journal of Psycholinguistic Research, 26,* 109–126.

Ho, C., & Bryant, P. (1997b). Learning to read Chinese beyond the Logographic Phase. *Reading Research Quarterly, 32,* 279–289.

Lundberg, I., Frost, J., & Petersen, O. (1988). Effects of an extensive program for stimulating phonological awareness in preschool children. *Reading Research Quarterly, 23,* 263–284.

Nunes, T., Bryant, P., & Bindman, M. (1997). Spelling and grammar: The necsed move. In C. Perfetti, L. Rieben, & M. Fayol (Eds.), *Learning to spell.* Hillsdale, NJ: Erlbaum.

Nunes, T., Buarque, L., & Bryant, P. (1992). *Dificuldades na aprendizagem da leitura: teoria e pratica.* Sao Paulo, Brazil: Cortez Editora.

Read, C. (1971). Pre-school children's knowledge of English phonology. *Harvard Educational Review, 41,* 1–34.

Read, C. (1986). *Children's creative spelling.* London: Routledge & Kegan Paul.

Rutter, M., & Yule, W. (1975). The concept of specific reading retardation. *Journal of Child Psychology and Psychiatry, 16,* 181–197.

Snowling, M. (1987). *Dyslexia: A cognitive developmental perspective.* Oxford: Blackwell.

Snowling, M. (1996). Contemporary approaches to the teaching of reading. *Journal of Child Psychology and Psychiatry, 37,* 139–148.

Stevenson, H. W., Stigler, J. W., Lee, S.-Y., Kitamura, S., & Hsu, C.-C. (1985).

Cognitive performance and academic achievement of Japanese, Chinese and American children. *Child Development, 56,* 718–734.

Stevenson, H. W., Stigler, J. W., Lucker, G. W., Lee, S.-Y., Hsu, C. C., & Kitamura, S. (1986). Mathematics achievement of Chinese, Japanese and American children. *Science, 231,* 693–699.

Totereau, C., Thevenin, M.-G., & Fayol, M. (1997). The development of the understanding of number morphology in French. In C. Perfetti, L. Rieben, & M. Fayol (Eds.), *Learning to spell.* Hillsdale, NJ: Erlbaum.

7

Assessing Young Children's Literacy Strategies and Development

Scott G. Paris and Christina E. van Kraayenoord

The education of children is a concern of parents, teachers, and policy makers around the globe. Education provides a legacy of cultural beliefs, values, practices, and knowledge that allows each successive generation to adapt to changing world conditions. Some people view education as a gateway to social opportunity and equality; others view it as a necessary stepping stone to good jobs and economic success; and still others view education as a foundation for lifelong learning and self-fulfillment. Regardless of one's perspective, educational beliefs and practices have been informed immensely by psychological research on fundamental aspects of teaching, learning, and developing students' competencies and motivation around the world. Harold Stevenson's research in particular has shown the value of cross-cultural studies of human development and cross-national comparisons of educational achievement for identifying similarities and differences among educational practices in countries with widely different educational philosophies. In addition, his work has shown the tremendous benefits of international collaboration among researchers who gain insights from each other and from working in new educational environments. This chapter is dedicated to Harold Stevenson and his emphases on international scholarly collaboration, empirical analyses of children's learning, and the value of developmental approaches for understanding children's educational achievement.

THE AUSTRALIAN CONTEXT

My coauthor and I have corresponded about issues in children's literacy development for 15 years and have collaborated on several projects in the 1990s. We share an interest in studying children's reading comprehension with a focus on the strategies and insights that children of different ages and abilities bring to the tasks of reading and writing. Over the years, we have discussed the similarities and differences between literacy instruction and assessment that we have observed in schools in the United States and Australia. We have identified how preservice education, professional development activities, assessment, and other factors differ in schools in the United States and Australia (van Kraayenoord & Paris, 1994). Because those factors motivated us to design new literacy assessment tasks, we identify some of the prominent features of literacy education that we have observed in Australia.

We noted five general characteristics of literacy education in primary schools in Australia that are not always evident in American schools (van Kraayenoord & Paris, 1994). The first characteristic is a *developmental view of learning*, in which Australian educators view children's literacy experiences as situated in a developmental continuum of their growth in multiple academic areas, including mathematical, scientific, and artistic skills. Literacy skills and literacy instruction are embedded in the child's general development and not treated as discrete subject areas in the elementary school, as in the United States. This leads directly to the second characteristic: *integration of language arts with content learning*. Because literacy is defined as *language in use* or language applied to meaningful goals, teachers in Australian classrooms incorporate language arts into content learning. A third characteristic is the use of a *holistic approach to language learning* that does not focus instruction on component skills or delay introduction of literacy uses until subskills have been mastered. Communication of meaning is the main goal, and Australian educators believe that invented spelling, incomplete decoding, text memorization, and other so-called errors in performance should be accepted in children's developing uses of literacy. A fourth feature is an emphasis on *classroom environments with multiple print resources*. Classrooms provide diverse examples of text, from environmental print to a wide range of genres. Furthermore, Australian educators value public demonstrations of children's literacy achievements and creativity, so it is common to display children's writing prominently throughout the school and to have daily book reports, oral reading, and conferences. A fifth characteristic is *social collaboration for learning*. Classrooms are organized to foster cooperative learning in pairs or small groups. Many Australian elementary classrooms are large rooms containing more than one class or two interconnected rooms so that teachers may regroup students in flexible ways and create independent learning centers.

Although these features also characterize some American elementary schools, they contrast sharply with the majority of classrooms in which reading is taught as a separate subject to children, frequently in ability-based reading groups, and often guided by a basal reading series with a strong emphasis on decoding skills, building vocabulary, and answering questions about the information. The materials-centered approach to teaching and the skills-oriented approach to learning in many American classrooms have a strong tradition and history through the 1980s (Paris, Wixson, & Palincsar, 1986). Many reform movements in the United States in the 1990s, including whole language, emergent literacy, and Reading Recovery, moved literacy instruction away from materials-driven and skills-based approaches, although the pendulum may be starting to swing in the other direction at the close of the decade.

In addition, literacy instruction in the United States has changed in response to the kinds of assessments imposed on teachers and students. Historically, norm-referenced achievement tests have been used to gauge the achievement of students, but many states have now created new criterion-referenced tests, portfolio assessments, or performance-based assessments of reading comprehension and writing (Calfee &

Hiebert, 1990). The cross-national adoption of various literacy practices seems ironic to us. On the one hand, American educators enthusiastically embraced features of literacy instruction in Australia and New Zealand, such as whole language, beginning book series, journal writing, book logs, and genre-based approaches to literacy while maintaining a tradition of accountability by testing. On the other hand, Australian educators have moved toward state-mandated testing of students' literacy achievement while maintaining their tradition of individually tailored instructional practices.

In both countries, the newly adopted approaches are inconsistent with previous practices and have created uproars among educators and parents. Australian instruction reflects an integrated, developmental approach to learning that is not easily measured by a uniform state test. Conversely, American educators who adopt classroom literacy practices more consistent with those of Australian schools are frustrated because the traditional standardized tests that follow a one-test-fits-all-curricula approach are inconsistent with the new instruction they provide.

THE ASSESSMENT CONTEXT

One reason for the paradoxical problem in these countries (and others) is the need for alternative literacy assessments that are congruent with instructional practices. Literacy researchers and educators in both Australia and the United States are wrestling with the same issues as they reform assessment to serve multiple functions (Paris & van Kraayenoord, 1992). Our goal was to design assessment tasks that promote students' thoughtful and motivated literacy development. Such tasks often are loosely structured and open-ended to allow students to construct meaning and to engage in conversations about the meanings they create. We believe that assessment tasks can be embedded in everyday classroom situations to connect instruction and assessment. These assessments are formative not summative, uniform but not standardized, and are designed to promote learning and teaching, not accountability. These tasks may be appropriate for large-scale assessment, but our main goal was to design tasks suitable for classroom assessment that would help students and teachers on a daily basis.

Our research identified three key problems that new literacy assessments ought to address: First, most assessments designed to measure young children's early literacy depend on the child's decoding abilities and phonological awareness. We wanted to assess children's thinking about text, so we tried to create tasks to assess children's comprehension as they listened to stories, examined picture books, and read text. Second, many literacy assessments are narrowly focused on discrete skills. We wanted to create richer tasks to assess more dimensions of literacy than word recognition, decoding fluency, and retelling. For example, we saw a need to assess how children choose books to read and how they reflect on their own literacy accomplishments. Third, we recognized that traditional assessments are often time-consuming, inflexible, or demanding in the amount of record keeping required, so we designed pragmatic tasks that teachers could adapt and embed in daily activities. Clay (1979) and Kemp (1990) have designed assessment activities to counter these problems as well, and our work follows in their tradition.

Researchers' reviews of current literacy tests support the need for new literacy assessments (Teale, 1990). According to Stallman and Pearson (1990), who analyzed hundreds of commercially available tests of early literacy, formal assessments rarely measure appropriate concepts or behavior of young children. These researchers drew five conclusions from their review of readiness tests: First, the tests are typically administered to groups, rather than to individuals. Second, most tests emphasize sound–symbol knowledge rather than the ability to construct meaning or think about the text. Third, the tests require several hours spread over many days to administer. Fourth, students rarely provide personal or elaborate responses to text, but instead fill in bubbles on multiple choice answer sheets. Fifth, the main type of cognitive processing assessed is the student's recognition of correct answers.

One consequence of testing students by traditional tests is that parents and teachers form a conceptual understanding that is often inaccurate of literacy, based on component skills and test scores. Because a fragmented and componential view is in stark contrast to emergent literacy perspectives, whole language instruction, and constructivist views of literacy learning, teachers and parents often resist new approaches in the classroom that are inconsistent with traditional tests. However, we believe that when teachers and parents are able to discuss children's thinking, metacognition, strategic literacy, and motivation on the basis of performance assessments, they will be more likely to create developmental theories of literacy learning and foster this development with appropriate activities at home and school (Paris & Ayres, 1994).

Traditional literacy testing may also teach children distorted views of literacy. For example, they might learn that pronouncing the words correctly is more important than understanding the meaning, or that getting the answers right is more important than understanding how to figure out what new words and sentences mean. When emphasis is placed on a specific correct answer, reading speed, accurate pronunciation, punctuation, and the number of items correct on a test, children construct counterproductive notions of literacy learning.

The need for new literacy assessments for young children is fueled by practical concerns as well as theoretical advances in literacy research (Morrow & Smith, 1990). For example, teachers are encouraged to use performance measures and portfolios of literacy to document children's progress (Tierney, Carter, & Desai, 1991), yet there is a dearth of information about what to include in portfolios and which performance measures give meaningful assessments of children's literacy development. Another stimulus for change is the instructional movement away from basal readers toward integrated language arts and whole language instruction that emphasize children's independent reading and writing, reading from trade books, and thinking about text as they listen and view, as well as read. There simply are not enough assessment tasks consistent with the new instructional approaches.

Our first study was designed to test the appropriateness, feasibility, and usefulness of a variety of literacy assessments for young children. Together we devised a series of early literacy tasks from our experiences in New Zealand, Australia, and the United States that we thought might be useful for teachers and researchers. Our choices were guided by both theoretical and practical criteria. We were interested in tasks that emphasized young children's abilities to construct meaning from text— that is, using information that they read, hear, view, and write to create plausible interpretations—as well as tasks that foster reflection, meta-cognition about literacy strategies, and conversations about literacy that intermingle a focus on personally constructed meaning with a focus on personally deployed strategies. Because the focus of early literacy is often on decoding accuracy, tasks that assessed how children think about narrative and expository texts independently of their abilities to decode the words were our concern.

The tasks we designed were also intended to be easily adapted by teachers for use in their daily instruction. Thus, the comprehension tasks were modeled after successful instructional activities in early grades so that they could be used interchangeably for assessment or instruction. We wanted the assessments to be diagnostic and the results to be sensible and easy to interpret. The tasks also needed to be brief and easy for teachers to administer without a lot of preparation. Finally, we wanted to create a battery of tasks that teachers and researchers could adapt to different grade levels and purposes. Some of the assessments were given in identical form to all students, but other assessments were appropriate only for older or younger children. For example, we designed listening comprehension and story construction tasks for children in Years 1 and 2 classrooms. Although Year 1 is the first year of formal school in Australia, it includes mostly 5- and 6-year-olds, similar to American children in kindergarten rather than first grade. We examined performance differences among the tasks due to age, gender, and ability to establish the developmental sensitivity of the measures, and we correlated children's performance on various tasks to assess the tasks' concurrent validity and to examine the children's similarities in reasoning. We also correlated the children's performance on the tasks in the first study with their performance 2 years later to assess the usefulness of the tasks to predict longitudinal literacy development.

THE RESEARCH CONTEXT

The research was conducted at a public primary school in Brisbane, Queensland, Australia. The school is located in a middle-class suburb in native bush surroundings. Some children walked to school, but many others arrived by public bus or private car because the school is set in an open area with few surrounding houses. The school is comprised of several single story buildings linked to each other by covered walkways. The classrooms are large with some double teaching rooms linked by storage areas and small withdrawal rooms. The school enrolled approximately 250 children in Years 1–6, although we assessed only students in Years 1–4 in the first study. A total of 158 children and eight classroom teachers participated in the first study. The teachers were female and had all taught at the school for at least 1 year prior to the study. Three reading tasks were designed to measure the children's awareness and use of strategies for choosing books, comprehension of literal and inferential meaning, and construction of meaning as they listened to or read text. Later, we created an interview about children's work samples to assess how well they reviewed and evaluated their own work. This interview was designed as a self-assessment task similar to a portfolio review or student–teacher conference. These tasks were compared with each other, to teacher's evaluations of students' comprehension and motivation, to a measure of metacognition about reading, and to a standardized test of reading comprehension. We describe each task separately and discuss some of the results of the research to show the usefulness of the assessments.

Book Selection

All students were given the task of examining a variety of books and selecting those that were personally interesting. We created this "authentic" task because it represents a common cognitive choice that children make about books and provides insight about literacy strategies that teachers often nurture but seldom assess. The task was a modification of the book selection interview described by Kemp (1990). As the children examined different books, a research assistant observed how they skimmed text, how they identified their interests, and how they gauged the difficulty of books. We abbreviated Kemp's interview protocol and designed the task so that it provided quantitative assessments of children's book selection skills. We selected six books for students in Years 1 and 2 to examine and seven books for students in Years

3 and 4. We were careful to choose books that represented a variety of genres with topics and titles appropriate to the children's interests and ages. We provided books that varied in attractiveness, size, density of print, and gender-related interests. Teachers confirmed that the books were appropriate for each grade level.

The task included two phases, one to assess children's spontaneous behaviors while examining books, and the second to assess explicitly their knowledge about skimming books, identifying genres, and evaluating their interests by asking direct questions. In the first phase, Spontaneous Behaviors, children were asked to think aloud as they examined the books and sorted them into two piles, one pile representing books they would like to read now (the most preferred), and one pile for the books that they might read later. Children were asked to tell the examiner why they put books into each pile as they examined and sorted the books. Five kinds of spontaneous behaviors were recorded: whether students (1) skimmed the texts for meaning; (2) identified the genre; (3) expressed familiarity or interest; (4) commented on the difficulty of the books; and (5) identified clear preferences. A checklist allowed the examiner to identify whether the reasons for familiarity or interest related to the topic, author, or series, and whether students' remarks about difficulty were related to length, print, pictures, vocabulary, or comprehension. Some children became so absorbed in sorting the books that they needed to be reminded to think aloud. The cue, "Remember to tell me what you think about each book," was used on many occasions.

The second phase, Prompted Questions, included five questions that explicitly queried students about the same knowledge and skills used in the first phase. We designed the task in this manner to assess differences between what students do spontaneously and what they are able to report with prompting. The questions were asked after children examined the books and included: (1) "What kinds of books do you like?"; (2) "What do you look for when you skim through a book?"; (3) "How do you know if you'll like a book before you read it?"; (4) "How can you tell if a book is going to be easy or hard before you read it?"; and (5) "Can you tell me what kind of book this is?". The last question required students to identify the genre of each book in both piles. The ten items in the two phases were each scored 0, 1, or 2 points (according to scoring rubrics) which yielded two subscale scores from 1–10 points that could be aggregated. Higher scores indicate that students have better strategies and knowledge for selecting books.

There were two measures derived from this task, the mean aggregated total of the five spontaneous behaviors observed as children selected books (Spontaneous Behaviors) and the mean aggregated total of the five prompted questions (Prompted Questions). The means for each subscale and each year are shown in Table 1. It is evident that book selection skills and knowledge increased with age and that students' answers to prompted questions revealed better understanding than observations of their spontaneous behaviors alone. Although performance was higher in response to prompted questions, it was not at floor or ceiling levels for any grade in either phase. It was surprising to note that students in Year 2 received higher scores than students in Years 3 and 4.

Table 1
Mean Scores for Book Selection Task

Grade level	Spontaneous behaviors	Prompted questions	Total
Year 1			
M	2.0	2.5	4.5
SD	1.2	1.5	1.4
Year 2			
M	3.2	4.2	7.4
SD	2.0	1.3	1.7
Year 3			
M	2.5	3.7	6.2
SD	1.3	1.3	1.3
Year 4			
M	2.7	4.1	6.8
SD	1.5	1.4	1.5

Students in Years 1 and 2 examined different sets of books than students in Years 3 and 4, but the scoring systems were identical so the data were analyzed together. Of the five spontaneous behaviors, the most frequent behavior was identifying the topic, and the most infrequent behavior was identifying text difficulty. This pattern was found for students in all grades. Of the five prompted questions, the most difficult item for children at all grade levels was correctly identifying the genre of books. The easiest question for students in Years 2, 3, and 4 was naming preferred books: Year 1 students showed about equal mean correct answers for all questions. The five spontaneous behaviors and five prompted questions were aggregated into separate scales and analyzed in a Year (4) × Gender (2) MANOVA. Year was the only significant effect in the MANOVA and univariate F tests revealed significant effects due to year for Spontaneous Behaviors and Prompted Questions. Planned contrasts between grade levels revealed that Year 1 < Years, 2, 3, and 4 on both scales and Year 2 > Years 3 and 4 on Spontaneous Behaviors.

The individual items on the task were then examined in a Year × Gender MANOVA using all 10 items as dependent variables. Again, only the year effect was significant in the overall MANOVA. Univariate tests showed significant year effects for all the spontaneous items except identifying difficulty and for all the prompted items except showing how to skim books and identifying familiar books (all $ps < .05$). These differences were consistently observed in the planned contrasts between Year 1 and older grades, although scanning books and identifying genre showed significantly better performance by Year 2 students than students in Years 3 and 4.

In general, the Book Selection task revealed that students had modest knowledge and skills for choosing books. Although scores could range from 0–2 for each of the 10 items, most cell means were less than 1, indicating that appropriate book handling techniques were observed infrequently in spontaneous behaviors and that fewer than half the prompted questions were answered correctly. Students in Year 2 were much better than students in Year 1, and students in Year 4 were slightly better than students in Year 3 when comparisons were limited to students handling the same books. Overall, increasing age was accompanied by better skills and knowledge for selecting books. The high performance of Year 2 students relative to Years 3 and 4 students might be explained by different teaching practices in the classrooms or by the greater difficulty of the task for older students (i.e., they had more books of greater difficulty to examine).

Think Along Passages

Two different passages were used to assess children's comprehension strategies and their metacognition about constructing meaning. The task for children in Years 1 and 2 was designed as a listening comprehension task because (a) few of the 5- and 6-year-olds were fluent readers, and (b) listening to authentic, expository text allowed us to assess their comprehension strategies with challenging text. The passage was entitled "Bats: Our Fast-Flying Friends" and was adapted for Australian students from a passage in the Creative Assessments of *Heath Reading* (1991) for second graders. The passage for students in Years 3 and 4 was adapted from "The Peabody Ducks," a passage in the Creative Assessments of *Heath Reading* (1991) for third graders. This passage, and its use as a think along passage (TAP), is described in Paris (1991).

It is important to note that we used expository passages for all students and that the structure of the tasks was similar. Students were asked five specific questions about the passages before, during, and after they read or listened to the passages. The first question asked students to identify the topic of the passage; the second asked them to make a prediction about the passage content; the third asked them to monitor the meaning of a nonsense word inserted in text; the fourth asked them to make a within-text inference; and the fifth question asked for a summary of the passage. Immediately after each comprehension question, another question was asked to determine students' metacognition about constructing meaning from the passage. If they answered the comprehension question correctly, they were asked, "How did you know that?" or "Why do you think so?" If they did not attempt to answer the question, usually by saying "I don't know," they were asked, "If you don't know, what could you do to find out?" or "If you're not sure, what could you do?" The wording was adjusted for each question, but the metacognitive questions consistently asked students to explain their reasoning.

Three scores were derived for the TAP at each grade level: The number out of five comprehension questions answered correctly (comprehension), the number out of five metacognitive questions answered correctly (metacognition), and the total of these two variables (TAP total). The mean scores for these measures for each grade level are shown in Table 2.

Although the younger students listened to one passage and older students read aloud a different passage, the structure of the tasks was identical, so the results were analyzed together. In the MANOVA, there were overall significant effects due to year and gender. The univariate F tests revealed significant effects of year for metacognition and for TAP total, all $ps < .001$. The subsequent planned contrasts between years

Table 2
Mean Scores for Think Along Passages

Grade level	Comprehension	Metacognition	TAP total
Year 1			
M	1.9	1.2	3.1
SD	1.1	1.0	1.7
Year 2			
M	2.1	1.8	3.9
SD	.9	1.1	1.4
Year 3			
M	2.8	2.5	5.3
SD	1.0	1.1	1.7
Year 4			
M	3.1	2.7	5.8
SD	.9	1.0	1.6

NOTE: TAP total scores are the combined means of five comprehension and five metacognitive items. TAP = think along passages.

for metacognition showed that Year 1 < Years 2, 3, and 4, and also Year 2 < Years 3 and 4. Planned contrasts on the TAP total revealed that Year 1 < 2, 3, and 4, and that Year 2 < 3. The ANOVA on comprehension confirmed this pattern with a significant main effect of year and significantly lower scores at Years 1 and 2 than at Years 3 and 4. There was also a significant interaction of Year × Gender due to Year 3 boys > Year 3 girls, but the opposite pattern at Year 4. The TAP results show consistent increases on comprehension and metacognition with increasing age. The task appears sensitive to developmental improvements in strategic comprehension regardless of whether the modality is listening or reading. The TAP may be particularly useful for teachers working with beginning readers because it can provide assessments of thinking strategies independently of children's decoding abilities.

Story Construction From a Picture Book

There are relatively few instruments that assess comprehension strategies and metacognition of early readers. Nevertheless, many nonreaders and beginning readers are able to construct meaning from viewing pictures or "reading" wordless picture books. Many have an awareness that books tell stories, that they make sense, and that stories have particular features or conventions. Many children are also able to create stories from sequences of pictures. Therefore, we created the task Story Construction From a Picture Book to assess the comprehension abilities of students in Years 1 and 2. The task can be used to assess children's awareness of story themes and features independent of their decoding abilities and is described more fully in van Kraayenoord and Paris (1996).

We selected a book that had clear pictures and told a coherent story involving temporal and causal sequences of events: *Our Dog* by Helen Oxenbury (1984). We deleted the words that accompanied the story, eliminated some redundant pictures, photocopied the remaining pictures, and created a 16-page picture book that included the cover. The front cover with the title and author's name were the only printed words in the book. We wanted to give children two opportunities to learn about the story so we devised two phases to the task. In the first phase, Spontaneous Meaning Construction, children were directed to look through the book and tell the examiner what they thought. The second pass through the text was the phase Prompted Comprehension, in which children had another opportunity to go through the book and answer questions about the story. During both phases, six different aspects of meaning-making were assessed: initial examination of the book, comments about the pictures, elaboration and personal involvement, metalinguistics, revision strategies, and identification of themes or morals. During the first phase, the assessments were made through observations, although in the second phase, students answered specific questions. The second phase also required children to suggest an alternative title for the story.

In the second phase, Prompted Comprehension, students were asked to construct meaning from the pictures. For example, on page 9 of the story the mother and the child are bathing the dog in a basin which is surrounded by puddles. The examiner asked, "If this book had words in it, what do you think the people would be saying here? Pretend that you are reading it to me." Here we were interested to learn whether children had an awareness of metalinguistic aspects of stories such as book language, story telling intonation, dialogue construction, and story structure. The other five questions, interspersed throughout the book, were: (1) "What does the first page tell about the story?"; (2) "If you were telling someone this story, what would you say here?"; (3) "Tell me what is happening at this point in the story?"; (4) "How do you think the people in the story feel in this picture?"; and (5) "This is the last picture in the story but what do you think happens next? Why do you think so?" There were six items in each phase, and each one was scored 0 or 1 point. Thus, the range for both scales was 0–6. (The last prompted question about an alternative title was scored separately as either 0 or 1 point.) The Story Construction total score (0–13) was the sum of the three measures.

There were four measures derived from this task, the mean of aggregated spontaneous comments made during the first examination of the picture book, the mean of aggregated answers to prompted questions about the story during the second pass through the book, the alternative titles made by children, and the sum of all three variables (Story total). These measures were analyzed in separate Year (2) × Gender (2) MANOVAs but no significant gender or age effects were found on any variable. A subsequent MANOVA of all individual items also revealed no significant differences due to year or gender. However, there were some differences among 5- and 6-year-olds in their abilities to construct a story from a wordless picture book when different literacy skills were considered rather than year and gender. The correlations between story total and other variables revealed several interesting relations. For example, story total and the number of strategies that children used during the TAP were significantly correlated ($r = .30$) as was story total and teachers' ratings of children's comprehension skills ($r = .31$) and children's motivation ($r = .27$), all $ps < .05$.

Metacognition About Reading Strategies

The Index of Reading Awareness (IRA), a 20-item multiple-choice assessment of children's knowledge about reading strategies (see Jacobs & Paris, 1987), was given to students in only Years 3 and 4 in the first study and to all students in the second study. It is designed to assess children's awareness of evaluation, planning, regulation, and perceived utility of strategies for reading. The task was given individually to students to insure comprehension of the items and alternatives (although it was designed for group administration). Each item was scored 0, 1, or 2 points. The aggregated score of the 20 items was used as an index of metacognition about reading strategies. Scores ranged from 0 to 40. Greater awareness of strategic reading is reflected in higher scores.

The multiple-choice test of children's metacognitive knowledge about reading was given to students in only Years 3 and 4. Each item on the IRA received 0, 1, or 2 points. The means for all 20 items ranged from 0.8–1.6, with only two item means falling below 1.0 for both years. Thus, students' knowledge was adequate, and the measure was unaffected by ceiling or floor effects but the range was compressed. Metacognition improved with age, however. Students in Year 4 had higher mean scores ($M = 28.4$) than students in Year 3 ($M = 25.3$) and also higher mean scores on 18 of the 20 questions. Girls knew more about reading strategies than boys. In the univariate ANOVA, both year and gender were significant.

Reading Comprehension

The Test of Reading Comprehension (TORCH) is an untimed, standardized reading test that was developed in Australia (Mossenson, Hill, & Masters, 1987). The TORCH was given to students in only Years 3 and 4 in the first study and to all students in the 2-year follow-up. The test assesses the extent to which readers are able to obtain meaning from text by examining how well they fill in blank spaces in a paraphrased retelling of the passage. Thus, it is similar to a cloze task, but the TORCH deals with larger segments of text and ideas. We selected Passage A3, "Lizards Love Eggs," for our study because it was at the appropriate level of difficulty for students in Years 3 and 4. The TORCH was administered to the entire class as a silent reading task to be completed individually. The students were given the passages to read, which were collected when all students had finished. Students were then given a printed retelling of the passage in words that contained gaps corresponding to details in the original text. The students were required to complete the retelling by filling in the gaps using one or more of their own words. The administration and scoring procedures were followed according to the manual.

The individual raw scores (the total number of correct responses out of 20) were converted to scaled scores according to conversion charts in the manual. The scaled scores were used in the data analyses. The TORCH scaled scores reflect the numbers of 20 blanks correctly completed in the reading task. As expected, students in Year 4 ($M = 38.1$) scored higher than students in Year 3 ($M = 37.4$). TORCH scores were analyzed in a MANOVA with other variables given to students in only Years 3 and 4. The TORCH scores revealed a significant difference only for gender, because the girls scored higher than boys.

Teachers' Ratings of Students' Reading

The eight teachers involved in the study were asked to provide evaluations of their students' reading in five different domains: (1) comprehension, (2) awareness about reading strategies, (3) self-confidence, (4) effort, and (5) interests or experiences. Each domain was defined briefly for teachers who were asked to assess each child in their class on a 5-point Likert scale. The options indicated whether the child was in the *bottom 10%* of children at this year level, *below average, average, above average,* or in the *top 10%* of students at this year level. On the evaluation scale, 1 represented the *bottom 10%*, and 5 represented the *top 10%*. Two subscales were constructed from teachers' evaluations, one for comprehension and one for motivation. One subscale, total comprehension (TCOMP), was the aggregate of ratings for comprehension and awareness, and the second subscale, total motivation (TMOT), aggregated teachers' assessments of self-confidence, effort, and interests and experiences. Scores for the comprehension subscale (TCOMP) range from 2 to 10, and for the motivation subscale (TMOT), they ranged from 3 to 15. Higher scores indicate more positive evaluations by teachers.

One would not expect differences in teachers' ratings across grades if teachers used the same implicit scales of grade-level appropriateness for their judgments. Indeed, that appears true for teachers in three of the grades, but not for the teachers in Year 3 who had an average rating of only 3.2. Teachers in the other grades had average ratings of 3.4 or 3.5. It appears that teachers rated students on approximately the same scales of judgments and dispersed their ratings across students in their classes but either students were poorer readers and less motivated in Year 3, or these teachers had more negative evaluations of their students than other teachers had of theirs.

One way to verify the accuracy of teachers' ratings is to compare their judgments with performance on the TORCH. Students in Years 3 and 4 were divided into top and bottom quartiles ($n = 21$ at the top and $n = 20$ at the bottom), and mean ratings were compared in t tests for each of the five rated dimensions. There were significant differences between the top and bottom students on each dimension. The accuracy of teachers' ratings was also confirmed by the correlations with TORCH scores. TCOMP, the aggregated rating for comprehension and awareness, was correlated significantly with the TORCH scaled scores. At Year

3, $r = .41$, and at Year 4, $r = .69$. Thus, teachers apparently rated students accurately according to their reading ability, at least at Years 3 and 4. However, the cohort of students at Year 3 may have been less able or less motivated than students in other grades.

CORRELATIONS AMONG ASSESSMENT TASKS

A correlation matrix provides one way to determine the relatedness of tasks to each other, a type of concurrent validity for children who completed similar tasks. We calculated the correlation matrices separately for children in Years 1 and 2 and those in Years 3 and 4 because the tasks were not completely crossed with grade. Also, even when the tasks were similar, many of the actual passages and materials differed in order to be equated in difficulty and familiarity across a wide age range. Unfortunately, the power of the statistical tests decreases because of the smaller sample sizes involved. Only 40 children from Years 1 and 2 and 83 children from Years 3 and 4 are included in the correlation matrix shown in Table 3.

Nevertheless, there are several interesting patterns in Table 3. First, comparing the two halves of the table reveals that the correlations were stronger among older children, perhaps because of greater stability of reading skills or because of the greater range of scores and larger sample size. Second, the tasks assessing comprehension and strategic reading were correlated with each other. Third, the teachers' ratings of students were strongly correlated with the students' performance. Even though teachers were asked to rate students after only 4 months of the school year, and even though the ratings were simple holistic judgments, the ratings were correlated with many other tasks. The high correlations indicate that teachers were good assessors of their students' abilities and motivation.

Our initial study demonstrated how a variety of new tasks can assess young children's literacy strategies, construction of meaning from pictures and text, and metacognition about reading. These tasks can be administered individually or in groups in 10 to 30 minutes and can provide a wealth of useful information to teachers and parents. The

Table 3
Correlations Among Tasks for Younger and Older Children

Children, Years 1 & 2 (n = 40)

Subscale (tasks)	1	2	3	4	5	6	7
1. CA	—	.22	.22	—	—	.34*	.37*
2. Bk Sel		—	.37*	—	—	.30	.30
3. TAP Total			—	—	—	.22	.17
4. TORCH				—	—	—	—
5. IRA					—	—	—
6. TCOMP						—	.93*
7. TMOT							—

Children, Years 3 & 4 (n = 83)

Subscale (tasks)	1	2	3	4	5	6	7
1. CA	—						
2. Bk Sel	.14	—					
3. TAP Total	.12	-.01	—				
4. TORCH	.12	.28*	.46*	—			
5. IRA	.26*	.25*	.22*	.28*	—		
6. TCOMP	.11	.25	.29*	.55*	.33*	—	
7. TMOT	.22*	.28*	.22*	.53*	.32*	.86*	—

NOTE: CA = Chronological Age; Bk Sel = book selection task; TAP Total = Think-along-passages total score; TORCH = Test of Reading Comprehension; IRA = Index of Reading Awareness; TCOMP = Total Comprehension; TMOT = Total Motivation.
*$p < .05$.

comprehension tasks emphasize assessments of children's abilities to make sense of cohesive and authentic text whether through listening to passages, reading text, or viewing a series of pictures. Several of the tasks allow simultaneous and on-line assessments of children's meta-cognitive knowledge about searching for answers to questions in text, understanding how to select books appropriately, or understanding how and why to apply various strategies. The tasks appear to be reasonably correlated with teachers' judgments of students' literacy development and with concurrent assessments of similar cognitive processes. The intent of this study was not to create psychometric instruments, but rather to design prototypes of authentic tasks that teachers could use for diagnostic assessment and instruction. The value of the tasks is not in their standardized application, but rather in their flexible use with materials appropriate for the age and abilities of individual students. Thus, books of varying difficulty, topics, and genres can be used in the Book Selection task, as TAPs, or as the bases for story construction. We are advocating the value of the tasks for supporting interactive conversations about books, constructed meaning, and literacy strategies that provide teachers with relevant information about children's thinking. More research is needed to determine if using such tasks increases teachers' understanding of students' literacy strategies and improves classroom instruction and assessment.

A 2-YEAR FOLLOW-UP

When we began this project, we did not know if we would be able to assess the children in subsequent years, but, in order to allow for that possibility, we assessed every child in every classroom who had parental permission. Two years later, we were able to return to the same school and give most of the children a similar battery of literacy assessment tasks. The purpose of this second wave of data collection was to test the predictive validity of the tasks and to create some new tasks appropriate for older children. Thus, we retained many of the original tasks, revised others, and added a few new ones in order to assess the usefulness of the tasks for predicting subsequent literacy development.

This study was conducted exactly 2 years after Study 1, using 75% of the original students and many of the same teachers. The literacy strategy assessments included a variety of the following tasks:

Book Selection

The Book Selection task was virtually identical to the one described in Study 1 except that books were used that were appropriate for the older children in Years 3–6. The total score for this task was the sum of the five spontaneous behaviors and answers to the five prompted questions. Because each question was scored 0, 1, or 2 points, the range was 0–20 for the total scores. The means for students in Years 3–6 respectively, were: 9.3, 13.2, 11.5, and 14.2. All of these means were higher than the means in Study 1, which ranged from 4.5 to 7.4, perhaps because the students were older and more skilled. These data were analyzed with data from other tasks in a Year × Gender MANOVA separately for Years 3 and 4 and then Years 5 and 6 because the tasks involved different, grade-appropriate materials for these groups of younger and older subjects. Both MANOVAs revealed significant effects due to year but not gender, and there were no significant interactions. Year 4 students displayed better book selection skills than Year 3 students, and students in Year 6 were better than students in Year 5 at book selection skills, although students in Year 4 actually had a higher mean score than students in Year 5. This could be due to the use of more difficult books for the older students or possibly an idiosyncrasy of the Year-5 students. Whatever the reason for the Year-5 anomaly, when children used the same materials, there were clear developmental improvements with age in the skills involved in scanning, selecting, and identifying books appropriately.

Think Along Passages

We used the same expository passage, "The Peabody Ducks," for students in Years 3 and 4. For students in Years 5 and 6, we modified an expository passage about science called "Oceanographers Explore the Titanic," that is included in the Creative Assessments of *Heath Reading* (1991). As in the initial study, we wrote five comprehension questions to determine if students could (1) use titles and pictures to identify the genre and topic, (2) make predictions, (3) make inferences, (4) monitor the meaning of an unfamiliar word, and (5) make summaries of the main ideas. After each question, students' explanations of their thinking (how they knew the answer or how they could find out the answer) were used to determine their metacognitive scores.

Three measures were used to assess students' thinking about their reading: comprehension, metacognition, and the TAP total score, which is the sum of the answers to comprehension questions and the on-line metacognitive explanations of their answers. These data are shown in Table 4, which shows that in general, older children scored higher than younger children on comprehension and metacognition when the same materials were used. The Year × Gender MANOVAs were conducted on students who used the same materials, calculating Years 3 and 4 separately from Years 5 and 6. The performance of Year-6 students was

Table 4
Means and Standard Deviations for Think Along Passages: Study 2

Grade level	Comprehension	Metacognition	TAP total
Year 3			
M	2.5	3.0	5.5
SD	1.0	1.2	1.9
Year 4			
M	3.0	3.4	6.5
SD	1.1	1.2	2.1
Year 5			
M	2.3	3.0	5.3
SD	1.1	.9	1.6
Year 6			
M	3.4	3.8	7.2
SD	1.1	.8	1.6

NOTE: TAP total scores are the combined means of five comprehension and five metacognitive items. TAP = think along passage.

higher than that of Year-5 students on all four measures ($ps < .001$), whereas the performance levels of Years 3 and 4 only differed on observed strategies (because Year-3 students actually exhibited more overt strategies than Year-4 students). There was also a significant effect due to gender in the TAP total score for students in Years 5 and 6, because boys at both grades performed slightly better than girls. In general, the TAP appears sensitive to grade differences in comprehension and metacognition.

Metacognition About Reading Strategies

This 20-item multiple-choice task was identical to the one used in Study 1. Children's metacognitive knowledge about reading increased at each grade level. The means for Years 1–4 were: 23.7, 26.5, 30.7, and 31.3, respectively. These scores are similar to scores obtained by American third and fifth graders (Paris & Jacobs, 1984). In the Year (4) × Gender (2) MANOVA, the only significant effect was due to year. The planned contrast revealed that Year 3 < Years 4, 5, and 6, and that Year 4 < Years 5 and 6. Thus, this task is sensitive to differences in metacognitive knowledge about reading strategies between children in successive grade levels, except for Years 5 and 6.

Reading Comprehension

Passage A3, "Lizards Love Eggs," from the Test of Reading Comprehension (TORCH) was again used to assess children's reading comprehension in Years 3 and 4. In Years 5 and 6, a slightly more difficult passage was used, A5, "Feeding Puff." However, the procedures for administering and scoring the passages were identical. The TORCH scaled scores were progressively higher at each grade level. From Years 3–6, the mean scores were: 30.9, 45.2, 52.1, and 54.0, respectively. When these data were analyzed with other measures in a Year (4) × Gender (2) MANOVA, the only significant effect was year. The planned contrast revealed that Year 3 < Years 4, 5, and 6, and that Year 4 < Years 5 and 6, which did not differ. Thus, TORCH scores were generally sensitive to grade-level differences in reading ability.

Correlations Among Tasks

The correlations among tasks were higher in the follow-up study than in the original, perhaps because there was greater stability among older children in the knowledge, skills, and attitudes that were assessed. Book Selection was correlated significantly with the total TAP ($r = .40$), TORCH ($r = .50$), and the IRA ($r = .42$). The total TAP was also correlated significantly with the TORCH ($r = .38$) and the IRA ($r = .32$). The TORCH was also significantly correlated with the IRA ($r = .67$). This suggests that the strategies used in selecting books, understanding reading strategies, and comprehending text may involve similar cognitive skills and knowledge. Furthermore, age was correlated significantly with all the reading performance and metacognition measures except the total TAP, which indicates that the tasks generally discriminate literacy development by age.

Correlations Between Tasks in Study 1 and Study 2

To examine the longitudinal relations in the data, two correlation matrices were constructed, one for students who were in Years 1 and 2 in Study 1 and the other for students who were in Years 3 and 4 in Study 1. These are shown in Tables 5 and 6, respectively. This split is necessary because many of the tasks in Study 1 employed different materials for different grade levels, or many of the tasks were not given to all students, and unfortunately, this weakens the power of the statistical tests. Because some of the tasks were given only to students in Years 1 and 2, or only to students in Years 3 and 4, in the original study (Study 1), some of the intercorrelations among tasks cannot be calculated and are missing in the tables.

Table 5 reveals several correlations of interest. First, the Book Selection task had a high test–retest correlation ($r = .64$). Second, the ability to select books appropriately for students in Years 1 and 2 was strongly correlated 2 years later for these students (now in Years 3 & 4) with metacognitive knowledge about reading ($r = .46$). Third, Story Construction at Years 1 and 2 predicts strategic reading performance and knowledge 2 years later with moderately high correlations with TAP ($r = .47$), TORCH ($r = .43$), and IRA ($r = .47$).

Table 5

Correlations Among Tasks in Study 1 and Study 2 for Younger Children ($N = 28$)

Subscale	Bk Sel	TAP	TORCH	IRA
		Study 2 tasks		
Study 1 Tasks				
Bk Sel	.64*	.29	.30	.46*
TAP	.30	.21	.33	.09
Story Tot	.27	.47*	.43*	.47*
TCOMP	.51*	.37	.49*	.42*
TMOT	.52*	.43*	.37	.45*

NOTE: Tasks were completed by children in Years 1 & 2 for Study 1, and again 2 years later at Years 3 & 4 for Study 2. Bk Sel = Book selection task; TAP = Think-along passages; Story Tot = Story Total; TORCH = Test of Reading Comprehension; IRA = Index of Reading Awareness; TCOMP = Total Comprehension; TMOT = Total Motivation.
*$p < .05$.

Fourth, teachers' ratings of children's comprehension and motivation are very good predictors of children's reading performance 2 years later.

Some of the same patterns are evident in Table 6, which shows the correlations among tasks for older students, that is, those students in Years 3 & 4 in Study 1 who were retested 2 years later at Years 5 & 6 for Study 2. First, there is modest test–retest reliability for the Book Selection, TAP, and IRA, and there is higher reliability for the TORCH. Second, the Book Selection and TAP tasks at Years 3 and 4 are modest predictors of reading performance 2 years later. Third, the TORCH is a strong predictor of subsequent literacy development with good correlations with Book Selection ($r = .40$), TAP ($r = .37$), and IRA ($r = .43$). Fourth, teachers' ratings of students' comprehension and motivation continue to be related to children's subsequent literacy performance, which may lend further credibility to teachers' judgments.

Table 6

Correlations Among Tasks in Study 1 and Study 2 for Older Children ($N = 60$)

	Study 2 tasks			
Subscale	Bk Sel	TAP	TORCH	IRA
Study 1 Tasks				
Bk Sel	.28*	.15	.20	.21
TAP	.23	.22*	.29	.13
TORCH	.40*	.37	.53*	.43*
IRA	.40*	.21	.18	.37*
TCOMP	.35	.30	.52*	.37*
TMOT	.35	.32	.44*	.39*

NOTE: Tasks were completed by children in Years 3 & 4 for Study 1, and again 2 years later at Years 5 & 6 for Study 2. Bk Sel = Book selection task; TAP = Think-along passages; Story Tot = Story Total; TORCH = Test of Reading Comprehension; IRA = Index of Reading Awareness; TCOMP = Total Comprehension; TMOT = Total Motivation.
*$p < .05$.

CHILDREN'S SELF-ASSESSMENT

As we conducted research on tasks for assessing children's early literacy skills, we were also conducting research on literacy portfolios. Portfolios are collections of students' work samples that provide authentic evidence about their accomplishments. One important feature of portfolios is the responsibility placed upon students to collect, review, evaluate, exhibit, and explain their own achievements. We wanted to create a straightforward way for teachers to assess whether children were taking this responsibility and assessing their own work appropriately, so we designed a brief interview to measure children's self-assessment. The Work Samples Interview was a modified version of a questionnaire developed by Paris, Turner, Muchmore, and Perry (1995). Students were asked to bring work samples that they had done in class over the preceding 2–3 weeks for discussion in an interview with one of the research assistants. No restrictions were put on the scope of the work that was collected, and we expected the work samples to include artifacts from all curriculum areas. The samples provided the stimuli and focus for the interview. Each question asked students to consider their work samples in terms of a different feature. These features were chosen to assess cognitive, motivational, and developmental aspects of learning. The examiner recorded the number and kinds of work samples on the interview form. The target features and interview items follow.

1. *Pride.* Which one of these things are you really proud of? Why are you proud of it?
2. *Difficulty.* Which one of these things was very difficult? What made it so difficult for you?
3. *Self-review.* How often do you look back at work you did earlier and think about your own learning? How do you feel when you review your work?
4. *Sharing with parents.* Have you shown any of these things to your parents? Do you like to show your work to your parents?
5. *Evaluation by teachers.* Did the teacher give you marks on any of this work or tell you what work was good and what needed improving? How do you feel when the teacher evaluates your work?
6. *Personal progress.* Are you getting better with your reading and writing? How can you tell if your reading and writing are improving?
7. *Ability in reading.* Show me one piece of work here that shows that you are a good reader. How does it show your reading ability?
8. *Ability in writing.* Show me one piece of work here that shows that you are a good writer. How does it show your writing ability?
9. *Self-assessment in nonlanguage arts domains.* What other things are you trying to improve on in school? How do you know what you need to do better on?
10. *Future development.* How do you think you will do as a student in the next few years? What will you be very good at? How can you tell?

Each item had several parts to allow students to discuss specific features of work samples or their own development. Students had little difficulty selecting work samples or providing relevant information and were quite willing to share their reactions because of the conversational nature of the interview. The questions were restricted to self-assessment of literacy development and limited in number for this study, but they could be revised to fit other subject areas and purposes. Our goal was to determine if a brief metacognitive interview would yield useful information from students and if the data were correlated with other measures of students' metacognition and literacy abilities.

Most students brought between 6 and 15 artifacts with them to the interview. The range of work samples for the Year-4 students included 3-dimensional pictures, poetry, narrative writing, writing and illustrations related to a social studies topic, math exercise books and worksheets, "retrieval" charts completed in science, retellings of narrative stories, poems they had read or heard, spelling tests, "word finds," self-made calendars, summaries, and science reports. Students in Year 5 based their appraisals and responses on work samples that included their camp books, math exercise books, "reading friends' folders," reading contracts, narrative writing, homework books, social studies projects, letters of thanks (e.g., to camp parents), poetry, spelling tests, self-made comic books, language arts worksheets, math worksheets, and written notes for a speech. The work samples from the Year 6 students included math worksheets, theme work, science, poetry, camp books, self-made brochures, history projects, letters (related to a social studies theme), math exercise books, diaries (related to a language arts activity), Japanese worksheets (many schools in the state of Queensland have classes in a foreign language for all students at the Year-6 level), library search activities, written reports, crosswords, and retellings. All of the work samples were required activities in the various curriculum areas and had been set by the classroom teacher or school librarian and, in Year 6, by the Japanese-language teacher. Parenthetically, the richness of the work samples attests to the integrated language arts focus of Australian teachers.

A (3) Grade Level × (2) Gender MANOVA was conducted on students' responses to the interview items, with three grade levels (Years 4, 5, & 6) and two levels of gender. It revealed significant main effects for grade and gender, but no interaction effect. An examination of the univariate F tests for the individual items revealed that the main effect of grade was evident for Item 4, *Sharing with parents*; Item 7, *Reading ability*; Item 8, *Writing ability*; Item 9, *Self-assessment*; and Item 10, *Future development*. The main effect for gender was evident for Item 9, *Self-assessment*, and Item 10, *Future development*. Girls apparently were slightly better at self-assessment than boys and used more tangible evidence to discuss their future achievements. The interview appears to assess students' metacognitive appraisals of their accomplishments and progress and it was correlated with some aspects of students' motivation as well as literacy (see van Kraayenoord & Paris, 1997). For example, the scores on the Work Samples Interview were correlated significantly with the TORCH ($r = .36$) and with the IRA ($r = .56$). Thus, students' reading comprehension and metacognition about reading strategies are related to their abilities to reflect on their work and assess their own progress.

CONCLUSIONS

These studies substantiate the usefulness of several new tasks for assessment of young children's literacy strategies and development. Although the data were stronger for some tasks than others, we hope that these prototype tasks encourage researchers to generate new measures of children's literacy strategies and metacognition that extend traditional assessments of children's decoding and vocabulary to their thoughtful engagement with text and books. As teachers revise their literacy instruction and assessment to be more congruent, there is a pressing need to use classroom literacy activities that combine diagnostic assessment with instructional opportunities.

The TAP was designed to be consistent with instructional practices in which teachers intersperse questions before, during, and after students experience a passage and ask students to explain their thinking rather than simply to provide answers. The task was designed to be used either as a listening or reading comprehension task, and can be used for individual or group administration for assessment or instruction. We designed the task to yield quantitative measures of children's comprehension and metacognition so that researchers and practitioners would be able to use the TAP as a basis for summative assessment. Alternatively, the TAP can be used for formative assessment and does not require quantification. One strength of the TAP is that it is suitable for both summative and formative assessment. Another is that the TAP can be adapted for listening or reading using authentic text from the regular curriculum. The data indicate that the TAP is significantly correlated with the TORCH reading comprehension test, book selection skills, and coherent story construction, and it provides useful information to teachers about children's reasoning while reading.

The Book Selection task was also reliably related to other characteristics of young children's literacy. In Study 1, the ability to examine and select books was significantly related to the TORCH and metacognitive knowledge about reading for children in Years 3 and 4, while it was also significantly related to the TAP for children in Years 1 and 2. In Study 2, the Book Selection task was even more strongly related to measures of reading among older children and was significantly correlated with all measures of literacy strategies for students in Years 3 and 4. The Book Selection task is closely related to instructional practices that teach children how to skim books, how to identify familiar topics and authors, how to identify genre, and how to identify children's reading interests and abilities. That there are no assessment tasks like this is surprising because most teachers regard book handling as an important aspect of early literacy development. The task is easily modified to assess children's knowledge about different kinds of books, and the interview can be adapted for use by parents, teachers, and librarians. Apparently the ability to select books appropriately is related to literacy development but is dissimilar to traditional tests that emphasize vocabulary, sound–symbol correspondence, and comprehension.

The multiple-choice test of children's metacognitive knowledge about reading, the IRA, was originally reported by Paris and Jacobs (1984) in the context of an instructional study and later discussed in the context of problems with the assessment of metacognition (Jacobs & Paris, 1987). This research provides additional support for the usefulness of the measure to discriminate among children by age and reading ability. Indeed, the confirmation of the IRA with Australian children who experience different literacy practices suggests that the IRA is not only measuring the effects of classroom practices, but also is assessing some developmental aspects of children's emerging awareness about reading. In Study 1, children's metacognitive knowledge about reading was significantly correlated with Age, Book Selection, TAP, and TORCH scores. All these correlations were also significant in Study 2. Although we prefer to assess children's meta-cognitive knowledge about literacy in the context of ongoing reading and writing activities, such as the TAP and story construction tasks, there are occasions when a multiple-choice survey of children's knowledge can be informative for teachers and parents. Because it is related to other aspects of children's literacy development, their metacognitive knowledge about planning, evaluation, regulation, and utility of strategies are important characteristics of young children's knowledge that need to be assessed and taught (Paris & Winograd, 1990).

The Work Samples Interview was designed because of our growing interest in portfolios as classroom assessment activities (Paris & Ayres, 1994). The point of portfolios, in our opinion, is to encourage students to collect and review their own work so that they will become aware of their strengths and weaknesses and begin to regulate their efforts accordingly. Self-assessment can be motivating and empowering for students if supported by teachers and parents. The interview we designed was intended to be a tool to foster greater self-assessment among students during portfolio reviews or student–teacher conferences. We were encouraged to discover that a relatively brief interview was correlated significantly with the TORCH and the IRA, reliable measures of reading ability and metacognition. The interview apparently discriminates students by age and reading ability and may be modified easily by teachers to suit their curricula and students.

For older children in Study 1, teachers' judgments of students' comprehension and motivation were consistently and strongly related to children's actual literacy performance. That this simple holistic judgment on a 5-point scale proved so accurate surprised us, especially because the teachers had only known the children in their classrooms for a few months. In Study 1, for example, teachers' ratings of students' comprehension and motivation correlated greater than $r = .50$ with their TORCH scores. In Study 2, teachers' judgments were strongly correlated with literacy development 2 years later. For example, the correlations with their TORCH scores 2 years later ranged from $r = .37$ to $r = .52$. This suggests that teacher judgments can be both accurate and predictive of children's development. The findings suggests that more articulate teacher ratings, such as those that can be included in report cards, may be excellent predictors of children's literacy development. Although open to charges of subjectivity and bias, teachers' judgments may be as reliable and valid as other measures of young children's literacy development.

We were surprised at the strength of the correlations among tasks in both Study 1 and Study 2, and at the good predictive validity of some of the tasks over a 2-year period. We see this research as evidence for the usefulness of a variety of new assessments for young children's literacy development and encourage others to modify these tasks. Such tasks should be adaptable by teachers to suit their students and curricula and require brief administration time. The information from these tasks is directly beneficial to parents and teachers because it is diagnostic and lends itself to instruction with authentic texts that emphasize constructing meaning, using appropriate strategies, and adopting appropriate motivational orientations (Paris, Wasik, & Turner, 1991). When such tasks become commonplace for teachers and parents, the gulf between literacy research and practice will narrow, and early childhood educators, teachers, and parents will share more compatible views of literacy development. The use of such assessment activities in classrooms in the United States and Australia may also help to make instruction and assessment practices more consistent and sensible to children, parents, and teachers.

REFERENCES

Calfee, R., & Hiebert, E. H. (1990). Classroom assessment of reading. In R. Barr, M. Kamil, P. Mosenthal, & P. D. Pearson (Eds.), *Handbook of reading research* (2nd ed., pp. 281–309). New York: Longman.

Clay, M. M. (1979). *The early detection of reading difficulties.* Auckland, NZ: Heinemann.

Heath Reading. (1991). Lexington, MA: D. C. Heath & Co.

Jacobs, J. E., & Paris, S. G. (1987). Children's metacognition about reading: Issues in definition, measurement, and instruction. *Educational Psychologist, 22,* 255–278.

Kemp, M. (1990). *Watching children read and write.* Portsmouth, NH: Heinemann.

Morrow, L. M., & Smith, J. K. (1990). *Assessment for instruction in early literacy.* Englewood Cliffs, NJ: Prentice Hall.

Mossenson, L., Hill, P., & Masters, G. (1987). *Test of reading comprehension (TORCH).* Hawthorne, Victoria: Australian Council for Educational Research.

Oxenbury, H. (1984). *Our dog.* London: Walker Books.

Paris, S. G. (1991). Assessment and remediation of metacognitive aspects of reading comprehension. *Topics in Language Disorders, 12,* 32–50.

Paris, S. G., & Ayres, L. R. (1994). *Becoming reflective students and teachers: How portfolios and performance assessment promote children's learning, teachers' instruction, and parents' involvement.* Washington, DC: American Psychological Association.

Paris, S. G., & Jacobs, J. E. (1984). The benefits of informed instruction for children's reading awareness and comprehension skills. *Child Development, 55,* 2083–2093.

Paris, S. G., Turner, J. C., Muchmore, J., & Perry, N. (1995). Teachers' and students' perceptions of portfolios. *Journal of Cognitive Education, 5,* 7–40.

Paris, S. G., & van Kraayenoord, C. E. (1992). New directions in assessing students' reading. *Psychological Test Bulletin, 5,* 20–27.

Paris, S. G., Wasik, B. A., & Turner, J. C. (1991). The development of strategic readers. In R. Barr, M. Kamil, P. Mosenthal, & P. D. Pearson (Eds.), *Handbook of reading research* (2nd ed., pp. 609–640). New York: Longman.

Paris, S. G., & Winograd, P. W. (1990). How metacognition can promote academic learning and instruction. In B. J. Jones & L. Idol (Eds.), *Dimensions of thinking and cognitive instruction* (pp. 15–51). Hillsdale, NJ: Erlbaum.

Paris, S. G., Wixson, K. K., & Palincsar, A. M. (1986). Instructional approaches to reading comprehension. In E. Rothkopf (Ed.), *Review of research in education* (pp. 91–128). Washington, DC: American Educational Research Association.

Stallman, A. C., & Pearson, P. D. (1990). Formal measures of early literacy. In L. Morrow & J. Smith (Eds.), *Assessment for instruction in early literacy* (pp. 7–44). Englewood Cliffs, NJ: Prentice Hall.

Teale, W. H. (1990). The promise and challenge of informal assessment in early literacy. In L. Morrow & J. Smith (Eds.), *Assessment for instruction in early literacy* (pp. 45–61). Englewood Cliffs, NJ: Prentice Hall.

Tierney, R. J., Carter, M. A., & Desai, L. E. (1991). *Portfolio assessment in the reading–writing classroom*. Norwood, MA: Christopher-Gordon.

van Kraayenoord, C. E., & Paris, S. G. (1992). Portfolio assessment: Its place in the Australian classroom. *Australian Journal of Language and Literacy, 15*, 93–104.

van Kraayenoord, C. E., & Paris, S. G. (1994). Literacy instruction in Australian primary schools. *The Reading Teacher, 48*, 218–228.

van Kraayenoord, C. E., & Paris, S. G. (1996). Story construction from a picture book: A comprehension assessment for young learners. *Early Childhood Research Quarterly, 11*, 41–61.

van Kraayenoord, C. E., & Paris, S. G. (1997). Children's self-appraisal of their worksamples and academic progress. *Elementary School Journal, 97*(5), 523–537.

8

Literacy Retention: Comparisons Across Age, Time, and Culture

Daniel A. Wagner

In 1972, Harold Stevenson began his classic volume, *Children's Learning*, with the key notion that some of our most important questions about human beings are among the most compelling and complex issues in science. A point often lost on educational policy makers in this country and abroad is that many of the most fundamental problems in human nature are closely linked with the real, everyday, and basic questions of human development. In the nearly quarter century of his research that followed, Stevenson has been a leader among those who wish to make fundamental psychological science into applicable principles for the improvement of human development and educational practice. Anyone who has been involved in straddling these two worlds—science and policy—knows how difficult this balancing act can be.

Partial support for this paper was provided by the National Center on Adult Literacy (NCAL) at the University of Pennsylvania, in part by funding from the Education Research and Development Center Program (Grant no. R117Q00003) as administered by the Office of Educational Research and Improvement, U.S. Department of Education. The opinions expressed in this chapter do not necessarily reflect the views or policies of any federal agency. Parts of this chapter are based on an NCAL technical report (Wagner, 1994). I thank Scott Paris and two anonymous reviewers for their editorial comments on an earlier version of this chapter.

Yet, there is another quotation in *Children's Learning* that forecasts a major change in Stevenson's career interests: "The [study of the] child in school . . . has been omitted on the grounds that it appears to have greater implication for educational practice than it does for the understanding of learning" (Stevenson, 1972, p. xiii). Here, Stevenson suggests that children "in school" will not be covered in the book, as they do not represent the fundamental nature of learning in children. Perhaps even more startling, especially to those who have followed Stevenson's work in Asia over the last 2 decades, is the absence of the word *culture* in his book. Cultural variation in children's learning is nowhere represented. Clearly, Stevenson's work over the last quarter century has made an important turn toward the study of human variation and cultural diversity and its application to educational policy. His work also has demonstrated the importance of linkages—across disciplines, paradigms, and national boundaries. In this effort, Stevenson was less restricted by the domain of learning itself, which ranged from children learning how to drop marbles into holes (in the early part of his career) to the nature of learning mathematics in China and Japan (later on). At least part of the attraction of Stevenson's work and personality is his ability to cover such a broad substantive territory, while keeping his focus on what matters most in the articulation of research and policy in education. Personally I doubt if I was very aware of this point of view when I first came to Ann Arbor to study in psychology in 1970, after 2 years in the Peace Corps in North Africa. Fortunately for me, Harold Stevenson moved from the University of Minnesota to the University of Michigan within the following year.

While at Michigan and studying with Stevenson, I specialized in the area of cognitive development. Within a year or two, Harold and I led a graduate seminar (apparently the first of its kind at Michigan) in the area of culture and cognitive development. During this time, I also undertook a number of studies of how children develop memory skills, both in this country and in Africa (see, e.g., Wagner, 1974). Most of my graduate and early career research work tended to focus on cross-cultural dimensions of cognitive development, with relatively little focus on educational policy or practice. Over time, however, my path has been

akin to (and followed) Stevenson's in the sense of trying to create linkages across intellectual territories, while at the same time trying to find
areas of learning that, when explored in comparative context, can en-
lighten our efforts to improve education and human development.

This chapter on literacy retention devolves from Stevenson's perspective, although he focused mostly on young children, and more on
learning than retention. Literacy skill retention, as will be discussed in
the following, is an area of cognition and education that is most often
taken for granted, so much so that it has been left relatively untouched
by researchers. In the 1980s, I undertook an empirical study of children's school-based learning and retention in Morocco (a follow-up, in
some ways, of my dissertation work with Professor Stevenson). In that
work, I began to realize that in many parts of the world the issue of
skill retention was nearly as important as skill acquisition; indeed, there
was evidence that children in schools in poor countries appeared to
retain little of what they learned in school. There was (and continues
to be) a degree of alarm that large expenditures on children's education
were being "wasted" by inadequate school instruction in developing
countries; meanwhile skill retention was largely taken for granted in
children in countries such as the United States. By contrast, considerably more research interest exists in skill retention among adults, in
both industrialized and nonindustralized nations, but for different reasons.

In the discussion that follows, the focus is primarily on the skill
learning and retention of adult basic skills (especially literacy skills),
and the linkages between research and policy. It is also important to
understand at the outset that this educational niche represents a vari-
egated landscape. There are many gaps in what we know, and only a
few subareas have been relatively well explored. What is significant is
that this area—from a perspective of lifespan development—receives
the critical attention it deserves. It makes little sense to focus exclusively
on the acquisition parameters of learning if one has little notion of
what is retained following instruction.

This chapter has several sections: (a) cognitive skill retention across
the life span, (b) studies of literacy and basic skills retention, and (c)

policy implications of skill retention work. Research is reviewed covering such diverse topics as foreign language learning, summer education programs, and adult literacy campaigns—both in laboratory-type studies as well as in studies of education in national and international contexts. The chapter title—referring to age, time, and culture—is intended to signal the diverse perspectives that follow from the age of the learner, the time during and following instruction, and cultural variation in learning contexts.

WHAT IS SKILL RETENTION?

The results of the U.S. National Adult Literacy Survey (NALS; Kirsch, Jungeblut, Jenkins, & Kolstad, 1993) indicate that a large percentage of American high-school graduates perform poorly on reading and calculating tasks, so poorly that many commentators refer to these individuals as functional illiterates with diplomas. It is commonly thought that such persons never really learned what was taught in school. However, another hypothesis exists: namely, that these high-school graduates simply failed to retain what they once learned. Some educators term this the "use-it-or-lose-it" phenomenon. Skill retention, in the domain of learning and cognition, refers to the ability to retain learned skills across time, and retention studies typically consider skills that are learned in formal or informal educational settings.

As in the case of foreign language studies, many of us know that we have forgotten much of what we may have known in various areas at one time or another. We have a sense that if we had practiced more regularly, with more intensity, and so forth, we would have retained this knowledge or skill. In the field of adult learning, most researchers have focused on the acquisition of various skills and abilities, but very little attention has been devoted to skill retention. Indeed, in developmental psychology and in children's education, the very idea that cognitive and basic learning skills (as contrasted with specific items of factual knowledge) can be lost is anathema (at least in countries such as the U.S.). The metaphor often invoked for literacy work is that of the bicycle: Once you learn how to ride, it's impossible to forget. Specialists would say that not forgetting is due to overlearning of some sort. But how does this fit with the use-it-or-lose-it perspective? In my view, it doesn't, because many of the educationally learned skills are not overlearned, but rather poorly learned.

COGNITIVE SKILL RETENTION ACROSS THE LIFE SPAN

Learning, Memory, and Practice

One way to think about the broad fields of learning and literacy is to consider the cognitive component skills, such as memory abilities. The beginning of the scientific study of memory in humans is largely credited to Ebbinghaus (1913), who in the late 19th century began to test how quickly he (as his primary human subject) could memorize lists of words, moving eventually from words with meaning (i.e., real words) to words that would be "independent" of previous learning (i.e., nonsense words). This latter trend in isolating items-to-be-recalled became a dominant theme in the field of learning and memory up until the last couple of decades (cf. Baddeley, 1990).

An important turning point came with the work of Bartlett (1932), who argued for an emphasis on memory for real-world phenomena. It took several decades for his work to be recognized as truly significant; however, over the last 20 years, there has been dramatic growth in research focused on everyday or real memory events, such as eyewitness testimony, memory for school facts, memory of autobiographical occurrences in real lives, and so forth (Gruneberg, Morris, & Sykes, 1978; Neisser, 1982). This research on memory was paralleled by a similar trend in broader domains of the psychology of learning, which focus on situational and everyday contexts.

In this realm, the issue of practice is widely used for all kinds of repetition of human behavior. From such disparate works as sociologist Pierre Bourdieu's (1977) *Outline of a Theory of Practice*, to anthropologist Jean Lave's (1988) *Cognition in Practice*, to psychologist Howard Gardner's (1983) *Frames of Mind*, there is a renewed effort not only to describe what people do in their everyday lives, but also the possible consequences of doing these things repeatedly, through practice. In the domain of literacy skills, one would want to know how practice over varying conditions and intervals of time affects skilled performance. For example, can relatively low levels of practice over intermittent time periods succeed in maintaining low levels of original competencies in literacy? Before attempting to address this question in educational settings, it is useful to review what is known about various constraints on skill retention.

Constraints on Retention: Capacity, Forgetting, Transfer

Capacity

A classic issue in the study of memory is that of capacity. In the models of human memory previously described, investigators typically assume that short-term memory would store only a limited amount of information and for relatively brief periods of time (from ms to min), while long-term memory would be almost limitless in capacity and maintenance of the information (cf. Baddeley, 1990). In addition to the numerous experimental studies supporting these capacity models, a wide variety of compelling anecdotal evidence exists. In the latter category, it seemed obvious to many observers that memorizing unfamiliar names, telephone numbers, and other unrelated bits of information was an exceedingly difficult task, and that such information disappeared and remained virtually irretrievable once the mind began to concentrate on other cognitive tasks.

By contrast, many clinical observers, including Sigmund Freud, have commented that human memory performance is often greater than our conscious minds suppose. A massive body of evidence that humans retain a great deal of information that is not consciously or volitionally retrievable at any given time now exists. Yet, under the right conditions, such as psychoanalysis or in drug-induced states, many of these remembrances (or memory traces) can be retrieved. Such data suggest that the brain continually stores incredibly large amounts of information unknown to the conscious mind, but that can be retrieved under the right circumstances.

What, then, is the capacity of human memory? In a comprehensive and insightful review, Landauer (1986) provides an integrated analysis of both learning rates and forgetting rates of individuals as a function of a lifetime of learning. Although many assumptions are required in such an analysis, Landauer found that the average person acquires about one billion bits of information by midlife, with learning and forgetting remaining roughly stable or constant until older age. Just as interesting is his claim, based on studies of the physiology of the brain, that the human brain's hardware (i.e., synapses) is capable of storing at least 1,000 times more information than the billion-bit estimate of current memory usage. This conclusion supports claims that massive redundancy is physiologically possible within the brain, providing helpful backup resources in cases of forgetting, physical damage, aging, and so on.

The implication of this brief review on memory capacity is that there is room for much greater growth in memory than humans normally believe possible. Although adults in adult basic education programs (as well as older adults more generally) complain about difficulties in learning new information and new skills (and they then relate this back to less-than-successful formal schooling experiences), the cognitive reality may be quite different. It is reasonably safe to say that there are few known limits on learning capacity, and there is no evidence to support the notion that poor retention is a function of reaching some type of asymptote in memory capacity.

Forgetting

The usual scientific term for what is lost or not retained in memory is *forgetting*. As noted previously, a large body of research literature covers this phenomenon, a phenomenon that naturally affects all human beings. The theoretical issues that surround forgetting are similar to those related to memory research, such as conscious versus unconscious knowledge, the role of meaning in the rate of forgetting, modality of original learning (e.g., via words or pictures), length of time since last repetition of information, and so forth (cf. Baddeley, 1990).

The issue of what can enhance the staying power of information, or concomitantly, reduce that of forgetting, is central to understanding

of retention. Yet, as with the early research on memory, the vast majority of studies of forgetting are based on experiments with bits of information, usually of little relevance to everyday life. There is a significant literature, for example, on the influence of *proactive* and *retroactive* interference on forgetting, that is, how prelearning and postlearning experiences interfere with the retrieval of accurate remembrances.

The literature on skill retention, in contrast to the retention of units of related or unrelated information, is much smaller and will be described later. However, it is useful to consider for a moment why this is so. To some extent, skill retention can be seen as largely overlapping with information retention, especially in the areas of math, language, content learning, and so on. Yet there are areas that do not overlap, especially after the termination of sustained practice. One such area is that of physical skills, as for example in bicycle riding or piloting an airplane, where it is commonly thought that skilled performance needs very little in the way of refresher training in order to achieve high performance.

Transfer

The issue of skill transfer is another major research domain with implications for the study of retention. Generally speaking, educational research on transfer tends to focus on the importance of teaching and learning of specific versus general information or skills. For example, the study of classical languages (e.g., Latin or Greek) is often thought of as training the mind in a rigorous way, a way that then could be transferred to other types of learning and thinking. Similarly, there is a strong focus in mathematics-learning research that supports the notion of learning general principles rather than specific pieces of information or facts. Anyone who has gone to school has a sense of the importance that teachers place on the transfer of knowledge and skill.

The importance of transfer to skill retention concerns the role that additional practice (if different in kind from the original behavior) has on skilled performance. For example, what would the impact be of using literacy skills in church for the maintenance of literacy skills that are being learned in a workplace literacy program, or, to be more concrete, the role of practice in flying a one-prop plane on relearning how to fly two-prop planes? (Work on this issue has been undertaken; see Mengelkoch, Adams, & Gainer, 1971.) This second example makes it obvious that the questions of near and far transfer—words originally coined for studying rats and pigeons in laboratory experiments—still have relevance in today's psychological study of learning and retention.

Indeed, the topic of transfer has been the subject of a number of major syntheses in recent years (e.g., Cormier & Hagman, 1987; Detterman & Sternberg, 1993; Saloman & Perkins, 1989). While there is still a great deal of ongoing research on transfer issues, there are those who now believe that transfer, at least for education and training purposes in the real world, has rather little value. In a major introductory chapter to *Transfer on Trial* (Detterman & Sternberg, 1993), Detterman claims that there is a dearth of solid data that can confirm the real transfer from the general to the specific, but "if you want somebody to know something, you teach it to them" (Detterman, 1993, p. 15). There is still considerable debate in this domain, a debate that is mirrored in many of our models of school instruction. What is relevant to discussions of skill retention is the role that additional learning (if not identical repetitive practice) can play on the retention of skills.

One important area in education where transfer studies have direct relevance is in second-language learning, since both the skills and contents of language learning are similar in certain ways to those of literacy learning. In a major review of second-language learning, Odlin (1989) provides strong and comprehensive evidence for cross-linguistic transfer. He has found evidence that transfer occurs roughly equally among children and adults, in formal and informal settings, and in virtually all areas of language use, including morphology, phonetics, phonology, and semantics. Of specific relevance to the present report is Odlin's conclusion that literacy skill in the native language can have an important impact on second-language and literacy learning. This finding is similar to that found in our own work among Moroccan youth learning French language and literacy, having already learned to read in Arabic (Wagner, Spratt, & Ezzaki, 1989), as well as in recent work in the United States among adult immigrants (Carlo & Skilton Sylvester, 1996).

Transfer is an area that has received some attention in adult literacy work as well, and a recent report by Mikulecky, Albers, and Peers (1994) provides a comprehensive review. In this report, the authors make clear that transfer of literacy learned in adult literacy programs is likely to be quite limited. They distinguish between skill transfer at lower levels and what they term more "mindful" or higher level skills, suggesting that at either level, transfer is rather limited. In applying these results to the study of skill retention, it is important not to lose sight of the need to carefully delineate what needs to be retained and how to know what has indeed been retained.

SCHOOL LEARNING AND RETENTION STUDIES

It is in the area of formal education that retention would seem to have its greatest policy significance. Schooling is not only an attempt to put information into people's heads, but also is supposed to be related to how much of the information gets retained before going out the pro-verbial "other ear." While all of us are generally aware of how much we cannot recall or retain from previous instruction in school, few of us have much sense about the effectiveness of the original instruction in helping the learned material to remain in a state of usable memory. Of course, as has been pointed out many times, there are numerous *mne-monics* (specialized memory strategies) that can help information be retained for limited amounts of time, but we still know rather little about what is remembered (following instruction) over longer time intervals (such as weeks and months). In the areas of school-based research, the length of the retention interval appears to be a significant factor in retention. There are two areas that have a substantial corpus of published research, and each of these will be addressed in turn.

Studies of Summer Retention: A Season for Forgetting?

The growth of compensatory education and intervention programs for American children has led to an increase in the number of programs available in the summer months for children from disadvantaged homes. There are at least two related reasons for these summer programs. First, social planners feel that students who are at risk of school failure could and should get additional instruction during the summer, and that this would help them catch up to students who achieve more. Thus, summer schooling could help overcome inequalities in home support of children's achievement. Second, there is some research that suggests that there is a loss of school-based skills that occurs during the summer, and that this occurs more frequently in disadvantaged homes than in advantaged ones. Evidence in support of both of these arguments is provided in comprehensive reviews by Heyns (1987, 1988). In her synthesis, Heyns describes a series of major "summer effects" studies that show conclusively that American children tend to lose some basic skills (reading, writing, math) over the summer, skills that they spend the first month or two relearning at the beginning of the following school year. Furthermore, the data show that disadvantaged and minority youth lose more skills than do the more advantaged children. Finally, Heyns found that compensatory programs can stem the loss of skills among disadvantaged youth through summer intervention programs.

For the purpose of the present review, there are several points worth underscoring. First, even with sustained learning over almost 9 months and at least several hours on task per day, studies show that a 3-month interval without formal instruction does generally lead to a loss of basic skills. Second, the skills that suffer most of the loss tend to be ones that are taught through drill, as well as those that require the learning of specific facts such as dates and vocabulary (Heyns, 1987). Third, the relearning or the maintenance of these school-learned skills is not difficult with additional practice. Finally, the overall efficiency of learning is reduced by the fact that previously learned material has to be relearned at a later date, causing weeks and months of time lost for new learning.

Foreign Language Learning and Retention

There now exists a small but growing field of research into what is termed *second-language attrition*. Although stimulated by a book resulting from a conference entitled *The Loss of Language Skills* (Lambert & Freed, 1982), this subfield has its origins much earlier among teachers of classical languages. For example, in the early days of educational psychology, research was undertaken by Kennedy (1932) on Latin learning and attrition over summer vacation periods. Among the relevant findings was that Latin syntax skills were lost over the three summer months, and that those students with poorer initial skills and lower IQ scores tended to lose the most syntactic forms.

A half-century later, this type of study was repeated on a much larger database of nearly 800 adults who had earlier in life learned Spanish to varying degrees of expertise. In this well-known empirical study, Bahrick (1984) were able to shed light on some important problems in second-language attrition, with implications for the present topic of literacy retention. With such a large sample of adults, most of whom reported little or no practice over long periods of time, Bahrick was able to show the impact of differing degrees of original skill on second-language skill attrition. Initial Spanish skill was measured by both grades and number of courses taken, while subsequent testing, undertaken as long as 50 years later, was measured through a battery of tests including grammar recall, idiom recall, vocabulary, and reading comprehension. Bahrick's most important finding was that considerable skill was retained over longer periods of time (from 5 to 25 yrs), in what he termed *permastore*, where little was forgotten in spite of little practice. Important for the present discussion are his findings on short-term retention over the first year and up to five years postinstruction. Here, Bahrick found considerable attrition in skill. For example, he found that a single course in Spanish was unlikely to leave much permanent store at all, and that the forgetting rates of individuals over the first 5 years following the end of language instruction was generally constant. This latter finding he interpreted as being due to the losses in recently learned information among individuals at all different levels.

Although there have been different interpretations of the Bahrick findings (Neisser, 1984) and more recent research has been undertaken (Lanoue, 1991; Moorcroft & Gardner, 1987; Vechter, Lapkin, & Argue, 1990; Weltens, Van Els, & Schils, 1989), the Bahrick study has had a major impact on the field of second-language acquisition. It is clear, for example, that even though there may be an asymptote in forgetting over many years, there are important losses that most learners at different levels of expertise are subject to in the initial time period after the termination of instruction. Most important is the somewhat provocative finding that there is considerable loss in skill for beginning language learners, but relatively stable maintenance of skill of intermediate learners with little practice. Of course, it must be emphasized that the Bahrick study was limited to English-speaking Americans who learned Spanish as a second language in high school or college, a rather specific middle-class population learning a limited range of skills.

The field of literacy has only just begun to address such a specific set of retention issues with empirical research. Much of the relevant research derives from concerns about the quality and duration of adult literacy programs in developing countries, as follows.

LITERACY SKILL RETENTION

International Studies

In the international education literature, the problem of retention of complex cognitive skills has been the focus of a considerable amount of discussion. As noted earlier, policy makers in developing countries have been especially concerned that the limited years of primary schooling available for children might be insufficient for them to retain basic literacy skills. Indeed, it is sometimes claimed for developing countries that at least 4–6 years of primary school for children is the intellectual human resources "floor" upon which national economic growth is built. The argument is that a threshold number of years of education is required for more-or-less permanent reading and math skills to be acquired by the school-aged child or adolescent (Fagerlind & Saha, 1983; Hamadache & Martin, 1987). This is one of the reasons that international organizations such as the United Nations and the World Bank have called for greatly increased access to primary schooling in Third World countries.

Within this line of reasoning, the concept of literacy retention

241

(sometimes termed *cognitive retention*; see Simmons, 1976) is central, since what children learn and retain from their school years (likewise for adults in informal and adult basic education programs) is thought to be what can be utilized in productive economic activities later on. When learners fail to retain what is taught in an educational program, educational *wastage* (a term often used by international agencies; UNESCO, 1984) occurs. Those individuals (children or adults) will not reach the presumed threshold of minimum learning required to ensure retention of acquired knowledge, or the threshold required for self-sustained learning to be maintained.

Thus, the retention of literacy is a key goal of educational planners around the world, particularly in Third World societies where only modest amounts of education can be (and are) provided to a large and growing portion of the population. In such contexts, it is critical to know how much is likely to be retained from a given input of instructional time and financial resources. Since basic literacy skills have been the prime educational target for most developing countries, apprehension about *literacy relapse* (falling back into a state of illiteracy) has received the most attention from national and international policy makers. Furthermore, this concern has been particularly apparent in discussions about the quality of retention in adult literacy campaigns in developing countries (International Development Research Centre, 1979; Hamadache & Martin, 1987; Lind & Johnston, 1986; Wagner, 1992, 1995).

Given the centrality of the assumption of literacy retention in policies governing basic education programs in developing countries, it is surprising to find how little attention has been devoted to its empirical study. Only a small amount of empirical research deals directly with literacy skill retention in developing countries (Gadgil, 1955; Hartley & Swanson, 1986; National Educational Testing Center, 1982; Roy & Kapoor, 1975; Simmons, 1976). A recent review by Comings (1995) pulled together a number of contemporary evaluations of adult literacy programs, with a focus on skill retention. Unfortunately, the Comings review, along with previous studies, encompass or accept serious flaws in methodology or project design, and none of these studies used a multiyear longitudinal design with participants as their own controls (where there is testing at program completion and further downstream)—a feature that is central to the credibility of the study of skill retention (as was utilized, for example in Heyns 1987, 1988; and Bahrick 1984; studies mentioned earlier). In the Third World, an appropriate research design for literacy retention is further complicated by the fact that primary school leavers may already be assumed to be among the lowest achievers in a school, making it difficult to compare their performance with those who remain in school. This is a limiting feature of most cross-sectional studies. Longitudinal designs are generally more rigorous in such work, so that an individual's school achievement may be compared with his or her own performance in the years after leaving school.

To date, the only adequately designed longitudinal study of literacy skill retention was carried out in Morocco in the 1980s (Wagner, Spratt, Klein, & Ezzaki, 1989). The study focused on the retention of literacy skills among adolescents, all of whom dropped out of school before completing the fifth grade of their studies, and all of whom were followed into everyday settings over a 2-year, postschooling period. The Moroccan students in the study ($N = 72$) were part of a larger study on the acquisition of literacy, so that the measures involved had considerable checking for validity and reliability, and substantial information was available on the social backgrounds of the youths, based on individual interviews in the home. The skill retention outcomes of this study were unequivocal; overall, Arabic literacy (reading and writing) skills were not lost over the 2 years after the termination of schooling. Indeed, depending on the nature of postschooling experience (e.g., work outside the home as contrasted with household chores mainly within the home), many adolescents actually increased their literacy skills. The only significant loss in skill was in schoollike math or computational tasks, although general cognitive function (as measured by a logical reasoning task) showed no change over time. One additional finding of some relevance was that French literacy skill, although studied much less than the national language of Arabic, was retained with only minimal loss after school dropout, a finding somewhat in contradiction to Bahrick's foreign-language attrition work cited earlier. Thus, these findings raise interesting questions about the skill level, or threshold, required before skills are permanently acquired.

Although the Morocco study lays to rest the myth that primary school dropouts who do not complete their studies will necessarily relapse into a state of illiteracy (as had been claimed), the study nonetheless leaves open many issues relevant to the present review. Most important, it did not study short-term and intermittent study by adults, but rather only the continuous study of a full, primary-school curriculum among children and youth.

Studies in the United States

As noted previously, the study of both the acquisition and retention of literacy skills among youth and adult learners has been the subject of considerable speculation. Several recently completed studies in the United States provide data of relevance to the question of literacy retention among adults.

The first is the National Adult Literacy Survey (NALS; Kirsch et al., 1993), which collected in-depth information (including literacy assessment items) on a broad and representative sample of nearly 26,000 American adults, with a wide variety of background characteristics. The results provide some important clues about the retention of literacy skills, beyond the well-publicized finding that nearly one half of the sample (and by extension, one half of the entire U.S. adult population) functioned at the two lowest levels of literacy skill, low enough to be considered lacking in fundamental skills (prose, document, quantitative) for the American workplace. This highly charged finding made the news around the world, but it masked additional key results that are relevant for the present review. For example, the NALS found that nearly 20% of adults who possessed a high-school diploma were also in the lowest literacy level, along with nearly 80% of those with 8 or fewer years of schooling. This means either that these individuals, as school-aged students, did not learn the basic literacy skills that were taught, or they failed to retain these skills once they left school. Furthermore, of the adults who had obtained the GED diploma (high-school equivalency), usually following some type of adult education program, nearly 15% were in the lowest literacy level, although more than half still scored in the lowest two levels. The performance of these adults, in other words, was roughly indistinguishable from that of high-school graduates, even though their training was necessarily later in life and closer to the time of the survey administration. Since the NALS was not a longitudinal study, it is impossible to know whether these perceived differences across time are due to retention issues or original lack of learning. Yet the study does suggest that whatever the inputs, in formal or informal education programs, the results (in terms of skills retained) are far less than policy makers and educators had expected or desired.

Another national study, the National Evaluation of Adult Education Programs, completed its work in 1994 (Development Associates, 1992, 1993, 1994). This research provides the profiles of a nationally representative sample of ABE programs and the adult students that they served, providing a compendium of useful background information, including the markedly limited amount of instruction received by many adults who enter these programs. For example, the 1993 report found that nearly 36% of all new adult learners left their programs of study before completing 12 hours of instruction, essentially before any meaningful literacy learning could take place. Indeed, in the 1994 final report, detailed assessment information on adult learners indicated that little gain was found among most learners.

Finally, an empirical study of adult literacy retention, undertaken by the National Center on Adult Literacy, has recently been completed (Wagner, Stites, & Foley, 1997). This research involved a tracer study based on the Development Associates (1994) study sample, with an additional assessment to measure skill retention after program completion; unfortunately, as with the larger Development Associates study itself, problems with the initial data collection and with the subsequent dataset led to the analysis of only a relatively small sample of complete cases. The results of this empirical study suggest, as in the Morocco study, that skill loss is relatively minimal. However, the fact that the acquisition curves (learning gains) were also relatively flat, means these results could also be interpreted by assuming that the sample adults learned relatively little and therefore had little skill to "lose." This study, as with the others described in this section, confirms the methodological difficulties endemic in skill retention studies with low-literate adults in real (as contrasted to experimental or laboratory) settings.

CONCLUSIONS AND POLICY IMPLICATIONS

As pointed out at the beginning of this chapter, complex scientific problems are often linked to questions of importance to fundamental policy. The domain of literacy retention provides a good case in point. Research on human skill retention spans many decades and much has focused on laboratory-like studies. There is a small but growing domain of retention studies focused on what is retained following basic skills instruction for children, youth, and adults. At the same time, there is a rising interest among policy makers about the effectiveness of investments in education. This nexus of research domain and policy interest is a good example of the kind of territory that needs further exploration in the coming years.

In the specific domain of adult literacy, policy makers lack information on the maintenance of skills learned in the short-term and intermittent programs that characterize adult education in contemporary America, as well as in other countries. Yet, public interest and support of literacy programs depends, as in public education, on the claim that learners learn efficaciously and can retain enough to apply new skills to improve their life circumstances. The funding of such important areas of education is dependent on research and evaluation studies that can support the relationship between these inputs and outputs.

The present review of the literature suggests that in spite of considerable ancillary information there remains a serious gap in our knowledge concerning literacy skill retention. The empirical findings on skill retention cover a wide range of subareas, but they are limited in generalizability. Nonetheless, such findings will provide important informational guideposts to future investigators. A brief listing of some of these key research questions is listed as follows:

- Are different types of skills (such as reading, writing, and calculating) retained to differing degrees? differently? Are there specific components of broader skills (e.g., vocabulary, speed of reading) that are retained in different ways?
- Do levels of skill at program entry determine, in part, the retention of skill acquired in a given type of program? Are there certain kinds of programs (e.g., ESL, workplace, family) that enhance (or could enhance) the level of literacy skill retained?
- Do thresholds of expertise exist for certain skills that allow them to be better maintained over time? What is the role of overlearning and automaticity on the retention of skills?
- What kinds of concurrent or postinstructional practice are conducive to skill retention? What might be the role played by metacognitive beliefs and affective attitudes toward learning?

In summary, as work continues in this area, researchers in the field ought to be able to resist anecdotal claims about "relapse" into illiteracy, just as Harold Stevenson has taught us to resist the easy and anecdotal claims (of only a decade ago) that "Japanese children don't have learning problems" (cf. Stevenson & Stigler, 1992). Rather, we need to be able to focus our attention on specific (and answerable) questions that can be addressed by researchers possessing not only adequate scientific skills, but also a sensitivity to the kinds of results that will be pertinent (and influential) among policy makers. The linkage between research and policy—cutting across age, time, and culture—is one of the important legacies of Harold Stevenson's approach to human development.

REFERENCES

Atkinson, R. C., & Shiffrin, R. M. (1968). Human memory: A proposed system and its control processes. In K. W. Spence (Ed.), *The psychology of learning and motivation: Advances in research and theory* (Vol. 2, pp. 89–195). New York: Academic Press.

Baddeley, A. (1990). *Human memory: Theory and practice.* New York: Allyn & Bacon.

Bahrick, H. P. (1984). Fifty years of second language attrition: Implications for programmatic research. *Modern Language Journal, 68,* 105–118.

Bartlett, F. C. (1932). *Remembering.* London: Cambridge University Press.

Bourdieu, P. (1977). *Outline of a theory of practice.* Cambridge: Cambridge University Press.

Carlo, M. S., & Skilton Sylvester, E. E. (1996). *A longitudinal investigation on the literacy development of Spanish-, Korean-, and Cambodian-speaking adults learning to read English as a second language* (Tech. Rep.). Philadelphia, PA: University of Pennsylvania, National Center on Adult Literacy.

Comings, J. (1995). Literacy skill retention in adult students in developing countries. *International Journal of Educational Development, 15*(1), 37–46.

Cormier, S. M., & Hagman, J. D. (Eds.). (1987). *Transfer of learning: Contemporary research and applications.* San Diego, CA: Academic Press, Inc.

Detterman, D. K. (1993). The case for the prosecution: Transfer as an epiphenomenon. In D. K. Detterman & R. J. Sternberg (Eds.), *Transfer on trial: Intelligence, cognition and instruction* (pp. 1–24). Norwood, NJ: Ablex.

Detterman, D. K., & Sternberg, R. J. (Eds.). (1993). *Transfer on trial: Intelligence, cognition and instruction.* Norwood, NJ: Ablex.

Development Associates. (1992). *National evaluation of adult education programs, first interim report: Profiles of service providers.* Washington, DC: U.S. Department of Education.

Development Associates. (1993). *National evaluation of adult education programs, first interim report: Profiles of client characteristics.* Washington, DC: U.S. Department of Education.

Development Associates. (1994). *National evaluation of adult education programs. Final Report.* Washington, DC: U.S. Department of Education.

Ebbinghaus, H. (1913). *Memory.* New York: Columbia University.

Fagerlind, I., & Saha, L. J. (1983). *Education and national development: A comparative perspective.* New York: Pergamon.

Gadgil, D. R. (1955). Report of investigation into the problem of lapse into illiteracy in the Satara District. In D. R. Gadgil & V. M. Dandekar (Eds.), *Primary education in the Satara Districts: Reports of two investigations* (Pub. No. 31). Gokhale Institute of Politics and Economics.

Gardner, H. (1983). *Frames of mind.* New York: Basic Books.

Gruneberg, M. M., Morris, P. E., & Sykes, R. N. (Eds.). (1978). *Practical aspects of memory.* London: Academic Press.

Hamadache, A., & Martin, D. (1987). *Theory and practice of literacy work: Policies, strategies and examples.* Paris: UNESCO/Code.

Hartley, M. J., & Swanson, E. V. (1986). *Retention of basic skills among dropouts from Egyptian primary schools* (Education and Training Series, Report No. EDT40). Washington, DC: The World Bank.

Heyns, B. (1987). Schooling and cognitive development: Is there a season for learning? *Child Development, 58,* 1151–1160.

Heyns, B. (1988). *Summer learning and the effects of schooling.* New York: Academic Press.

International Development Research Centre. (1979). *The world of literacy: Policy, research and action.* Ottawa: Author.

Kennedy, L. R. (1932). The retention of certain Latin syntactical principles by first and second year Latin students after various time intervals. *Journal of Educational Psychology, 23,* 132–146.

Kirsch, I. S., Jungeblut, A., Jenkins, L., & Kolstad, A. (1993). *Adult literacy in America: A first look at the results of the National Adult Literacy Survey.* Washington, DC: U.S. Department of Education.

Lambert, R., & Freed, B. (Eds.). (1982). *The loss of language skills.* Rowley, MA: Newbury House.

Landauer, T. K. (1986). How much do people remember? Some estimates of the quantity of learned information in long-term memory. *Cognitive Science, 10,* 477–493.

Lanoue, G. (1991). Language loss, language gain: Cultural camouflage and social change among the Sekani of Northern British Columbia. *Language in Society, 20,* 87–115.

Lave, J. (1988). *Cognition in practice: Mind, mathematics and culture in everyday life.* New York: Cambridge University Press.

Lind, A., & Johnston, A. (1986). *Adult literacy in the Third World: A review of objectives and strategies* (Education Division Documents, No. 32). Stockholm: Swedish International Development Authority.

Mengelkoch, R. F., Adams, J. A., & Gainer, C. A. (1971). The forgetting of instrument flying skills. *Human Factors, 13,* 397–405.

Mikulecky, L., Albers, P. N., & Peers, M. (1994). *Literacy transfer: A review of the literature* (Tech. Rep. No. TR94-05). Philadelphia: University of Pennsylvania, National Center on Adult Literacy.

Moorcroft, R., & Gardner, R. C. (1987). Linguistic factors in second-language loss. *Language Learning, 37,* 327–340.

National Educational Testing Center. (1982). *Literacy retention among dropouts from the Philippine elementary schools.* Manila, The Philippines: Philippine Ministry of Education, Culture, and Sports.

Neisser, U. (1982). *Memory observed.* San Francisco: Freeman.

Neisser, U. (1984). Interpreting Harry Bahrick's discovery: What confers immunity against forgetting. *Journal of Experimental Psychology: General, 113,* 32–35.

Odlin, T. (1989). *Language transfer: Cross-linguistic influence in language learning.* New York: Cambridge University Press.

Roy, P., & Kapoor, J. M. (1975). *The retention of literacy.* Delhi, India: Macmillan of India.

Saloman, G., & Perkins, D. (1989). Rocky roads to transfer: Rethinking mechanisms of a neglected phenomenon. *Educational Psychologist, 24,* 113–142.

Simmons, J. (1976). Retention of cognitive skills acquired in primary school. *Comparative Education Review, 20,* 79–93.

Stevenson, H. W. (1972). *Children's learning.* New York: Appleton-Century-Crofts.

Stevenson, H. W., & Stigler, J. W. (1992). *The learning gap: Why our schools are failing and what we can learn from Japanese and Chinese education.* New York: Summit.

UNESCO. (1984). *Evolution of wastage in primary education in the world between 1970 and 1980* (Document ED/BIE/CONFINTED/39/Ref. 2). Paris: UNESCO.

Vechter, A., Lapkin, S., & Argue, V. (1990). Secondary language retention: Summary of the issues. *The Canadian Modern Language Review, 46,* 289–303.

Wagner, D. A. (1974). The development of short-term and incidental memory: A cross-cultural study. *Child Development, 45,* 389–396.

Wagner, D. A. (1992). *Literacy: Developing the future.* UNESCO Yearbook of Education (1992, Vol. 43). Paris: UNESCO.

Wagner, D. A. (1994). *Use it or lose it? The problem of adult literacy skill retention.* National Center on Adult Literacy (NCAL) (Tech. Rep. No. TR94-97). Philadelphia: University of Pennsylvania.

Wagner, D. A. (1995). Literacy and development: Rationales, myths, innovations, and future directions. *International Journal of Educational Development, 15,* 341–362.

Wagner, D. A., Spratt, J. E., & Ezzaki, A. (1989). Does learning to read in a second language always put the child at a disadvantage? Some counterevidence from Morocco. *Applied Psycholinguistics, 10,* 31–48.

Wagner, D. A., Spratt, J. E., Klein, G. D., & Ezzaki, A. (1989). The myth of literacy relapse: Literacy retention among Moroccan primary school leavers. *International Journal of Educational Development, 9,* 307–315.

Wagner, D. A., Stites, R., & Foley, E. (1997). *Skill retention in adult basic education.* National Center on Adult Literacy (NCAL) (Tech. Rep.). Philadelphia: University of Pennsylvania.

Weltens, B., Van Els, T. J., & Schils, E. (1989). The long-term retention of French by Dutch students. *Studies in Second Language Acquisition, 11,* 205–216.

Yates, F. A. (1966). *The art of memory.* Chicago: University of Chicago Press.

9

Literacy Experiences and the Shaping of Cognition

Keith E. Stanovich, Anne E. Cunningham, and
Richard F. West

Reading is a popular topic in cognitive development and education. Within cognitive developmental psychology, for example, there is considerable literature on the individual differences in the cognitive processes that support efficient reading performance (Carr & Levy, 1990; Gough, Ehri, & Treiman, 1992; Perfetti, 1985; Share & Stanovich, 1995). A popular research strategy has been the cognitive correlates approach (see Pellegrino & Glaser, 1979; Sternberg, 1990) in which investigators attempt to determine whether individual differences in particular cognitive processes or knowledge bases can serve as predictors of reading ability (e.g., Carr & Levy, 1990; Jackson & McClelland, 1979). The causal model that is implicit in such analyses locates individual differences in the cognitive subprocesses prior to reading ability. The focus of this chapter tends to invert the causal model implied in most of this research. That is, many researchers have attempted to specify individual differences in the cognitive processes that support efficient

This research was supported by Grant No. 410-95-0315 from the Social Sciences and Humanities Research Council of Canada to Keith E. Stanovich; a postdoctoral fellowship from the James S. McDonnell Foundation to Anne E. Cunningham; and a James Madison University Program Faculty Assistance Grant to Richard F. West.

reading performance. In contrast, very little attention has been focused on the reciprocal possibility that exposure to print itself, *print exposure*, affects the development of cognitive processes and declarative knowledge bases.

In contrast to the relative inattention to the consequences of reading experience displayed by developmental psychologists, the literature on the cognitive consequences of literacy in the humanities and social sciences outside of psychology is large (Gee, 1988; Goody, 1977, 1987; Graff, 1986, 1987; Havelock, 1963, 1980; Kaestle, 1991; Ong, 1967, 1982; Stock, 1983). Over the past 3 decades, scholars such as Goody (1977, 1987), Olson (1977, 1994), and Ong (1982) have promulgated a view that has come to be called the Great Divide theory, which proposes that literacy fosters logical and analytic modes of thought, critical attitudes, propositional knowledge, and abstract uses of language. However, in the 1980s, the Great Divide theory received what seemed like a death blow from the much publicized study of Scribner and Cole (1981), who examined literacy effects among the Vai people in Africa. The fact that some unschooled individuals in this society were familiar with an indigenous script allowed researchers to separate schooling effects from literacy effects. Scribner and Cole (1981) found no specific effect of literacy on a number of tasks tapping general cognitive processes, including taxonomic categorization tasks, memory tasks, and syllogistic reasoning problems. The extremely innovative separation of literacy and schooling in the Scribner and Cole investigation led to an almost instant acceptance in the literature of their main conclusions on the consequences of literacy.

The seeming conclusiveness of the Scribner and Cole (1981) investigation dampened enthusiasm for new empirical studies of the effects of literacy. Unfortunately, Scribner and Cole's (1981) innovative and costly project is unlikely to be replicated, so resolving the issues using a variant of their methodology will not be possible. However, the cognitive consequences of literacy can be studied without necessarily using a cross-cultural comparison. Our methodology exploits the fact that even within a generally literate culture, individuals vary tremendously in their degree of exposure to print. Furthermore, even among a group of individuals who have the same level of assessed reading comprehension ability, remarkably large differences are found in their degrees of engagement in print-related activities (Stanovich & West, 1989), and, most important, the correlates of this natural variation can be studied. Comparing literate and illiterate people is the exclusive design of choice only if the effects of literacy are believed to be completely discontinuous—with no cognitive consequences of variation in the amount of exposure to print found among literate individuals. Our research program is predicated on the view that this discontinuity assumption is false, and that there is important cognitive variation among people who differ in only the *amount* of reading that they do. We do not dispute the fact that there may be important cognitive implications of the literacy–illiteracy divide, but point out that other, more continuous variability in literacy practices deserves exploration. Our research conclusions are thus restricted to the more continuous variation in reading experience.

INDIVIDUAL DIFFERENCES IN DECLARATIVE KNOWLEDGE: ALTERNATIVE VIEWS

Theories of cognitive development that have strongly emphasized the importance of declarative knowledge provide an important theoretical motivation for this research program (Alexander, 1992; Bjorklund, 1987; Ceci, 1990, 1993; Chi, 1985; Chi, Hutchinson, & Robin, 1989; Hoyer, 1987; Keil, 1984; Scribner, 1986). Given that the knowledge-dependency of cognitive functioning is a central tenet of many contemporary developmental theories, it is surprising that more attention is not directed to a question that such theories seem naturally to prompt: Where does knowledge come from? This question seems to be addressed only implicitly by theories emphasizing knowledge-dependency, the most common implication being that individuals' differences in domain knowledge are, for the most part, a product of experiential differences. In contrast, some investigators have explicitly argued against the experiential assumption implicit in the declarative knowledge literature. These alternative hypotheses can be illustrated by using vocabulary knowledge as an example.

255

Vocabulary is an important knowledge base for many aspects of psycholinguistic processing, and it is certainly tempting to attribute readers' variability in knowledge of vocabulary to experiential differences. For example, there is considerable evidence indicating that the size of children's vocabularies is correlated with parental education and indicators of environmental quality (Hall, Nagy, & Linn, 1984; Mercy & Steelman, 1982; Wells, 1986). Thus, it has been argued that vocabulary differences are primarily the result of differential opportunities for learning words. This conjecture might be termed the *environmental opportunity hypothesis*.

The environmental opportunity hypothesis is countered by theorists who emphasize that differences in vocabulary are caused by variation in the efficiency of the cognitive mechanisms responsible for inducing meaning from context. Proponents of what we might call the *cognitive efficiency hypothesis* argue that experiential factors are not implicated—or at least are of secondary importance—in explaining differences in size of vocabulary. For example, Sternberg (1985) has argued that

> Simply reading a lot does not guarantee a high vocabulary. What seems to be critical is not sheer amount of experience but rather what one has been able to learn from and do with that experience. According to this view, then, individual differences in knowledge acquisition have priority over individual differences in actual knowledge. (p. 307)

Jensen (1980) has stated the cognitive efficiency hypothesis in even stronger form:

> Children of high intelligence acquire vocabulary at a faster rate than children of low intelligence, and as adults they have a much larger than average vocabulary, not primarily because they have spent more time in study or have been more exposed to words, but because they are capable of educing more meaning from single encounters with words. . . . The vocabulary test does not discriminate simply between those persons who have

and those who have not been exposed to the words in context. ... The crucial variable in vocabulary size is not exposure per se, but conceptual need and inference of meaning from context. (pp. 146–147)

It is important to realize that cognitive efficiency explanations of this type are generic and are not necessarily restricted to the domain of vocabulary acquisition. They could, in theory, apply to knowledge acquisition in virtually any domain. Ceci (1990) has discussed how in an attempt to undermine developmental theories that emphasize the importance of knowledge structures in determining intelligent performance, advocates of the cognitive efficiency hypothesis argue that "intelligent individuals do better on IQ tests because their superior central-processing mechanisms make it easier for them to glean important information and relationships from their environment" (p. 72). The cognitive efficiency hypothesis thus undercuts all developmental theories that emphasize the importance of knowledge structures in determining intelligent performance by potentially trivializing them. According to the cognitive efficiency view, these differences in individuals' knowledge bases may affect certain cognitive operations, but the knowledge differences themselves arise merely as epiphenomena of differences in the efficiency of more basic psychological processes. Differences in acquired knowledge thus become much less interesting as explanatory mechanisms of developmental differences, because they are too proximal a cause.

MEASURING THE SPECIFIC EFFECTS OF PRINT EXPOSURE

As part of a broad-based research program examining the impact of reading experience on cognitive development (Echols, West, Stanovich, & Zehr, 1996; Stanovich, 1993; Stanovich & Cunningham, 1992, 1993), we have put to the test the cognitive efficiency hypothesis by examining the experiential variable that presents perhaps the most serious challenge to it: exposure to print. Before embarking on these investigations, we were faced with two fundamental problems: (a) How do you measure individual differences in exposure to print? and (b) How should you interpret any associations between cognitive outcomes and print exposure that are observed? We turn first to the former question.

A variety of methods have been used to assess individual differences in exposure to print (Guthrie & Greaney, 1991; Smith, 1996). For example, many different questionnaire and interview techniques have been used, but many of these are encumbered with reliability and validity problems. A more valid method—but also a more logistically complicated one—is the use of daily activity diaries filled out by subjects. Activity diaries yield estimates of the actual amount of time spent each day on literacy activities and are generally more valid than interview or questionnaire instruments.

Anderson and colleagues (Anderson, Wilson, & Fielding, 1988) pioneered the use of the activity diary method to estimate the amount of time that fifth graders (10–11-year-olds) spent reading in their nonschool hours, and we have used the activity diary method in some of our own studies. Our method of collecting daily activity records was adapted from that used in the Anderson et al. (1988) investigation, but we also attempted to improve on their methods in several respects (see Allen, Cipielewski, & Stanovich, 1992). Our daily activity record-keeping procedure was designed to minimize the time students would need to spend on it; to minimize the necessity for adding and subtracting minutes or converting hours into minutes; and to maximize student time judgment accuracy. We collected data over a 3-week period and thus obtained estimates of the average number of minutes per day that the children in our fifth-grade (10–11-year-olds) sample spent in various activities when they were outside of school.

Although some of our categories were different from those of the Anderson et al. (1988) study, those that were common were ordered similarly in the two studies. For example, television watching was the most frequent activity, and book reading was far down the list in both studies. Our fifth-grade students watched less television (83.2 min vs. 131.1 min) and did more homework (49.0 min vs. 18.9 min) than the Anderson et al. fifth-grade students. These differences might reflect the use of different populations: a private school in our study, and public schools in the Anderson et al. (1988) study. Previous studies have shown private versus public school differences in television and homework habits (Coleman, Hoffer, & Kilgore, 1982).

Despite differences in the estimates in other categories, our estimates of book reading time (mean and median of 10.2 and 5.0 min, respectively) were very close to those obtained in the Anderson et al. study (10.1 and 4.6 min). Certain rough generalizations thus hold across the two studies: Fifth-grade students (10–11-year-olds) spend around 5 min per night reading books for pleasure outside of school, less than one tenth the amount of time they spend watching television. These figures call to mind the many studies of school achievement in which American children have scored poorly and in which their poor performance has been linked to excessive television watching, low levels of homework, and little reading (Applebee, Langer, & Mullis, 1988; Chen & Stevenson, 1989; Stevenson & Lee, 1990; Stevenson, Stigler, Lee, Lucker, Kitamura, & Hsu, 1985).

Our specific concern, however, was to find whether the amount children read related to their achievement and whether such a linkage could be shown to have any specificity. In our study, time spent reading books (logarithmically transformed, see Allen et al., 1992, and Anderson et al., 1988) displayed a significant correlation of .39 with a standardized test of vocabulary knowledge. However, the significant zero-order correlation is not, by itself, enough to establish that vocabulary size is specifically linked to reading experience. The cognitive efficiency hypothesis is simply one way of framing the basic problem, which is that levels of print exposure are correlated with many other cognitive and behavioral characteristics. Avid readers tend to be different from nonreaders on a wide variety of cognitive skills, behavioral habits, and background variables. Attributing any particular outcome only to print exposure is extremely difficult.

We have used a regression logic to deal with this problem. In our analyses, we first regress out general measures of cognitive ability before examining the relationship between print exposure and criterion variables. The logic of our analytic strategy is conservative because, in certain analyses we have actually partialled out variance in abilities that are likely to be developed by reading itself. However, the explanatory ambiguities surrounding a variable such as print exposure have led us to continue to structure the analyses in a so-called worst case manner, as far as print is concerned.

In this study, we assessed the specificity of the relation between reading books and development of vocabulary by conducting a hierarchical regression analysis in which a standardized vocabulary test was the criterion measure and in which performance on a standardized mathematics test was forced into the equation first, as a control for general scholastic learning ability. When entered second, time spent reading books explained an additional 9.7% of the variance, and this unique variance was statistically significant ($p < .01$). Thus, the linkage between vocabulary and book reading time remains even when variability in general academic performance is partialled out.

Alternative Methods for Assessing Exposure to Print

Before embarking on further tests using this logic, we needed to develop an alternative methodology for measuring print exposure that was less logistically taxing than the activity diary technique. The latter requires extensive participant cooperation over a number of weeks. Children must record their activities from the day, either at the end of the day or on the following morning, and these recordings must be checked by a teacher or another adult to assure that the scale is being used properly. Such a level of participant involvement may discourage many investigators from using the technique.

A further problem is that the retrospective estimation of periods of time is a notoriously difficult task, even for adults (Bradburn, Rips, & Shevell, 1987; Burt & Kemp, 1991). This difficulty places some limits on how valid such estimates can be, even for a group of conscientious and well-motivated children. Finally, social desirability is a potential confound: Responses may be distorted because of tendencies to over-report socially desirable behaviors (Furnham, 1986; Paulhus, 1984). In this case, the effect would be to report more reading than actually takes place. Independent evidence indicates that social desirability does distort self-reports of time spent reading books by adults (Ennis, 1965;

Sharon, 1973–1974; Zill & Winglee, 1990). The extent to which it is a factor in children's self-reports of reading time is unknown.

However, we were not constrained to use the diary method because the correlates of differential exposure to print can be studied without estimating absolute amounts of reading in terms of minutes per day. Only an index of *relative* differences is required for the regression logic to be employed. Thus, one can use measures of print exposure that do not have some of the drawbacks of the activity diary method. Our research group has attempted to develop and validate measures of individual differences in print exposure that were designed: (a) to yield estimates of relative differences in exposure to print in a single 5–10 minute session; (b) to have very simple cognitive requirements (i.e., not require retrospective time estimates); and (c) to be immune from contamination from the tendency to give socially desirable responses.

The first measures we developed (Stanovich & West, 1989) were designed for use with adult participants. The Author Recognition Test (ART) and the Magazine Recognition Test (MRT) both exploited a signal detection logic whereby actual target items (real authors and real magazines) were embedded among foils (names that were not authors or magazine titles, respectively). Participants simply scan the list and check the names they know to be authors on the ART and the titles they know to be magazines on the MRT. The measures thus have a signal detection logic. The number of correct items checked can be corrected for differential response biases that are revealed by the checking of foils. Although checklist procedures have been used before to assess print exposure (Chomsky, 1972), our procedure is unique in using foils to control for differential response criteria (see Stanovich & Cunningham, 1993; Stanovich, West, & Harrison, 1995 for examples of the stimuli).

In constructing the list of ART authors, we selected items that were most likely to be encountered outside the classroom, so that the ART would be a proxy measure of out-of-school print exposure rather than of curriculum content. Thus, an attempt was made to avoid authors who are regularly studied in the school curriculum. In short, the ART was intentionally biased toward out-of-school reading, because it was intended as an indirect measure of the amount of free reading participants engaged in.

The checklist method has several advantages. First, it is immune to the social desirability effects that may contaminate responses to subjective self-estimates of socially valued activities such as reading. Guessing is not an advantageous strategy, because it is easily detected and corrected for by an examination of the number of foils checked. Furthermore, the cognitive demands of the task are quite low. The task does not necessitate frequency judgments, as do most questionnaire measures of print exposure, nor does it require recalling time spent, as does the use of daily activity diaries. Finally, the measures can be administered in a matter of a few minutes.

The checklist tasks are, of course, proxy indicators of a person's print exposure rather than measures of absolute amounts of reading in terms of minutes or estimated words (Anderson et al., 1988). The fact that the measures are very indirect indicators is clearly problematic in some contexts. For example, a participant's hearing about a magazine or author on television without having been exposed to the actual written work is problematic. The occurrence of this type of situation obviously reduces the validity of the tasks. However, a postexperimental comment sometimes made by adult participants in our studies is revealing: Some participants said they knew that a certain name was that of an author but, nevertheless, had never read anything that the author had written. When questioned about how they knew that the name was a writer, the participants often replied that they had seen one of the author's books in a bookstore; had seen an author's book in the New Fiction section at the library; had read a review of the author's work in *Newsweek*; had seen an advertisement in the newspaper, and so forth. In short, individuals' knowledge of that author's name was a proxy for reading activities, despite the fact that the particular author had not actually been read. Thus, although some ways of gaining familiarity with author names would reduce validity (e.g., TV, radio), most behaviors leading to familiarity with the author names are probably reflections of immersion in a literate environment.

We have developed analogous checklist measures for assessing children's exposure to print. One task is the Title Recognition Test (TRT), a measure that has the same signal detection logic as the adult ART and MRT, but involves children's book titles rather than authors as items. This children's measure shares the same advantages of immunity from socially desirable responding, objective assessment of response bias, low cognitive load, and lack of necessity for retrospective time judgments. In selecting the items to appear on the TRTs used in our investigations, we attempted to choose titles that were not prominent parts of classroom reading activities in the schools in which our studies were conducted. Because we wanted the TRT to reflect out-of-school rather than school-directed reading, we attempted to avoid books that were used in the school curriculum. Thus, if the test is used for this purpose, versions of it will necessarily differ somewhat in item content from classroom to classroom and from school to school.

Although the checklist measures have some obvious drawbacks as indices of children's exposure to print and degree of immersion in a literate environment, just how much their obvious limitations impair their performance as probes of environmental print exposure is not known. For example, to get credit for a correct item on the TRT, one clearly need have only some familiarity with the title. Children do not need to have read the entire book or to remember any of the contents. However, this seemingly problematic feature—that responses can be based on general familiarity rather than a more complete reading of the book—may be a strength just as often as a drawback. The possibility of responding on the basis of a shallow familiarity means that the TRT is not cognitively demanding and that it does not stress memory as much as some other tasks (in which children might be asked to recall titles or information about plot or characters). The response demands of such tasks would necessarily implicate name retrieval and memory processes of considerable complexity (Bradburn et al., 1987; Burt & Kemp, 1991) that may affect performance and make such measures weaker indices of print exposure. Also, requiring recall of children may fail to index books read so long ago that they are partially forgotten. Title recognition appropriately allows such imperfectly recalled items to influence the obtained print-exposure score.

Validation of Checklist Measures

We have validated all the recognition checklist measures in a variety of ways. First, we have shown that they are convergent with diary estimates of absolute reading time (Allen et al., 1992). In another study (West, Stanovich, & Mitchell, 1993), we attempted to validate the checklist print-exposure measures by seeing if they were associated with individual differences in reading observed in a nonlaboratory setting where reading occurs. The setting chosen for our study was an airport passenger waiting lounge at National Airport in Washington, DC. Reading occurs in this setting by way of the free choice of the participant. If individual differences in free reading in a setting such as this could be related to performance on the recognition checklist tasks, it would bolster the construct validity of the checklist measures as indicators of individual differences in print exposure.

Individuals sitting by themselves were the potential participants and were monitored unobtrusively by the experimenter for 10 min consecutively. If participants were not reading at the beginning of the observation period and continued sitting by themselves without reading or having reading matter in sight for the entire 10-minute period, they were classified as *nonreaders*. If they were reading at the beginning of the observation period and continued reading for the entire 10-minute period, they were classified as *readers*. Individuals whose behavior did not fall into one of these categories did not enter the sample. Subsequent to the observation, the individual was approached by the experimenter, was asked for consent to participate in the study and to fill out several experimental measures, and then was debriefed. Over 90% of the potential subjects agreed to participate.

Table 1 displays the results of a comparison of the 111 readers and 106 nonreaders on a few of the checklist measures. The groups were significantly different on the ART, the MRT, and a newspaper recognition test. However, they were not different on measures of exposure to television and film. This pattern of differences provides evidence of ecological validity for the print-exposure measures. They were reliably linked to direct observations of free reading in a situation where investigators do not intrude upon the process.

Table 1
Differences Between Readers and Nonreaders

Variable	Nonreaders	Readers	t value
Author Recognition Test	.401	.635	7.75*
Magazine Recognition Test	.598	.751	5.21*
Newspaper Recognition Test	.370	.529	6.12*
Television Recognition Test	.426	.468	1.87
Film Recognition Test	.292	.320	1.10
Vocabulary checklist	.516	.731	7.57*
Cultural Literacy Recognition	.600	.770	7.00*
Age	35.3	41.4	3.28*
Education	15.2	16.5	4.25*

NOTE: df = 211 for the vocabulary checklist; 213 for the Magazine Recognition Test (MRT); 214 for film recognition; and 215 for all other variables.
*$p < .01$.

The data presented in Table 1 illustrate additionally that the readers were also superior on measures of vocabulary and general knowledge (a cultural literacy test). However, as the last two rows of Table 1 show, the readers were also older and had more education. It is thus possible that age or education might have resulted in a spurious link between airport reading and performance on the vocabulary and cultural literacy measures.

The results of the two hierarchical regressions presented in Table 2 address this possibility. In these regressions, age and education were entered prior to airport reading (scored dichotomously) as predictors of vocabulary and general knowledge. In both analyses, airport reading remained a significant predictor even after age and education had been partialled out. These regressions demonstrate that we have discovered, in essence, a "10-minute airport test" that predicts vocabulary, independent of educational level. Studies such as this and indications that the checklist measures converge with diary estimates of reading activity (Allen et al., 1992) gave us confidence in employing the

Table 2
Airport Reading as a Predictor of Vocabulary and Cultural Literacy

Step/Variable	R	R^2	R^2 change	F to enter
		Vocabulary checklist		
1. Age	.257	.066	.066	14.91*
2. Education	.562	.315	.249	76.52*
3. Airport reading	.638	.408	.093	32.50*
		Cultural literacy test		
1. Age	.211	.045	.045	10.04*
2. Education	.495	.245	.200	56.65*
3. Airport reading	.574	.329	.084	34.81*

*$p < .01$.

former as measures of individual differences in print exposure in some of our other studies.

PRINT EXPOSURE AS A CONTRIBUTOR TO GROWTH IN VERBAL SKILLS

In several studies, we have attempted to link print exposure to specific cognitive outcomes after controlling for relevant general abilities—in short, to test the cognitive efficiency hypothesis. In a study of fourth-, fifth-, and sixth-grade children (Cunningham & Stanovich, 1991), we examined whether print exposure accounts for differences in vocabulary development when controls for both general and specific (i.e., vocabulary relevant) abilities were invoked. The analyses displayed in Table 3 illustrate some of the outcomes of this study. Three different vocabulary measures were employed as dependent variables: a word checklist measure of the written vocabulary modeled on the work of Anderson and Freebody (1983; see also White, Slater, & Graves, 1989); a verbal fluency measure where the children had to say as many words as they

Table 3

Unique Print Exposure Variance After Age, Performance on Raven Progressive Matrices, and Phonological Coding Were Partialled Out

Step/Variable	R	R^2	R^2 change	F to enter
			Word checklist	
1. Age	.103	.011	.011	1.41
2. Raven	.457	.209	.198	32.57**
3. Phonological coding	.610	.372	.163	33.49**
4. TRT	.683	.466	.094	22.52**
			Verbal fluency	
1. Age	.043	.002	.002	0.24
2. Raven	.231	.053	.051	6.89**
3. Phonological coding	.477	.228	.175	28.47**
4. TRT	.582	.339	.111	21.02**
			PPVT	
1. Age	.230	.053	.053	7.29**
2. Raven	.393	.154	.101	15.60**
3. Phonological coding	.403	.162	.008	1.21
4. TRT	.516	.266	.104	18.19**
			Spelling	
1. Age	.179	.032	.032	4.31*
2. Raven	.414	.172	.140	21.95**
3. Phonological coding	.656	.430	.258	58.51**
4. TRT	.713	.509	.079	20.42**
			General information	
1. Age	.224	.050	.050	6.84**
2. Raven	.362	.131	.081	12.05**
3. Phonological coding	.410	.168	.037	5.68*
4. TRT	.492	.242	.074	12.37**

NOTE: The spanner headings identify the dependent variables in the regression analyses. TRT = Title Recognition Test; PPVT = Peabody Picture Vocabulary Test.
$*p < .05.$ $**p < .01.$

could that fit into a particular category (e.g., things that are red; see Sincoff & Sternberg, 1987); and a group-administered version of the Peabody Picture Vocabulary Test (PPVT). Age was entered first into the regression equation, followed by scores on the Raven Progressive Matrices as a control for general intelligence.

As a second control for ability that would be more closely linked to vocabulary acquisition mechanisms, we entered phonological coding ability into the equation. A variable such as phonological coding skill might mediate a relationship between print exposure and a variable such as vocabulary size in numerous ways. High levels of decoding skill—certainly a contributor to greater print exposure—might provide relatively complete verbal contexts for the induction of word meanings during reading. Decoding skill might also indirectly reflect differences in short-term phonological storage that are related to vocabulary learning, particularly in the preschool years (Gathercole & Baddeley, 1989, 1993). Thus, print exposure and vocabulary might be spuriously linked by way of their connection with decoding ability: Good decoders read a lot and have the best context available for inferring new words. This spurious linkage is controlled by entering phonological coding into the regression equation prior to the TRT. If print exposure were only an incidental correlate of vocabulary because of its linkage with phonological coding skill, then the TRT would not serve as a unique predictor of vocabulary once phonological coding was partialled out.

The results of the first three analyses displayed in Table 3 indicate that for each of the vocabulary measures, the TRT accounted for significant variance after the variance attributable to performance on the Raven Matrices and the phonological coding measure had been removed. The last two regressions indicate that this was also true for two additional criterion variables in the study: spelling ability and performance on the general information subtest of the Wechsler Intelligence Scale for Children (WISC).

We have conducted an even more stringent test of whether exposure to print is a unique predictor of verbal skill in a study of college subjects (Stanovich & Cunningham, 1992). Table 4 summarizes the re-

Table 4
Unique Print Exposure Variance After Nonverbal Abilities and Reading Comprehension Ability Are Partialled Out

Step/Variable	Dependent variables					
	N–D Voc.	PPVT	NAEP	CLR	Sp Com	Vb Fl
	Multiple R					
1. Figural analogies	.316	.278	.280	.270	.238	.205
2. Raven	.488	.405	.369	.363	.362	.243
3. Nelson–Denny Comprehension	.684	.541	.599	.600	.582	.323
4. ART	.738	.688	.677	.803	.625	.423
4. MRT	.725	.636	.660	.770	.589	.356
	R^2 change					
1. Figural analogies	.100**	.077**	.079**	.073**	.057**	.042**
2. Raven	.138**	.087**	.057**	.059**	.074**	.017*
3. Nelson–Denny Comprehension	.230**	.129**	.222**	.227**	.208**	.045**
4. ART	.076**	.180**	.100**	.286**	.052**	.075**
4. MRT	.058**	.112**	.077**	.234**	.008	.023*

NOTE: Dependent variables: N–D Voc. = Nelson–Denny Vocabulary; PPVT = Peabody Picture Vocabulary Test; NAEP = history and literature (from National Assessment of Education Progress); CLR = cultural literacy recognition; Sp Com = spelling composite; Vb Fl = verbal fluency; ART = Author Recognition Test; MRT = Magazine Recognition Test.
*$p < .05$. **$p < .001$.

sults of this study. In this hierarchical forced-entry regression analysis two nonverbal measures of general ability were entered first into the equation: performance on a figural analogies test and on the Raven Matrices. Next, performance on the Nelson–Denny Reading Comprehension Test is entered subsequent to the two nonverbal ability tasks but prior to the measure of print exposure. By structuring the analyses in this way, we do not mean to imply that print exposure is not a determinant of reading comprehension ability. Indeed, we would argue that there are grounds for believing that exposure to print does facilitate growth in comprehension ability. However, in recognition of the correlational nature of our data, we have attempted to construct the most conservative analysis possible by deliberately allowing the Nelson–Denny comprehension measure to steal some variance that is rightfully attributed to the print-exposure measure. The results illustrated in Table 4 indicate that print exposure was able to account for additional variance in two measures of vocabulary, and two measures of general knowledge, spelling, and verbal fluency even after reading comprehension ability had been partialled along with nonverbal ability.

That these analyses are conservative in entering reading comprehension before the print-exposure measure is illustrated in a longitudinal study that we have conducted (Cipielewski & Stanovich, 1992), which indicates that exposure to print is related to growth in reading comprehension ability. The regression analyses presented in Table 5 display the results of this study in which growth in reading comprehension ability was tracked by administering the comprehension tests from the Stanford Diagnostic Reading Test and the Iowa Test of Basic Skills (ITBS) to 82 fifth graders who had been administered the comprehension subtest from the ITBS in the third grade (as 8–9-year-olds). The regressions are hierarchical forced-entry analyses for prediction of fifth-grade reading comprehension ability. Third-grade reading comprehension was entered first, followed by the recognition checklist measure of print exposure. Thus, the analyses are essentially addressed to the question of whether exposure to print can predict individual differences in growth in reading comprehension from third to fifth grade. In both cases, print exposure predicted variance in fifth-grade reading

Table 5				
Hierarchical Regressions Predicting Fifth-Grade Reading Ability				
Step/Variable	R	R^2	R^2 change	F to enter
Fifth-grade Stanford Reading Comprehension				
1. Iowa Comprehension (third grade)	.645	.416	.416	54.06**
2. Title Recognition Test	.725	.526	.110	17.38**
Fifth-grade Iowa Reading Comprehension				
1. Iowa Comprehension (third grade)	.545	.297	.297	33.78**
2. Title Recognition Test	.609	.371	.074	9.25**

NOTE: The spanner headings identify the dependent variables in the regression analyses.
**$p < .01$.

comprehension ability after third-grade reading comprehension scores had been partialled out. Thus, in partialling reading comprehension ability in our adult studies, we are undoubtedly removing some of the variance in the criterion variable that is rightfully attributed to print exposure.

EXPOSURE TO PRINT AND DECLARATIVE KNOWLEDGE

In other studies, we have focused even more directly on content knowledge by addressing the question "Where Does Knowledge Come From?" Stanovich and Cunningham (1993) examined general ability, print exposure, and exposure to other media sources as determinants of individual differences in content knowledge. This study contained a particularly stringent test of the cognitive efficiency explanation of individual differences in the acquisition of knowledge. The subjects were 268 college students, and the test is displayed in Table 6. The criterion variable

Table 6
Hierarchical Regression Analyses Predicting General Knowledge Composite Among 268 College Students

Step/Variable	R	R^2 change	F to enter	Final β	Final F
1. HS GPA	.372	.139	42.82**	.020	0.32
2. Raven Matrices	.447	.061	20.30**	.016	0.20
3. Mathematics test	.542	.094	35.07**	.165	18.19**
4. N–D Comp.	.630	.103	45.11**	.112	9.87**
5. Television composite	.630	.000	0.06	−.039	1.68
6. Print composite	.876	.371	417.63**	.720	417.63**

NOTE: HS GPA = high school grade-point average. N–D Comp. = Nelson–Denny Comprehension Test.
**$p < .01$.

is a composite index of performance on five general knowledge measures. Four measures of general ability were entered prior to print exposure: high school grade-point average, performance on the Raven Matrices, performance on an SAT-type mathematics test, and the score on the Nelson–Denny Reading Comprehension Test. This set of tasks surely exhausts the variance attributable to any general ability construct, and general ability does account for a substantial proportion of variance in the general knowledge composite (multiple R of .63). When entered as the fifth step, a composite measure of exposure to television accounted for no additional variance. However, a composite index of exposure to print accounted for a substantial 37.1% of the variance when entered after the four ability measures and television exposure.

This pattern replicated in each of the five measures of general knowledge we employed, including a homemade instrument we called the Practical Knowledge Test. This task was designed to address the criticism that our other measures of general knowledge were too academic, that they tapped knowledge that was too esoteric or elitist, information that was not useful in daily life. We thought this a dubious criticism—many items on these measures were mundane and concrete questions such as "In what part of the body does the infection called pneumonia occur?", hardly esoteric. Nevertheless, in the Practical Knowledge Test, we addressed these criticisms by devising questions that were directly relevant to daily living in a technological society in the late 20th century. For example, "What does the carburetor in an automobile do?"; "If a substance is carcinogenic it means that it is _____?"; "After the Federal Reserve Board raises the prime lending rate, the interest that you will be asked to pay on a car load will generally increase/decrease/stay the same?"; "What vitamin is highly concentrated in citrus fruits?"; "When a stock exchange is in a "bear market," what is happening?"; and so forth.

The results indicate that more avid readers in our study—independent of their general abilities—knew more about how a carburetor worked, were more likely to know their U.S. senators, were more likely to know how many teaspoons are equivalent to one tablespoon, were more likely to know what a stroke was, what a closed-shop was in a factory, and so forth. One would be hard pressed to deny that at least some of this knowledge is relevant to living in the United States in the late 20th century.

In other questions asked of these same subjects, we attempted to probe areas that we thought might be characterized by misinformation. We then attempted to trace, in our individual difference analyses, the "cognitive anatomy" of this misinformation. One such question concerned the sizes of the world's major religions and was designed to assess awareness of the multicultural nature of the modern world. The question was phrased as follows: "The 1986 Encyclopedia Britannica estimates that there are approximately nine hundred million people in the world (not just the United States) who identify themselves as Christians. How many people in the world (not just the United States) do you think identify themselves as _____?" Space was then provided on the form for the subjects to make estimates of the number of Moslem, Jewish, Buddhist, and Hindu people.

We will focus here on the estimates of Moslem and Jewish people because of our a priori hypothesis that availability effects caused by U.S.

273

television coverage of Israel has skewed the perception of this ratio. Although the median estimate in our sample of the number of Jewish people (20 million) was quite close to the actual figure of 18 million according to the 1990 *Universal Almanac*, the number of estimated Moslem people—a mean of 10 million—was startlingly low (817 million is the estimate in the *Universal Almanac*). For each subject, we calculated the ratio of the estimates of Moslem to Jewish people to see how many subjects were aware of the fact that the number of Moslem people is an order of magnitude larger (the actual estimated ratio is approximately 33:1 according to the *World Almanac*; 45:1 according to the *Universal Almanac*). The median ratio in our sample was 0.5. That is, 69.3% of our sample thought that there were more Jewish people in the world than Moslem people.

This level of inaccuracy is startling given that approximately 40% of our sample of 268 students were attending one of the most selective public institutions of higher education in the United States (the University of California, Berkeley). We have explored the correlates of this particular misconception in a variety of ways. In the following analysis, we scored a subject's ratio "correct" if it was 1.0 or greater—admittedly a ridiculously liberal scoring criterion, but one necessitated by the fact that only 8.2% of the sample produced a ratio of 20:1 or greater. Table 7 presents a breakdown of the scores on this question based on a median split of the print composite and television composite variables. There is a clear effect of print exposure on the scores on the question, and a significant effect of television viewing, but the effects were in

Table 7

Proportion of "Correct" Answers on the Estimates of Moslem and Jewish People as a Function of Print and Television Exposure

High print exposure		Low print exposure	
Low TV	High TV	Low TV	High TV
.614	.419	.298	.236

opposite directions. Print exposure was associated with higher scores on the question, but television exposure was associated with lower scores. Scores among the group comprising subjects who were high in print exposure and low in television exposure were highest (61.4% of this group got the item quote "correct"). The lowest scores were achieved by those subjects who were high in television exposure and low in print exposure (only 23.6% of the subjects in this group responded with a ratio of at least 1.0). Regression analyses confirmed that these relationships were not due to differences in general ability.

Similarly, we have analyzed a variety of other misconceptions in a number of other domains—including knowledge of World War II, the world's languages, and the components of the federal budget—and all of them replicate the pattern shown for this question. The cognitive anatomy of misinformation appears to be one of too little exposure to print and overreliance on television for information about the world. Although television viewing can have positive associations with knowledge when the viewing is confined to public television, news, or documentary material (Hall, Chiarello, & Edmondson, 1996; West & Stanovich, 1991; West et al., 1993), familiarity with the prime-time television material that defines mass viewing in North America is most often negatively associated with the acquisition of knowledge.

We conducted another study using a population of much older individuals to investigate the extent to which age-related difference in declarative knowledge can be accounted for by differential experience with print (Stanovich, West, & Harrison, 1995). Although much research effort has been expended on describing cumulative growth in crystallized intelligence, we know little about the experiential correlates of knowledge growth in older individuals. For example, educational experience is a predictor of intellectual functioning in older individuals (e.g., Schwartzman, Gold, Andres, Arbuckle, & Chaikelson, 1987). We assume that education (which is received early in life) in part determines the extent and quality of many intellectual activities later in life. Presumably these intellectual activities undertaken in later life are crucial to the preservation of cognitive capacities. Thus, while considerable development of cognitive skills and abilities can result from formal educational experiences, it is the lifelong use of these skills that we assumed has the beneficial effect.

In this study, we investigated the extent to which age-related growth in declarative knowledge can be accounted for by differential experience with print. We compared the performance of 133 college students (mean age = 19.1 years) and 49 older individuals (mean age = 79.9 years) on two general knowledge tasks, a vocabulary task, a working memory task, a syllogistic reasoning task, and several measures of exposure to print.

The older individuals outperformed the college students on the measures of general knowledge and vocabulary, but did significantly less well than the college subjects on the working memory and syllogistic reasoning tasks—the standard dissociation between fluid and crystallized intelligence found in the literature (Baltes, 1987; Horn & Hofer, 1992; Salthouse, 1988). However, a series of hierarchical regression analyses indicated that when measures of exposure to print were used as control variables, the positive relationships between age and vocabulary and age and declarative knowledge were eliminated (in contrast, the negative relationships between age and fluid abilities were largely unattenuated). The results are consistent with the conjecture that—in the domain of verbal abilities—print exposure helps to compensate for the normally deleterious effects of aging (see also, Smith, 1996).

DEVELOPING A LIFELONG READING HABIT

Given that lifelong reading habits are such strong predictors of verbal cognitive growth, what is it that predicts these habits? Thus far the analyses have treated exposure to print as a predictor variable of criterion abilities such as reading comprehension. However, it is generally agreed that comprehension ability and exposure to print are in a reciprocal relationship (Anderson et al., 1988; Stanovich, 1986, 1993), which we have examined in a longitudinal study using extensive cognitive profiles of a group of children who had been tested as first graders in 1981 (see Stanovich, Cunningham, & Feeman, 1984). About one half of the children in this sample were available 10 years later for testing as 11th graders. At that time, we administered a set of reading comprehension, cognitive ability, vocabulary, and general knowledge tasks, as well as several measures of exposure to print. We were thus able to examine what variables in the first grade predicted these cognitive outcomes in the eleventh grade.

Table 8 displays the results from an analysis in which we addressed the question: Could the speed of initial reading acquisition in the first grade predict the tendency to engage in reading activities 10 years later, even after the present level of reading comprehension ability is taken into account? Entered first in the hierarchical regression is 11th-grade reading comprehension ability (Nelson–Denny performance) in order to remove the direct association between print exposure and contem-

Table 8

Hierarchical Regression Analysis Predicting Amount of Print Exposure in the 11th Grade

Step/Variable	R	R^2 change	F to enter	Partial r
Forced Entry				
1. Grade 11, N–D Comp.	.604	.364	14.34**	—
2. Grade 1, Metropolitan	.696	.121	5.61*	.435
2. Grade 1, Gates	.681	.100	4.45*	.396
2. Grade 1, WRAT	.686	.106	4.78*	.408
2. Grade 1, Raven	.632	.035	1.39	.234
2. Grade 1, PPVT	.641	.047	1.89	.270
2. Grade 3, Metropolitan	.765	.221	11.09**	.588
2. Grade 5, Metropolitan	.719	.153	6.72*	.484

NOTE: N–D Comp. = Nelson–Denny Reading Comprehension Test; PPVT = Peabody Picture Vocabulary Test; WRAT = Wide Range Achievement Test; PPVT = Peabody Picture Vocabulary Test.
*$p < .05$. **$p < .01$.

STANOVICH, CUNNINGHAM, AND WEST

poraneous reading ability. Listed next in the table are seven alternative second steps in the regression equation. All three measures of first-grade reading ability (Metropolitan Achievement Test, Gates, Wide Range Achievement Test) predicted significant variance (slightly over 10%) in 11th-grade print exposure even after 11th-grade reading comprehension ability had been partialled out.

The table indicates that the two measures of cognitive ability administered in first grade (Raven & PPVT) did not account for unique variance in print exposure once 11th-grade reading-comprehension ability had been partialled out. Finally, third- and fifth-grade measures of reading ability account for even more variance in print exposure than do the first-grade measures. Thus an early start in reading is important in predicting a lifetime of literacy experience—and this is true regardless of the level of reading comprehension that the individual eventually attains. This is a strong finding because it indicates that, regardless of their level of reading comprehension in the 11th grade, students who got off to a fast start in reading (as indicated by their first-grade reading ability scores) are more likely to engage in more reading activity as adults. Early success at reading acquisition is thus one of the keys that unlocks a lifetime of reading habits. The subsequent exercise of this habit serves to develop further reading comprehension ability in an interlocking positive feedback logic (Juel, 1988; Juel, Griffith, & Gough, 1986; Snow, Barnes, Chandler, Goodman, & Hemphill, 1991; Stanovich, 1986, 1993).

CONCLUSION

Our work on the cognitive correlates of exposure to print has demonstrated that a strong version of the cognitive efficiency account of knowledge acquisition is clearly falsified by the data. Print exposure accounted for a sizable portion of variance in measures of vocabulary and general knowledge even after variance associated with general cognitive ability was partialled out. Thus, at least in certain domains, and at least as measured here, individual differences in declarative knowledge bases—differences emphasized by many contemporary theories of developmental growth—appear to be experientially based.

Researchers and practitioners in the reading education community are nearly unanimous in recommending that children be encouraged to spend more time engaged in literacy activities outside of school (e.g., Adams, 1990; Anderson, Hiebert, Scott, & Wilkinson, 1985). From a cultural standpoint, this recommendation is virtually unassailable. What has been less clear, however, is the empirical status of the tacit model of skill acquisition often underlying the recommendation to increase children's free reading. The tacit model is basically one of accelerating skill development by way of practice. It is thought that more exposure to print through reading at home will lead to further growth in reading comprehension and related cognitive skills. As plausible as this tacit model sounds, until quite recently, there was actually very little evidence to support it. Most of the available evidence was correlational—for example, research demonstrating that avid readers tend to be good comprehenders (see Guthrie & Greaney, 1991, for a review)—and most of the available evidence did not contain any statistical controls of possible third variables. These zero-order correlations are ambiguous because they are open to the interpretation that better readers simply choose to read more—an interpretation at odds with the tacit model of skill development through practice that underlies efforts to increase children's free reading. The pattern of regression results in our studies suggests that print exposure does appear to be both a consequence of developed reading ability and a contributor to further growth in reading ability and in other verbal skills, thus they bolster the emphasis on reading experience that currently prevails in the reading education community. The results also strengthen the case for advocating a more prominent role for reading activity in general theories of cognitive development (Booth & Hall, 1994; Guthrie, Schafer, & Hutchinson, 1991; Hayes, 1988; Olson, 1994; Stanovich, 1986, 1993; Stanovich & Cunningham, 1993).

Cognitive theories that view individual differences in basic processing capacities as at least partly determined by differences in knowledge bases (e.g., Ceci, 1990, 1993) elucidate a mechanism by which print exposure can be said to influence cognitive development. Print exposure is simply a more distal factor that determines individual differences in knowledge bases, which in turn influence performance on a variety of basic information processing tasks (see Ceci, 1990). If the theories of cognitive development in which declarative knowledge is emphasized have some truth to them, then demonstrating effects on such knowledge structures is an important finding, because whatever causal power accrues to content knowledge in these theories also partially accrues to exposure to print as a mechanism of cognitive change.

There are, in fact, several possible mechanisms by which print exposure could become a mechanism for the growth and preservation of crystallized knowledge. Reading is a very special type of interface with the environment, providing the readers with unique opportunities to acquire declarative knowledge. The world's storehouse of knowledge is readily available for those people who read, and much of this information is not usually attained from other sources. Personal experience provides only narrow knowledge of the world and is often misleadingly unrepresentative (Baron, 1985, 1994; Dawes, 1988; Gilovich, 1991; Nisbett & Ross, 1980; Stanovich, 1994, 1996). The most commonly used electronic sources of information (television, radio) lack depth (Comstock & Paik, 1991; Hayes & Ahrens, 1988; Huston, Watkins, & Kunkel, 1989; Iyengar & Kinder, 1987; Zill & Winglee, 1990). For example, most theorists agree that a substantial proportion of growth in vocabulary during both childhood and adulthood occurs indirectly through exposure to language (Miller & Gildea, 1987; Nagy & Anderson, 1984; Nagy, Herman, & Anderson, 1985; Sternberg, 1985, 1987). Obviously, the only opportunities to acquire new words occur when an individual is exposed to a word in written or oral language that is outside the current vocabulary. Work by Hayes (1988; Hayes & Ahrens, 1988; see also, Akinnaso, 1982; Biber, 1986; Chafe & Danielewicz, 1987; Corson, 1995) has indicated that moderate- to low-frequency words—precisely those words that differentiate individuals with large and small vocabulary sizes—appear much more often in common reading matter than in common speech. These relative differences in the statistical distributions of words in print and in oral language have direct implications for vocabulary development.

In summary, when speculating about variables in people's ecologies that could account for cognitive variability, print exposure is worth investigating because such variables must have the requisite potency to perform their theoretical roles. A class of variable that might have such potency would be one that has long-term effects because of its repetitive or cumulative action. Schooling is obviously one such variable (Cahan & Cohen, 1989; Ceci, 1990, 1991; Ferreira & Morrison, 1994; Morrison, Smith, & Dow-Ehrensberger, 1995; Varnhagen, Morrison, & Everall, 1994). However, print exposure is another factor that varies enormously from individual to individual and that accumulates over time. These individual differences are associated to a strong degree with individual differences in general knowledge across the life span and with individual differences among individuals of roughly similar age.

REFERENCES

Adams, M. J. (1990). *Beginning to read: Thinking and learning about print.* Cambridge, MA: MIT Press.

Akinnaso, F. N. (1982). On the difference between spoken and written language. *Language and Speech, 25,* 97–125.

Alexander, P. A. (1992). Domain knowledge: Evolving themes and emerging concerns. *Educational Psychologist, 27,* 33–51.

Allen, L., Cipielewski, J., & Stanovich, K. E. (1992). Multiple indicators of children's reading habits and attitudes: Construct validity and cognitive correlates. *Journal of Educational Psychology, 84,* 489–503.

Anderson, R. C., & Freebody, P. (1983). Reading comprehension and the assessment and acquisition of word knowledge. In B. Huston (Ed.), *Advances in reading/language research* (Vol. 2, pp. 231–256). Greenwich, CT: JAI Press.

Anderson, R. C., Hiebert, E. H., Scott, J. A., & Wilkinson, I. (1985). *Becoming a nation of readers.* Washington, DC: National Institute of Education.

Anderson, R. C., Wilson, P. T., & Fielding, L. G. (1988). Growth in reading and how children spend their time outside of school. *Reading Research Quarterly, 23,* 285–303.

Applebee, A. N., Langer, J. A., & Mullis, I. V. S. (1988). *Who reads best?* Princeton, NJ: Educational Testing Service.

Baltes, P. B. (1987). Theoretical propositions of life-span developmental psychology: On the dynamics between growth and decline. *Developmental Psychology, 23,* 611–626.

Baron, J. (1985). *Rationality and intelligence.* Cambridge: Cambridge University Press.

Baron, J. (1994). *Thinking and deciding* (2nd ed.). Cambridge, England: Cambridge University Press.

Biber, D. (1986). Spoken and written textual dimensions in English: Resolving the contradictory findings. *Language, 62,* 384–414.

Bjorklund, D. F. (1987). How age changes in knowledge base contribute to the development of children's memory: An interpretive review. *Developmental Review, 7,* 93–130.

Booth, J. R., & Hall, W. S. (1994). Role of the cognitive internal state lexicon in reading comprehension. *Journal of Educational Psychology, 86,* 413–422.

Bradburn, N. M., Rips, L. J., & Shevell, S. K. (1987). Answering autobiographical questions: The impact of memory and inference on surveys. *Science, 236,* 157–161.

Burt, C. D. B., & Kemp, S. (1991). Retrospective duration estimation of public events. *Memory & Cognition, 19,* 252–262.

Cahan, S., & Cohen, N. (1989). Age versus schooling effects on intelligence development. *Child Development, 60,* 1239–1249.

Carr, T. H., & Levy, B. A. (Eds.). (1990). *Reading and its development: Component skills approaches.* San Diego: Academic Press.

Ceci, S. J. (1990). On intelligence . . . more or less: A bio-ecological treatise on intellectual development. Englewood Cliffs, NJ: Prentice-Hall.

Ceci, S. J. (1991). How much does schooling influence general intelligence and its cognitive components? A reassessment of the evidence. *Developmental Psychology, 27,* 703–722.

Ceci, S. J. (1993). Contextual trends in intellectual development. *Developmental Review, 13,* 403–435.

Chafe, W., & Danielewicz, J. (1987). Properties of spoken and written language. In R. Horowitz & S. J. Samuels (Eds.), *Comprehending oral and written language* (pp. 83–113). San Diego: Academic Press.

Chen, C., & Stevenson, H. W. (1989). Homework: A cross-cultural examination. *Child Development, 60,* 551–561.

Chi, M. T. H. (1985). Changing conception of sources of memory development. *Human Development, 28,* 50–56.

Chi, M. T. H., Hutchinson, J. E., & Robin, A. F. (1989). How inferences about novel domain-related concepts can be constrained by structured knowledge. *Merrill-Palmer Quarterly, 35,* 27–62.

Chomsky, C. (1972). Stages in language development and reading exposure. *Harvard Educational Review, 42,* 1–33.

Cipielewski, J., & Stanovich, K. E. (1992). Predicting growth in reading ability from children's exposure to print. *Journal of Experimental Child Psychology, 54,* 74–89.

Coleman, J. S., Hoffer, T., & Kilgore, S. (1982). *High school achievement.* New York: Basic Books.

Comstock, G., & Paik, H. (1991). *Television and the American child.* San Diego: Academic Press.

Corson, D. (1995). *Using English words.* Boston: Kluwer Academic.

Cunningham, A. E., & Stanovich, K. E. (1991). Tracking the unique effects of print exposure in children: Associations with vocabulary, general knowledge, and spelling. *Journal of Educational Psychology, 83,* 264–274.

Dawes, R. M. (1988). *Rational choice in an uncertain world.* San Diego, CA: Harcourt, Brace & Jovanovich.

Echols, L. D., West, R. F., Stanovich, K. E., & Zehr, K. S. (1996). Using children's literacy activities to predict growth in verbal cognitive skills: A longitudinal investigation. *Journal of Educational Psychology, 88,* 296–304.

Ennis, P. H. (1965). *Adult book reading in the United States* (National Opinion Research Center Report No. 105). Chicago: University of Chicago.

Ferreira, F., & Morrison, F. J. (1994). Children's metalinguistic knowledge of syntactic constituents: Effects of age and schooling. *Developmental Psychology, 30,* 663–678.

Furnham, A. (1986). Response bias, social desirability and dissimulation. *Personality & Individual Differences, 7,* 385–400.

Gathercole, S. E., & Baddeley, A. D. (1989). Evaluation of the role of phonological STM in the development of vocabulary in children: A longitudinal study. *Journal of Memory and Language, 28,* 200–213.

Gathercole, S. E., & Baddeley, A. D. (1993). *Working memory and language.* Hove, England: Erlbaum.

Gee, J. P. (1988). The legacies of literacy: From Plato to Freire through Harvey Graff. *Harvard Educational Review, 58,* 195–212.

Gilovich, T. (1991). *How we know what isn't so: The fallibility of human reason in everyday life.* New York: Free Press.

Goody, J. (1977). *The domestication of the savage mind.* New York: Cambridge University Press.

Goody, J. (1987). *The interface between the written and the oral.* Cambridge, England: Cambridge University Press.

Gough, P. B., Ehri, L., & Treiman, R. (Eds.). (1992). *Reading acquisition.* Hillsdale, NJ: Erlbaum.

Graff, H. J. (1986). The legacies of literacy: Continuities and contradictions in Western society and culture. In S. de Castell, A. Luke, & K. Egan (Eds.), *Literacy, society, and schooling* (pp. 61–86). Cambridge: Cambridge University Press.

Graff, H. J. (1987). *The labyrinths of literacy.* London: Falmer.

Guthrie, J. T., & Greaney, V. (1991). Literacy acts. In R. Barr, M. L. Kamil, P. Mosenthal, & P. D. Pearson (Eds.), *Handbook of reading research* (Vol. 2, pp. 68–96). New York: Longman.

Guthrie, J. T., Schafer, W. D., & Hutchinson, S. R. (1991). Relations of document literacy and prose literacy to occupational and societal characteristics of young black and white adults. *Reading Research Quarterly, 26,* 30–48.

Hall, V. C., Chiarello, K., & Edmondson, B. (1996). Deciding where knowledge comes from depends on where you look. *Journal of Educational Psychology, 88,* 305–313.

Hall, W. S., Nagy, W. E., & Linn, R. (1984). *Spoken words: Effects of situation and social group on oral word usage and frequency.* Hillsdale, NJ: Erlbaum.

Havelock, E. A. (1963). *Preface to Plato.* Cambridge: Harvard University Press.

Havelock, E. A. (1980). The coming of literate communication to Western culture. *Journal of Communication, 30,* 90–98.

Hayes, D. P. (1988). Speaking and writing: Distinct patterns of word choice. *Journal of Memory and Language, 27,* 572–585.

Hayes, D. P., & Ahrens, M. (1988). Vocabulary simplication for children: A special case of "motherese"? *Journal of Child Language, 15,* 395–410.

Horn, J. L., & Hofer, S. (1992). Major abilities and development in the adult period. In R. J. Sternberg & C. A. Berg (Eds.), *Intellectual development* (pp. 44–99). Cambridge: Cambridge University Press.

Hoyer, W. (1987). Acquisition of knowledge and the decentralization of g in adult intellectual development. In C. Schooler & K. W. Schaie (Eds.), *Cognitive functioning and social structure over the life course* (pp. 120–141). Norwood, NJ: Ablex.

Huston, A., Watkins, B. A., & Kunkel, D. (1989). Public policy and children's television. *American Psychologist, 44,* 424–433.

Iyengar, S., & Kinder, D. R. (1987). *News that matters: Television and American opinion.* Chicago: University of Chicago Press.

Jackson, M., & McClelland, J. (1979). Processing determinants of reading speed. *Journal of Experimental Psychology: General, 108,* 151–181.

Jensen, A. (1980). *Bias in mental testing.* New York: Free Press.

Juel, C. (1988). Learning to read and write: A longitudinal study of 54 children from first through fourth grades. *Journal of Educational Psychology, 80,* 437–447.

Juel, C., Griffith, P. L., & Gough, P. B. (1986). Acquisition of literacy: A longitudinal study of children in first and second grade. *Journal of Educational Psychology, 78,* 243–255.

Kaestle, C. F. (1991). *Literacy in the United States.* New Haven, CT: Yale University Press.

Keil, F. C. (1984). Mechanisms of cognitive development and the structure of knowledge. In R. Sternberg (Ed.), *Mechanisms of cognitive development* (pp. 81–99). New York: Freeman.

Mercy, J., & Steelman, L. (1982). Familial influence on the intellectual attainment of children. *American Sociological Review, 47,* 532–542.

Miller, G. A., & Gildea, P. M. (1987). How children learn words. *Scientific American, 257*(3), 97–99.

Morrison, F. J., Smith, L., & Dow-Ehrensberger, M. (1995). Education and cognitive development: A natural experiment. *Developmental Psychology, 31,* 789–799.

Nagy, W. E., & Anderson, R. C. (1984). How many words are there in printed school English? *Reading Research Quarterly, 19,* 304–330.

Nagy, W. E., Herman, P. A., & Anderson, R. C. (1985). Learning words from context. *Reading Research Quarterly, 20,* 233–253.

Nisbett, R. E., & Ross, L. (1980). *Human inference: Strategies and shortcomings of social judgment.* Englewood Cliffs, NJ: Prentice-Hall.

Olson, D. R. (1977). From utterance to text: The bias of language in speech and writing. *Harvard Educational Review, 47,* 257–281.

Olson, D. R. (1994). *The world on paper.* Cambridge, England: Cambridge University Press.

Ong, W. J. (1967). *The presence of the word.* Minneapolis, MN: University of Minnesota Press.

Ong, W. J. (1982). *Orality and literacy.* London: Methuen.

Paulhus, D. L. (1984). Two-component models of socially desirable responding. *Journal of Personality and Social Psychology, 46,* 598–609.

Pellegrino, J. W., & Glaser, R. (1979). Cognitive correlates and components in the analysis of individual differences. In R. J. Sternberg & D. K. Detterman (Eds.), *Human intelligence: Perspectives on its theory and measurement* (pp. 61–88). Norwood, NJ: Ablex.

Perfetti, C. A. (1985). *Reading ability.* New York: Oxford University Press.

Salthouse, T. A. (1988). Resource-reduction interpretations of cognitive aging. *Developmental Review, 8,* 238–272.

Schwartzman, A., Gold, D., Andres, D., Arbuckle, T., & Chaikelson, J. (1987). Stability of intelligence: A 40-year follow-up. *Canadian Journal of Psychology, 41,* 244–256.

Scribner, S. (1986). Thinking in action: Some characteristics of practical thought. In R. J. Sternberg & R. K. Wagner (Eds.), *Practical intelligence* (pp. 13–30). Cambridge: Cambridge University Press.

Scribner, S., & Cole, M. (1981). *The psychology of literacy.* Cambridge, MA: Harvard University Press.

Share, D. L., & Stanovich, K. E. (1995). Cognitive processes in early reading development: Accommodating individual differences into a model of acquisition. *Issues in Education: Contributions From Educational Psychology, 1,* 1–57.

Sharon, A. T. (1973–1974). What do adults read? *Reading Research Quarterly,* *9,* 148–169.

Sincoff, J. B., & Sternberg, R. J. (1987). Two faces of verbal ability. *Intelligence,* *11,* 263–276.

Smith, M. C. (1996). Differences in adults' reading practices and literacy proficiencies. *Reading Research Quarterly, 31,* 196–219.

Snow, C. E., Barnes, W., Chandler, J., Goodman, I., & Hemphill, L. (1991). *Unfulfilled expectations: Home and school influences on literacy.* Cambridge, MA: Harvard University Press.

Stanovich, K. E. (1986). Matthew effects in reading: Some consequences of individual differences in the acquisition of literacy. *Reading Research Quarterly, 21,* 360–407.

Stanovich, K. E. (1993). Does reading make you smarter? Literacy and the development of verbal intelligence. In H. Reese (Ed.), *Advances in child development and behavior* (Vol. 24, pp. 133–180). San Diego, CA: Academic Press.

Stanovich, K. E. (1994). Reconceptualizing intelligence: Dysrationalia as an intuition pump. *Educational Researcher, 23*(4), 11–22.

Stanovich, K. E. (1996). *How to think straight about psychology* (4th ed.). New York: HarperCollins.

Stanovich, K. E., & Cunningham, A. E. (1992). Studying the consequences of literacy within a literate society: The cognitive correlates of print exposure. *Memory & Cognition, 20,* 51–68.

Stanovich, K. E., & Cunningham, A. E. (1993). Where does knowledge come from? Specific associations between print exposure and information acquisition. *Journal of Educational Psychology, 85,* 211–229.

Stanovich, K. E., Cunningham, A. E., & Feeman, D. J. (1984). Intelligence, cognitive skills, and early reading progress. *Reading Research Quarterly, 19,* 278–303.

Stanovich, K. E., & West, R. F. (1989). Exposure to print and orthographic processing. *Reading Research Quarterly, 24,* 402–433.

Stanovich, K. E., West, R. F., & Harrison, M. (1995). Knowledge growth and maintenance across the life span: The role of print exposure. *Developmental Psychology, 31,* 811–826.

Sternberg, R. J. (1985). *Beyond IQ: A triarchic theory of human intelligence.* Cambridge: Cambridge University Press.

Sternberg, R. J. (1987). Most vocabulary is learned from context. In M. G. McKeown & M. E. Curtis (Eds.), *The nature of vocabulary acquisition* (pp. 89–105). Hillsdale, NJ: Erlbaum.

Sternberg, R. J. (1990). *Metaphors of mind: Conceptions of the nature of intelligence.* Cambridge: Cambridge University Press.

Stevenson, H. W., & Lee, S. (1990). Contexts of achievement. *Monographs of the Society for Research in Child Development, 55*(1–123, Serial No. 221).

Stevenson, H. W., Stigler, J. W., Lee, S. Y., Lucker, G. W., Kitamura, S., & Hsu, C. C. (1985). Cognitive performance and academic achievement of Japanese, Chinese, and American children. *Child Development, 56,* 718–734.

Stock, B. (1983). *The implications of literacy.* Princeton, NJ: Princeton University Press.

Varnhagen, C. K., Morrison, F. J., & Everall, R. (1994). Age and schooling effects in story recall and story production. *Developmental Psychology, 30,* 969–979.

Wells, G. (1986). *The meaning makers.* Portsmouth, NH: Heinemann Educational Books.

West, R. F., & Stanovich, K. E. (1991). The incidental acquisition of information from reading. *Psychological Science, 2,* 325–330.

West, R. F., Stanovich, K. E., & Mitchell, H. R. (1993). Reading in the real world and its correlates. *Reading Research Quarterly, 28,* 34–50.

White, T. G., Slater, W. H., & Graves, M. F. (1989). Yes/no method of vocabulary assessment: Valid for whom and useful for what? In S. McCormick & J. Zutell (Eds.), *Cognitive and social perspectives for literacy research and instruction* (38th Yearbook of the National Reading Conference, pp. 391–397). Chicago: National Reading Conference.

Zill, N., & Winglee, M. (1990). *Who reads literature?* Cabin John, MD: Seven Locks Press.

PART THREE

Developmental Psychology, Social Policy, and Education

10

Japanese Collectivism and Education

Hiroshi Azuma

WHAT WE OWE TO HAROLD STEVENSON

Harold Stevenson has made notable contributions to educational research and processes, and to cross-cultural research and methods. Not the least of these are his contributions to and support for Japanese educational practices.

First, Stevenson and his colleagues have clearly shown that Japanese and Chinese educators have much to teach to American educators. This has helped balance earlier trends when the direction of influence was from the United States to Japan and China not the other way around. A European–American modern school system was introduced in Japan in 1872 by its new reform government, only a few years after the termination of the feudalistic Shogunate. The committee that wrote the master plan for education was composed of those people who were knowledgeable about Western world systems rather than those knowledgeable about traditional Japanese education. American influence was particularly strong in the plans for curriculum and instruction, while the centralized system of education itself was patterned after the French model. From this beginning, Japan's educational system tended to look to Western, and especially American, methods and curricula as more advanced. Further, after World War II, the U.S. occupation headquarters began the introduction of American progressive education methods throughout Japan. The goal was to help train the future generations of Japanese people in the ways and values of democracy.

Against this historical backdrop, Stevenson's empirically based arguments that American education could learn from Japanese and Chinese education (Stevenson, Lee, & Stigler, 1986; Stigler, Lee, Lucker, & Stevenson, 1982) were as fresh to the Japanese as they were to the Americans. Although the superiority of Japanese students in mathematics achievement had been shown earlier (Husen, 1967), Stevenson's research more comprehensively documented this and was the first to link this superior achievement to educational practices. These findings encouraged the emergence of process-oriented empirical evaluations of Japanese education (Rohlen, 1983; Peak, 1991). They also prompted Japanese educators to outgrow a longstanding belief in the idea of "progressive United States, backward Japan."

Second, Stevenson's research, beginning with his three cities study that compared students and schools in Sendai, Taipei, and Minneapolis, has established an exemplary standard for cross-national comparisons of educational outcome. He began with a careful and systematic method for equating the achievement test items used to compare the three cultures. Clearly, a test constructed in one country and then translated for the other would be inadequate. Differences across the languages as well as across curriculum contents, school practices, and cultural meaning systems could undermine the putative similarity of cultural versions of such tests created merely by translation or back translation. Stevenson and his group, therefore, made a thorough study of U.S., Japanese, and Chinese school textbooks, curriculum goals, and cultural backgrounds in order to develop a more culturally valid and equitable set of tests. In their tests, items could be different from culture to culture, but the meaning of the test scores could be argued to be basically equivalent, and the statistical characteristics of the tests were the same across cultures.

This validation of the tests, which we will call *cultural validation*, is a refined form of construct validation, a classic consideration for test construction. Cultural validation is impossible without well-defined concepts of the constructs to be tested and thorough knowledge of the target cultures. With his training and expertise as a rigorous experimental researcher; with his knowledge of Japan and China (including his fluency in the local languages); and with his collaboration with researchers, educators, and native speakers in all the target countries, Stevenson set an impressive model for the cultural validation of tests.

Third, although Stevenson has been rigorously theoretical and empirical, he addresses actual needs in educational practice whenever possible. His coworkers include teachers in various schools, government officials, and housewives. Instead of isolating a small number of factors to conduct a neat and simple study, he investigates a complex array of cultural factors including the teachers, family, community, and administration systems, as well as interactions among them that impact on school achievement. With this kind of broad view of the contexts responsible for educational achievement, practical recommendations for policy and educational practices were possible. People certainly disagreed with his suggestions, often for political reasons, but even his critics have had to admit the solidity and clarity of his findings and the practicality of his arguments.

With these contributions as background, I propose that the advantages of Japanese education that Stevenson has documented are related in various ways to what I call *Japanese collectivism.*

JAPANESE COLLECTIVISM

The individualism–collectivism dichotomy is a well known and often useful conceptual frame in cultural psychology (Markus & Kitayama, 1991; Triandis, 1989). A number of Stevenson's findings of the advantages of Japanese educational practices, such as effective group management, may be attributable to the collectivistic mentality of the Japanese people. Whether Japan is a typical example of the collectivistic culture, however, can be questioned. Although individualism is a well-defined concept with its stress on individual autonomy, collectivism is an omnibus category that lacks such a clear common denominator. A couple of recent studies show that the Japanese are collectivistic in some aspects but not in others. For example, Yamagishi and Yamagishi found that Japanese scores on interpersonal trust were actually lower than American scores (1994), seemingly contradicting the expectation based on the assumption of Japanese as collectivists. Kashima and others found that the Japanese and Koreans' priorities contrast with the Americans' in that they value group goals over individual goals, but at the same time the Japanese values contrast with those of the Koreans and Americans in their low score on a scale of empathy, which they called relationism (Kashima et al., 1995). To say the least, the concept of collectivism needs to be separately defined in terms of the social structure, industrial status, sociocultural history, and moral philosophy of each target group. For this reason, I specify Japanese collectivism as the group orientation that developed as an adjustment to the historical and current social situations of Japan.

The core features of Japanese collectivism are role attachment and receptive diligence. As feudalism matured in Japan during the isolation of the Edo era (1590–1868), it turned into a stable hierarchical structure of roles where people were to live up to their role expectations and not to trespass role boundaries. What one would and could do depended not necessarily on one's calibre or merit but more on one's role in the hierarchy, a role usually assigned by one's family heritage but sometimes assigned by top-down appointment or even by sheer chance. Concentration on one's role was the guarantee of one's security in the society. If one did not have a role, one did not have a place in that society.

Once a role was assigned, the person had to do his or her best to perform it. In a feudal society where the room for competition in productivity was limited, the evaluation of a person's work was often measured by how intensively that person worked in the process rather than in the quantity of the product produced. The role was assigned, and its recipient was expected by people of other roles to carry it out conscientiously with intensive effort but without the aggressiveness of trespassing into others' roles. This leads to what I call *receptive diligence*, which combines a fatalistic attitude toward the assigned task with the obsession to perform the job with intense effort and methodical perfection.

The Meiji Reform (1868) terminated feudalism and introduced an industrially competitive society. But the industrial development of Japan has capitalized on the Japanese deep-rooted involvement with and attachment to roles. Thus, role attachment and receptive diligence have remained as requirements for good citizenship. Older ways of thinking about the group, about role acceptance, and a traditional work ethic remain alongside rapid adoption of Westernized ideology. Studies of Japanese second-, third-, and fourth-generation immigrants to the United States suggest that although ideologies and explicit customs may change within a short period, it takes several generations to change more basic values, preferences, and feelings (Catherine Cooper, personal communication, August, 1994). Thus, Japanese collectivism is a collectivism in that group goals have priority over personal goals, but it is a collectivism that also involves role attachment and receptive diligence. As Yamagishi and Yamagishi have pointed out (1994), the personal interrelatedness comes as part of a commitment to a role so that interpersonal preference, trust, and empathy play a lesser part. For this reason, and without implying that this sort of collectivism is applicable only to the Japanese, I will qualify my use of the term *collectivism* with the adjective *Japanese*, because the commonly used meaning of collectivism is too broad and imprecise in that it can mean little more than "less individualistic than the western individualism."

The following describes a few studies showing that Japanese collectivism has a strong influence upon Japan's educational practices as well as upon the attitudes of Japanese students.

Japanese Collectivism in Japanese Schools

The achievement goals of Japanese students are framed within an interpersonal role. In 1993, we tested the predictive validity of the Control, Agency, Means-End Instrument (CAMI) with Japanese fifth and seventh graders (Karasawa, Littoe, Miyashita, Mashima, & Azuma, 1997). The CAMI was developed at the Max Planck Institute for Human Development in Berlin under Paul Baltes' direction to measure control, agency, and means-end beliefs of students with regard to school achievement. It has proven to be a good predictor of school achievement in Europe. With a West Berlin sample, the raw product–moment correlation (r) of the CAMI with school achievement was .41 for control beliefs (the belief that one can be a good achiever), $r = .50$ for agency-effort beliefs (the belief that one works hard), and $r = .55$ for agency-ability beliefs (the belief that one has high ability). With East Berlin and other European samples, the figures were equal or higher. Those predictors together accounted for more than 80% of the non-error variance of school achievement (Oettingen, Littoe, Lindenberger, & Baltes, 1994).

In Japan, however, the corresponding correlations are much lower. The correlation between these beliefs and school achievement was $r = .27$ for control, $r = .28$ for agency-effort, and $r = .42$ for agency-ability beliefs. There was no difference between West Berlin and Japan in the reliability of the CAMI or in the target achievement variables (Karasawa, Littoe, Miyashita, Mashima, & Azuma, 1997), yet the predictive validity of CAMI was significantly lower in Japan.

We hypothesized that what was missing in the CAMI was an assessment of efficacy beliefs related to role taking and role expectations. Accordingly, we created new items designed to measure the following three factors: the expectation construct, the teaching-role construct, and the peer-support construct. The expectation construct was designed to be a measure of the student's belief that he or she is expected by significant others to earn good grades. The teaching-role construct was designed to measure the student's belief that one can and does help one's peers in their studies. The peer-support construct targeted students' beliefs about the availability of peers as helpers for their studies. New items measuring these constructs were administered to 11th graders in Japan along with the traditional CAMI items. The factors that showed the strongest correlations with school achievement were: agency-control ($r = .14$), agency-effort ($r = .33$), agency-ability ($r = .37$), expectation ($r = .33$), and teaching-role ($r = .42$). The teaching-role measure had higher predictive validity than any other CAMI constructs for these Japanese students. When all other CAMI constructs were partialled out, the partial correlation with school grade was .15 for expectation and .23 for teaching-role. The partial correlation after partialling out the contribution of all other CAMI and new constructs was significant only with teaching-role, with the value of .22. The R^2 of all predictors was significant at the level of .21. While significant, this was still lower than those found in European countries, perhaps due to the difference in the age level of the subjects tested (Miyashita, Karasawa, Mashima, & Azuma, 1997).

To my mind, teaching-role beliefs are a specific form of the belief in one's agency-ability, and therefore, this finding does not refute the importance of agency-ability as a construct, but clarifies it for Japanese students. As I have argued, the cross-cultural adaptation of these measures requires deeper considerations of construct validity. People's agency beliefs about their ability can be expressed in several ways, for the Japanese, in terms of role and relation rather than in terms of personal achievement.

Group Management Practices

The effective management of classroom groups within Japanese schools also depends heavily on Japanese collectivistic values and practices among students and teachers. Stevenson and others reported that Japanese teachers spend a higher percentage of classroom time actually leading children as compared to American teachers (Stevenson & Stigler, 1992). Although the data must be interpreted with caution considering the differences in general teaching strategy between the two countries, the findings probably reflect the belief of Japanese and Chinese teachers that "teachers are to teach." As a counterpart to this belief, teaching methods of Japanese teachers tend to presuppose that children are and should be receptive to teaching (Stevenson et al., 1986).

As a part of a cross-cultural project I codirected with Robert Hess, children's behavior at age four in free interaction with their mothers was examined (Azuma, Kashiwagi, & Hess, 1981). Among other measures, children's behavior was coded in terms of *originality* and *persistence*. The originality score represented the tendency of the child to start or change the task according to his or her desires. Persistence represented the tendency to accept the suggested task and to persist in working on it with involvement. Correlations of these measures with school performance 8 years later at age 12 revealed a sharp contrast between Japanese and the U.S. children. Originality correlated with later school performance at .39 in the United States, but only .14 in Japan. Persistence, on the other hand, correlated only at an insignificant .13 in the United States, but at a highly significant .56 in Japan. Notice that persistence seems close to receptive diligence, as I have defined it. Receptive diligence is an important component to successfully profiting from a Japanese education. Perhaps the teaching methods of Japanese teachers presuppose receptive diligence on the part of their students.

In the same project, we correlated mothers' expectations about their children's education, assessed when the children were four-year-olds, with children's school achievement at age 6 and at age 12 (the 5th–6th grade). With the American group, there was no significant partial correlation left after the achievement at age 6 had been partialled out. With the Japanese subjects, on the other hand, the partial correlation was as high as .43. This would mean that the maternal expectation of educational success influences the child's progress after entering school only in Japan and not in the United States. The readiness of Japanese children to identify with their mothers until a late age could be a part of the explanation for this difference.

Stevenson and Stigler noticed that both in Japan and China the goals and methods of parental socialization differ depending on the developmental stage of the person (Stevenson et al., 1982). The goals differ for people of different age levels because their roles are geared to age level. Instead of conceiving psychological development as involving monotonic growth and decline along a single dimension, the dimensions along which growth is appreciated in Japan differ depending on the life stage. There is one role expectation for early childhood, another for later childhood, another for adolescence and so on, until a final role expectation for the elder years. As a part of another project, we have asked American ($n = 1,562$) and Japanese ($n = 1,842$) respondents ranging from late childhood to age 66 and over to choose the kind of person they wanted to be from a list of 20 descriptions. Subsequently each participant was to pick three most important characteristics out of items she had chosen. The one chosen as most important was scored as 2 points, those chosen at the first stage were given 1 point, and the rest of the items were given 0 points.

The scores of items showed clear cross-national differences. With 18 out of 20 items, American averages were significantly higher than those of the Japanese, suggesting that Americans were more demanding in defining ideal self images. More closely related to the present discussion was that Japanese ideals changed more markedly with age level than those of the Americans. For 14 out of 20 items, the age related variance of the score was greater in Japanese respondents than in American respondents (Karasawa, Kojima, & Azuma, 1994). Figures 1, 2, and 3 show representative patterns. They also show the desirability for various personal characteristics as a function of increasing age. The childhood ideal, adolescent ideal, middle age ideal, and old age ideal differ more sharply from each other in Japan than in the United States. Our inference is that this reflects the age-geared role expectations taken almost for granted in Japan.

Role attachment is useful in education because a person who accepts a so-called student's role will be motivated to behave like a student and fulfill its expectations. In practice, for example, at the beginning of each school term, Japanese teachers divide their classes into several small groups, and the groups will take turns in tasks like room cleaning, lunch service, care of class flowers and small pets, meeting organization, and so forth. This practice helps children feel that their place and role is both defined and guaranteed in the class.

The receptive diligence of the students makes the task of instructing a large group easier. The teacher may assign tasks that students should experience without being restricted by the diversity of each child's interests.

PROBLEMS WITH JAPANESE COLLECTIVISM

Although Japanese collectivism in terms of role attachment and receptive diligence helps to increase the efficiency of Japanese school edu-

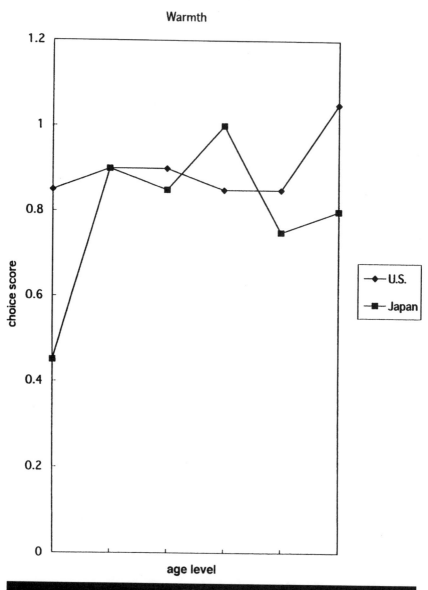

Figure 1

Popularity

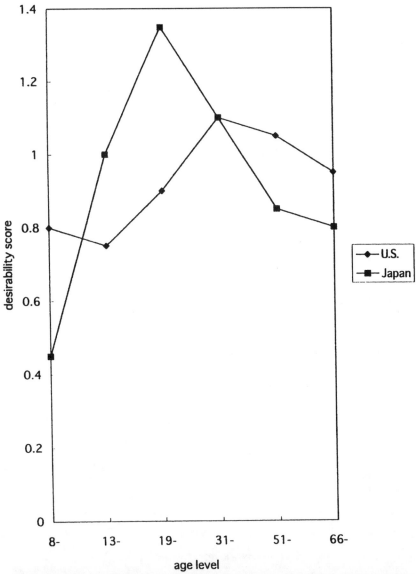

Figure 2

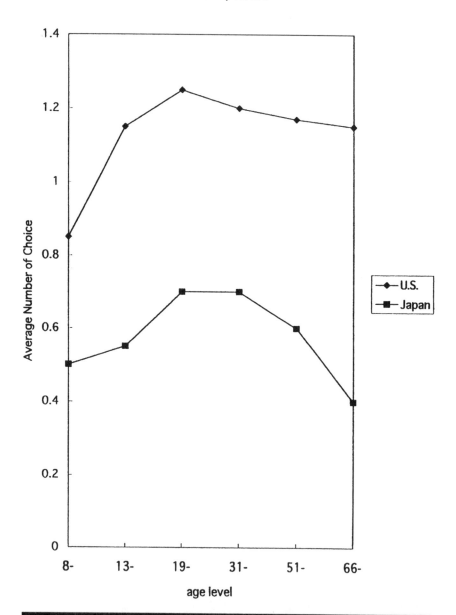

Job Competence

Figure 3

cation, there are also problems related to the influence of Japanese collectivism within education. Thus, although we acknowledge the beneficial influences of Japanese collectivism upon our education, we need to consider potential negative effects, as well.

One negative manifestation of Japanese collectivism is the intense competition surrounding the Japanese college entrance examinations. The importance of these exams results in the domination of the college entrance examination over school curricula, over teaching practices, and over the everyday life of young people. In actuality, the capacity of all colleges in Japan considered together is sufficient to accommodate all who want tertiary education. The competition thus involves not entrance to college per se, but entrance to the so-called top ranking colleges. This concern with college ranking does not accurately reflect the quality of teaching and research of the universities involved. Rather, it reflects a traditional ranking of universities in terms of entrance to a competitive and conservative job market. People take it for granted that, beyond one's effectiveness on the job being accepted for a particular career track depends on the ranking of the college from which one graduates. Thus, this college ranking is one of the most influential factors in determining the kind of role one can take on in Japanese society. For example, almost all top bureaucrats of the Ministry of Finance as well as many of the managers of top industries are graduates of the University of Tokyo. Many top industries, until recently, recruited career-track employees only from leading universities.

Because success in the college entrance examination is so very important for young people, it becomes the most salient goal of high-school education. In spite of government guidelines and experts' warning that the schools' curricula should *not* be overburdened with piecemeal items of knowledge useful on the exams, teachers are pressed to cover every item that could be a part of the entrance examination, and time and effort are spent in coaching students for that examination. Many students further attend *juku*, the after-school schools, for better preparation, and this can mean sacrificing other important experiences that otherwise serve to enrich youthful lives. About half of the applicants to leading universities are repeaters, some of whom have spent 3 or more years after high-school graduation just preparing for the entrance examination.

Because the competition is so important, the procedural fairness of the college examination is pushed to an extreme with a resulting obvious loss of validity. The examination becomes a test of piecemeal knowledge, rather than creative thinking, and this influences the teaching in senior-high schools. The reputation of the high school and parents' satisfaction with the school depend on the number of graduates who pass the exam. These figures, together with individual names of those students who passed, will be reported in several nationwide weekly magazines equivalent to *Time* or *Newsweek* in the United States. This preoccupation with the entrance examination spreads downward to junior-high and elementary schools, affecting their curricula, teaching methods, and students' lives.

In Japan if one could move easily from one employer to another and from one college to another, then it would not matter much where one first gets employed or where one goes to college as a freshman. However, as one's self is structurally defined by her or his affiliations in Japan (Markus & Kitayama, 1991), such changes of affiliation are considered immoral or unethical. When a person's first employment is by Mitsubishi, there is a very high likelihood that person will stay as a Mitsubishi employee throughout his or her career.

Likewise, there are institutionalized strict restrictions that make it difficult for a student of one university to move to another, and even when this is possible, it will involve a loss of one or two academic years, and therefore, substantial amounts of tuition. This mentality is reminiscent of the Edo period when social, occupational, and geographical mobility was strictly restricted.

A second serious problem within Japanese education is that of bullying in the schools. Almost every week there is a report of a junior-high school or even an elementary-school pupil committing suicide after a prolonged victimization. There are two kinds of such bullying: One is where a gang of delinquent or demoralized youngsters intimidates a member or an outsider as a "sucker." Although this is serious, I will not discuss it here because it is a type of bullying that can be found everywhere. The second type is more structurally connected to Japanese collectivism.

This second type of bullying is a form of ostracization, where the entire class isolates a member and either neglects, ridicules, or makes fun of that victim. This form of bullying, too, may be common in several different cultures. Such isolation, however, is particularly traumatic and intolerable for a victim who has been socialized into a collectivistic self-perception. For these people, losing a good standing within the interpersonal net of a group or being without an accepted role in one's group is to have no place to live in the world. Independent-minded individuals may think of finding a new niche outside the group, but those individuals who see the self as defined within a given interpersonal net cannot.

A girl who was such a victim has told me her story (personal communication, Summer, 1981). In her first-grade class, one child refused to drink the milk, which was a part of the school lunch. For the teacher, this refusal of something everyone was supposed to take was unacceptable, and he forced the child to drink. That child gagged and choked on the milk. The girl who spoke with me vomited with fear and disgust while watching the scene. This caused her to be subject to a long isolation. A few influential children stigmatized her as a dirty vomiter and said that anybody who approached her would also become unclean. Since then, she has been alone and removed from peer interaction except for occasions when other children hide her belongings in order to ridicule her further.

Not all other children were unsympathetic to her plight. But they knew that if she was not the target, one of them might be. When a new child moved into her class from another school, that child would often approach her without knowing the taboo. Feeling happy, she would be pleased and would enjoy a nice friendship for a couple of weeks. But the new child would soon know the taboo and then begin to keep his or her distance from her. This she called a *turnover*, and she would feel even more miserable. The childhood taboo placed on her weakened and faded in the upper grades, but by that time she was not comfortable even with the approach of well-intended children. She expected the turnover again, and felt that would be more damaging to her than the isolation. She developed anorexia, then school phobia, and she has taken many years to recover.

CONCLUSIONS

Japanese collectivism has certainly helped our schooling to be effective. At the same time, however, it has certain negative consequences. Understanding Japanese education requires understanding these problems as well. A complete picture is needed in order to know the full lessons that Japanese education may have for schooling practices and effectiveness elsewhere in the world. Deeper understanding is needed for us in Japan as well, as we strive to maintain the advantages of a traditional work ethic and school practices in the face of increasing individualization and competition.

REFERENCES

Azuma, H. (1994). *Socialization and education of the Japanese: A US–Japan comparison of development* (text in Japanese). Tokyo: University of Tokyo Press.

Azuma, H., Kashiwagi, K., & Hess, R. D. (1981). *Hahaoya no taido-kodoto kodomo nochitek; hattatsu* [Mother's attitude and behavior in relation to child's cognitive development]. Tokyo: University of Tokyo Press.

Husen, T. (Ed.). (1967). *International study of achievement in mathematics: A comparison of twelve countries* (Vols. 1 & 2). New York: Wiley.

Kashima, Y., Yamaguchi, S., Kim, U., Choi, S. C., Gelfand, M. J., & Yuki, M. (1995). Culture, gender, and self: A perspective from individualism-collectivism research. *Journal of Personality and Social Psychology, 69,* 925–937.

Karasawa, M., Kojima, A., & Azuma, H. (1994). The life course development of ideal selves in Japan and the United States. *Human Developmental Research, 10,* 62–72.

Karasawa, M., Littoe, T. D., Miyashita, T., Mashima, M., & Azuma, H. (1997). Japanese children's action-control beliefs about school performance. *International Journal of Behavior Development, 20,* 385–404.

Kashiwagi, K. (1984). A psychological study of the cognitive and emotional influences of examination pressure (text in Japanese). Unpublished Ministry of Education grant report.

Markus, H. R., & Kitayama, S. (1991). Culture and self: Implications for cognition, motivation and self. *Psychological Review, 98,* 224–253.

Miyashita, T., Karasawa, M., Mashima, M., & Azuma, H. (1997). CAMI and relationistic items: Cultural specificity of Japanese? Paper presented at the 14th Biennial Conference of International Society for the Study of Behavioral Development, Quebec city, Canada.

Oettingen, G., Little, T. D., Lindenberger, U., & Baltes, P. B. (1994). Causality, agency, and control beliefs in East versus West Berlin children: A natural experiment on the role of context. *Journal of Personality and Social Psychology, 66,* 579–595.

Peak, L. (1991). *Language to go to school: Transition from home to preschool life.* Berkeley, CA: University of California Press.

Rohlen, T. P. (1983). *Japan's high schools.* Berkeley, CA: University of California Press.

Stevenson, H. W., Stigler, J. W., & Lee, Shin-Ying. (1986). Achievement in mathematics. In H. Stevenson, H. Azuma, & K. Hakuta (Eds.), *Child development and education in Japan.* New York: Freeman.

Stevenson, H. W., & Stigler, J. W. (1992). *The learning gap.* New York: Simon & Schuster.

Stigler, J. W., Lee, S-Y., Lucker, W., & Stevenson, H. W. (1982). Curriculum and achievement in mathematics: A study of elementary school children in Japan, Taiwan, and the United States. *Journal of Educational Psychology, 74,* 315–322.

Triandis, H. C. (1989). The self and social behavior in differing cultural contexts. *Psychological Review, 96*(3), 506–520.

Yamagishi, T., & Yamagishi, M. (1994). Trust and commitment in the United States and Japan. *Motivation and Emotion, 18,* 129–166.

11

Beyond Reform Slogans: Linking Developmental Psychology and Teacher Education Reform

Frank B. Murray

Harold Stevenson was among the first of the modern developmental psychologists to see and act on the link between his discipline and education. In 1960 he chaired a study group for the National Society for the Study of Education (NSSE) that synthesized some 2,000 recent research studies of children's behavior, the lessons from which they felt had the potential for improving schooling. These studies, unlike the prevailing longitudinal and observational studies of the past, were largely short-term laboratory studies in which the effects of defined variables could be precisely determined. The book that resulted, *Child Psychology: The Sixty-Second Yearbook of the National Society for the Study of Education*, set a new standard for educators for the presentation of material in the discipline (Stevenson, Kagan, & Spiker, 1963). It broke from the limiting tradition of organizing developmental information by the age of the child or by a prevailing theoretical perspective. Instead, the literature was organized by research topic and task, wisely deferring statements about practical applications of the laboratory research until the appropriate field studies could be done.[1]

---

[1]In his *Children's Learning* (1972), Stevenson synthesized the rapidly expanding experimental research literature on the developmental changes in children's learning again with the hope that it

Faced with the documented poor performance of the American schools, Stevenson and his colleagues began a 10-year series of field studies in school achievement in selected cities in the United States, China, and Japan. These provided a kind of existence proof of the educational practices and cultural attitudes that are associated with superior educational attainment (Stevenson, 1992; Stevenson & Stigler, 1992). They are *existence proofs* in the sense that they demonstrate, or prove, that superior school achievement can occur under conditions that are often rejected by policy makers in the United States. Stevenson found, for example, that high levels of schooling could be obtained when teachers teach for shorter periods of time during the school day, when pupils have more recess play during the school day, when a higher value was placed on pupil effort than on ability, when a stable national curriculum was in place, when groups of teachers crafted and polished lessons, and when a greater emphasis was placed on cooperative rather than individual achievement (Stevenson, 1992; Stevenson & Stigler, 1992; Stigler & Stevenson, 1991).

These findings, and others from research in developmental psychology, would seem to support the consensus of modern educational reform schemes manifested in such reform slogans as: *all kids can learn, less is more, teaching for understanding, authentic assessment, student as worker, any subject can be taught at any time with integrity, teacher empowerment, standards-based reform, developmentally appropriate teaching,* and so on. We find, however, that these slogans are often detached from their intellectual roots and defined by educators only in the negative, as what they are *not* rather than what they *are* (Murray, 1989).

Authentic assessment is not a standardized test, for example, but it is not clear exactly what it is and why it couldn't be standardized. We have some idea about *less* content coverage, but very little idea of the *more* that might result. We have no approach to finding the *less* or how to sort out the essential from the not-so-essential curriculum content. The slogan, *all kids can learn* usually translates to an end to tracking

---

would "serve students in psychology and education as a guide through the profusion of studies and divergent theoretical positions that are represented in the experimental literature on children's learning" (p. v).

and segregated ability grouping, but it is not so clear what positive practices replace these or what forms special education or gifted education would take if the slogan were taken seriously. What is clear is that none of these slogans is understood deeply enough for the reformers to respond to these kinds of questions. This lack of understanding, more than any other factor, impedes school reform. At the same time there are bodies of scholarship, rarely invoked in the reform literature, that can illuminate the positive dimensions of these reform slogans. Developmental psychology, as Stevenson noted nearly 40 years ago, is such a literature. Its current implications for school and teacher education reform are the subjects of this chapter.

DEVELOPMENTALLY APPROPRIATE SCHOOLING AND DEVELOPMENTAL THEORY

There is no doubt that children do come to know and understand more each year they attend school (Austin & Garber, 1982; Educational Testing Service (ETS), 1990). Moreover, unlike the fairly universal patterns of the young child's thought, which have precarious and fragile connections with schooling (Cole, 1992), the advanced forms of thought seem to be associated exclusively with formal schooling (e.g., Cole & Scribner, 1977; Goodnow & Bethon, 1966; Kuhn, 1992; Stevenson, Parker, Wilkinson, Bonnevaux, & Gonzalez, 1978).

Developmental theories can be expected to specify the degree to which schooling is a necessary, sufficient, or an irrelevant factor in our intellectual accomplishment. Schooling speaks to the fundamental phenomenon in all developmental theory, namely, that there is an asymmetrical pattern in the most important intellectual changes. They go only in one direction, for example from nonconservation to conservation, and never the other way around.[2] The pervasive long-lasting

---

[2]Children who understand that the number of objects in an array is unaffected by the configuration of the objects in the array (conservation) almost never return to their prior belief (nonconservation) that changes in the configuration of the objects also change the number of objects—even when they are pressured to do so by powerful training techniques (Murray, Ames, & Botvin, 1977).

effects of schooling also need to be accounted for by any theory of development that hopes to win acceptance. Similarly, successful theories of schooling inevitably include theoretical propositions about the development of the unschooled mind, about which very little is actually known (Kuhn, 1992). Schooling and developmental theory, in other words, are inextricably connected.

Surprisingly, developmental theorists write little about education or schooling, and they claim that their theories have only the most general implications for schooling (e.g., Ginsburg, 1981; Murray, 1981; Smith, 1985; Parke, Ornstein, Rieser, & Zahn-Waxler, 1994). Nevertheless, because Piaget had written about children's understanding of concepts that were actually part of the school's curriculum, educators turned to developmental theory when education and schooling were thought to be in crisis after Sputnik and during the Civil Rights movements that followed Sputnik.

Regrettably, they often came away with only slogans to guide their efforts to reform the schools. The most pernicious and seductively attractive of these is that the content and method of schooling must be *developmentally appropriate*. It is pernicious because neither the findings, nor the theoretical propositions from developmental psychology, warrant strong statements about what a child is *unable* to do in some context. What a child is able to do is more firmly established and documented, of course, but the connections between what children are able to do, because of the variability in children's behavior, rarely support a confident claim about what they are unable to do, particularly in a different context (Siegler, 1996).

The theoretical warrants for the developmentally appropriate intervention are often similarly uncertain. J. McVicker Hunt (1961), for example, argued for a developmentally appropriate match between the pupil's level or stage of cognitive development and demands of the curriculum, although Hans Alebi (cited in Flavell, 1963) saw that the developmentally appropriate pedagogical approach was basically the opposite of what Hunt recommended. Alebi took developmental theory to mean that the pupil, regardless of grade level, would need to have curriculum material presented in a way that recapitulated the entire set of stages. Thus, for Hunt, the teacher of adolescent children could presume that the students' formal operational competence could be addressed directly in the lesson. On the other hand, Alebi would require that the teacher begin the lesson with some sensorimotor representation, followed by a figural representation of the lesson's content, and so forth, until the lesson could be approached in the way the teacher following Hunt's recommendations had assumed in the first place.

THE ROLE OF DEVELOPMENTAL THEORY IN SOME REFORM SLOGANS

From the nation's beginning, when the Puritans in 1647 required each village of 100 households to establish a school to "delude old Satan" and thereby build a new nation, education has been the American secular religion, the means by which the country would transform itself and its citizens. More than 300 years later, in 1957, when the Soviet Union demonstrated an engineering and scientific competence sufficient to do what the United States had not yet accomplished, the nation identified its schools as the source of its competitive failure. Jerome Bruner, 2 years later, convened a group of natural scientists, psychologists, and educators in Woods Hole, Massachusetts, to study the ways in which American schools might be reformed to compete in the Space Race (Bruner, 1961).

Any Subject at Any Time

The group's conclusions, summarized by Bruner in *The Process of Education* (1961), introduced developmental theory to the wider American academic and educational community. At one level the book merely acknowledged a centuries-old argument that schooling should be responsive to the stages and characteristics of the pupil's developing mind (see, e.g., Carter, 1926). What was new this time, however, was that the reformers could point to a sweeping theory that described how the structure of the child's thinking about school tasks changed throughout the school years. Unlike so much of educational theory before, the new approach seemed to be grounded empirically, particularly when buttressed by the experimental literature Stevenson had marshalled about children's learning (Stevenson, 1968, 1970).

As a result, several school curricula were developed in the 1960s and 1970s that attempted to lay bare the structure of each discipline in the same way that developmental theory attempted to lay bare the structure of the child's reasoning and thought. Each of these curricula was based upon a notion of the sequential stages in the structure of knowing that were associated with childhood and adolescence. The driving slogan behind the curricular reforms of the 1960s and early 1970s, taken by Bruner and the others as fairly direct implications of developmental theory, was that "any subject can be taught effectively in some intellectually honest form to any child at any stage of development" (Bruner, 1961, p. 33). Thus, a way could be found to work into the curriculum the difficult physics and mathematics needed for the United States to reestablish its position as an economic and military leader.

Spiral Curricula

The way, of course, was the developmentally appropriate *spiral curriculum* in which each subject worth an adult's attention would be taught throughout the school years in ways that were sensitive to the particular constraints and power of each stage of intellectual development. Ironically, the hypothesis that any subject can be taught at any age with integrity could just as well be seen as incompatible with developmental theory. The postulated discontinuities between each stage, that is, the qualitative changes that legitimize the declaration of a new stage, also threaten the integrity and honesty of any discipline. The link, for example, between geo-board activities and Euclid, or between learning the letters of the alphabet and the *Scarlet Letter*, is too distant to support an intellectually valid or interesting developmental connection. Yet other links, equally strained on first appearance, seemed to have a deep root in cognitive development that justified a spiral curriculum approach, despite the strain it would put on the epigenic requirement that subsequent stages are inherently unpredictable from prior stages and not fully decomposable into the elements of the prior stages.

By virtue of epigenesis, presumably, some school subjects cannot be taught with integrity across the life span because they are intrinsically different at different periods of intellectual development. The links between each stage are *emergent*, that is, by definition there is nothing in the earlier stage from which the later stage can be deduced or predicted. On the other hand, there are thematic links between each stage such that the earlier stages provide a necessary, even if insufficient, base for the later stages. These links presumably have pedagogical value and support the notion of a spiral curriculum.

For example, one important school lesson informed by developmental theory is that some things remain constant and intrinsically themselves, even though some of their aspects change over time. The notion of a spiral curriculum is rooted in a context-dependent theory of developmental stage that leads educators to see that this concept of invariance in change is addressed at several times in the child's development. In the first years of life, the child appreciates the perceptual constancies in which wide ranges of visual stimuli, for example, a line, an oval, an ellipse, and a circle (each a possible retinal image of a coin), are recognized immediately as a round coin. Thereafter, with some instruction, children know the perceptual constancies metacognitively, that is, by thinking about their own perceiving. They go on to understand that the coin is always round because its shape is unchanged by changes in its location or orientation (identity). Later, and usually without direct instruction, the child comes to understand more about the coin. The child understands, after first believing the contrary, that the number of coins in a row is unaffected by the distances between them, or the amount of metal in them, or the weight of the metal, or the space each coin takes up, or the age of the coin, and so forth (conservation). Nor are children's judgments of the coin's weight, and so forth, affected by whether a coin is flat, on its edge, or pounded thinner, and so on. Somewhat later, but again after first asserting the contrary, the pupil finally comes to understand, despite changes in the coin's appearance or position, that there are still other constancies about the coin, for example, its density, its value, its acceleration in free fall, the likelihood that it will land on its head or tail in a random toss, and so

FRANK B. MURRAY

forth. Throughout the course of the school curriculum, the pupil comes
to see that appearances differ in their status—some are taken as misleading appearances, others are seen as signs of an underlying and stable
reality, and still others are seen as a necessity (Murray, 1990).

Less Is More

The lesson that some aspects of things remain constant, although other
aspects vary, is a lesson, like many important lessons, that cannot be
learned at once. It is a lesson that must be revisited in each stage and
each grade. It is the lesson that also stands behind another reform
slogan, *less is more*, in the sense that by attending to fewer less-
important ideas, the pupil will gain more through understanding powerful and pivotal concepts, like invariance, number, cause, justice, proportion, or necessity. The spiral notion, or the revisiting of important
—or big—ideas, is similar to the Genevan notion of *reflective
abstraction*, in which the mental accomplishments of earlier stages are
reconstructed and extended upward into more consolidated later stages.

Regrettably these structures of the disciplines and spiral curricula
failed to win a permanent place in the American public schools, although some found enduring places in the private schools and abroad.
In America this failure to take hold partly was due to a crisis of social
justice, but mostly it was because the reforms did not address the
teacher, and more important, the education of the teachers. For whatever misguided reasons, the spiral curriculum reformers attempted to
build teacher-proof curriculum materials that would bypass the teacher
entirely and speak directly to the pupil.

As we shall see, the current educational reforms have the teacher,
and by implication teacher education, at the center of the reform initiative. As in the structure of the discipline reformers, proponents of
current educational reforms insist that the pupil understand, as opposed
to merely learn, the contents of the curriculum (Holmes Group, 1990,
1995; National Commission on Teaching & America's Future, 1996).
Thus, some important goals of the structure-of-the-disciplines and spiral curricular innovations have been preserved in the current reform
movement as part of its slogan, *teaching for understanding* (sometimes

called *tofu*): the *more* of the *less is more* slogan is the addition of "understanding" to the learning of fewer topics.

All Children Can Learn

Unfortunately, the responses to the Sputnik crisis left more out of the proposed solutions to the nation's problems than the teacher, or the teacher's education. Like educational reform efforts before, they left out entire groups of pupils, despite the slogan that any concept could be taught to any child with integrity. The civil rights movement made it clear that the schools had not attended to the needs of all their pupils and had not optimized the intellectual development of all the pupils in the school (e.g., Irvine, 1990). For whatever reason, poor children and children from some minority groups were overrepresented in special education, school dropout, and suspensions, and were underrepresented in gifted programs and college attendance (e.g., Goodlad & Keating, 1990; Howe, 1990). The legacy of decades of legal and de facto racial discrimination in schooling was evident in educational policies such as tracking, ability grouping, and property-tax school financing. These policies simply segregated schools once more along racially and economically identifiable lines with the result that educational opportunities for some poor and minority pupils were reduced (Oakes, 1985).

As with the Sputnik crisis, the prevailing theories of intelligence and learning proved an inadequate source for the reform of the schools. The laboratory conditioning and verbal learning paradigms that dominated inquiry in psychology were too distant from the schools to provide any guidance, except of the most general sort, about how to teach mathematics, science, language, and so forth. Laboratory tasks such as oddity learning, reversal and nonreversal shifts, and transposition, although informative cognitive tasks, were not closely related to school tasks.[3] Similarly, the conditions under which the data were obtained in the laboratory were so unlike the classroom, as Stevenson had noted earlier, that generalization for school practice was difficult and unwise (Stevenson, Kagan, & Spiker, 1963).

---

[3]See Stevenson (1972) for an explication of these and related experimental learning tasks.

317

The reform question grew into how to help all young pupils grasp the newly implemented structure-of-the-disciplines curricula, particularly children who began school without having mastered some seemingly prerequisite cognitive tasks (Stevenson, Chen, & Uttal, 1990). The prevailing psychometric determinations of intellectual potential and achievement, like the learning paradigms, were simply not about the kinds of preschool cognitive skills that mattered in subsequent intellectual accomplishment. Moreover, the standardized tests of ability, apart from their designers' insistence that intellectual ability was normally distributed and that sex differences in performance were trivial, were essentially atheoretical. More to the point, the tests revealed the kinds of differences in abilities that the civil rights reformers wished to minimize. The kind of intellectual difference the tests uncovered between categories of children, while substantial, was only modestly related to schooling, accounting for no more than 25% of the variance in school grades, for example (Brody & Brody, 1976). There were also severe problems of underprediction insofar as these tests tended to underestimate the academic performance and potential of some low scorers (Nettles, Thoeny, & Gosman, 1986).

Theories of intellectual development, such as Piaget's theory of intelligence, hold that the structure of intelligence and its development are universal and should be largely insensitive to cultural and social differences. Because they also seem to focus on what children could do as opposed to what they could not do, developmental theory proved attractive to school reformers as an ideological alternative to the psychological models prevailing in the 1960s (Hunt, 1961).

The civil rights movement in American education, although it turned to developmental theory for a new and more generous view of intelligence, also undermined the newly developed structure-of-the-disciplines curricula. Because of the emerging success of the American space program, these curricula were increasingly seen as needlessly difficult and as an unnecessary barrier to universal schooling and to equity in educational achievement throughout the kindergarten through 12th-grade system. There was, as a result, a shift from the individual pupil to inclusive groups of pupils, toward cooperation and collaboration in classroom instruction. This shift drew upon the developmental theory of Vygotsky (Moll, 1990), and focused on basic skills that all children could readily master, drawing in part upon advances in instructional technology.

A Nation at Risk

Throughout the 1980s the direct influence of developmental theory on the American schools was less evident as the schools invested in their pupils' mastery of the basic academic skills and in other ways of making universal education work. Having all pupils succeed in school was the legacy of the civil rights movement, and the slogan, *all kids can learn*, supplanted the earlier slogan, *any subject in an honest form at any grade*.

About the year 1981, the nation's parents, politicians, and educators finally became aware of the painful fact that the performance on the Scholastic Aptitude Test (SAT) had declined steadily each year since the end of the school year in 1963. The facts of the decline are more or less as follows: Between 1952 and 1963, at a time when the percentage of high-school candidates taking the test rose from 6.8% to 50%—or from 81,000 to 933,000 students—the scores fluctuated randomly from year to year. Between 1963 and 1982, the scores fell 90 points (55 verbal and 35 math out of a possible 600 points on each test), representing a drop in about 11 actual items, 7 from the verbal test and 4 from the mathematics test.

That the tests became harder was not the case: If anything they had become easier (e.g., 3,000 students from 66 schools who took both the 1963 and the 1973 versions scored 8–12 points higher on the later version). About one half the total drop, and almost all of the drop between 1960 and 1970, can be explained by changes in the composition of the group who took the tests. During the 1960s, for example, proportionately more students with lower scores aspired to college and took the test, and a small number of would-be high scorers elected not to attend college and therefore did not take the test (Eklund, 1982).

The declines after 1970 (about 50 points) are more difficult to explain because they happened in all types of schools (private, public, large, small, high- and low-socioeconomic neighborhoods) and to all kinds of people (men, women, Whites, Blacks, and valedictorians). By 1976 there were about 80,000 fewer students than there were in 1970 who scored above 600 on either the math or verbal tests.

This decline and the relatively poor performance of the nation's best high-school students in international comparisons (Berliner & Biddle, 1995; Ogle & Alsalam, 1990; Stevenson, 1992), bolstered by the nation's weakened economic position, led a special federal commission to conclude that, owing to the low quality of schooling, and especially of teacher education, the entire nation was at risk. The commission, along with the authors of scores of subsequent reports, called for the restructuring of American schools (Elmore & Associates, 1990). They sought to do this by the assertion of another set of slogans— *high stakes standards, more time on task,* for example—and the rigorous assessments of academic achievement, as well as by improvements in the education of teachers, whose SAT scores also had declined, but more sharply in this period than those of the typical college-bound student.

REDUCING THE NATION'S RISK

Initially, the nation-at-risk reformers thought the schools could remain pretty much as they were and meet the nation's needs by simply increasing the amount of time available for instruction. Restructuring in both the political and developmental senses was finally called for because the very form or structure of education had to be changed to accommodate the full and diverse range of pupils, massive amounts of new curricular information, and the centrality of the empowered teacher.

The current American educational crisis is defined almost entirely by the poor performance of American students on standardized tests of academic information and skill (Stevenson & Stigler, 1992). The poorest performance on the National Assessment of Education Progress (NAEP) tests is on those items that require the student to use higher levels of cognitive functioning. Scores on the basic skills items, a target of the civil rights movement, are good by comparison with higher level skill items but still lower than they are in other countries (Stevenson, 1992). Nearly every school district in the nation, on the other hand, is performing above average, the so-called Lake Woebegone effect, in comparison to normed basic skills test results a decade earlier (Linn, Graue, & Sanders, 1990; Shanker, 1989). The Lake Woebegone effect could have been taken as good news, ironically, because students were actually performing better than the normative sample of American students upon whom the tests had been standardized earlier. Instead it was taken as a sign that the tests were corrupt (Cannell, 1987).

Apparently the schools are succeeding in the basic skills areas, the areas that are easiest to teach and evaluate and the areas that were emphasized in Head Start and other early childhood interventions (Grissmer, Kirby, Berends, & Williamson, 1994). However, the areas that had been addressed by the post-Sputnik reforms, and subsequently ignored in the reforms of the 1970s, now stand out as the areas of greatest educational weakness (ETS, 1990).

At the moment, classical developmental theory, being clearer in proscription than in prescription, would seem to be of little use in addressing the crisis identified by the nation-at-risk reformers. For example, developmental theory makes it clear that pupils in the preoperational stage will probably not succeed in understanding traditional lessons about the product-moment relationships in the beam balance, even though they may learn the terms and formula associated with the relationship, and even though the child may have noted each separate factor in the relationship (Inhelder & Piaget, 1958). But the theory is not as clear about what lessons the preoperational child should take in place of the traditional product-moment beam-balance lesson. The neo-Piagetians, however, most notably Case and his colleagues, (e.g., Case, 1985, 1988; Case & Okamoto, 1996), have made clear prescriptions for sequences of school lessons that lead the pupil to understand the beam-balance relationships and other concepts that are central to the elementary school curriculum.

DEVELOPMENTAL THEORY AND THE
POST-NATION-AT-RISK REFORM SOLUTIONS

Despite these qualifications, and the fact that no developmental theorist was mentioned in the nation-at-risk report, there are lessons from developmental theory for the current crisis. John Carroll's (1989) model of school learning provides an instructive way of organizing the current implications of developmental theory for educational practice.

The model sets out four main variables, none startlingly new, that control the degree to which a school task will be mastered. The model holds that

Degree of school learning = f (time spent/time needed for learning).

Time spent in learning is a function of the time the pupil is engaged and willing to work on the school task (perseverance), or the time the teacher allocates for the lesson (allocated time), whichever is less. The time needed for learning is a function of the pupil's ability. This is taken as the time the pupil needs to learn the task on his or her own, minus the time the pupil saves as a result of instruction (or the time that is added owing to low-quality instruction).

In sum, the time the pupil needs to learn the lesson is a function of two general factors: the pupil's ability, as measured by unassisted learning time, and instructional quality, as measured by time the pupil saves as a result of the school and teacher's efforts.

Increasing the Numerator

The national effort, inspired by the report *A Nation at Risk* (National Commission on Excellence in Education, 1983), targeted the numerator of Carroll's model. It focused on fairly crude ways to increase the time allocated for schoolwork, either through lengthening the school day beyond 6 hours, or the school year beyond 180 days. In some cases this was done by increasing the number of years the pupil attends school by mandating preschool and kindergarten, or by raising the dropout age limit, or by making school attendance a condition of having a driver's license, and so forth (Barrett, 1990).

The attempts to increase the amount of time the pupil actually spends on mastering the lesson, once the time has been allocated by the teacher and the school, have not been influenced by any account of human development (Ben-Peretz & Bromme, 1990). Instead, they have been inspired by straightforward programs of research that analyze the relationships between the time the teacher allocates (a surprisingly small amount in some instances), the amount of time the pupil is actually engaged in attempting to learn the lesson, and the brief time interval in which the pupil actually learns what the lesson requires. The key factor in determining the pupil's perseverance appears to be the success the pupil has in the initial attempts to grasp what the lesson calls for. For example, Berliner (1990) reports that a construct, academic learning time (ALT), defined as that part of allocated time in which the pupil is successfully engaged in an academic task that will be tested, is a powerful predictor of final academic achievement. For example, in one sample (Berliner, 1990) daily ALT in reading averaged between 4 and 52 min over 25 days and accurately predicted final reading grades, especially for weaker students.

Decreasing the Denominator

Because the time spent in learning will always be determined by the smallest value in the numerator, reformers finally have come to see that the greatest changes in school-based learning are likely to come from efforts to affect the time the pupil needs to learn the lesson. Of course, educators have always known that the pupil's ability and the quality of instruction determine the outcome of many lessons. The question is whether developmental theory has anything new to add at this time.

Pupil's Ability

The full power of developmental theory has not been realized with regard to pupil's ability. Piaget's theory, for example, especially as it has been extended by so-called neo-Piagetian researchers, does provide a comprehensive account of the child's developing intellectual competence (Demetriou, 1988).

The basic cognitive building block in the Genevan account is the child's growing ability to invent the opposite of any event, action, or attribute the child has in mind. Two forms of opposite occur: In the simplest, *negation*, the child conceives of the undoing of the attribute, event, or action; in the more complex, *the reciprocal*, the child must invent another idea, attribute, or event that undoes or cancels the original one. The entire mental system of necessary links and connections that stands at the heart of logic, mathematics, physics, and so forth depends upon the child's ability to invent some mental entity, imagine its being undone, invent yet another way to cancel it, and then see that these two means of reversing or undoing the entity are themselves bound together in a system of mutual implication. Thus in time, the child understands that an object can be made heavier, for example, by adding to its width, and that the object can be returned to its original weight by subtraction from its width. In addition, the child realizes it can be returned to its original weight by conceiving of another attribute, height, that can also be altered to restore the object to its original weight. More important, the child, through these alterations in width, height, and so on, comes to see that they are necessarily related to each other insofar as the very idea, width, implies—*of necessity*—the idea of height, just as the idea of *three* implies the existence of the other numbers, and just as the notion of *addition* implies *subtraction* in the system of arithmetic.

The Genevan account, unlike others, does not make a provision for individual differences because the epistemic subject[4] has no individual characteristics. Although this is a crippling limitation to its utility to educational theory, the approach, following the findings of Stevenson's field studies, draws the teacher's attention to the features of the school task, not the pupil's inherent ability, as a more important feature of the school's curriculum. The slogan, *all children can learn*, means that the normal school curriculum is well within the grasp of all but the seriously challenged child; consequently, all regularly enrolled pupils are expected to master the curriculum, and the school cannot be excused

---

[4]The epistemic subject is the pure knower; the theory is about his or her competence to know and understand. The theory, in other words, is solely about the mechanisms and structures that yield this kind of competence.

from ensuring that all its pupils do on the grounds that the pupils were not able, did not try, had the wrong background, and so forth (Goodlad & Keating, 1990; Holmes Group, 1990, 1995). When the school tasks have the characteristics Case (1988; Case & Okamoto, 1996) and others have specified, each pupil, at the appropriate stage, has the competence to do the work required. More to the point, when the school accepts the goal that the curriculum will be understood by the students, and not merely learned or imitated, cognitive developmental theory has a special role because it is about the acquisition of ideas that are both extraordinarily resistant to forgetting and that increase in power over time.

The developmental perspective, as a result, is in line with another of the current reform slogans, namely the calls for understanding, not just learning. The year-by-year comparisons of the national tests of the school's accomplishments indicate that pupils learn a great deal each year. We know also that, as adults, high-school graduates know more than grade-school graduates, and that college graduates know more than either of the lower school graduates (Murray, 1985). The problem is that pupils *understand* very little of what they have learned (ETS, 1990).

Cognitive developmental theory, for example, is precisely about how we come to understand what we know. Thus, the theory is ideally suited to provide the guiding rationale for school reformers who have set as their goal the pupil's understanding of what is learned in school as well as other puzzling phenomena that are encountered in everyday life. The guidance comes from a close examination of the children in the Genevan experiments, who develop the confidence of intellect to plunge into the problem armed only with their abilities to use their minds well.

One of the lessons of Inhelder and Piaget's seminal book, *The Growth of Logical Thinking from Childhood to Adolescence* (1958), was that pupils' school learning did not serve them well. When they had to confront novel versions of the same problem they had learned in school, such as the angle of incidence and reflection equality, or the floating body principle, few used their school knowledge to solve the problems.

body principle, few used their school knowledge to solve the problems. They had to draw upon other resources, quite apart from specific school lessons.

In summary, developmental theory has strong claims to make about the intellectual competence of school children and how that competence can be expected to vary by age and by grade level. In addition, and more important, the theory tends to shift the pedagogical issues from the consideration of the child's competence to the characteristics of the school task itself.

Quality of Instruction

Because the importance of pupils' ability is minimized in the current reform effort, the burden of reform has shifted to the quality of instruction (Elmore & Associates, 1990). Of course, reformers as well as traditional educators and administrators have always acknowledged the importance of pupils' ability when they delay instruction in some topics so that the more mature pupils are assigned the more difficult school tasks, or when they simply segregate the school's pupils by measures of intellectual ability.

Developmental theorists have written almost nothing about pedagogy, other than to generally endorse the discovery and collaboration methods that were the standard feature of progressive education (Ginsburg, 1981). Piagetian theory, however, gave rise to 3 decades of research on the teaching procedures that advance a child from one stage to another. In addition, developmental psychologists uncovered scores of variables that influenced whether a child or adolescent would give evidence that he or she truly understood a concept or that a correct solution indicated genuine understanding (as in the claims and counterclaims of pseudo-operativity).

Flavell and Wohlwill (1969) proposed a model to capture the relationships between these variables that can still serve educators. In their model, the probability that a child would solve a developmental task, or an important educational task, was expressed as:

$$p = p_a \cdot (p_b)^{l-k}$$

by p_a, and p_b is the probability that the relevant task variables will be attended to and influence the outcome.

The exponential term, k, which like the other terms, varies between 0 and 1, is an individual difference factor, such as IQ, memory, or learning style. It weights the probability that the task variables will influence the outcome, p, which is the probability that the pupil's performance will indicate that the concept in question is truly understood. Clearly, if p_a or p_b is zero, the child will be unable to give any evidence of understanding. When p_a has some value, however, the child's performance can be enhanced as k approaches 1. When the child is very bright and attentive, and remembers all the task variables, the p_b factors raise the probability that the idea will be understood.

A number of task variables have been discovered and each presents itself as a candidate upon which some pedagogical device can be constructed, because each will increase the probability that the concept or relationship in question will be understood. Murray (1981) reviewed a comprehensive set of task variables that affect whether the child will give evidence that the conservation relationship has been understood. Although the manipulation of these variables can be quite helpful in promoting understanding, the variables also signify conceptual errors that must be corrected at some point in the course of schooling. Thus, in a good school, the errors, or misconceptions, of childhood constitute a scaffold of imperfect understanding, so to speak, that forms the core of a so-called spiral toward fuller understanding.

For example, it makes a difference in the conservation-of-amount task whether the substance whose amount is to be conserved is discontinuous (e.g., sand or pebbles) or continuous (e.g., water). The discontinuous material is often found to be easier for children. This difference has been featured in attempts to teach conservation to preoperational children (e.g., Murray, 1978, 1981).

Instructional Strategies and Developmental Theory

As it happens, since 1961 about 180 carefully executed attempts to teach young children to understand the conservation relationship were published. Rarely were their authors motivated by a desire to improve the

lished. Rarely were their authors motivated by a desire to improve the schools; more often than not, they were motivated by a desire to test a claim in developmental theory, usually the alleged immutable character of the Genevan stages. The Genevan claim was that learning and experience, the benefits of the "Vygotsky" social milieu, and maturation, although necessary for cognitive development, were not—separately or collectively—sufficient for it. The results of the training literature, as it was called, are still instructive, however, for the design of pedagogical strategies within the *zone of proximal development*, that is, within the period during which the student is most receptive to instruction.

On the whole the results of these studies were remarkably consistent. There is evidence of cohort effects because children in the late 1970s learned their lessons more easily than those in the 1960s. Nevertheless, overall, only half the number of the pupils in these laboratory experiments changed in a significant way, and they made only half the gains that could have been made in the lesson. Not surprising, children who were in the zone of proximal development, that is, who had some grasp of the concept in question (as assessed by pretests), invariably made greater gains than those who were genuine novices (Beilin, 1971; Brainerd, 1973; Glaser & Resnick, 1972; Peill, 1975; Strauss, 1972, 1974–1975).

These are not encouraging results for the schools insofar as the concepts could not be considered difficult. Even in fairly ideal teaching situations (small groups and few distractions), only about one half of the class's pupils actually learned something along the lines of what was intended. Some children, of course, scored perfectly on tests of what they were taught, and some could solve similar problems, and even other problems that were related but quite different from those that were explicitly taught in the lesson.

Over the 30-year period, eight generic methods for teaching these concepts emerged in the developmental literature. Each has a wide application in education because conservation is a feature of every curricular concept, not just those examined by Piaget and his colleagues. In fact, conservation can be seen as a prototypical test of the under-

know whether a concept has changed when some attributes associated with the concept have changed.

Consequently, teaching methods that were directed toward the child's understanding of the conditions under which any concept is, or is not, altered ought to be an important part of teachers' education. Even though these strategies have been developed in another academic tradition and for other reasons, many of them are clearly in line with how classroom teachers might approach teaching the concepts in question.

The lessons developmental psychologists have devised for their nonconserving pupils in these experimental studies follow.

Teacher Feedback

These were straightforward conditioning approaches in which the pupil was simply rewarded for stating the correct answer and "punished" for incorrect answers.

Discovery

Here, the reward or reinforcement comes from the pupil's manipulation of the materials themselves and from the measurement instruments. If the child is to understand that the weight of an object is independent of changes in its shape, then the child might be exposed to a series of transformations of an object into various shapes. She would see from the readings on a scale, or some other device, that the reading was unaffected by each change of shape. Or the child might produce the transformations, weigh the results of each transformation, and thereby *see* that the weight of the object was not affected by the transformations.

The weakness in the method, as in nearly all the others, is that it does not require, or even lead, the child to conclude that the weight *has* to be the same, but only that it *is* the same in each case. The method, like so many others in the schools, promotes learning more effectively than understanding, because understanding requires an appreciation of the inherent necessity in the concept and how the concept is linked to other notions. In the end, one wants the pupil to understand that the weight of the object is necessarily unaffected by changes in the object's shape, for example, not merely that the weight did not change on this occasion.

Verbal Rule Instruction

Of all the methods, this procedure is closest to traditional school instruction because the pupil is simply given the rule for the solution to the problem. For example, the child might be told that "the only way to change the weight of an object is to add or take some part of it away." Apart from the fact that the rule is incomplete, as most oversimplified school rules have to be, the rule does not address the underlying structure of the task that is needed for there to be understanding.

Cue Reduction or Scaffolding

Here, the pupil is actually prevented from making an error because the factors that would otherwise lead to the error are either hidden from the pupil or introduced at such a gradual and slow pace that their effects are negligible on the pupil's reasoning. To some degree, this method allows the child to answer correctly by ignoring much of the problem that was presented, and like the methods above, the child may correctly respond without understanding the systematic relationships among all the factors in the problem. The method attempts to slow the process down sufficiently so that the pupil can grasp more easily the nature of the events. Thus, the child would be asked about the ball's weight, then an oval shape of pressed ball, then a more flattened shape, and so forth, until the pancake shape is presented.

Analogy and Apperception

These methods presume that the pupil has acquired a prior distinction, most often the distinction between appearance and reality. The problem is made an instance of the earlier distinction by means of an analogy or metaphor. For example, the pupil's attention could be directed to the fact that the clay ball simply looked heavier, but really was not, just as a ball under a magnifying glass only looks larger.

Cognitive Conflict

This method is an instance of the *reductio ad absurdum* argument in which the procedure, or transformation, that ostensibly makes the clay ball appear heavier actually (through duplicity on the teacher's part) makes the ball lighter (see Murray, 1983b). Thus, the pupil is confronted with a powerful contradiction between his expectations, based upon an immature reasoning structure, and the outcome of the lesson. The hope is that the contradiction will be resolved in favor of the teacher's lesson, but there are other somewhat risky outcomes. The contradiction could be unnoticed, maintained as a mystery or paradox, or the pupil could acquiesce and thereby avoid thinking further about the problem. Or the contradiction could be resolved in the direction of the teacher's duplicity (i.e., the pupil, instead of concluding that the ball would not change, would believe flattening the ball made it lighter instead of heavier as the pupil had originally thought).

Training on Theoretical Prerequisites

These procedures, of course, vary with the theory. They range from training on every step previously uncovered in an empirical analysis of a learning paradigm, such as a "Gagne" hierarchy, to training on abstract Genevan or neo-Piagetian factors such as reversibility, reciprocity, M-space, decentration, concrete groupings, prior tasks from the vertical or horizontal *décalage*, and so forth.

Social Interaction Methods

These procedures introduce interactions between the pupil and the other members of the pupil's class either through planned disagreements, cognitive dissonance, imitation, role playing, or cooperation on a common goal. Originally, these methods were little more than a strategy to break down the child's presupposed *egocentrism*, or inability to take the point of view of another. In that sense they were but a variation of methods based upon other theoretical perspectives. More recently, these methods have been situated in Vygotskian accounts of development (Moll, 1990).

Basically, the teacher places two pupils who disagree about the answer to a problem in a group and tells them to work together until they can agree or come to a common answer. Once the pupils agree, usually in about 5 min, the teacher tests the children alone and usually finds that the pupils who initially do poorly on the problem, when on their own, solve the problem in a way that is indistinguishable from the way a correct problem solver solved it in the first place (see Murray, 1986 for a review of this literature). In some instances teachers may also instruct the pupils in the dyad to simply imitate a correct problem solver, and on other occasions, the teacher may instruct one child, in the presence of the other, to pretend to reason in a mature way—in other words the teacher places the pupil in some social situation where he or she is forced to take a viewpoint that conflicts with his or her own point of view. The practice works best if the teacher ensures that one pupil understands the task. Some cognitive growth also occurs when neither child knows the correct answer to the problem, but only when each initially offers an incorrect answer that contradicts the other's answer.

QUALITY OF INSTRUCTION, TEACHER EDUCATION, AND DEVELOPMENTAL THEORY

Clearly, the quality of instruction hinges on a teacher's understanding of the discipline. Developmental theory's most significant role in educational reform may be in the field of teacher education. The study of genetic epistemology, for example, could provide the prospective teacher with precisely the kind of understanding educational reformers envision when they point out that pedagogical technique is specific to a particular domain of knowledge (Shulman, 1986, 1987).

In this approach to teacher education, the prospective teacher studies the developmental psychological literature from the perspective of the development of the concepts that make up the curriculum. The teacher learns the relevant developmental constraints upon the pupil's acquisition of the curriculum, and learns, as an unavoidable part of the discussion, the nature of the subject itself. The story of how the young child develops the notion of number, for example, is valuable in its own right, but also reveals salient portions of number theory, the arithmetical algorithms, and other aspects of mathematics. Similarly, the account of the child's moral development reveals the principal issues in moral philosophy and political theory.

The study of the development of the child's concept of weight is an instructive example because it entails studying the same notion as it appears in Newtonian mechanics and other branches of physics. The young child can be shown to operate with the following "system" for weight where weight is a function of the following aspects of an object (Murray & Johnson, 1970, 1975):

1. The object's mass, with additions of mass yielding greater weight, and so forth, and no change in mass yielding no change in weight;
2. Size, with larger objects weighing more;
3. Shape, with some shapes weighing more and some less (e.g., flattening increases weight);
4. Texture, with the rougher weighing more and the smoother weighing less;
5. Temperature, with the colder weighing more and the warmer weighing less;
6. Hardness, with the harder weighing more and the softer weighing less;
7. Continuity, with a whole weighing more than the sum of the components;
8. Label, with the object labeled *bigger* weighing more than the object labeled *smaller.*

Some factors that are potential members of the system can be shown to have no influence on the child's physics of weight of an object, for example:

1. An object's horizontal position, with an object weighing the same at either end of the table;
2. An object's vertical position, with an object weighing the same in a deep hole or at the top of the tallest mountain.

The young child's view of weight is based upon a consistent child-logic in which the factors above influence weight lawfully and dependably (Murray, 1982; Murray & Markessini, 1982).

Adolescents and many adults operate with the following simpler and to some degree more sophisticated "system" where weight is a function of only the object's mass, the only influential factor to survive the child's system. In other words, the only way adults can think of to change an object's weight is to alter its mass, that is, add something or take something away from the object. The young child can imagine many other ways for altering weight, all unfortunately incorrect.

The educated person operates within another system where the following factors are organized as a mathematical expression of the product of the first two factors divided by the square of the third factor:

1. Mass of the object (as above);
2. Mass of the planet (the largest, nearest object), with larger planets yielding increased weight;
3. The distance between the centers of the above two factors, with weight decreasing disproportionately with increases in the distance.

In addition, the educated person may be able to convert the expression into a genuine equation by way of a value, [g], for the gravitational constant, which permits algebraic manipulation of the terms in the expression. At this point other factors may be introduced into the expression to treat certain buoyant forces, variations in the earth's g, or variations in the location and movement of an object (as when it might be falling, etc.). With further education, gravitation is seen as an aspect of a space-time continuum in relativity physics.

There is a similar developmental progression for the child's understanding of the beam balance in which the young child's understanding of the concept of "weighing" is controlled solely by the effects of adding or subtracting weight from a pan without the influence of any other factor (Siegler, 1981). Later the distance of the balance pan from the fulcrum is gradually factored into the child's scheme for the operation of the balance, and after several more developmental steps, the product-moment law is in place in the adolescent's thinking. All concepts and relations in the curriculum can be profitably approached from this perspective. The approach also has face validity in teacher education because it contains the kinds of information that prospective teachers accept as clearly relevant for their future work.

The prospective teacher's study of genetic epistemology, however, is more than a device by which students in teacher education might learn their academic disciplines. It goes to the core of the kind of knowledge the teacher needs, namely generative ways of organizing information and knowledge. It entails the search for structures, ways of representing the subject matter, such as analogies and metaphors, that will take each pupil well beyond what can be maintained temporally and spatially through rote memorization. Pedagogical content knowledge (Shulman, 1986, 1987) is fundamentally about the structures of genetic epistemology that confer some appropriate level of understanding, and it is ultimately about those structures that actually advance our understanding (see Murray & Fallon, 1989).

The knowledge of what is a telling example, a good analogy, a provocative question, or a compelling theme is a proper object of study in an academic major and could yield the kind of understanding of the disciplines that is deep and generative. To have multiple ways of representing subject matter, to have more than one example or metaphor, to have more than one mode of explanation, requires a high order and demanding form of understanding.

Consider teaching the division of $1\frac{3}{4}$ by $\frac{1}{2}$ and going beyond the mindless algorithm, "invert and multiply." If the teacher were asked for some real world examples of this arithmetical operation, what would the teacher have had to study to develop a repertoire of different representations of the arithmetical expression, $1\frac{3}{4} \div \frac{1}{2}$? (For example, "how many 50-cent tickets can be bought with $1.75," or "how many half-yard ruffles can be sewn from $1\frac{3}{4}$ yards of ruffles," or "how many half slices of pizza can be served from $1\frac{3}{4}$ pizzas," or "how many dips of a $\frac{1}{2}$ quart container of oil are needed to exactly fill an engine that holds only $1\frac{3}{4}$ quarts," and so on.) Whatever the discipline might be called, it is a new kind of knowledge that is dependent upon a knowledge of fractions, but is not directly derivable from it, and as such it is qualitatively different from it.

Not every pedagogical technique needs to be as content specific as those above. Virtually every reform report (e.g., Holmes Group, 1986, 1990, 1995) endorses cooperative learning as a modern teaching strategy or procedure that is superior to traditional methods. The strategy also has clear links to developmental theory and to other accounts of mental functioning and may provide the most convincing example of the usefulness of the link between developmental theory and schooling (see Murray, 1990 for a review of the link between cooperative learning techniques and developmental psychology).

Assessment and Developmental Theory

Unfortunately, we know very little about how teachers actually think about their teaching. This fact yields a final arena for a developmental theoretical approach to one of the current educational reform slogans, *authentic assessment*. Virtually the entire corpus of experimental designs in cognitive development outlined by Stevenson (1972, 1992) could be seen as an alternative to the typical classroom and standardized tests of the student's understanding of some aspect of the curriculum. The objective in each experimental study of cognitive development is to determine the genuine nature of the child's thought about the child's grasp of a concept, such as transitivity, justice, shadow, number, or some other aspect of the child's thinking. These designs, not all of them restricted to laboratory investigations, tease apart the subtleties of understanding and learning. All would constitute an improvement upon the typical educational test or assessment.

Teachers need a way to formulate standards for their student's intellectual accomplishment, especially standards delineating the degree to which each pupil has understood each subject studied in the school's curriculum. These standards, implicitly applied in the teacher's traditional and daily evaluation of each pupil's work, unfortunately are rarely made explicit. What is lacking are the criteria by which all educators, parents, teachers, and researchers can know whether a student's work meets the standard, is well below it, or is well above it.

The scoring rubric, by which the student's accomplishments and progress are noted, is at the heart of the matter and is dependent upon the teacher's theory of at least two domains: (a) a theory of children's and adolescents' cognitive development and understanding, and (b) a theory of the complexity and sophistication of the subject matter itself.

If a child who had pluralized the word *mouse* as *mice*, to take a well-worn example, suddenly pluralizes it as *mouses*, a naive teacher might score the event as an unfortunate regression that requires re-mediation, whereas a professional teacher will see the so-called error as temporary and actually a sign of cognitive advancement in which the pupil is exhibiting a newly developed appreciation of a linguistic rule that is merely overgeneralized.

Upon what theory, to take another example, is the teacher to score the pupil who arrives at the correct answer to a multiplication problem through serial addition? Should that pupil's score be lower or higher than the pupil who arrives at an incorrect answer through multiplica-tion? Similarly, how is the teacher to grade the child who believes the weight of an object is affected by its texture or temperature?

The teacher's evaluation of the pupil's correct and incorrect re-sponses provides a telling and targeted arena for distinguishing naive and professional teachers. A pupil's reasoning may look illogical to a naive teacher, while the educated teacher will see that the pupil's rea-soning is intact, but has operated on different premises from those of the set problem. Other decrements in performance may also indicate education progress; for example, some 6-year-old pupils not only main-tain incorrectly that the longer row of two rows of five beans has more beans, but also maintain that the longer row must have more beans and would always have more beans. These errors occur even after the pupil has just counted the equal number of beans in each row. It hap-pens that the error "there *must* be more beans," which seems the more serious error, is indicative of more developed reasoning than the error "there are more beans." Naturally, it is very difficult for the naive teacher to accept any error and poor performance as a marker of prog-ress, yet the failure to see some errors as markers of progress is a serious pedagogical mistake that stems from the naive theory of teaching and learning (Bruner, 1961).

CONCLUSION

For more than 3 decades educational reformers and policy makers have reacted with changes to unsettling events in the nation's history, such as the space race, urban riots, declining test scores, and so forth, with changes. Each time, the nation's schooling's practices and outcomes are barely altered (Pogrow, 1996). What is it that holds the country back from implementing the compelling ideas represented in such reform slogans as *any subject to any child, less is more, all kids can learn, developmentally appropriate teaching,* and so on?

The answer seems to be that these slogans are not well understood by the reformers. As a result, the slogans do not provide guidance about the implementation of educational reform. They are deprived of the flexibility that accrues to ideas that are understood. The claim of this chapter is that the deeper understanding of these worthy slogans has its roots, as Harold Stevenson advised decades ago, in the study of developmental theory and the empirical findings generated within the various developmental theories. This deeper understanding, as Stevenson's recent work demonstrates (Stevenson & Stigler, 1992), is not only needed by school reformers, but also by the individual classroom teacher. This is why the connections between teacher education and developmental theory and research are critical for the reforms of school practices, and ultimately, the alteration of school outcomes. It is also why a new teacher education curriculum based upon developmental psychology (namely, genetic epistemology and pedagogical content knowledge) is recommended (Holmes Group, 1995; Murray & Fallon, 1989).

REFERENCES

Austin, G., & Garber, H. (1982). *The rise and fall of national test scores.* New York: Academic Press.

Barrett, M. (1990). The case for more school days. *Network News & Views,* 9(12), 25–37.

Beilin, J. (1971). The training and acquisition of logical operations. In M. F. Rosskopf, L. P. Steffe, & S. Taback (Eds.), *Piagetian cognitive-development research and mathematical education.* Washington, DC: National Council of Teachers of Mathematics, Inc.

Ben-Peretz, M., & Bromme, R. (1990). *The nature of time in schools: Theoretical concepts, practitioner perceptions.* New York: Teachers College Press.

Berliner, D. (1990). What's all the fuss about instructional time? In M. Ben-Peretz & R. Bromme (Eds.), *The nature of time in schools: Theoretical concepts, practitioner perceptions*. New York: Teachers College Press.

Berliner, D., & Biddle, B. (1995). *The manufactured crisis*. Reading, MA: Addison-Wesley.

Brainerd, C. J. (1973). Judgments and explanations as criteria for the presence of cognitive structures. *Psychological Bulletin, 79*, 172–179.

Brody, E., & Brody, N. (1976). *Intelligence: Nature, determinants, and consequences*. New York: Academic Press.

Bruner, J. (1961). *The process of education*. Cambridge, MA: Harvard University Press.

Cannell, J. (1987). *Nationally normed achievement testing in America's public schools: How all fifty states are above the national average* (2nd ed.). Daniels, WV: Friends of Education.

Carroll, J. (1989). The Carroll Model: A 25-year retrospective and prospective view. *Educational Researcher, 18*(1), 26–31.

Carter, J. (1926). Essays on popular education in the *Boston Patriot*, 1825. In A. O. Norton (Ed.), *The first state normal school in America: The journals of Cyrus Pierce and Mary Swift*. New York: Arno Press.

Case, R. (1985). *Intellectual development: Birth to adulthood*. New York: Academic Press.

Case, R. (1988). Structure and process of intellectual development. In A. Demetriou (Ed.), *The neo-Piagetian theories of cognitive development: Toward an integration* (pp. 65–101). Amsterdam: Elsevier.

Case, R., & Okamoto, Y. (1996). The role of central conceptual structures in the development of children's thought. *Monographs of the Society for Research in Child Development, 61*(1–2, Serial No. 246).

Cole, M. (1992). Culture in development. In M. Bornstein & M. Lamb (Eds.), *Developmental psychology: An advanced textbook*. Hillsdale, NJ: Erlbaum.

Cole, M., & Scribner, S. (1977). Cross-cultural studies of memory and cognition. In R. Kail & J. Hagen (Eds.), *Perspectives on the development of memory and cognition*. Hillsdale, NJ: Erlbaum.

Demetriou, A. (1988). *The neo-Piagetian theories of cognitive development: Toward an integration*. Amsterdam: Elsevier.

Educational Testing Service. (1990). *The educational reform decade.* Princeton, NJ: ETS Policy Information Center.

Eklund, B. (1982). College entrance examination trends. In G. Austin & H. Garber (Eds.), *The rise and fall of national test scores.* New York: Academic Press.

Elmore, R., & Associates. (1990). *Restructuring schools: The next generation of educational reform.* San Francisco: Jossey-Bass.

Flavell, J. (1963). *The developmental psychology of Jean Piaget.* New York: Van Nostrand.

Flavell, J., & Wohlwill, J. (1969). Formal and functional aspects of cognitive development. In D. Elkind & J. Flavell (Eds.), *Studies in cognitive development: Essays in honor of Jean Piaget* (pp. 67–120). New York: Oxford University Press.

Ginsburg, H. (1981). Piaget and education: The contributions and limits of genetic epistemology. In I. Sigel, D. Brodzinsky, & R. Golinkoff (Eds.), *New direction in Piagetian theory and practice* (pp. 315–330). Hillsdale, NJ: Erlbaum.

Glaser, R., & Resnick, L. (1972). Instructional psychology. In P. H. Mussen & M. Rosenweig (Eds.), *Annual Review of Psychology.* Palo Alto, CA: Annual Reviews.

Goodlad, J., & Keating, P. (1990). *Access to knowledge: An agenda for our nation's schools.* New York: College Entrance Examination Board.

Goodnow, J., & Bethon, G. (1966). Piaget's tasks: The effects of schooling and intelligence. *Child Development, 37,* 573–582.

Grissmer, D., Kirby, S., Berends, M., & Williamson, S. (1994). *Student achievement and the changing American family.* Santa Monica, CA: Rand.

Holmes Group. (1986). *Tomorrow's teachers.* East Lansing, MI: Author.

Holmes Group. (1990). *Tomorrow's schools: Principles for the design of professional development schools.* East Lansing, MI: Author.

Holmes Group. (1995). *Tomorrow's School of Education.* East Lansing, MI: Author.

Howe, H. (1990). Thinking about the *forgotten half. Teachers College Record, 92,* 293–305.

Hunt, J. (1961). *Intelligence and experience.* New York: Ronald Press.

Inhelder, B., & Piaget, J. (1958). *The growth of logical thinking from childhood to adolescence.* New York: Basic Books.

Irvine, J. (1990). *Black students and school failure: Policies, practices, and prescriptions.* New York: Greenwood Press.

Kuhn, D. (1992). Cognitive development. In M. Bornstein & M. Lamb (Eds.), *Developmental psychology: An advanced textbook.* Hillsdale, NJ: Erlbaum.

Linn, R., Graue, A., & Sanders, T. (1990). *Comparing state and district test results to national norms: Interpretations of scoring "above the national average."* (Tech. Rep. No. 307). Los Angeles: University of California at Los Angeles, Center for Research on Evaluation, Standards, and Student Testing.

Moll, L. (1990). *Vygotsky and education: Instructional implications and applications of sociohistorical psychology.* New York: Cambridge University Press.

Murray, F. (1978). Teaching strategies and conservation training. In A. M. Lesgold, J. W. Pellegrino, S. Fokkema, & R. Glaser (Eds.), *Cognitive psychology and instruction* (pp. 419–428). New York: Plenum.

Murray, F. (1981). The conservation paradigm: Conservation of conservation research. In I. Sigel, D. Brodzinsky, & R. Golinkoff (Eds.), *New directions and applications of Piaget's theory* (pp. 143–176). Hillsdale, NJ: Erlbaum.

Murray, F. (1982). The pedagogical adequacy of children's conservation explanations. *Journal of Educational Psychology, 74*(5), 656–659.

Murray, F. (1983a). Learning and development through social interaction and conflict: A challenge to social learning theory. In L. Liben (Ed.), *Piaget and the foundations of knowledge* (pp. 231–247). Hillsdale, NJ: Erlbaum.

Murray, F. (1983b). Equilibration as cognitive conflict. *Developmental Review, 3,* 54–61.

Murray, F. (1985). Paradoxes of a university at risk. In J. Blits (Ed.), *The American University: Problems, prospects and trends* (pp. 101–120). Buffalo, NY: Prometheus Books.

Murray, F. (1986). Micro-mainstreaming. In J. Meisel (Ed.), *The consequences of mainstreaming handicapped children* (pp. 43–54). Hillsdale, NJ: Erlbaum.

Murray, F. (1987). Necessity: The developmental component in school mathematics. In L. Liben (Ed.), *Development and learning* (pp. 51–69). Hillsdale, NJ: Erlbaum.

Murray, F. (1989). Explanations in education. In M. Reynolds (Ed.), *Knowledge base for the beginning teacher* (pp. 1–12). New York: Pergamon.

Murray, F. (1990). The conversion of truth into necessity. In W. Overton (Ed.), *Reasoning, necessity and logic: Developmental perspectives* (pp. 183–204). Hillsdale, NJ: Erlbaum.

Murray, F., Ames, G., & Botvin, G. (1977). Acquisition of conservation through cognitive dissonance. *Journal of Educational Psychology, 69*(6), 519–527.

Murray, F., & Fallon, D. (1989). *The reform of teacher education for the 21st century: Project 30 year one report.* Newark, DE: University of Delaware.

Murray, F., & Johnson, P. (1970). A note on using curriculum models in analyzing the child's concept of weight. *Journal of Research in Science Teaching, 7,* 377–381.

Murray, F., & Johnson, P. (1975). Relevant and some irrelevant factors in the child's concept of weight. *Journal of Educational Psychology, 67,* 705–711.

Murray, F., & Markessini, J. (1982). A semantic basis of nonconservation of weight. *The Psychological Record, 32,* 375–379.

National Commission on Teaching & America's Future. (1996). *What matters most: Teaching for America's future.* New York: Author.

Nettles, M., Thoeny, A., & Gosman, E. (1986). Comparative and predictive analyses of black and white students' college achievement and experiences. *Journal of Higher Education, 57,* 289–318.

Oakes, J. (1985). Keeping track: How schools structure inequality. New Haven, CT: Yale University Press.

Ogle, L., & Alsalam, N. (1990). *The condition of education 1990: Vol. 1. Elementary and secondary education.* Washington, DC: U.S. Department of Education.

Parke, R., Ornstein, P., Rieser, J., & Zahn-Waxler, J. (1994). *A century of developmental psychology.* Washington, DC: American Psychological Association.

Peill, E. J. (1975). *Invention and discovery of reality: The acquisition of conservation of amount.* New York: Wiley.

Pogrow, S. (1996). Reforming the wannabe reformers: Why education reforms almost always end up making things worse. *Phi Delta Kappan, 77*(10), 656–663.

Shanker, A. (1989). The social and educational dilemmas of test use. In *The uses of standardized tests in American education.* Princeton, NJ: Educational Testing Service.

Shulman, L. (1986). Those who understand: Knowledge growth in teaching. *Educational Researcher, 15*(2), 4–14.

Shulman, L. (1987). Knowledge and teaching: Foundations of the new reform. *Harvard Educational Review, 57*(1), 1–22.

Siegler, R. (1981). Developmental sequences within and between concepts. *Monographs of the Society of Research in Child Development, 46* (Serial No. 189).

Siegler, R. (1996). *Emerging minds: The process of change in children's thinking.* New York: Oxford University Press.

Smith, L. (1985). Making educational sense of Piaget's psychology. *Oxford Review of Education, 11*(2), 181–191.

Stevenson, H. (1968). Studies of children's learning: A bibliography. *Psychonomic Monographs Supplements, 2*(11, Whole No. 27).

Stevenson, H. (1970). Learning in children. In P. H. Mussen (Ed.), *Carmichael's manual of child psychology: Vol. 1.* (3rd ed., pp. 849–983). New York: Wiley.

Stevenson, H. (1972). *Children's learning.* New York: Appleton-Century-Crofts.

Stevenson, H. (1992). Learning from Asian schools. *Scientific American* (December), 70–76.

Stevenson, H., Chen, C., & Uttal, C. (1990). *Beliefs and achievement: A study of Black, White and Hispanic children. Child Development, 61*(2), 508–523.

Stevenson, H., Kagan, J., & Spiker, C. (1963). *Child psychology: The sixty-second yearbook of the National Society for the Study of Education.* Chicago: University of Chicago Press.

Stevenson, H., Parker, T., Wilkinson, A., Bonnevaux, B., & Gonzalez, M. (1978). Schooling, environment, and cognitive development: A cross-cultural study. *Monographs of the Society for Research in Child Development, 43* (3, Whole No. 175).

Stevenson, H., & Stigler, J. (1992). *The learning gap: Why our schools are failing and what we can learn from Japanese and Chinese children.* New York: Summit Books.

Stigler, J., & Stevenson, H. (1991). How Asian teachers polish each lesson to perfection. *American Educator, 15*(1), 43–47.

Strauss, S. (1972). Inducing cognitive development and learning: A review of short-term training experiments I, the organismic-developmental approach. *Cognition, 1*, 329–357.

Strauss, S. (1974–1975). A reply to Brainerd. *Cognition, 3*, 155–185.

12

Applying the Findings of Developmental Psychology to Improve Early Childhood Intervention

Edward Zigler and Sally J. Styfco

S ocial scientists have long studied the effects of poverty on children's development. A translation of an 1870 survey by the Pedagogical Society of Berlin noted that "the conditions of the various parts of the city exercise different influences . . . in consequence of which the mental receptivity of children of different wards show a noticeable inequality" (in Bronfenbrenner & Crouter, 1983, p. 360). In roughly the century between that survey and the time Bronfenbrenner developed his ecological model, a lot of data were gathered to show how "different social addresses" affect children and their rearing (p. 361). During these years psychologists built an understanding of how addresses in poverty-stricken neighborhoods adversely impact the children living there. The scientist's job, however, was only to study the risks associated with poverty. Helping children to overcome these risks was a task assumed by church women and social reformers (Cahan, 1989).

A turning point came in 1969, when George Miller delivered his presidential address to the American Psychological Association. He admonished psychologists to "give psychology away" by providing intel-

Preparation of this chapter was supported by the Carnegie Corporation of New York.

lectual leadership in solving the behavioral and social problems they worked so hard to understand (Miller, 1969, p. 1071). His message was acted upon by Harold Stevenson. In 1971, when Harold was president of the Society for Research in Child Development, he chose to forego the traditional presidential address and instead held a forum among policy makers and leading developmentalists. The discussion convinced many who attended that the two interests had much to offer one another (Zigler, 1996). A few years later, Harold headed the second in the network of Bush Centers in Child Development and Social Policy. His leadership and example over the years have encouraged many scholars and students to apply their science to developing programs and policies for the benefit of children.

Theirs was not always an easy course to take, because children's causes have not always been high on the national agenda. As a case in point, when the War on Poverty was launched in 1964, the effort targeted adults. Among the new antipoverty initiatives, only the Job Corps, an employment and training program for severely disadvantaged teenagers and young adults, and Head Start, a preschool intervention, considered the needs of children living in poverty. Interestingly, although most of the War's programmatic weapons have been dismantled, the Job Corps and Head Start remain.

Applied developmental psychology, a field that Harold helped stake, has devoted a great deal of attention to the Head Start model and has generated knowledge that can be used fruitfully throughout early care and education systems. For these reasons, Head Start will be the focus of this chapter.

Now entering its 4th decade, Head Start has helped millions of children with economic disadvantages enter school healthier and better prepared to learn. Their parents have acquired better child-rearing skills, have become involved in their children's education, and many have gained job skills and a better quality of life. Social scientists involved in the Head Start experiment have learned a great deal about the needs of children affected by poverty and how to meet them. These accomplishments have earned the program a broad base of grass-roots support and the approbation of policy makers. A widespread hope is that if Head Start is made available to all preschoolers who live below the federal poverty level, they will not grow up to be poor.

But Head Start did not end poverty in the 1960s, nor can it conquer the crueler circumstances of poverty that have taken hold in the 1990s. The program instead showed that it is possible to enhance the educational outcomes of children who have economic disadvantages and to boost some aspects of their families' functioning. These are no small accomplishments. Updated and improved, Head Start has the potential to become even more effective and to serve as a model for new intervention efforts.

Surprisingly, after operating for over 30 years, graduating more than 15-million children, and progressing to an annual budget of over \$3.5 billion, Head Start is still widely misunderstood and often confused with other types of intervention. Therefore, we will briefly describe the program before we offer our ideas for enhancing Head Start's services and leadership role.

HISTORICAL OVERVIEW OF HEAD START

Head Start opened in 1965, just months after its planners first convened to develop the idea of a program for impoverished preschoolers. The project began on a massive scale, serving over one-half million children in its first summer. It was actually a summer program, lasting 6–8 weeks before children entered kindergarten. It soon became a school-year program, which it essentially is today.

Head Start currently serves over 750,000 children in some 42,500 classrooms around the nation. The majority are 3- and 4-year-olds whose families have incomes below the poverty line. Nearly 13% are children with disabilities. Each Head Start center must focus on three major activities: child development services (physical and mental health, nutrition, preschool education); family and community partnerships (including parent involvement and social support services); and program design and management (to improve quality and accountability). Although these components must conform to a national set of performance standards, centers are encouraged to adapt their services to local needs and resources. Thus, Head Start is the prototype of comprehensive, two-generation, community-based service programs that scholars today endorse.

The wisdom of the Head Start approach took some time to be appreciated. One aspect of the program that was unheard of and highly controversial back in the 1960s was the central role accorded parents. They were invited to participate in their children's classrooms and were given the opportunity to attend classes of their own. They were also included in the planning and administration of their local centers. One reason for the decision to involve parents on so many levels was that Head Start originated in the War on Poverty's Community Action Programs, which were to provide "maximum feasible participation" by people of low incomes in programs designed to serve them. Another reason is that one member of the planning committee was Urie Bronfenbrenner, who was just beginning to develop his ecological approach to human development. Bronfenbrenner (1979) argued that there is a complex interrelationship among children, their families, and communities, so an intervention must touch all of these areas to be effective. This insight was astute, and far ahead of its time. Today, parent participation is considered crucial to the effectiveness of early intervention as well as to later schooling.

The basic goal of Head Start is, and always was, to prepare children for school (Zigler & Styfco, 1997). But instead of providing the academic skills and concepts that are the standard fare of nursery schools, Head Start takes a whole-child approach to school readiness. Children receive inoculations, physical and dental exams, and follow-up treatment if needed. They are served hot meals and nutritious snacks, while their parents are taught to provide healthy diets at home. The preschool education component is developmentally and culturally appropriate; it includes language and other school readiness skills as well as experiences to promote social and emotional development. Parents volunteer in the classrooms, attend classes of their own, and serve on the Parent Committee and the Policy Council (the governing bodies of Head Start centers and grantees). Family needs and goals are assessed and support services are provided through the program and links to community agencies. Head Start also initiates the development of community partnerships to enhance the availability and delivery of needed human services.

The reasoning behind these many services is that children who are healthy, have the academic and social skills they need, have parents who are involved in their education, and have familes whose basic needs are met will be more socially competent when they arrive at school. The program's methods are thus quite complex, and its purpose somewhat modest.

The goal of Head Start was indeed too modest for the 1960s, a time of over-optimism and "can do" attitudes. Just think about the fact that we launched a *war* on poverty. Not a program to reduce poverty, not an antipoverty initiative, but a war. Americans were not used to losing wars, and we fully expected to win this one. A sense of the times can be gained from the speech President Johnson gave in the Rose Garden to announce the opening of the Head Start summer program: "This program this year means that 30 million man-years—the combined lifespan of these youngsters—will be spent productively and rewardingly, rather than wasted in tax-supported institutions or in welfare-supported lethargy" (in Califano, 1997, p. 68). This certainly is a lot to ask of a program that is so brief in the life of a child.

The exuberance of the sixties also invaded the social sciences community, where psychologists were enthralled with the possibility of raising IQ scores. This was the time when parents were buying crib mobiles to give their infants superior minds and books about teaching 2-year-olds to read. They themselves were reading media articles about how to raise their children's IQs by 20 points and J. McVicker Hunt's (1971) claims that IQ gains of 70 points were possible. Given society's infatuation with intelligence, it is not surprising that IQ tests became central in the evaluation of Head Start and other early interventions. This enthusiasm ballooned when results showed that just about any program —even the 6-week Head Start—raised children's IQs by 10 points or more. When these gains were found to fade out shortly after children began school, the balloon burst. Arguments much like those presented recently in *The Bell Curve* (Herrnstein & Murray, 1994) were made, and pessimism set in that little could be done to help underprivileged children do better in school. The Head Start "lovefest" came to an end, and the program was nearly dismantled.

In hindsight, it is easy to see the emptiness of the promise inherent in the inoculation model. The notion that psychologists could take children who have lived their whole young lives in poverty, provide them with a few weeks or months of intervention, and forever immunize them against the ill effects of continuing economic disadvantage was absurd. And as rebuttals to *The Bell Curve* are now making clear, IQ is not the only feature responsible for a person's success in life (Gardner, 1995; Sternberg, Wagner, Williams, & Horvath, 1995). The Head Start program's goal of helping children be more socially competent—improving their behavioral functioning instead of their IQs—is beginning to make sense.

The scientific literature now has given us insights into the true effects of intervention and has thereby shaped more realistic expectations. In brief, quality early intervention programs do help prepare children for school. Once there, they are better able to meet the expectancies of school by having better attendance, less grade retention, and fewer special class placements (Barnett, 1995; Consortium for Longitudinal Studies, 1983). Longitudinal studies of some programs also suggest the possibility of lowered juvenile delinquency and welfare dependency and better high-school graduation rates (Schweinhart, Barnes, & Weikart, 1993). These effects are not as exciting as turning children into geniuses, but they are certainly worthwhile outcomes.

REQUIREMENTS FOR PROGRAM SUCCESS

In the 30 years since the Head Start program and the early intervention movement began, the field has matured tremendously and the theories have become increasingly sophisticated. There is now general agreement on the necessary elements of effective intervention and a sense of how they should be delivered (National Head Start Association, 1990; Price, Cowen, Lorion, & Ramos-McKay, 1988; Schorr, 1988; Zigler & Berman, 1983; Zigler & Styfco, 1993b). First, programs must be comprehensive in scope, attending to the needs of the whole child and supporting families in their roles. Second, programs must involve parents, who are the child's first and most influential teachers. Third, program services must be of high quality to produce desired outcomes. Finally, programs must last longer than the year or so before a child enters school. There is no inoculation against poverty. We must commit to a sustained effort that dovetails services throughout a child's developing years. The following discussion expands on these points.

The first lesson is the need for *comprehensive services*, that is services that address physical and mental health, age-appropriate learning experiences, and social support for the children and their families. Each area is important in its own right, but here we will focus on mental health and family-support services. There are many threats to the psychological well-being of poor children, many of whom have witnessed or have been victims of violence, have myriad unmet needs, and may have been abused or neglected by the adults who are supposed to nurture them. Unfortunately, practitioners in the field of mental health services have focused more on adults and older children than on the very young. This void was recently addressed by the American Orthopsychiatric Association's Task Force on Head Start and Mental Health (1994). Although the group focused on strengthening the mental health component in Head Start, their work is applicable to early childhood programs in general. Their efforts are an example of the applied science advocated by Harold Stevenson.

Family-support services are not that common in early childhood programs, but they should be. Many parents with low or limited incomes move from place to place frequently and become socially isolated. They do not have nearby relatives or friends to advise them about child rearing or help them solve problems. Assistance with basic needs such as housing, food, and medical and child care may be available in their communities, but they do not know how to access it. By linking families with the support services they need, early intervention personnel can help to strengthen the family and thus improve the child's rearing environment.

The second lesson from the early intervention literature is the need for *parent involvement.* It took psychologists a long time to step down from their professional pedestals and acknowledge that parents raise children, not teachers or those who design preschool programs. Parents can carry on the goals of the intervention long after the child graduates from the program. There is now some evidence from other types of intervention that there are diffusion effects to siblings (Seitz & Apfel, 1994), because the mothers became better socializers of all their children. If so, the benefits of parental involvement are more far-reaching than we ever imagined.

As for the third lesson, the need for *high quality services* is a given for any childhood program, but it must be stressed in programs that serve at-risk children. Simply put, good programs are better for children than bad ones. The early care and education literature clearly defines the characteristics of good programs (Bredekamp, 1987; Cost, Quality, & Child Outcomes Study Team, 1995). For example, the physical environment must be free of safety hazards; group sizes should not be too large; child-to-staff ratios should be high; teachers should be trained in early childhood development; and the program should be appropriate to the developmental level of each child. Such criteria have been found to relate to children's developmental outcomes (see Cost, Quality, & Child Outcomes Study Team, 1995; Peisner-Feinberg, 1995).

The imperative of quality was underscored during the recent Head Start expansion, when it became evident that not all centers were delivering good services (Chafel, 1992; Inspector General, 1993; Zigler & Styfco, 1994). Inconsistent quality in Head Start has actually existed from the very beginning. The program started off so big and so fast that quality controls were left behind. Funding levels that fell further and further behind inflation later eroded the ability of many centers to provide quality programs. It is important to stress this is not the case in all centers. Many Head Start programs are excellent (Brush, Gaidurgis, & Best, 1993; Sibley, VandeWiele, & Herrington, 1996). Yet there are some that are only mediocre, and a few that are not good at all. Congress and the Clinton administration have now taken steps to enhance quality throughout Head Start, an effort that will be discussed in the next section.

The final lesson, the need for programs that last longer, derives from what we now know about the importance of *developmental continuity*. We must never again be so naive to believe that a preschool education will guarantee all children success in school and later life. Child development does not begin and end at the age of four. Most of it occurs during prior and succeeding years. Head Start's planners were aware of this, at least they were aware that not much could be accomplished in 6 weeks. Head Start was therefore designed as a national laboratory for the development of further means of intervention. It immediately began to test models for serving very young children and to dovetail services into the early years of elementary school. Both efforts are now well enough developed to be integrated into the national Head Start program. Steps in this direction have already begun, and are described in the context of modernizing Head Start.

TOWARD A SYSTEM OF PREVENTIVE INTERVENTION

Our vision of the Head Start of the future is actually a system of early care and education that spans the age range from birth to 8 years. It begins with Early Head Start, a program that has recently been mounted for families and children from the prenatal period through age 3. This is followed by preschool Head Start that is universally of high quality. Finally, there is a Head Start Transition to School program that continues appropriate services from kindergarten through third grade.

Infants and Toddlers

Early Head Start grew out of the work of the Carnegie Task Force on Meeting the Needs of Very Young Children (1994) and a paper requested of us by the Clinton transition team (Zigler & Styfco, 1993a). The project was designed by the Advisory Committee on Services for Families with Infants and Toddlers (1994). Unlike the planners of the original Head Start, this committee had an established knowledge base and a wealth of expertise from which to draw. The culmination of this knowledge in Early Head Start represents the most promising chance we have had since 1965 for our society to attempt new ways to address the ills of poverty and the causes of school failure.

The general structure of the new program includes all the components that experience has proven necessary for good developmental outcomes. The content of these services will, of course, be adjusted to the special needs of infants and toddlers. Because parents are the child's first teachers and socializers, many aspects of the intervention are parent-focused. In response to recent policies to reduce welfare and send welfare recipients to work, the 0-to-3 programs are encouraged to make quality child care services available. A research and evaluation component is written into the program's design.

Early Head Start services are to be guided by national quality standards adapted to the needs of very young children. The standards cover qualifications of personnel, adult-to-child ratios, group sizes, and program features that promote sound development. These quality elements are absolutely necessary for at-risk children to have a chance at optimal development. Today too many young children are in care settings that are horrific, devoid of so many environmental nutrients that their development is being compromised (Cost, Quality, & Child Outcomes Study Team, 1995). For children whose futures are already threatened by poverty, such care only gives them a start on the road leading to their own socioeconomic failure. We hope the federal standards will do more than ensure quality in Early Head Start. They can set an example for the entire nation of how to improve the quality of care delivered to millions of children, including those who are not economically disadvantaged.

Preschoolers

The basic features and administration of the preschool Head Start program remain sound and are often used as the comparative standard for early childhood services (General Accounting Office, 1995). However, many Head Start centers have had difficulties meeting the needs of their children and families because of inadequate funding and changes in the population they serve. For example, teachers earn an average of $15,000 a year, and aides earn $9,500. It can be hard to attract and retain qualified staff with such low wages. Social services workers have caseloads that are far too high, averaging 91 families, and staff in charge of parent involvement are assigned to over 175 families (Verzaro-O'Brien, Powell, & Sakamoto, 1996). These large caseloads are particularly troublesome because Head Start now serves a high proportion of dysfunctional families with myriad needs. Parental involvement needs to be strengthened throughout Head Start, which is a challenge now that so many mothers work outside the home or are still children themselves. Finally, research, evaluation, and dissemination—so necessary to guiding Head Start's evolution—once diminished to the point where they consumed less than 1% of the budget.

Congress took steps to address quality problems in Head Start when it passed the Human Services Reauthorization Act of 1990 and subsequent legislation. The Act began the practice of reserving one quarter of Head Start's budget increases after inflation for quality improvements. Half of the set-aside money is used for raising salaries and benefits. Training and technical assistance are being expanded. Soon all classrooms must have at least one teacher with a Child Development Associate credential. Facilities and transportation are also being upgraded.

When rapid expansion threatened implementation of these improvements, Health and Human Services Secretary Donna Shalala appointed the Advisory Committee on Head Start Quality and Expansion (1993). Their ideas built upon the enhancements covered by the Reauthorization Act and also addressed evaluation, management, and administration. Secretary Shalala and Administration on Children, Youth and Families (ACYF) Commissioner Olivia Golden also had the courage to do something that has rarely been done before: close bad centers. With the full support of President Clinton, they are standing behind their regional directors' efforts to deny Head Start grants to poor performers and give the money to grantees who can do a better job. Finally, four Research Centers on Head Start Quality have been funded recently to guide the development of more effective services. All these efforts, along with better monitoring, are bringing us closer to the time when every Head Start center will deliver the quality services that children deserve and that are necessary for positive developmental outcomes. The rate of improvement may have slowed with the minimal budget increase (and hence quality set-aside) Head Start received in fiscal year 96, but the program is now headed in the right direction.

One reason that policy makers have been supportive of expanding and improving Head Start is that they see it as a step toward achieving the national education goals. The first goal is that all children will enter school ready to learn, and Head Start has been demonstrably successful in this regard. Its accomplishments have inspired the growth of public school prekindergartens nationwide, but whether these will help to realize Goal One is uncertain. A survey by the Children's Defense Fund showed that 32 states now fund preschool programs (Adams & Sandfort, 1994). Like Head Start, most of the state programs are for children deemed at-risk of having problems in public school. However, many of these programs do not provide the quality and services that are absolutely necessary to produce benefits. In Texas, for example, teacher-to-child ratios in public preschools are greater than 1:20, more than twice the ratio recommended for Head Start (Mitchell, Seligson, & Marx, 1989). A study by the General Accounting Office (1995) showed that although some public preschools provide services that go beyond education, none approaches the level of services in Head Start. Only 35%, for instance, offer any type of health services. Even Head Start's educational component generally surpasses the state preschools in that it is more appropriate to the developmental needs of young children. In sum, despite the criticisms of quality in Head Start, the program has been found superior to many public as well as private preschools (Layzer, Goodson, & Moss, 1993). To achieve the national education goals, the Head Start model should be followed more closely by public schools that are serving at-risk preschoolers.

Transition to School

The third component of an early intervention system applies to children beginning elementary school. In the early years of Head Start, studies showed that the preschool graduates began school with better academic skills than comparison children who did not attend (Datta, 1997). This initial advantage soon appeared to fade, however, leaving critics to argue whether Head Start or the public-school system was to blame. Later research showed that Head Start and similar programs do have lasting benefits in the areas of social and academic adjustment (Barnett, 1995; Consortium, 1983), but that sustained improvement in academic performance is better achieved when preschool services are followed by coordinated programming in elementary school. The Head Start Transition Project, conceptualized by Senator Edward Kennedy (1993) and mounted by ACYF, is such an effort.

This program begins at the time of transition from the preschool to the elementary school environment and lasts through third grade. Comprehensive services are continued for these 4 years, giving children more protection against common health and social problems that can interfere with learning. Also continued are Head Start's individualized and developmentally appropriate programs. Preschool and elementary school educators are required to coordinate their curricula and pedagogies, making the two school experiences less fragmented for young learners. Parental involvement is assured because, as in Head Start, each Transition Project grantee must have a plan for including parents in the design, management, and operation of the program.

The Transition Project clearly contains all the elements known to make intervention effective. Further, there is a small but very convincing body of evidence (reviewed by Zigler & Styfco, 1993b; see also Reynolds, 1996) that supports the project's premise that continuous intervention for an adequate length of time can help children who live in poverty succeed in school. Expansion of the Transition Project to serve all Head Start graduates would seem to be the next logical step. This will take money, however, money that can be found by redirecting the massive Title I education program. Title I receives over $7 billion annually— almost twice as much as Head Start—but it has had only minor impact on the achievement levels of children in low income families (Arroyo & Zigler, 1993; U.S. Department of Education, 1996).

The reason is that the program contains none of the elements that are necessary for successful intervention: It is remedial rather than preventive, services are academic rather than comprehensive, and parent involvement and developmental continuity are minimal. To improve its benefits and cost-effectiveness, we have developed a proposal for Title I to adopt the model of the Transition Project and become the school-age version of Head Start (Zigler & Styfco, 1993b).

As Head Start expands to serve all eligible children, Title I programs can continue their interventions in grammar school. Coordinated curricula and continued parent involvement and comprehensive services will then be firmly placed in schools that serve populations of students whose parents are below the poverty level. The merger will also help shape a coherent federal policy about how to help children with economic disadvantages succeed in school. With some 11 federal agencies and 20 offices funding over 90 programs for at-risk children (General Accounting Office, 1994), the need for such a policy is clear.

The three-stage intervention system described here would constitute a meaningful effort to enable children and families to overcome the negative effects of poverty. A parent–child program would begin prenatally and continue through age 3. Quality preschool services would then be provided, overlapping with the start of elementary school to assure a smooth transition between the two learning environments. To keep the momentum toward success going in the long process of public education, dovetailed services would continue from kindergarten through third grade. Each phase of the intervention would provide health care and nutrition, developmentally appropriate social and educational experiences, parent involvement, and family support. Our current knowledge strongly suggests that such a system would be successful.

SOME LIMITS OF INTERVENTION

Although efforts are being planned to improve, expand, and extend Head Start services, there are several issues that need to be contemplated. One is the frequently heard plea that Head Start become a full-day, all-year program to provide child care for working parents. This idea is gaining more attention now that federal and state policies are phasing out welfare entitlements. Wartime excepted, national support of child care has, in fact, always been linked to welfare reform. But Head Start is not a child-care program. It is a comprehensive, two-generation intervention. A small percentage of centers do provide child care as part of their mission to meet the needs of participating families. In an ideal world with unlimited finances, all Head Start centers could offer child care. But finances are limited, and lawmakers must be careful to preserve the Head Start model as it exists and not overextend it.

Linkages between Head Start and community child-care services are being tried in some places (Koppel, 1995; Poersch & Blank, 1996). Such collaborations have the advantage of ensuring the quality of care by holding it to Head Start's performance standards. They help Head Start to meet family needs and allow participants the opportunity to interact with children from other socioeconomic groups. Another plus is that they permit Head Start to concentrate on its primary mission.

Another issue to ponder as Head Start is renovated and increasing funds are spent on it and other early childhood programs concerns our expectations. The nationwide preschool movement and the massive Head Start expansion have occurred amidst a clamor of exaggerated claims. Many people seem to believe that preschool programs will improve IQ, high-school graduation rates, and the nation's productivity. These programs are also supposed to lower rates of delinquency, teenage pregnancy, and welfare use. Some of these outcomes were actually reported for the Perry Preschool, which was a small project run in the 1960s that provided quality preschool education and some parent involvement activities (Schweinhart et al., 1993). Although the Perry graduates did better than they would otherwise have done, the absolute level of their functioning remains quite low. The reality is that no program offered to young children for a brief portion of their lives can solve deep-rooted problems such as underachievement and poverty.

So what can early intervention accomplish? Head Start and similar programs have had some success in preparing children for school. If society wants to do more, it must mount a comprehensive prevention system that involves the child, family, and community and lasts long enough to make a difference. Such a system could conceivably prevent more than school failure. The risks associated with poor school performance include child factors, such as ability and motivation; family factors, such as parenting skills and economic status; and community factors, such as the quality of education and health services. These factors also coincide with a model developed by Yoshikawa (1994) to describe the risks associated with juvenile delinquency. If intervention can alleviate some of the risks that make a child likely to fail, it might also lessen the likelihood that a child will turn to crime. A number of workers have now discussed early childhood intervention as a possible tool in delinquency prevention (Farrington, 1994; Watson, 1995; Wilson, 1987; Yoshikawa, 1995; Zigler & Hall, 1987; Zigler & Styfco, in press; Zigler, Taussig, & Black, 1992). A great deal of research is needed to examine this possibility, of course, but the hypothesis is certainly promising.

CONCLUSION

The ideas presented here about the future of early childhood intervention derive from an extensive literature and broad knowledge base. They are built on the findings of sound empirical work and will depend on the same to realize their potential. Developmentalists have accomplished much, but there is still much to accomplish. We are indebted to Harold Stevenson for showing us how to do good research and how to put it to good use.

REFERENCES

Adams, G., & Sandfort, J. (1994). *First steps, promising futures. State prekindergarten initiatives in the early 1990s*. Washington, DC: Children's Defense Fund.

Advisory Committee on Head Start Quality and Expansion. (1993). *Creating a 21st century Head Start*. Washington, DC: U.S. Department of Health and Human Services.

Advisory Committee on Services for Families with Infants and Toddlers. (1994). *Statement of the Advisory Committee on Services for Families with Infants and Toddlers*. Washington, DC: U.S. Department of Health and Human Services.

Arroyo, C. G., & Zigler, E. (1993). America's Title I/Chapter 1 programs: Why the promise has not been met. In E. Zigler & S. J. Styfco (Eds.), *Head Start and beyond: A national plan for extended childhood intervention* (pp. 73–95). New Haven, CT: Yale University Press.

Barnett, W. S. (1995). Long-term effects of early childhood programs on cognitive and school outcomes. *Future of Children, 5*(3), 25–50.

Bredekamp, S. (Ed.). (1987). *Accreditation criteria and procedures.* Washington, DC: National Association for the Education of Young Children.

Bronfenbrenner, U. (1979). *The ecology of human development.* Cambridge, MA: Harvard University Press.

Bronfenbrenner, U., & Crouter, A. C. (1983). The evolution of environmental models in developmental research. In P. H. Mussen (Series Ed.) & W. Kessen (Vol. Ed.), *Handbook of child psychology: Vol. 1. History, theory and methods* (4th ed., pp. 357–414). New York: Wiley.

Brush, L., Gaidurgis, A., & Best, C. (1993). *Indices of Head Start program quality.* Report prepared for the Administration on Children, Youth and Families, Head Start Bureau. Washington, DC: Pelavin Associates.

Cahan, E. (1989). *Past caring: A history of U.S. preschool care and education for the poor, 1820–1965.* New York: National Center for Children in Poverty.

Califano, J. A., Jr. (1997). Head Start, a retrospective view: The founders. Section 1: Leadership within the Johnson administration. In E. Zigler & J. Valentine (Eds.), *Project Head Start: A legacy of the War on Poverty* (2nd ed., pp. 43–72). Alexandria, VA: National Head Start Association.

Carnegie Task Force on Meeting the Needs of Young Children. (1994). *Starting points: Meeting the needs of our youngest children.* New York: Carnegie Corporation.

Chafel, J. A. (1992). Funding Head Start: What are the issues? *American Journal of Orthopsychiatry, 62,* 9–21.

Consortium for Longitudinal Studies. (Ed.). (1983). *As the twig is bent: Lasting effects of preschool programs.* Hillsdale, NJ: Erlbaum.

Cost, Quality, & Child Outcomes Study Team. (1995). *Cost, quality, and child outcomes in child care centers, Public report* (2nd ed.). Denver: University of Colorado at Denver, Economics Department.

Datta, L. (1997). Another spring and other hopes: Some findings from national evaluations of Project Head Start. In E. Zigler & J. Valentine (Eds.), *Project Head Start: A legacy of the War on Poverty* (2nd ed., pp. 405–432). Alexandria, VA: National Head Start Association.

Farrington, D. P. (1994, April). *Delinquency prevention in the first few years of life.* Plenary address, Fourth European Conference on Law and Psychology, Barcelona, Spain.

Gardner, H. (1995). Cracking open the IQ box. In S. Fraser (Ed.), *The bell curve wars: Race, intelligence, and the future of America* (pp. 23–35). New York: Basic Books.

General Accounting Office. (1994, October). *Early childhood programs. Multiple programs and overlapping target groups* (GAO/HEHS-95–4FS). Washington, DC: Author.

General Accounting Office. (1995, March). *Early childhood centers. Services to prepare children for school often limited* (GAO/HEHS-95-21). Washington, DC: Author.

Herrnstein, R. J., & Murray, C. (1994). *The bell curve. Intelligence and class structure in American life.* New York: Free Press.

Hunt, J. McV. (1971). Parent and child centers: Their basis in the behavioral and educational sciences. *American Journal of Orthopsychiatry, 41,* 13–38.

Inspector General (Office of). (1993). *Evaluating Head Start expansion through performance indicators* (Rep. No. OEI-09-91-00762). Washington, DC: U.S. Department of Health and Human Services.

Kennedy, E. M. (1993). The Head Start Transition Project: Head Start goes to elementary school. In. E. Zigler & S. J. Styfco (Eds.), *Head Start and beyond: A national plan for extended childhood intervention* (pp. 97–109). New Haven, CT: Yale University Press.

Koppel, S. G. (1995). *Head Start and child care: Partners not competitors.* Lumberville, PA: Support Services for Child Care Professionals.

Layzer, J. I., Goodson, B. D., & Moss, M. (1993). *Life in preschool: Vol. 1. An observational study of early childhood programs for disadvantaged four-year-olds.* Final report (Contract No. EALC 890980, U.S. Dept. of Education). Cambridge, MA: ABT Associates.

Miller, G. A. (1969). Psychology as a means of promoting human welfare. *American Psychologist, 24,* 1063–1075.

Mitchell, A., Seligson, M., & Marx, F. (1989). *Early childhood programs and the public schools.* Dover, MA: Auburn House.

National Head Start Association. (1990). *Head Start: The nation's pride, a nation's challenge.* Report of the Silver Ribbon Panel. Alexandria, VA: Author.

Peisner-Feinberg, E. (1995). Child care quality and children's developmental outcomes. In *Cost, quality, and child outcomes in child care centers. Public report* (2nd ed., pp. 305–310). Denver: University of Colorado at Denver, Economics Department.

Poersch, N. O., & Blank, H. (1996). *Working together for children: Head Start and child care partnerships.* Washington, DC: Children's Defense Fund.

Price, R. H., Cowen, E., Lorion, R. P., & Ramos-McKay, J. (Eds.). (1988). *Fourteen ounces of prevention: A casebook for practitioners.* Washington, DC: American Psychological Association.

Reynolds, A. J. (1996). *Chicago Child-Parent Centers: A longitudinal study of extended early childhood intervention.* New York: Foundation for Child Development.

Schorr, L. B. (1988). *Within our reach: Breaking the cycle of disadvantage.* New York: Doubleday.

Schweinhart, L. J., Barnes, H. V., & Weikart, D. P. (1993). *Significant benefits: The High/Scope Perry Preschool study through age 27. Monographs of the High/Scope Educational Research Foundation, 10.* Ypsilanti, MI: High/Scope Press.

Seitz, V., & Apfel, N. H. (1994). Parent-focused intervention: Diffusion effects on siblings. *Child Development, 65,* 677–683.

Sibley, A., VandeWiele, L., & Herrington, S. (1996). *Quality initiative, year one report. Georgia Head Start.* Atlanta, GA: Quality Assist.

Sternberg, R. J., Wagner, R. K., Williams, W. M., & Horvath, J. A. (1995). Testing common sense. *American Psychologist, 50,* 912–927.

Task Force on Head Start and Mental Health. (1994, April). *Strengthening mental health in Head Start: Pathways to quality improvement.* New York: American Orthopsychiatric Association.

U.S. Department of Education. (1996). *Mapping out the national assessment of Title I: The interim report.* Washington, DC: Author.

Verzaro-O'Brien, M., Powell, G., & Sakamoto, L. (1996). *Investing in quality revisited. The impact of the Head Start Expansion and Improvement Act of 1990 after five years of investment.* Alexandria, VA: National Head Start Association.

Watson, J. (1995). Crime and juvenile delinquency prevention policy: Time for early childhood intervention. *Georgetown Journal on Fighting Poverty, 2,* 245–270.

Wilson, J. Q. (1987). Strategic opportunities for delinquency prevention. In J. Q. Wilson & G. C. Loury (Eds.), *From children to citizens: Vol. 3. Families, schools, and delinquency prevention* (pp. 291–312). New York: Springer-Verlag.

Yoshikawa, H. (1994). Prevention as cumulative protection: Effects of early family support and education on chronic delinquency and its risks. *Psychological Bulletin, 115,* 28–54.

Yoshikawa, H. (1995). Long-term effects of early childhood programs on social outcomes and delinquency. *Future of Children, 5*(3), 51–75.

Zigler, E. (1996). *Child development and social policy.* Unpublished manuscript, Yale University, New Haven, CT.

Zigler, E., & Berman, W. (1983). Discerning the future of early childhood intervention. *American Psychologist, 38,* 894–906.

Zigler, E., & Hall, N. (1987). Preventing juvenile delinquency. In E. Aronowitz & R. Sussman (Eds.), *Issues in community mental health: Youth.* Canton, MA: Prodist.

Zigler, E., & Styfco, S. J. (1993a). An earlier Head Start: Planning an intervention program for economically disadvantaged families and children ages zero to three. *Zero to Three, 14*(2), 25–28.

Zigler, E., & Styfco, S. J. (1993b). Strength in unity: Consolidating federal education programs for young children. In E. Zigler & S. J. Styfco (Eds.), *Head Start and beyond: A national plan for extended childhood intervention* (pp. 111–145). New Haven, CT: Yale University Press.

Zigler, E., & Styfco, S. J. (1994). Head Start: Criticisms in a constructive context. *American Psychologist, 49,* 127–132.

Zigler, E., & Styfco, S. J. (in press). Can early childhood intervention prevent delinquency? A real possibility. In *Constructive and destructive behavior: Implications for family, school, and society. A Festschrift in honor of Seymour and Norma Feshbach.*

Zigler, E., & Styfco, S. J. (1997). A "Head Start" in what pursuit? IQ vs. social competence as the objective of early intervention. In B. Devlin, S. E. Fienberg, D. Resnick, & K. Roeder (Eds.), *IQ, race, and public policy: An analysis of* The Bell Curve (pp. 283–314). New York: Springer-Verlag.

Zigler, E., Taussig, C., & Black, K. (1992). Early childhood intervention: A promising preventative for juvenile delinquency. *American Psychologist, 47,* 997–1006.

Chronological List of Publications by Harold W. Stevenson

Stevenson, H. W. (1954). Latent learning in children. *Journal of Experimental Psychology, 47,* 17–21.

Stevenson, H. W., & Weiss, E. S. (1954). Overtraining and transposition in children. *Journal of Experimental Psychology, 47,* 251–255.

Stevenson, H. W., Iscoe, I., & McConnell, C. (1955). A developmental study of transposition. *Journal of Experimental Psychology, 49,* 278–280.

Stevenson, H. W. (1955). Experimental studies of children's learning. *Journal of Genetic Psychology, 87,* 323–330.

Stevenson, H. W., & Weiss, E. S. (1955). Time as a variable in transposition. *American Journal of Psychology, 68,* 285–288.

Stevenson, H. W., & Iscoe, I. (1955). Transposition in the feeble-minded. *Journal of Experimental Psychology, 49,* 11–15.

Stevenson, H. W., & Bitterman, M. W. (1955). The distance effect in the transposition of intermediate size by children. *American Journal of Psychology, 68,* 274–279.

Stevenson, H. W., & Iscoe, I. (1956). Anxiety and discriminative learning. *American Journal of Psychology, 69,* 113–114.

Stevenson, H. W., & Moushegian, G. (1956). The effect of instructions and degree of training on shifts of discriminative responses. *American Journal of Psychology, 69,* 281–284.

Stevenson, H. W., & Zigler, E. F. Discrimination learning and rigidity in normal and feebleminded individuals. *Journal of Personality, 25,* 699–711.

Capaldi, E. J., & Stevenson, H. W. (1957). Response reversal following different amounts of training. *Journal of Comparative and Physiological Psychology,* *50,* 195–198.

Stevenson, H. W., & Lankford, T. (1957). Time as a variable in transposition by children. *Child Development, 28,* 366–370.

Stevenson, H. W., & Stewart, E. C. (1958). A developmental study of racial awareness in your children. *Child Development, 29,* 399–409.

Stevenson, H. W., & Pirojinikoff, L. A. (1958). Discrimination learning as a function of pretraining reinforcement schedules. *Journal of Experimental Psychology, 56,* 41–44.

Zigler, E. F., Hodgden, L., & Stevenson, H. W. (1958). The effect of support on the performance of normal and feebleminded children. *Journal of Personality, 26,* 106–122. (Reprinted in *Research readings in child psychology,* L. Lipsitt & D. Palermo, Eds., New York: Holt, Rinehart, & Winston.)

Stevenson, H. W., & McBee, G. (1958). The learning of object and pattern discriminations by children. *Journal of Comparative and Physiological Psychology, 51,* 752–754.

Stevenson, H. W., & Zigler, E. F. (1958). Probability learning in children. *Journal of Experimental Psychology, 56,* 185–192.

Weir, M. W., & Stevenson, H. W. (1959). The effect of verbalization on children's learning as a function of chronological age. *Child Development, 30,* 143–149.

Stevenson, H. W., Weir, M. W., & Zigler, E. F. (1959). Discrimination learning in children as a function of motive-incentive conditions. *Psychological Reports, 19,* 95–98.

Stevenson, H. W., & Weir, M. W. (1959). Response shift as a function of overtraining and delay. *Journal of Comparative and Psychological Psychology, 52,* 327–329.

Stevenson, H. W., & Weir, M. W. (1959). Variables affecting children's performance in a probability learning task. *Journal of Experimental Psychology, 57,* 403–412.

Steigman, M. J., & Stevenson, H. W. (1960). The effect of penetrating reinforcement schedules on children's learning. *Child Development, 31,* 53–58.

Stevenson, H. W. (1960). Learning of complex problems by normal and retarded subjects. *American Journal of Mental Deficiency, 64,* 1021–1026.

Stevenson, H. W., & Snyder, L. G. (1960). Performance as a function of the interaction of incentive conditions. *Journal of Personality, 28,* 1–11.

Stevenson, H. W., & Stevenson, N. G. (1960). Social interaction in an interracial nursery school. *Genetic Psychology Monographs, 61,* 37–75.

McCullers, J. C., & Stevenson, H. W. (1960). Effects of verbal reinforcement in a probability learning situation. *Psychological Reports, 7,* 439–445.

Iscoe, I., & Stevenson, H. W. (Eds.). (1960). *Personality development in children.* Austin, TX: University of Texas Press.

Stevenson, H. W., & Fahel, L. S. (1961). The effect of social reinforcement on the performance of institutionalized and noninstitutionalized normal and feebleminded children. *Journal of Psychology, 24,* 135–147.

Stevenson, H. W. (1961). The effect of pretraining reinforcement schedules on probability learning in the rat. *Journal of Comparative and Psychological Psychology, 54,* 556–559.

Stevenson, H. W., & Cruse, D. B. (1961). The effectiveness of social reinforcement with normal and feebleminded children. *Journal of Personality, 29,* 124–135.

Stevenson, H. W., & Stevenson, N. G. (1961). A method for simultaneous observation and analysis of children's behavior. *Journal of Genetic Psychology, 99,* 253–260.

Stevenson, H. W., & Weir, M. W. (1961). Developmental changes in the effects of reinforcement and nonreinforcement of a single response. *Child Development, 32,* 1–5.

Stevenson, H. W., & Knights, R. M. (1961). Effect of visual reinforcement on the performance of normal and retarded children. *Perceptual and Motor Skills, 13,* 119–126.

Kass, N., & Stevenson, H. W. (1961). The effect of pretraining reinforcement conditions on learning by normal and retarded children. *American Journal of Mental Deficiency, 66,* 76–80.

Stevenson, H. W., & Odom, R. D. (1961). Effects of pretraining on the reinforcing value of visual stimuli. *Child Development, 32,* 739–744.

Stevenson, H. W. (1961). Social reinforcement with children as a function of chronological age, sex of experimentor, and sex of subject. *Journal of Abnormal and Social Psychology, 63,* 147–154.

Stevenson, H. W. (1962). Piaget, behavior theory, and intelligence. In W. Kessen

& C. Kuhlman (Eds.), Thought in the young child. *Monographs of the Society for Research in Child Development, 27,* 113–135.

Stevenson, H. W. (1962). Studies in racial awareness in young children. *Journal of Nursery Education, 17,* 118–122.

Stevenson, H. W., & Knights, R. M. (1962). The effectiveness of social reinforcement after brief and extended institutionalization. *American Journal of Mental Deficiency, 66,* 589–594.

Stevenson, H. W., & Knights, R. M. (1962). Social reinforcement with normal and retarded children as a function of pretraining, sex of experimentor, and sex of subject. *American Journal of Mental Deficiency, 66,* 866–871.

Stevenson, H. W., & Odom, R. D. (1962). The effectiveness of social reinforcement following two conditions of social deprivation. *Journal of Abnormal and Social Psychology, 65,* 429–431.

Stevenson, H. W. (1963). Discrimination learning. In N. R. Ellis (Ed.), *Handbook of mental deficiency* (pp. 424–437). New York: McGraw-Hill.

Stevenson, H. W., Keen, R., & Knights, R. (1963). Parents and strangers as reinforcing agents for children's performance. *Journal of Abnormal and Social Psychology, 67,* 183–186.

Stevenson, H. W., & Weir, M. W. (1963). The role of age and verbalization in probability learning. *American Journal of Psychology, 76,* 295–305.

Stevenson, H. W., (Ed.). (1963). *62nd Yearbook of the National Society for the Study of Education, Child Psychology.* Chicago: University of Chicago Press.

Hill, K. T., & Stevenson, H. W. (1964). The effectiveness of social reinforcement following social and sensory deprivation. *Journal of Abnormal and Social Psychology, 68,* 579–584.

Stevenson, H. W., & Allen, S. (1964). Adult performance as a function of sex of experimenter and sex of subject. *Journal of Abnormal and Social Psychology, 68,* 214–216.

Stevenson, H. W., & Hoving, K. L. (1964). Probability learning as a function of age and incentive. *Journal of Experimental Child Psychology, 1,* 64–70.

Stevenson, H. W., & Odom, R. D. (1964). Visual reinforcement with children. *Journal of Experimental Child Psychology, 1,* 248–255.

Stevenson, H. W., & Odom, R. D. (1964). Children's behavior in a probabilistic situation. *Journal of Experimental Child Psychology, 68,* 261–268.

Ruebush, B. K., & Stevenson, H. W. (1964). The effects of mothers and strangers on the performance of anxious and defensive children. *Journal of Personality, 32,* 587–600.

Stevenson, H. W., & Odom, R. D. (1965). Interrelationships in children's learning. *Child Development, 36,* 7–19.

Stevenson, H. W., & Hill, K. T. (1965). The effects of social reinforcement and nonreinforcement following success and failure. *Journal of Personality, 33,* 418–427.

Hill, K. T., & Stevenson, H. W. (1965). The effects of social reinforcement and nonreinforcement and sex of experimentor on the performance of adolescent girls. *Journal of Personality, 33,* 30–36.

Stevenson, H. W., & Wright, J. C. (1965). Experimental child psychology. In J. Sidowski (Ed.), Methods and instrumentation in psychological research. New York: McGraw-Hill.

Stevenson, H. W. (1965). Social reinforcement in children's behavior. In L. P. Lipsitt & C. C. Spiker (Eds.), *Advances in child development and behavior* (Vol. 2, 97–126). New York: Academic Press.

Terrell, C., & Stevenson, H. W. (1965). The effectiveness of normal and retarded peers as reinforcing agents. *American Journal of Mental Deficiency, 70,* 373–381.

Stevenson, H. W., & Odom, R. D. (1965). The relation of anxiety to children's performance on learning and problem-solving tasks. *Child Development, 36,* 1003–1012.

Seigel, A. W., & Stevenson, H. W. (1966). Incidental learning: A developmental study. *Child Development, 37,* 811–817.

Stevenson, H. W., Hill, K. T., Hale, G. A., & Moely, B. E. (1966). Adult ratings of children's behavior. *Child Development, 37,* 929–941.

Stevenson, H. W., & Hill, K. T. (1966). The use of rate as a measure of response in studies of social reinforcement. *Psychological Bulletin, 66,* 321–326.

Stevenson, H. W. (Ed.). (1966). Concept of development. *Monographs of the Society for Research in Child Development, 31,* (Serial No. 107).

Allen, S. A., Dubanoski, R. A., & Stevenson, H. W. (1966). Children's performance as a function of race of experimentor, race of subject, and type of verbal reinforcement. *Journal of Experimental Child Psychology, 4,* 248–256.

Stevenson, H. W., Hess, E. H., & Rheingold, H. L. (Eds.). (1967). *Early behavior: Comparative and developmental approaches.* New York: Wiley.

Stevenson, H. W., Hale, G. A., Hill, K. T., & Moely, B. E. (1967). Determinants of children's preferences for adults. *Child Development, 38,* 1–14.

Stevenson, H. W. (1967). Developmental psychology. *Annual Reviews, 32,* 87–128.

Olson, G. M., Bibelheimer, D., & Stevenson, H. W. (1967). Incentive effects and social class in children's probability and discrimination learning. *Psychonomic Science, 9,* 249–250.

Klein, R. E., Hale, G. A., Miller, L. K., & Stevenson, H. W. (1967). Children's paired-associate learning of verbal and pictorial material. *Psychonomic Science, 9,* 203–204.

Stevenson, H. W., & Allen, S. A. (1967). Variables associated with adult's effectiveness as reinforcing agents. *Journal of Personality, 35,* 246–254.

Stevenson, H. W., Hale, G. A., & Miller, L. K. (1967). Children's ability to guess the ages of adults. *Psychological Reports, 20,* 1265–1266.

Stevenson, H. W., Hale, G. A., & Miller, L. K. (1967). Developmental changes in children's concepts of probability. *Psychonomic Science, 9,* 229–230.

Stevenson, H. W. (1968). Developmental psychology. In D. Sills (Ed.), *International Encyclopedia of the Social Sciences* (pp. 136–140). New York: Macmillan.

Hale, G. A., Miller, L. K., & Stevenson, H. W. (1968). Incidental learning of film content: A developmental study. *Child Development, 39,* 69–77.

G. M., Miller, L. K., Hale, G. A., & Stevenson, H. W. (1968). Long-term correlates of children's learning and problem-solving behavior. *Journal of Educational Psychology, 59,* 227–232.

Stevenson, H. W., Hale, G. A., Klein, R. E., & Miller, L. K. (1968). Solution of anagrams: A developmental study. *Child Development, 39,* 905–912.

Stevenson, H. W., Hale, G. A., Klein, R. E., & Miller, L. K. (1968). Interrelations and correlates in children's learning and problem-solving. *Monographs of the Society for Research in Child Development, 33,* (Serial No. 7).

Stevenson, H. W. (1968). Studies in children's learning: A bibliography. *Psychonomic Monograph Supplements, 2,* (Serial No. 77).

Miller, L. K., Hale, G. A., & Stevenson, H. W. (1968). Learning and problem-solving in normal and retarded children. *American Journal of Mental Deficiency, 72,* 681–689.

Stevenson, H. W. (1969). Learning and reinforcement effects. In T. Spencer & N. Kass (Eds.), *Perspectives in child psychology: Research and review.* New York: McGraw-Hill.

Stevenson, H. W., & Siegel, A. W. (1969). Effects of instructions and age on retention of filmed content. *Journal of Experimental Psychology, 60,* 71–74.

Stevenson, H. W. (1970). Learning in children. In P. Mussen (Ed.), Manual of child psychology (3rd ed., pp. 849–938). New York: Wiley.

Stevenson, H. W., Friedrichs, A. G., & Simpson, W. E. (1970). Interrelations and correlates over time in children's learning. *Child Development, 41,* 625–637.

Stevenson, H. W., Friedrichs, A. G., & Simpson, W. E. (1970). Learning and problem-solving by the mentally retarded under three testing conditions. *Developmental Psychology, 3,* 307–312.

Hill, K. T., & Stevenson, H. W. (1970). Effectiveness of social and visual reinforcement following social and nonsocial deprivation. *Journal of Experimental Research in Personality, 4,* 100–107.

Friedrichs, A. G., Hertz, T. W., Moynahan, E. D., Simpson, W. E., Arnold, M. R., Christy, M. D., Cooper, C. R., & Stevenson, H. W. (1971). Interrelations among learning and performance tasks at the preschool level. *Developmental Psychology, 4,* 164–172.

Stevenson, H. W., Williams, A. M., & Coleman, E. (1971). Interrelations among learning and performance tasks in disadvantaged children. *Journal of Experimental Psychology, 62,* 179–184.

Stevenson, H. W. (1971). The study of children's learning. In M. E. Meyer (Ed.), *Early learning.* Bellingham, WA: Western Washington State College Press.

Stevenson, H. W. (1972). Television and the behavior of preschool children. In J. P. Murray, E. Rubenstein, & G. Comstock (Eds.), *Television and social behavior* (Vol. 2 pp. 346–371). Rockville, MD: National Institute of Mental Health.

Stevenson, H. W. (1972). *Children's learning.* New York: Appleton-Century-Crofts. (Japanese translation, 1981)

Stevenson, H. W. (1972). The taxonomy of tasks. In F. Monks, W. Hartup, &

J. deWit (Eds.), *Determinants of behavioral development* (pp. 75–88). New York: Academic Press.

Stevenson, H. W. (1975). The young child: Learning and recognition. In J. Payne (Ed.), *Mathematics yearbook.* Reston, VA: National Council of Teachers of Mathematics.

Stevenson, H. W., & Others. (1975). The Chinese kindergarten. In W. Kessen (Ed.), *Childhood in China* (pp. 73–115). New Haven: Yale University Press.

Stevenson, H. W. (1975). Research in children's learning. In J. Gallagher (Ed.), *The application of child development research to exceptional children* (pp. 118–135). Reston, VA: Council for Exceptional Children.

Stevenson, H. W., Parker, T., Wilkinson, A., Hegion, A., & Fish, E. (1976). Predictive value of teachers' ratings of young children. *Journal of Educational Psychology, 68,* 507–517.

Stevenson, H. W., Parker T., Wilkinson, A., Hegion, A., & Fish, E. (1976). Longitudinal study of individual differences in cognitive development and scholastic achievement. *Journal of Experimental Psychology, 68,* 377–400.

Stevenson, H. W. (1977). Vorbilder und leitspruche: Beobachtungen und sprache und ihre bedeutung fur Kinder. In G. Nessen (Ed.), *Lern und Lernstorungen in Kindern* (pp. 120–125). Heidelberg: Springer Verlag.

Zuckerman, P., Ziegler, M., & Stevenson, H. W. (1978). Children's viewing of television and recognition memory of commercials. *Child Development, 49,* 96–104.

Stevens, H. W., Parker, T., Wilkinson, A., Bonnevaux, B., & Gonzales, M. (1978). Schooling, environment, and cognitive development: A study in Peru. *Monographs of the Society for Research in Child Development, 43* (Serial No. 175, Whole No. 3).

Stevenson, H. W. (1978). *Psychology: From research to practice.* New York: Plenum.

Stevenson, H. W. (1979). Children's learning. In M. Rutter (Ed.), Scientific foundations of developmental psychiatry (pp. 110–117). London: Heinemann.

Wilson, R., Wilkinson, A., Parker, T., & Stevenson, H. W. (1979). Differential roles of individual transformations in a perceptual learning task. *Journal of Educational Psychology, 71,* 220–225.

Wilkinson, A., Parker, T., & Stevenson, H. W. (1979). The influence of schooling and environment on the development of selective attention. *Child Development*, 50, 890–894.

Stevenson, H. W. (1979). kindheit in China nach der Kulturrevolution. In L. Montada (Ed.), *Brennpunkteder entwinklungspsychologie*. Stuttgart: Verlag.

Stevenson, H. W., Parker, T., Wilkinson, A., Bonnevaux, B., & Gonzales, M. (1979). Escolaridad, medio ambiente y dessarrollo: Un estudio transcultural. *Interamerican Journal of Psychology*, 13, 133–134.

Wagner, D., & Stevenson, H. W. (Eds.). (1981). *Cross-cultural studies of child development*. San Francisco: Freeman.

Stevenson, H. W. (1981). Influences of schooling on cognitive development. In D. Wagner & H. W. Stevenson (Eds.), *Cross-cultural studies of child development* (pp. 208–228). San Francisco: Freeman.

Stevenson, H. W., Lee, S. Y., & Stigler, J. W. (1981). The reemergence of child development in the People's Republic of China. *SRCD Newsletter*, Summer, 1–5.

Stevenson, H. W. (1981). Xuexiao jiaoyu yu renzhi fazhan [Schooling and cognitive development]. *Xinli Kexue Tongxun* [Information on Psychological Sciences], 1, 56–64.

Stevenson, H. W. (1981). Wenhua, zeng zifa, he yue du: Zhongwen he yingwen ke ye [Culture, orthography, and reading in Chinese and English]. *Xinli Kexue Tongxun* [Information on Psychological Sciences], 1, 28–35.

Stevenson, H. W. (1981). An eastern perspective. *UCLA Innovator*, 23, 38–41.

Stevenson, H. W. (1981). Education and social policy. In I. N. Berlin (Ed.), *Children and our future*. Albuquerque, NM: University of New Mexico.

Stevenson, H. W. (1981). Migration to the city: Influences on children's cognitive and academic performance. In C. Hwang & E. K. Yen (Eds.), *Family, child, and mental health* (pp. 119–126). Taipei: Chinese National Association for Mental Hygiene.

Stigler, J. W., Lee, S. Y., Lucker, G. W., & Stevenson, H. W. (1982). Curriculum and achievement in mathematics: A study of elementary school children in Japan, Taiwan, and the United States. *Journal of Educational Psychology*, 74, 315–322.

Stevenson, H. W., Stigler, J. W., Lucker, G. W., & Lee, S. Y. (1982). Reading disabilities: The case of Chinese, Japanese, and English. *Child Development*, 53, 1164–1182.

Paris, S., Olson, G. M., & Stevenson, H. W. (Eds.). (1982). *Learning and motivation in the classroom.* Hillsdale, NJ: Erlbaum.

Stevenson, H. W. (1983). How children learn: The quest for a theory. In P. H. Mussen (Ed.), *Manual of child psychology* (4th ed., pp. 213–236) New York: Wiley.

Stevenson, H. W., & Azuma, H. (1983). IQ in Japan and the United States: Methodological problems in Lynn's analysis. *Nature, 306,* 291–292.

Stevenson, H. W., Lee, S. Y., Lucker, G. W., Hsu, C. C., & Kitamura, S. (1984). Family variables and reading: A study of mothers of poor and average readers in Japan, Taiwan, and the United States. *Journal of Learning Disabilities, 17,* 150–156.

Stevenson, H. W. (1984). Orthography and reading disabilities. *Journal of Learning Disabilities, 17,* 296–301.

Stevenson, H. W., & Jing, C. C. (Eds.). (1984). *Conference proceedings: Issues in cognition.* Washington, DC: American Psychological Association.

Stevenson, H. W. (1984). Learning to read Chinese. In H. W. Stevenson & C. C. Jing (Eds.), *Conference proceedings: Issues in cognition* (pp. 163–178). Washington DC: American Psychological Association.

Stevenson, H. W., & Siegel, A. E., (Eds.). (1984). *Research in child development and social policy.* Chicago: University of Chicago Press.

Stevenson, H. W., Stigler, J. W., Lee, S. Y., Lucker, G. W., Kitamura, S., & Hsu, C. C. (1985). Cognitive performance and academic achievement of Japanese, Chinese, and American children. *Child Development, 56,* 718–734.

Stevenson, H. W., Stigler, J. W., Lee, S. Y., Lucker, G. W., Kitamura, S., & Hsu, C. C. (1985). Cognitive performance and academic achievement of Japanese, Chinese, and American children. *Child Development, 56,* 718–734.

Stevenson, H. W. (1985). Culture and reading disabilities. In Wolraich, M. & D. Routh (Eds.), Advances in developmental and behavioral pediatrics (Vol. 6). Greenwich, CT: JAI Press.

Stevenson, H. W., Azuma, H., & Hakuta, K. (Eds.). (1986). *Child development and education in Japan.* New York: Freeman.

Stevenson, H. W., Lee, S. Y., Stigler, J. W., Kitamura, S., Kimura, S., & Kato, T. (1986). Learning to read Japanese. In H. W. Stevenson, H. Azuma, & K. Hakuta (Eds.), *Child development and education in Japan.* New York: Freeman.

Stevenson, H. W., Stigler, J. W., Lee, S. Y., Kitamura, S., Kimura, S., & Kato, T. (1986). Achievement in mathematics. In H. W. Stevenson, H. Azuma, & K. Hakuta (Eds.), *Child development and education in Japan*. New York: Freeman.

Stevenson, H. W., Lee, S. Y., & Stigler, J. W. (1986). Mathematics achievement in Chinese, Japanese, and American children. *Science, 231*, 693–699.

Lee, S. Y., Stigler, J. W., & Stevenson, H. W. (1986). Beginning to read Chinese and English. In B. R. Foorman & A. W. Siegel (Eds.), *Learning to read: Cognitive universals and cultural restraints*. Hillsdale, NJ: Erlbaum.

Stevenson, H. W., & Newman, R. S. (1986). Long-term prediction of achievement and attitudes in mathematics and reading. *Child Development, 57*, 646–659.

Stigler, J. W., Lee, S. Y., & Stevenson, H. W. (1986). Digit memory among Chinese and Americans: Evidence for a temporally limited store. *Cognition, 23*, 1–20.

Lee, S. Y., Ichikawa, F., & Stevenson, H. W. (1987). Beliefs and achievement in mathematics and reading: A cross-national study of Chinese, Japanese, and American children and their mothers. In D. Kleiber & M. Maehr (Eds.) *Advances in motivation* (Vol. 7). Greenwich, CT: JAI Press.

Stevenson, H. W. (1987). America's math problems. *Educational Leadership, 45*, 4–10.

Stevenson, H. W. (1987). The Asian advantage: The case of mathematics. *American Educator, Summer*, 26–31, 47.

Stevenson, H. W. (1987). Child development in Asia. *SRCD Newsletter, Summer*, 1–3.

Stevenson, H. W., Lucker, G. W., Lee, S. Y., Stigler, J. W., Kitamura, S., & Hsu, C. C. (1987). Poor readers in three cultures. In C. Super & S. Harkness (Eds.), *The role of culture in developmental disorder* (Vol. 1, pp. 153–177). New York: Academic Press.

Stigler, J. W., Lee, S. Y., & Stevenson, H. W. (1987). Mathematics classrooms in Japan, Taiwan, and the United States. *Child Development, 58*, 1272–1285.

Stevenson, H. W., Stigler, J. W., Lucker, G. W., Lee, S. Y., Hsu, C. C., & Kitamura, S. (1987). Classroom behavior and achievement of Japanese, Chinese, and American children. In R. Glaser (Ed.), *Advances in instructional psychology* (pp. 153–204). Hillsdale, NJ: Erlbaum.

Chen, C., & Stevenson, H. W. (1988). Cross-linguistic differences in digit span of preschool children. *Journal of Experimental Child Psychology, 46,* 150–158.

Stevenson, H. W. (1988). Children's problems in learning to read Chinese, Japanese, and English. In D. A. Wagner (Ed.), *The future of literacy in a changing world.* New York: Pergamon.

Stevenson, H. W. (1988). Culture and schooling. In E. M. Hetherington, R. Lerner, & M. Perlmutter (Eds.), *Child development in a life-span perspective* (pp. 241–258). Hillsdale, NJ: Erlbaum.

Uttal, D. H., Lummis, M., & Stevenson, H. W. (1988). Low and high mathematics achievement in Japanese, Chinese, and American elementary school children. *Developmental Psychology, 24,* 335–342.

Chen, C., & Stevenson, H. W. (1989). Homework: A cross-cultural examination. *Child Development, 60,* 551–561.

Stevenson, H. W., & Chen, C. (1989). Schooling and achievement: A study of Peruvian children. *International Journal of Educational Research, 13,* 883–894.

Stevenson, H. W., Chen, C., & Booth, J. (1990). Influences of schooling and urban-rural residence on gender differences in cognitive abilities and academic achievement. *Sex Roles, 23,* 535–551.

Stevenson, H. W., Chen, C., & Uttal, D. (1990). Beliefs and achievement: A study of black, white and Hispanic children. *Child Development, 61,* 508–523.

Stevenson, H. W., Lee, S., Chen, C., Stigler, J. W., Hsu, C. C., & Kitamura, S. (1990). Contexts of achievement: A study of American, Chinese, and Japanese children. *Monographs of the Society for Research in Child Development, 221*(Whole no. 55), 1–2.

Stevenson, H. W., & Lummis, M. (1990). Gender differences in beliefs and achievement: A cross-cultural study. *Developmental Psychology, 26,* 254–263.

Stevenson, H. W., Lummis, M., Lee, S., & Stigler, J. (1990). *Making the grade in mathematics: Elementary school mathematics in the United States, Taiwan, and Japan.* Reston, VA: National Council of Teachers of Mathematics.

Stigler, J., Lee, S., & Stevenson, H. W. (1990). *Mathematical knowledge of Japanese, Chinese, and American elementary-school children.* Reston, VA: National Council of Teachers of Mathematics.

Stevenson, H. W. (1990). Adapting to school: Children in Beijing and Chicago. In *Annual Report, Center for Advanced Study in the Behavioral Sciences* (pp. 51–67). Palo Alto, CA: Center for Advanced Study in the Behavioral Sciences. (Translated and reprinted in Chinese in *Zhongguo Ertong Fazhang* [Child Development in China], *7*, 20–30)

Stevenson, H. W., Lee, S., Chen, C., Lummis, M., Stigler, J., Fan, L., & Ge, F. (1990). Mathematics achievement in children in China and the United States. *Child Development, 61*, 1053–1066.

Stevenson, H. W. (1990). Ertong xueyie chengji de bijiao yanjiu [A comparative study of children's academic achievement]. In The Committee on Developmental Psychology of the Chinese Psychological Society (Eds.), *Fazhang xinli zhuanti jiang yanji* (pp. 50–57) [Special topics on developmental psychology]. Beijing, China: Beijing Teacher's College Press.

Stevenson, H. W., Chen, C., Lee, S. Y., & Fuligni, A. J. (1991). Schooling, culture, and cognitive development. In R. J. Sternberg & L. Okagaki (Eds.), *Influences on the development of children's thinking* (pp. 243–268). Hillsdale, NJ: Erlbaum.

Crystal, D. S., & Stevenson, H. W. (1991). Mothers' perceptions of children's problems with mathematics: A cross-national comparison. *Journal of Educational Psychology, 83*, 372–376.

Kitamura, S., Stevenson, H. W., Kimura, S., Kato, T., & Takeda, E. (1991). Jido no seiseki. Noryoku ni tsuite no jikohyoka to fubo no hyotei ni kansuru Nichi-bei hikaku [Children's self-evaluation of their achievements and abilities and parents' rating of their children and themselves—a comparison of American and Japanese]. *Japanese Journal of Applied Psychology, 16*, 19–31.

Stevenson, H. W. (1991). Japanese elementary school education. *The Elementary School Journal, 92*, 109–120.

Stevenson, H. W. (1991). The development of prosocial behavior in large-scale collective societies: China and Japan. In R. A. Hinde & J. Groebel (Eds.), *Cooperation and prosocial behavior* (pp. 89–105). Cambridge, England: Cambridge University Press.

Stigler, J., & Stevenson, H. W. (1991). How Asian teachers polish each lesson to perfection. *American Educator, Spring*, 12–20, 43–47.

Stevenson, H. W., & Chen, C. (1992). Literacy acquisition in Peru, Asia, and the United States. *Annals of the American Academy of Political and Social Sciences, 520,* 174–185.

Stevenson, H. W., & Bartsch, K. (1992). An analysis of Japanese and American textbooks in mathematics. In R. Leetsma & H. Walberg (Eds.), *Japanese educational productivity* (pp. 103–133). Ann Arbor, MI: Center for Japanese Studies.

Stevenson, H. W., Chen, C., & Lee, S. Y. (1992). Chinese families. In J. L. Roopnarine & B. Carter (Eds.), *Parent-child socialization in diverse cultures* (pp. 17–33). Norwood, NJ: Ablex.

Stevenson, H. W., & Stigler, J. W. (1992). *The learning gap.* New York: Summit Books. (Japanese edition, 1994, Tokyo: Kaneko Shobo)

Stevenson, H. W. (1992). Don't deceive children through a feel-good approach. *The School Administrator, 49,* 23–30.

Stevenson, H. W. (1992). Measuring up to the competition: Looking to Asia for answers. *Technos, Winter,* 8–11.

Stevenson, H. W. (1992). Learning from Asian schools. *Scientific American, 267,* 70–76.

Stevenson, H. W., Chen, C., & Lee, S. Y. (1993). Mathematics achievement of Chinese, Japanese, and American children: Ten years later. *Science, 259,* 53–58.

Chen, C., Lee, S. Y., & Stevenson, H. W. (1993). Students' achievement and mathematics instruction. In G. Bell (Ed.), Asian perspectives on mathematics education (pp. 21–35). Lismore, Australia: The Northern Rivers Mathematical Association.

Stevenson, H. W., Lee, S. Y., & Graham, T. (1993). Chinese and Japanese kindergartens: Case study in comparative research. In B. Spodek (Ed.), *Handbook of research on the education of young children* (pp. 519–535). New York: Macmillan.

Stevenson, H. W. (1993). Why Asian students still outdistance Americans. *Educational Leadership, 50,* 63–68.

Stevenson, H. W., Chen, C., & Lee, S. Y. (1993). Motivation and achievement of gifted children in East Asia and the United States. *Journal for the Education of the Gifted, 16,* 223–250.

Stevenson, H. W., Lee, S. Y., & Chen, C. (1994). Education of gifted and talented students in Mainland China, Taiwan, and Japan. *Journal for the Education of the Gifted, 17,* 104–130.

Stevenson, H. W. (1994). Extracurricular programs in East Asian schools. *Teachers College Record, 95,* 387–407.

Stevenson, H. W. (1994). *Teachers preparation and professional development in the Asia-Pacific Region: A review of the literature.* Paper commissioned by Teachers College, Columbia University, for APEC Comparative Study, New York.

Stevenson, H. W., & Lee, S. Y., in collaboration with Carton, S., Evans, M., Meziane, S., Moriyoshi, N., and Schmidt, I. (1994). *International comparisons of entrance and exit examinations: Japan, United Kingdom, France, and Germany.* Paper commissioned by Jacob Javits Center for Gifted and Talented, U.S. Department of Education, Washington, DC.

Crystal, D. S., Chen, C., Fuligni, A. J., Stevenson, H. W., Hsu, C.-C., Ko, H.-J., Kitamura, S., & Kimura, S. (1994). Psychological maladjustment and academic achievement: A cross-cultural study of Japanese, Chinese, and American high school students. *Child Development, 65,* 738–753.

Stevenson, H. W., Lee, S. Y., Chen, C., Kato, K., & Londo, W. (1994). Education of gifted and talented students in China, Taiwan, and Japan. In P. O'Connell Ross (Ed.), *National excellence: An anthology of readings* (pp. 27–60). Washington, DC: U.S. Department of Education.

Stevenson, H. W. (1994). Moving away from stereotypes and preconceptions: Students and their education in East Asia and the United States. In P. R. Greenfield & R. R. Cocking (Eds.), *Cross cultural roots of minority development* (pp. 315–323). Hillsdale, NJ: Erlbaum.

Stevenson, H. W. (1994, October 11). 'Oscars' made of tin. *The New York Times,* p. C1.

Crystal, D. S., & Stevenson, H. W. (1995). What is a bad kid? Answers of adolescents and mothers in three cultures. *Journal of Research on Adolescence, 5*(1), 71–91.

Stevenson, H. W., & Lee, S. Y. (1995). The East Asian version of whole-class teaching. *Educational Policy, 9,* 152–168.

Chen, C., Lee, S. Y., & Stevenson, H. W. (1995). Response styles and cross-cultural comparisons of rating scales among East Asian and North American students. *Psychological Science, 6,* 170–175.

Fuligni, A. J., & Stevenson, H. W. (1995). Time-use and mathematics achievement among Chinese, Japanese, and American high school students. *Child Development, 66,* 830–842.

Stevenson, H. W. (1995). Mathematics achievements of American students: First in the world by Year 2000? In C. A. Nelson (Ed.), *Minnesota Symposia on Child Psychology, 27,* 131–149.

Stevenson, H. W., & Lee, S. Y. (1995). Academic achievement of Chinese students. In M. Bond (Ed.), *Handbook of Chinese psychology* (pp. 119–146). Hong Kong: Oxford University Press.

Chen, C., & Stevenson, H. W. (1995). Motivation and mathematics achievement: A comparative study of Asian-American, Caucasian-American, and East-Asian high school students. *Child Development, 66,* 1215–1234.

Stevenson, H. W. (1996). Self esteem: The myth of feeling good about oneself. *USA Today, 124,* 80–81.

Lee, S. Y., Graham, T., & Stevenson, H. W. (1996). Teachers and teaching: Elementary schools in Japan and the United States. In T. Rohlen & G. LeTendre (Eds.), *Teaching and learning in Japan* (pp. 157–189). Cambridge, England: Cambridge University Press.

Chen, C., Lee, S. Y., & Stevenson, H. W. (1996). Academic achievement and motivation of Chinese students: A cross-national perspective. In S. Lau (Ed.), *Growing Up the Chinese Way: Chinese Child and Adolescent Development* (pp. 69–92). Hong Kong: The Chinese University Press.

Chen, C., Lee, S. Y., & Stevenson, H. W. (1996). Long-term prediction of academic achievement of American, Chinese, and Japanese adolescents. *Journal of Educational Psychology, 88,* 750–759.

Fuligni, A., & Stevenson, H. W. (1997). Home environment and school learning. In T. Husen & N. Postlethwaite (Eds.), *Encyclopedia of Education.* New York: Macmillan.

Stevenson, H. W. (In press.). *Teacher preparation and professional development in the Asia-Pacific Region: A review of the literature.* Paper commissioned by Teachers College, Columbia University for APEC Comparative Study.

Stevenson, H. W. (In press). Cultural interpretations of giftedness: The case of East Asia. In R. Friedman & B. M. Shore (Eds.), *Gifted Children* (Vol. 2). Washington, DC: American Psychological Association.

Stevenson, H. W., Lee, S. Y., & Schweingruber, H. (In press). Home influences on early literacy. In D. Wagner (Ed.), *International Encyclopedia of Literacy.*

Stevenson, H. W., Lee, S. Y., & Nerison-Low, R. (In press). Case studies in mathematics and science (Vol. 1), *Contemporary research in the United States, Germany, and Japan on five education issues: Structure of the education system; Standards in education; The role of school in adolescents' lives; Individual differences among students; and Teachers' lives.* Washington, DC: U.S. Government Printing Office.

Stevenson, H. W., & Nerison-Low, R., (Series Eds.). (In press). Case studies in mathematics and science: Vol. 2, Japan; Vol. 3, Germany; Vol. 4, United States. Washington, DC: U.S. Government Printing Office.

Stevenson, H. W., & Nerison-Low, R. (In press). To sum it up: Case studies of education in Germany, Japan, and the United States, Vol. 5. Washington, DC: U.S. Government Printing Office.

Stevenson, H. W., & Lee, S. (In press). An examination of American student achievement from an international perspective. In D. Ravitch (Ed.), *The state of student performance in American schools.* Washington, DC: The Brookings Institution.

Stevenson, H. W. (In press). Human capital. In H. Rowen (Ed.), *The rise of East Asia.* Stanford: Stanford University Press.

Stevenson, H. W., & Lee, S. Y. (In press). *International comparisons of entrance and exit examinations: Japan, United Kingdom, France, and Germany.* Washington, DC: U.S. Government Printing Office.

Stevenson, H. W. (In press). *U.S. education and goals 2000.* In W. Evers (Ed.), Stanford: Hoover Institution.

Stevenson, H. W. (In press). The case study project of TIMSS. In G. Kaiser (Ed.), *Comparative studies of mathematics achievement.*

Stevenson, H. W., Lee, S. Y., & Mu, X. (In press). Successful achievement in mathematics: China and the United States. In C. van Lieshout (Ed.), *Festschrift for F. Monks.* Hillsdale, NJ: Erlbaum.

Author Index

Numbers in italics refer to listings in the reference sections.

Subject Index

Third International Mathematics
and Science Study (TIMSS),
47, 65, 143–167
background, 144
goals, 144
methodology, 144–151
coding, 148–156
multimedia database, con-
struction of, 146–148
sampling, 144–145
tapes, 145–146
teachers, 145
qualitative descriptors, 164–166
quantitative indicators, 157–164
concepts and applications,
160–162
global ratings, 162–163
mathematical content, 159–
160
seatwork, student thinking
during, 163–164
topics and topic segments
per lesson, 157–159
Third World, 241–243
Time tables, and leeway, 116–117
TIMSS. See Third International
Mathematics and Science
Study
Title Recognition Test (TRT), 263,
268
TORCH. See Test of Reading Comprehension
Tradeoffs, in academic achievement, 119–120
Training, inservice, 65–68
TRT. See Title Recognition Test

United Nations, 241
United States
academic achievement in, 26–
36
and intelligence, 28–31
motivational processes, 36
primary and secondary competencies, 27–28

schooling, 31–36
supporting primary systems,
36
Asian countries as model for,
98–101
civil rights movement in, 318
crisis in mathematics education
in, 45–46
literacy development in, vs.
Australia, 194–196
literacy retention studies in,
244–246
mathematics learning and
teaching in, 48–64
achievement levels, 49, 51
active learning, 54–56
instructional processes, 56,
59–64
teachers, 64–66, 68, 73–74
video survey results, 159–
166
U.S. National Adult Literacy Survey
(NALS), 232, 244–245

Vai (ethnic group), 254
Verbal explanations by students,
54–56
Verbal rule instruction, 330
Verbal skills, print exposure and
growth in, 266–271
Video surveys, 129, 135–143. See
also Third International
Mathematics and Science
Study (TIMSS)
advantages of, 136–138
complex processes, visibility
of, 137–138
concreteness, 136
durability, 136
merging of qualitative–
quantitative analysis,
137
new ideas, revelation of, 136
disadvantages of, 138–143

About the Editors

Scott G. Paris is a professor of psychology and education at the University of Michigan and a program director for the Center for the Improvement of Early Reading Achievement. His research examines children's literacy and learning in schools and community contexts, with special attention paid to the factors that influence children's motivation, strategies, and metacognition. He is a co-author of *Developmental Psychology Today* and *Becoming Reflective Students and Teachers With Portfolios and Authentic Assessment,* and the author of educational materials for grades 3 through 8 titled "Reading and Thinking Strategies."

Henry M. Wellman is a professor of psychology at the University of Michigan and a research scientist at the Center for Human Growth and Development. His research focuses on early cognitive development, including children's developing theories of the world and of people. A special interest is children's early understanding of people in terms of their internal mental states, their desires, emotions, hopes, and beliefs. He has authored numerous articles and several books including *The Child's Theory of Mind, Children Talk about the Mind,* and *The Emergence of Core Domains of Thought.*